"This book combines many of the best features of biography and Festschrift. The lives of Stanley and Ruth Burgess are recounted, celebrated, and then illuminated by the essays of distinguished scholars. This is a rich and rewarding read!"

—William K. Kay
Professor of Theology, Glyndŵr University, Plas Coch Campus, Wrexham, Wales

"*Children of the Calling* is a wonderful gift for the retirement of Stan and Ruth Burgess. It not only capsulizes their rich careers but also the great contribution that they both made to the study and practice of the theology of the holy spirit. In addition, the editors have gathered extremely qualified and interesting contributions to honor these two great missionary pioneers of the holy spirit. Whether one is a member of a charismatic or pentecostal experience or not, this collection of essays will be a most welcomed addition to one's desired reading list for personal growth and challenge."

—James F. Puglisi
Director, Centro Pro Unione, Rome, Italy

"One of the beautiful offerings of this volume is that we are reminded that Ruth was not the proverbial 'good woman behind the good man,' but serving as an equal partner, not only sharing his ministry, but influencing his scholarship and, yes, teaching him! How fitting that Stan and Ruth should be honored by this diverse and stellar group of scholars, recalling the multifaceted ministries of these creative, brilliant, and passionate people who embody what it means to be a part of the renewing work of the holy spirit in the church and world."

—Kimberly Ervin Alexander
Associate Professor of the History of Christianity,
Regent University School of Divinity, Virginia Beach, VA

Children of the Calling

Children of the Calling

Essays in Honor of Stanley M. Burgess and Ruth V. Burgess

Edited by
ERIC NELSON NEWBERG
and LOIS E. OLENA

Foreword by
RUSSELL P. SPITTLER

☙PICKWICK *Publications* • Eugene, Oregon

CHILDREN OF THE CALLING
Essays in Honor of Stanley M. Burgess and Ruth V. Burgess

Copyright © 2014 Wipf and Stock Publishers. All rights reserved. Except for brief quotations in critical publications or reviews, no part of this book may be reproduced in any manner without prior written permission from the publisher. Write: Permissions. Wipf and Stock Publishers, 199 W. 8th Ave., Suite 3, Eugene, OR 97401.

Pickwick Publications
An Imprint of Wipf and Stock Publishers
199 W. 8th Ave., Suite 3
Eugene, OR 97401

www.wipfandstock.com

ISBN 13: 978-1-62564-723-8

Cataloguing-in-Publication Data

Children of the calling : essays in honor of Stanley M. Burgess and Ruth V. Burgess / edited by Eric Nelson Newberg and Lois E. Olena ; foreword by Russell P. Spittler

X + Y p. ; 23 cm. Includes bibliographical references and index(es).

ISBN 13: 978-1-62564-723-8

1. Burgess, Stanley M., 1937–. 2. Burgess, Ruth V. 3. I. Newberg, Eric Nelson. II. Olena, Lois E. III. Spittler, Russell P. IV. Title.

CALL NUMBER 2014

Manufactured in the U.S.A.   12/22/2014

New Revised Standard Version Bible, copyright 1989, Division of Christian Education of the National Council of the Churches of Christ in the United States of America. Used by permission. All rights reserved.

Revised Standard Version of the Bible, copyright 1952 [2nd edition, 1971] by the Division of Christian Education of the National Council of the Churches of Christ in the United States of America. Used by permission. All rights reserved.

As an expression of their friendship and esteem,
the authors dedicate their essays to
Stan and Ruth Burgess
on the occasion of their retirement
from many years of distinguished service
on the faculties of
Evangel University,
Southwest Missouri State University, and Regent University.

Stan and Ruth, 2006 graduation, Regent University

Contents

Foreword by Russell P. Spittler | ix

Preface | xiii
—Lois E. Olena

Contributors | xv

Introduction | xxiii
—Eric Nelson Newberg

From Mavelikara and Pune to Springfield and Jerusalem

1   Stanley Milton Burgess and the Artifacts of Renewal | 3
    —Eric Nelson Newberg

2   Ruth Vassar Burgess: Many Cultures, Multiple Perspectives | 29
    —Lois E. Olena

Photos | 65

The Quest to Understand beyond Boundaries

3   Written with the Finger of God: Divine and Human Writing in Exodus | 81
    —Brian Doak

4   The Church of the East in the Tang Dynasty (635–907 CE): A Theological Assessment | 111
    —Paul W. Lewis

5   A Story about a Dishonest Manager | 133
    —Charles W. Hedrick

6   The Revolutionary Paradigm of Grace | 152
    —J. Lyle Story

7   Is the Origin of the Spirit Still a Theological Impasse? A Modest Ecumenical Proposal about the Derivation of the Spirit in the Trinity | 173
    —Veli-Matti Kärkkäinen

8   Salvation according to Luke | 186
    —Graham H. Twelftree

9   Apostolic Advice: 1 Corinthians 7 as Deliberative Rhetoric | 199
    —Charles Puskas

The Need to Expand, Preserve, and Restore Tradition

10 "Behind Every Successful Man . . .": Recovering God the Mother in the Search for Subjectivity | 219
    —Elaine R. Cleeton

11 The MissouriFind Project: A Labor of Love (And an Exercise in Patience, Perseverance, and Political Acumen) | 235
    —Steven W. Hinch and David Brown

12 Feuerstein's Cognitive Map: A Conceptual Framework for Analyzing Learning Tasks and Providing Effective Feedback | 256
    —Carolyn S. Nixon

13 The Keralite Diaspora | 262
    —Thomson K. Mathew

14 Strategizing in the Spirit in Time of War: The 1943 Assemblies of God Missionary Conference | 281
    —Malcolm R. Brubaker

15 Baptism in the Holy Spirit: A Spiritual and Theological Journey | 298
    —Peter Hocken

16 The Ecumenical Imperative and the Catholic Charismatic Renewal | 311
    —Kevin M. Ranaghan and Dorothy Garrity Ranaghan

17 Looking Back on the Forward Way | 328
    —Karl Luckert

Epilogue | 341
    —Stanley M. Burgess and Ruth Vassar Burgess

Index of Names and Subjects | 343

Foreword

A Festschrift for two? How many celebratory collections of essays have *ever* been presented by colleagues to a married pair of academics? That may be a statistic hard to come by, but these pages manifest just such double congratulations.

Both born in India as "MKs" (missionaries' kids), childhood friends at the same boarding school, married in Texas, both taking PhDs at the University of Missouri, simultaneous tenured faculty service at universities in Missouri and Virginia, and now together retired on a few acres in rural Missouri—Stanley and Ruth Burgess have formed an admirable and productive academic duet over a period that bridges five decades.

Readers first get the human stories. Five children, ten grandchildren. Parents of the pair were missionaries to India and friends. Stanley's parents: founders of the first Bible training institute of the Assemblies of God outside the United States. Ruth's parents: directors of an orphanage. Such activities, because they did not involve direct evangelism, drew scant support at home and imposed arduous struggles on the young families. For Ruth, a predeceased two-year-old brother and a stillborn baby sister lie untimely buried in India, both consequences of medical misdiagnosis.

To immersion in the cultures of India and the subsequent shock of adapting to American culture can be added, for Ruth, engagement with Native Americans in the tiny town of Pawhuska, Oklahoma, capital of the Osage Nation. Such intercultural mix homogenized this learned couple into an illustrative case study of a road sometimes travelled by missionary offspring, the *Children of the Calling*, as the book title puts it. These MKs critically sorted their religious roots gained from their families and, in doing so, extended refined Pentecostal Christian values into the university world.

Today, Stanley Milton Burgess stands widely recognized as perhaps the leading historian of the charismatic and Pentecostal movements who is expressly concerned with the entire two millennia of Christian history—ancient, medieval, Reformation, and modern. Given leading roles in the publication of several anthologies of texts and of three award-winning encyclopedias focused on this sector of the Christian movement, Stanley Burgess—if a lexical caper can be forgiven—might be said to have fomented a small *Stanpede* of such reference volumes. Surely Stanley Burgess warrants the title of Pentecostal/charismatic encyclopedist laureate.[1]

For her part, Ruth Vassar Burgess entered the academy with the PhD in speech pathology, flavored with language theory. Veering into the study of brain processes, she spent a sabbatical semester in Jerusalem with Reuven Feuerstein, a Romanian Jewish scholar who championed the view that human intelligence is not fixed but malleable. With multiple financial grants, Ruth Burgess not only explored Feuerstein's revolutionary ideas with her graduate students but also lectured on the subject around the globe. As well, she applied the theories and the related techniques in elementary school classrooms in Springfield, Missouri, during the years of teaching at Southwest Missouri State University (SMSU), now called Missouri State University—the same school where husband Stanley for some years chaired the Religious Studies department. She even produced a biography of the cognitive reformer: *Changing Brain Structure Through Cross-Cultural Learning: The Life of Reuven Feuerstein* (Lewiston, NY: Mellen, 2008).

Indeed, combing the biographies of Stanley and Ruth Burgess makes clear their lifelong connection with special-needs students and an abiding interest in caring advocacy and activism. Ruth's maternal grandmother was a suffragette and among the first women who voted in the American national elections. From 1978 to 1985, Stanley was the Director of Handicapped Student Services (now known as Disability Resource Center) at SMSU. A few publications reflect the same interests.

Quite expectedly, then, the cornucopia of chapters that follow reflects the varying interests, styles, and methods of the great cloud of witnesses to the joint impact of the Burgesses. Contributions range from biblical exegesis, at times with gripping sermonic effect, theological nuancing, mission history and demographics, personal recollections, maps of mind-shifts, with wisps of gender equity issues and pleas for social justice.

Some contributors to this volume would bear deep sympathies or lasting connections with the Pentecostal/charismatic tradition. Others may not. Such a pacific state of affairs attests mutual acceptance within the academy, a signal of rising participation of Pentecostals in the academic enterprise.

---

1. See the careful review of the literary legacy of Stanley Burgess in the biographic chapter 1 by Eric Nelson Newberg, to which can be added dozens of entries by Burgess in encyclopedic volumes edited by others.

The very fact that a Festschrift emerges for scholars so conspicuously connected with the Pentecostal and charismatic movements itself gives evidence of the emerging academic maturity in those allied traditions. Such noteworthy academic ripeness may surprise observers, given the deep-seated antipathy toward matters intellectual and academic within Pentecostal spirituality (but notably less so among charismatics). But now well into its second century, the Pentecostal movement has achieved measurable advance in serious academic publication. Scholars of the tradition, even if buoyed by the ubiquitous quest for diversity in higher education, can be found widely in leading seminaries, colleges, and universities. In these times, then, the dozen decades of the Pentecostal tradition are yielding completed academic careers, and with that, the emergence of Festschriften honoring academics who have emerged from the Pentecostal and charismatic traditions. Here, in this volume, arrives yet another one.[2]

In addition to the literary thanks implied in the chapters that follow, hundreds of students and scores of colleagues treasure grateful memories for the guidance provided and the example displayed through encounter with Stanley and Ruth Burgess. Personally, my wife, Bobbie, and I have enjoyed a recent season of renewed association with the Burgesses as Stan and I have served on the board of trustees for the revitalized Oral Roberts University. Within that board, Stanley chaired the Academic Affairs Committee, on which I also served under his splendid leadership.

May their remaining years be blessed and productive ones for this noble academic pair, Ruth and Stanley Burgess.

Russell P. Spittler
Provost Emeritus and Professor of New Testament Emeritus
Fuller Theological Seminary
Pasadena, California

---

2. Here are a few examples of Festschriften for Pentecostal or charismatic scholars (with apologies for worthy honorees not listed): Sven K. Soderlund, ed., *Romans and the People of God: Essays in Honor of Gordon Fee On the Occasion of His 65th Birthday* (Grand Rapids: Eerdmans, 1999); Jan A. B. Jongeneel, ed., *Pentecost, Mission, Ecumenism: Essays on Intercultural Theology, Festschrift in Honour of Walter J. Hollenweger* (Berlin: Lang, 1992); Paul Elbert, ed., *Faces of Renewal: Studies in Honor of Stanley M. Horton Presented on His 70th Birthday* (Peabody, MA: Hendrickson, 1980); Wonsuk Ma and Robert P. Menzies, eds., *Pentecostalism in Context: Essays in Honor of William W. Menzies* (Sheffield, UK: Sheffield Academic, 1997); Mark W. Wilson, ed., *Spirit and Renewal: Essays in Honor of J. Rodman Williams* (Sheffield, UK: Sheffield Academic, 1994).

Preface
—Lois E. Olena

Origination of the Festschrift for Stan and Ruth Burgess can be traced to Eric's sabbatical in 2002 at the Tantur Ecumenical Institute. While at Tantur, Father Thomas Stransky, rector emeritus, asked if he was acquainted with Drs. Stanley and Ruth Burgess, Pentecostal scholars who had spent two sabbatical leaves at Tantur. At that point Eric was not acquainted with the Burgesses. That would change two years later, when Eric commenced PhD studies at Regent University, and his first course was taught by Stan. When Eric opened Stan's *The Holy Spirit: Eastern Christian Traditions*, an assigned text, he read with amazement Stan's acknowledgment of Tantur's world-class theological library as the primary research site for the book. Eric went on to work with Stan as his teaching assistant, and Stan became his beloved doctor father.

During Eric's time at Regent (2004–2008), he worked closely with Stan and came to admire his scholarly acumen, whimsical humor, ecumenical spirit, passion for social justice, and intellectual honesty. For his class on renewal historiography, he wrote a paper on Stan's contribution to the historiography of Pentecostal spirituality, reading everything he had written. Stan's work convinced Eric of the continuance of the charismatic gifts of the Holy Spirit throughout Christian history. It also motivated him to tell the truth about the history of the Pentecostal mission in Palestine, Eric's dissertation topic. During his doctoral program in renewal studies, Eric also studied with Dr. Ruth Burgess. Her class on research-based pedagogy opened his eyes to various theories of learning. Ruth, a master teacher, equipped her Regent doctoral students with an approach to teaching and learning informed by Reuven Feuerstein's theories. Thanks to Ruth, Eric's teaching aims at nurturing the habits of mind and heart that make for free inquiry, ongoing transformation, and lifelong learning. Stan and Ruth became mentors for Eric in the craft of scholarship guided by Anselm's maxim—faith seeking understanding.

The actual idea for this Festschrift originated in 2008 prior to Eric's first teaching position in Australia. When he proposed a Festschrift to Stan and Ruth, they were positively disposed to the idea and brainstormed possible themes and contributors. After he commenced his position in Sydney, Ruth sent a thematic prospectus with a list of possible contributors. Bogged down by the demands of restructuring the curriculum of the pastoral theology department at Alphacrucis College, Eric had to put the project on the back burner.

In 2010 Eric returned to the United States to assume a one-year assignment at Regent University School of Divinity, covering for Stan while he was on sabbatical. At that time, Graham Twelftree, Charles L. Holman Professor of New Testament and Early Christianity, asked how the project was coming along and encouraged Eric to make it happen, insisting it would be a fitting tribute to his esteemed colleagues. Eric took Dr. Twelftree's cue and resumed work on the Festschrift.

Meanwhile Stan and Ruth retired to their home near Springfield, Missouri, in 2010 and in the fall of 2011 Eric moved from Regent to Oral Roberts University. Earlier that year, my husband Doug and I renewed acquaintance with the Burgesses, having met them through the Society for Pentecostal Studies. I first met Ruth at Duke University in 2008 when attending her SPS presentation, "A Call for a Cognitive Spiritual Renewal" and—as the Society's incoming Executive Director—I interviewed Stan at the 2011 SPS Annual Meeting in Memphis in preparation for his receiving the Lifetime Achievement Award.

Back in Springfield, Doug and I enjoyed spending time together through a reading group, in one another's homes, at Evangel Temple, and through my engaging Stan and Ruth as doctoral advisers at the Assemblies of God Theological Seminary. Impressed by their unique mixture of scholarship and kindness and desirous of telling their remarkable life stories, I proposed to them the possibility of a Festschrift in their honor. Since Eric had already birthed the idea in 2008, they conferred with him about a co-editing partnership, and the project went full steam ahead in August 2012.

Eric and I are thankful to Stan and Ruth for the privilege of honoring them in this way and look forward to cultivating our friendship with them for many years to come.

Contributors

David Brown (EdD, Oklahoma State) is Professor of Elementary Education in the department of Childhood Education and Family Studies, College of Education and family studies, college of education, Missouri State University. Dr. Brown teaches both graduate and undergraduate courses in the elementary program. He is the former associate dean, director of student services, and department head at MSU. He has been an elementary principal and fifth grade teacher in the Tulsa Union School District. Dr. Brown has published in areas of paradigmatic change effects on theory and practice in teaching and learning. He lives in Springfield, Missouri with his wife, Julie, who teaches kindergarten in Springfield Public Schools, and with their daughter, Carlee, who just graduated from fifth grade.

Malcolm R. Brubaker (PhD, Regent University) is Professor of Bible at Valley Forge Christian College, Phoenixville, Pennsylvania. His biblical interest is the Old Testament with a ThM from Westminster Theological Seminary, and he has published writings on the prophets. Brubaker's doctoral work under Stanley and Ruth Burgess led him to make the study of Assemblies of God missions history his current research interest. This turn from biblical studies to church history is a return to his undergraduate history major at Evangel University when Stanley Burgess taught there. He is a fourth-generation Pentecostal and was raised in the Assemblies of God church in Warren, Ohio, which his maternal great-grandfather, John Waggoner, had started. His grandparents, Harry and Helen Waggoner, spent thirty-three years in North India leper work.

Elaine R. Cleeton (PhD, Syracuse University; MDiv, Colgate Rochester Divinity School; MA, Northwestern University) is Associate Professor of Sociology at the State University of New York at Geneseo. She is visiting professor at Sun Yat-Sen University, Guangzhou, Guangdong Province, China. The daughter of Reverend Jack Cleeton and Louise Miles Cleeton, ministers in the Assemblies of God, ordained a United Church of Christ minister, she served as Pastor of the Grindstone Island United Methodist Church, Clayton, New York. A Speech Pathologist, she directed the Speech Clinic at the University of California, Santa Barbara. Dr. Cleeton and her husband, photographer William Gandino, reside in Pittsford, New York, with their sons, Benjamin and William.

Brian Doak (PhD, Harvard University) is Assistant Professor of Biblical Studies and Faculty Fellow in the William Penn Honors Program at George Fox University. Professor Doak is the recipient of the Aviram Prize for archaeological research (2012) as well as the George Fox University Undergraduate Researcher of the Year (2014). Among other publications, he is the author of three books, *The Last of the Rephaim: Conquest and Cataclysm in the Heroic Ages of Ancient Israel* (2012), *Consider Leviathan: Narratives of Nature and the Self in Job* (2014), and *The Bible: Ancient Context and Ongoing Community* (co-authored with Steve Sherwood, 2014).

Charles W. Hedrick (PhD, Claremont Graduate University) is Emeritus Distinguished Professor of Religious Studies, Missouri State University. An ordained Southern Baptist minister and retired U.S. Army Chaplain (Colonel), he has published numerous books and articles on Christian Origins. His most recent book is *Unlocking the Secrets of the Gospel According to Thomas: A Radical Faith for a New Age* (2010). Since 1980 he and his wife, Peggy, have lived in Springfield, Missouri, where he publishes a blog titled "Wry Thoughts about Religion."

Steven W. Hinch (PhD, University of Missouri-Columbia) is Associate Professor in the Reading, Foundations, and Technology department in the College of Education at Missouri State University. Steve has been at the university for the past twenty-three years, the last three years in the position of program coordinator for the Master of Arts in Teaching program. Dr. Steve Hinch has long been an advocate for Civic Education. As a result of that commitment, Dr. Hinch has been heavily involved at the state, national, and international levels in spreading that message. He was a member of a NCSS delegation that visited with educators in South Africa to explore the challenges of teaching civics in a post-apartheid society. He later was appointed to the Missouri Bar Advisory Committee for Citizenship Education. In this capacity, Dr. Hinch has served as the International Liaison to Civitas International, the global unit of the Center for Civic Education. Dr. Hinch traveled to Jakarta, Indonesia two years ago to represent Missouri at the 14th World Congress on Civic Education. More recently, Hinch traveled to South Korea to participate in the Asia-Pacific Forum on Civic Education.

Peter Hocken (PhD, University of Birmingham, UK) is an ordained Catholic priest for the diocese of Northampton, England, and has been a leader in Catholic charismatic renewal for many years. He is a former President of the Society for Pentecostal Studies (1985-86) and Executive Secretary (1988-97). He is author of several books, including *Streams of Renewal* (1986), *One Lord One Spirit One Body* (1987), *The Glory and the Shame* (1994), *The Strategy of the Spirit?* (1996), *The Challenges of the Pentecostal Charismatic and Messianic Jewish Movements* (2009), *Pentecost and Parousia: Charismatic Renewal, Christian Unity, and the Coming Glory* (2013). He was a major contributor to *The New International Dictionary of the Pentecostal and Charismatic Movements* (2002). He has lived in Austria since 2002.

Veli-Matti Kärkkäinen (Dr. Theol. Habil., University of Helsinki) is Professor of Systematic Theology at Fuller Theological Seminary, Pasadena, California, and Docent of Ecumenics at the University of Helsinki. Native of Finland, he has also lived and taught theology in Thailand. He has participated widely in the ecumenical, theological, and interreligious work of the World Council of Churches, Faith and Order, and several international bi-lateral dialogues. He travels widely to give lectures and participate in consultations and seminars. In addition to about two hundred articles and essays, Dr. Kärkkäinen has written or edited twenty books, including *Trinity and Religious Pluralism* (2004) and *The Trinity: Global Perspectives* (2007). He is also the editor of *Holy Spirit and Salvation*, in the series The Westminster Collection of Sources of Christian Theology, and coeditor of *The Global Dictionary of Theology* (2008). His most recent books are *Christ and Reconciliation* (2013) and *Trinity and Revelation* (2014), the first two of five volumes in the series Constructive Christian Theology for the Pluralistic World (2013-18).

Paul W. Lewis (PhD, Baylor University) is currently the Associate Professor of Historical Theology and Intercultural Studies, and the Admissions and Program Coordinator of the Intercultural Doctoral Studies at the Assemblies of God Theological Seminary where he also serves as the Editor of *Encounter: Journal for Pentecostal Ministry* and the *International Journal of Pentecostal Missiology*. Formerly, Paul also served as Editor of the *Asian Journal of Pentecostal Studies*, from 2008 to 2011. He is also an ordained Assemblies of God minister and has been an Assemblies of God World Missions missionary to East Asia for over nineteen years, during which time he served as Academic Dean of Asia Pacific Theological Seminary, Baguio, Philippines (2006-12). His articles have appeared in the *African Journal of Pentecostal Theology*, the *Asian Journal of Pentecostal Studies*, *Cyberjournal of Pentecostal-Charismatic Research*, *Mythlore*, and *The Spirit & Church*. His essays have appeared in *The New International Dictionary of Pentecostal and Charismatic Movements* and the *Encyclopedia of Pentecostal and Charismatic Christianity*. He, his wife, Eveline, and their two daughters, Rachel and Anastasia, currently reside in Springfield, Missouri, for the duration of their current missionary assignment at the Assemblies of God Theological Seminary.

Karl W. Luckert (PhD, University of Chicago) is a Professor Emeritus at Missouri State University, where he taught from 1979 to 1999 in the Religious Studies Department. He received his MA and PhD degrees in the History of Religions at the University of Chicago (1967, 1969). He has published extensively in his field—on Navajo Indian, Middle American, and ancient Egyptian religions, as well as on Chinese minority traditions. Among earth scientists he has argued his own Expansion Tectonics theory, and he has copublished two musicals for choir and organ with Jonas Nordwall. His most recent book is *Stone Age Religion at Göbekli Tepe: From Hunting to Domestication, Warfare and Civilization* (2013). He and his wife, Dora, live in Portland, Oregon, and watch their families and fruit trees grow.

Thomson K. Mathew (EdD, Oklahoma State University; DMin, Oral Roberts University) is Professor of Pastoral Care and Dean of the College of Theology and Ministry at Oral Roberts University. A third-generation Pentecostal minister from Kerala, India, he writes bilingually on pastoral care, leadership, and Spirit-led ministry. Several of his books, book chapters, and numerous articles are in print both in Malayalam and English. He is active in ministry among Indian Pentecostals in America and is involved in preaching/teaching ministries in India and other nations. Mathew's extended family and his wife's grandparents were pioneer Pentecostals who had significant contacts with missionary John Burgess and his ministry.

Eric Nelson Newberg (PhD, Regent University) is associate professor of Theological and Historical Studies at Oral Roberts University and adjunct instructor at Regent University School of Divinity. His doctoral dissertation was supervised by Stan and Ruth Burgess. Following his doctoral studies, Dr. Newberg lived in Sydney, Australia, and served as Head of Pastoral Theology at Alphacrucis College. His recently published book *The Pentecostal Mission in Palestine: The Legacy of Pentecostal Zionism* (2012) grapples with the challenges faced by Western missionaries in building intercultural bridges to the peoples of the Middle East. He is the author of a chapter on Philip Jacob Spener's vision for church renewal in *Servant Leadership* (1994). His articles have appeared in *Australasian Pentecostal Studies*, *International Bulletin of Missionary Research*, *European Pentecostal Theological Association Journal*, and *Expository Times*. He has made conference presentations on a variety of topics, including Eastern Christian iconography, Muslim-Christian relations, and Pentecostal missions. Dr. Newberg is an ordained minister of Word and Sacrament with the Evangelical Covenant Church. He lives with his wife, Carol, in Tulsa, Oklahoma.

Carolyn S. Nixon (BS, Communication Disorders; MS, Elementary Education, Missouri State University) is an instructional coach at Willard R-II School District, Willard, Missouri. A published poet and author, Carolyn has recently published two quilt books for Kansas City Star Publishing (*Memories of Christmas Past*, with nonfiction journals based on her childhood experiences growing up in the Ozark Mountains, and *Butterfly Fields*, a tribute to the creative spirit of her mother, Pearl Brown). With multiple areas of certification, her thirty-two-year career as a public educator includes teaching at the pre-school, elementary, middle school, high school, and college levels. She supervised regular education teachers at Southwest Missouri State University (SMSU), now Missouri State University, (MSU) and special education teachers at the University of Missouri. Ms. Nixon has a passion for personal learning and professional development for teachers. She has designed and presented workshops at local, state, national, and international levels. She is an active member of the Missouri State Teachers Association (MSTA) and works on the state level with that group for conference planning and other professional development endeavors. Throughout her career, she has been the nominee and winner of many teaching awards including the MSTA Outstanding Secondary Educator of the Year in 2012 and two nominations for Missouri Educator of the Year. Carolyn lives near Buffalo, Missouri, with her husband, Greg. She has three daughters—Donna, Laura, and Whitney—and one stepson, Darren.

Lois E. Olena (DMin, Assemblies of God Theological Seminary) is Associate Professor of Practical Theology and Jewish Studies at the Assemblies of God Theological Seminary, where she also serves as DMin Project Coordinator. An ordained AG minister, she has been involved in various aspects of local church ministry since her youth. In addition, Olena has published Holocaust curricula and poetry (most recently in *Blood to Remember: American Poets on the Holocaust*), articles for *AG Heritage* magazine, book chapters on the history of AG race relations, the official biography of Dr. Stanley M. Horton, *Stanley M. Horton: Shaper of Pentecostal Theology* (2009), the biography of Benny C. Aker in *But These Are Written* (2014), and a forthcoming coedited volume in the Global Pentecostal and Charismatic Studies series (Brill). She also teaches Jewish Studies and theology as an adjunct at Evangel University in Springfield, Missouri, where she and her husband, Doug, have lived since 2002 with their two daughters, Arwen and Eden. In 2011, Dr.

Olena accepted the post of executive director of the Society for Pentecostal Studies.

Charles Puskas (PhD, Saint Louis University) is a Field Sales Executive with Convivium Press, Miami, Florida. He has extensive experience in college teaching, religious publishing, and parish ministry. He is the author of *The Conclusion of Luke-Acts: The Significance of Acts 28:16–31* (2009); coauthor, with David Crump, of the volume *An Introduction to the Gospels and Acts* (2008); coauthor, with C. Michael Robbins, of *An Introduction to the New Testament* (2011); and coauthor, with Mark Reasoner, of *The Letters of Paul: An Introduction* (2013).

Dorothy Garrity Ranaghan (MA, University of Notre Dame) is a writer, editor, and retreat and conference speaker. She is a founding member and pastoral leader of the People of Praise Covenant Community. She served as a member of the National Service Committee for the Catholic Charismatic Renewal for six years and was the editor in chief of *Chariscenter USA* for eight years. She is a member of the Society for Pentecostal Studies. Her most recent publication is *Blind Spot: War and Christian Identity* (2011). Her husband, Kevin, and she live in South Bend, Indiana; they have six children and fifteen grandchildren.

Kevin M. Ranaghan (PhD, University of Notre Dame) is an ordained Roman Catholic Deacon in the diocese of Fort Wayne/South Bend, Indiana, since 1973. He is a founding member and coordinator of the People of Praise covenant community since 1971. Kevin is a former member and past vice president of the Council of the International Catholic Charismatic Renewal Services and the North American Renewal Service Committee. He served as a member of the National Service Committee of the Catholic Charismatic Renewal in the U.S. for fifteen years and as its executive director for eleven years. He currently serves on the boards of the International Charismatic Consultation, the Gathering of the Holy Spirit, and the Charismatic Leaders Fellowship and Trinity Schools. He is currently a member of the Society for Pentecostal Studies. He and his wife, Dorothy, coauthored *Catholic Pentecostals* (1969). They live in South Bend, Indiana, and have six children and fifteen grandchildren.

J. Lyle Story (PhD, Fuller Theological Seminary) is Professor of Biblical Languages and New Testament in the School of Divinity at Regent University in Virginia Beach and has taught courses in biblical studies for thirty-five years. He is an ordained pastor with Harvest Network International (HNI) and coauthor of *Greek to Me* as well as *The Greek to Me Multimedia Tutorial* (CD-ROM) and other teaching aids. He has also written numerous articles/

chapters in books, dictionaries, and academic journals, with special interest in the gospels, parables, Luke-Acts, women's studies, and social justice. He and his wife, Sherri, currently reside in Suffolk, Virginia.

Graham H. Twelftree (PhD, University of Nottingham) is Charles L. Holman Professor of New Testament and Early Christianity, and Director of the PhD program in the School of Divinity, Regent University. Recent publications include *People of the Spirit: Exploring Luke's View of the Church* (2009), *Paul and the Miraculous: A Historical Reconstruction* (2013) and, as editor, *The Cambridge Companion to Miracles* (2011). He is ordained, and a member of the Vineyard movement.

Introduction
—Eric Nelson Newberg

The essays in this Festschrift are dedicated to Stanley Milton Burgess and Ruth Vassar Burgess in appreciation of their scholarship, collegiality, and influence. In this volume, the authors celebrate Stan and Ruth's accomplishments together because of the many intersections in their family backgrounds, religious heritage, multi-cultural moorings, and academic endeavors. Stan and Ruth grew up in India in missionary families, imbibing a diverse religious and cultural worldview. Religiously they were inculcated with the values of classical Pentecostalism. Culturally they were immersed in the languages, food, and customs of India. Intellectually, they were shaped by streams of thought that took them far afield from their origins. As an historian of Pentecostalism, Stan's horizons were broadened by his study of the mystical spirituality of Eastern Christianity. As a teacher of teachers, Ruth's vision of pedagogy was expanded by Reuven Feuerstein's theory of mediated learning experience and tools of instrumental enrichment. The scholarly attainments of each were undergirded by shared values of family commitment, free inquiry, and social justice.

This book contains three sections: (1) personal and biographic, (2) historical and theological, and (3) applied venues, such as gender issues, education, India, and ecumenical and departmental recollections. Prior to a synopsis of the chapters, this Introduction will elucidate the book's theme, "children of the calling," in the following sequence: defining the notion of calling in general, outlining the specific characteristics of a missionary calling in a Pentecostal context, and exploring the calling of scholarship.

THE NOTION OF CALLING

Several meanings can be subsumed under the theme "children of the calling." Simply put, the notion of "calling" pertains to a strong inner impulse toward a particular course of action, especially when accompanied by conviction of divine influence. It can refer to a strong feeling of being destined to undertake a specific type of work, such as a sense of being chosen by God for religious work or a specific career. Christian writers construe calling in different ways. In *The Call,* Os Guinness distinguishes between primary and secondary callings. He defines primary calling as following Christ. First and foremost one is called to Someone (God), not to something (such as parenthood, politics, or teaching) or to somewhere (such as a university campus in Springfield, Missouri or a missionary field in India). Secondarily one is called to a particular task or career. It is therefore a matter of secondary calling that one is called to something like homeschooling or to the practice of law or to religious studies. But these and other things are always the secondary, never the primary calling. They are "callings" rather than the "calling." They are one's personal answer to God's address, one's response to God's summons. Secondary callings do matter, but the primary calling matters most.[3]

CHARACTERISTICS OF PENTECOSTAL MISSIONARY CALLING

Stan and Ruth Burgess are children of the calling of their Pentecostal missionary parents. They were nurtured in a cross-cultural setting in which the notion of calling, in its primary and secondary senses, was formative. Their parents felt they had "divine callings." Estelle Barnett Vassar, John Burgess, and Bernice F. Burgess interpreted this as a specific calling to the subcontinent of India. Ted Vassar felt a calling to ministry and went to India in respect to the Great Commission and love for his wife. As children of parents with divine callings, Stan and Ruth met in January 1948 at Kodaikanal, Tamil Nadu, South India. The crucible in which they were nurtured was a Pentecostal mission field in India.

From its beginnings Pentecostalism was a missionary movement. Although Pentecostalism had multiple points of origin, the case of the Azusa Street Revival (1906–1912) is indicative of the prodigious missionary impulse of Pentecostalism.[4] By October 1906, thirty-eight missionaries

---

3. Guinness, *The Call,* 31.
4. Robert Owens states, "The massive appeal of the revival had two peaks, from

had been sent overseas from Azusa, nineteen of whom were first-time missionaries. In 1907 Azusa sent out twelve additional first-time missionaries. By 1908 Azusa had sent out a total of forty-five first-time missionaries and re-commissioned a sizable number of veteran missionaries. In a short span of time, missionaries affiliated with the Azusa Street Mission were located in many countries, including Angola, Canada, Chile, China, England, India, Korea, Liberia, Palestine, and South Africa.[5]

The explosive growth of early Pentecostal missions brings to the fore the question of its motivating force. There is no doubt about how early Pentecostals would have answered this question. It was commonplace for early Pentecostal missionaries to attribute their calling to an inner directive from the Holy Spirit.[6] DeLonn Rance defines a missionary call as "a sense of divine direction and confirmation to cross geographical and/or cultural boundaries to communicate the gospel of Jesus Christ."[7] Rance holds that such a call is a life-changing and life-sustaining event and process directed by the Holy Spirit.[8] According to the published addresses and letters of Pentecostal missionaries, it is evident that the core of Pentecostal missionary motivation was pneumatological.[9] Among the early Pentecostals, there was a widely-held belief that the apostolic power of the Holy Spirit was being restored through the Pentecostal Revival, and Pentecostal missionaries understood they were playing an important role in the unfolding of this monumental restoration.[10]

Pentecostals posited that the *gateway for participation* in the new epoch was the experience of speaking in tongues. This they believed to be the initial physical evidence of the baptism of the Holy Spirit. Soon this theme achieved brand recognition and was accepted as normative for Pentecostal identity. Eventually it was thought necessary to safeguard Pentecostal identity with a doctrinal formulation, which has come to be known as "initial evidence."[11] The doctrine can be traced back to Charles Parham and the Azusa Street Revival, during which William Seymour inscribed the doctrine of "evidence" in a creedal statement circulated on a flyer, stating, "The

---

1906 to 1909 and again from 1911 to 1912." The Azusa Street Revival occurred in two phases, with William Seymour leading the first phase and William Durham taking over control during the second phase. Owens, "The Azusa Street Revival," 61.

5. Robeck, "Pentecostalism and Mission," 81–82.
6. Anderson, *Spreading Fires*, 65–68.
7. Rance, "Training Pentecostal Missionaries," 183.
8. Ibid.
9. McGee, "Assemblies of God Mission Theology," 168.
10. McClung, "Try to Get People Saved," 4–6.
11. See Flokstra, "Sources for the Initial Evidence Discussion," 79, 119–20, 164, 211.

Baptism of the Holy Ghost is a gift of power upon the sanctified life; so when we get it we have the same evidence as the Disciples received on the Day of Pentecost (Acts 2:3, 4), in speaking in new tongues."[12] In 1916, two years after the Assemblies of God (hereafter AG) was founded, its General Council adopted initial evidence in its statement of fundamental truths. Under the heading, "The Full Consummation of the Baptism in the Holy Spirit," the official AG statement reads, "The full consummation of the baptism of believers in the Holy Ghost is indicated by the initial physical sign of speaking with other tongues as the Spirit of God gives them utterance, Acts 2:4. This wonderful experience is distinct from and subsequent to the experience of the new birth."[13]

The doctrine of initial evidence performed three essential functions. First, it established a boundary marker by which to determine who was a Pentecostal and who was not. Second, it steered the charismatic impulse of Pentecostal spirituality within theological parameters. Third, it defined Pentecostalism over against other branches of Christian faith. Pentecostals were not shy about proclaiming the doctrine of initial evidence. They did not deny that other Christians had the Holy Spirit, for the most part, but rather affirmed that a Pentecostal had something that other Christians did not have, yet could if they were to seek it. Pentecostals claimed that this extra, added measure of charismatic power qualified them, more than other Christians, to carry out Christ's missionary commission. Stan and Ruth were indoctrinated with this dogma by virtue of the fact that they were children of Assemblies of God missionaries. However, another fact of their upbringing would prove to be more determinative in shaping their autonomy and calling to scholarship. That fact was the cultural milieu of the mission field in India.

THE CALLING OF SCHOLARSHIP

As North American missionary children growing up in India, Stan and Ruth internalized multiple worldviews. In traversing the cultural realities of India, Pentecostalism, and North America, Stan and Ruth developed a fluid sense of identity and a capacity for feeling at home with multiple perspectives. It is often apparent to children of missionaries living in a "foreign field" that their view of the world is different from those who grow up in the sending country. They often feel out of place when they return

---

12. Robeck, *Azusa Street Mission and Revival*, 120.
13. "Combined Minutes," 14.

"home" during furloughs or for education.[14] As difficult as this may seem, the children of missionaries often acquire a facility for global competency and cross-cultural sensitivity. They more likely feel at home in the presence of diverse peoples sometimes regarded by those with a unitary cultural identity as the "other." In the realm of ideas, Stan and Ruth openly entertained diverse worldviews. Though these children of missionaries did not personally take on board the specific missionary calling of their parents, they charted life maps that benefitted from the cross-cultural proficiencies developed in their childhoods in India. Assuredly, their global competency suited them well for lives of service in scholarship.

Stan and Ruth are exemplary scholars. The calling that each has pursued can be aptly described in terms of the schema advanced by Johann Gottlieb Fichte (1762–1814) in his 1794 lecture, "The Vocation of the Scholar."[15] The calling of the scholar entails serving as a learner, teacher, guide, and model. As a lifelong learner, the scholar remains current with research in his or her field and conversant with the work of those in his or her department. Knowledge of one's field is not an end in itself. The purpose of learning is to understand where we are and where we need to go to further human progress. Far more than the acquisition of knowledge, learning is about the blending of knowledge with purpose, direction, methodology, and praxis. Hence, the scholar is also a teacher. Because, as Fichte puts it, the scholar "exists only through society and for society,"[16] the communication of knowledge is incumbent upon him or her. Scholarly knowledge must be applied to the good of society in the interest of assisting students in becoming conscious of their true wants and acquainting them with the means of satisfying these wants. A search for truth is common to humankind, but it must be developed, proved, and purified. To this end, the task of the scholar as teacher requires that he or she be a guide, because, as Fichte states, the scholar "sees not merely the present, but also the future." A scholar "sees not merely the point which humanity now occupies, but also that to which it must next advance if it is to remain true to its final end, and not wander and turn back from its legitimate path."[17] Finally, the scholar is a model of integrity. According to Fichte, erudition without ethics is empty. An educated person is an ethical person.[18] A person of intelligence is a person of

---

14. For a summary of recent research on missionary children, including re-entry issues and identity formation, see Hawley, "Research on Missionary Kids."

15. Fichte, "The Vocation of the Scholar."

16. Ibid., 56–57.

17. Ibid., 57.

18. Ibid., 58–59.

integrity. The scholar shows respect for religious and social freedom and eschews deceptive schemes and manipulative techniques. He or she does not engage in indoctrination, propaganda, bullying, or the abuse of power. The scholar is an advocate of academic freedom, which is the heart and soul of the scholarly vocation.

The above characteristics of the scholarly calling are clearly evident in Stan and Ruth Burgess. First, as lifelong learners they remain competent and accomplished in their respective fields. Second, as consummate teachers they have gently plied the tools of cognitive transformation to get their students to acknowledge, "Hmm, you have a point there; I'm going to have to go home and think about that." Third, as trustworthy guides they have illuminated traditions of the past in order to keep them alive for future generations. Fourth, they stand as models of ethical integrity who prize the value of free inquiry. Keenly aware of the pitfalls associated with emotional manipulation and the cult of prosperity in their inherited confessional community, they do not force their views on others or participate in the idolization of wealth. They don't preach. They engage in a reasoned dialogue. They maintain safe and appropriate boundaries. Furthermore, they remain open and honest yet tolerant in speaking of their spirituality. University professors sometimes present a façade to the community and their students as a part of the public role they play. They fashion themselves as professional educators and dispassionate thinkers who are not supposed to express their emotions, least of all deepest emotions such as those that well up in moments of joy or loss. Stan and Ruth stand out because they do not espouse a misguided distinction between what the heart feels and the head thinks.

As Stan and Ruth Burgess are children of the callings of their parents, so too they have had a distinctive influence on their children, academic colleagues, and students, some of whom have submitted essays for this Festschrift.

SYNOPSIS OF CHAPTERS

This volume is concerned with a variety of topics, including religious studies, learning theory, and history. The diversity of subjects addressed in this Festschrift attests to the breadth of the scholarly work of Stan and Ruth Burgess. They have provided wise advisement and collegial encouragement for the exploration of various aspects of Christian spirituality, pneumatology, and pedagogy. The book contains three sections: Section 1 deals with the major highlights of Stan and Ruth's academic biographies. Section 2 presents pioneering studies of biblical studies and church history. Section

3 offers application-based research and personal reminiscences. In the Epilogue, Stan and Ruth share a brief response to the contributors.

Section 1: From Mavelikara and Pune to Springfield and Jerusalem

Chapter 1, "Stanley Milton Burgess and the Artifacts of Renewal," originated as a research paper prepared by Eric Newberg in Stan Burgess' Renewal Historiography seminar at Regent University. The chapter consists of three sections: (1) a brief biographical sketch, (2) a review of Stanley Burgess' published research, and (3) an assessment of Burgess' legacy. The major contention of this chapter is that Stan Burgess has made a groundbreaking contribution to the study of the historical roots of Pentecostal spirituality. By means of his numerous articles, books, and monumental reference dictionary, Burgess has unearthed historical artifacts documenting the renewing work of the Holy Spirit throughout the entire Christian era. In keeping with the title of this book, *Children of the Calling*, Burgess has shifted the focus of Pentecostal scholarship from a polemical emphasis on the legitimacy of Pentecostal doctrine to a critical reevaluation of Pentecostalism in its many forms.

In chapter 2, "Ruth Vassar Burgess: Many Cultures, Multiple Perspectives," Lois Olena presents an intellectual biography grounded in the theme of heritage. Dr. Olena depicts the heritage that shaped the course of Ruth's life and provided for her a multitude of perspectives as "a beautiful kaleidoscope for seeing, experiencing, and contributing to the world in ways characterized by grace, kindness, love of life and learning, and a strong sense of justice." The chapter is organized chronologically according to the cultural experiences and concomitant perspectives that Ruth Vassar developed in periods of her life: *childhood* in India (1937–52), *transition* to America for schooling (1952–57), *discovery* of the joys of academia, marriage, and family (1958–61), *vocation* in speech therapy (1962–85), *transformation* in Israel with Dr. Reuven Feuerstein (1986–88), *justice* relative to gender equity struggles (1990s), physical *suffering* with cancer (2001–2), and *ShantiStan*—the effort toward peace (2004–14). Dr. Olena concludes that the many cultures of Ruth Vassar Burgess's life provided multiple perspectives that continue to pour into and enrich the lives of all those with whom she comes in contact.

Section 2: The Quest to Understand Beyond Boundaries

In chapter 3, "Written with the Finger of God: Divine and Human Writing in Exodus," Brian Doak presents a study of writing and divine representation in the Book of Exodus with specific attention to the incident of the golden calf in Exodus 32. Against the backdrop of ancient Near Eastern sources, Dr. Doak presents a detailed study of the significance of divine and human writing in Exodus. He explores the connection of writing and cultic acts in passages relating to Amalek, the vision of God on the mountain, the golden calf episode, and the inscribing of cultic apparel. His thesis is that the act of writing and the products of writing in the Hebrew Scriptures are intimately involved in the search for God's physical representation on earth.

Paul Lewis contributes chapter 4, "The Church of the East in the Tang Dynasty (635–907 CE)," an informative description and revealing theological assessment of the material evidence of the missionary presence of the Nestorians in China. The evidence consists of monuments and documents, including the 'Xi'an Stele,' the Dunhuang manuscripts, and the Luoyang stele. Based on his analysis of the extant sources, Dr. Lewis deduces the theological perspectives of the Nestorian Christians in China, concluding that the Church of the East made a noteworthy attempt at constructing a contextualized Buddhist-Taoist Christology reminiscent of the poetic style of Ephrem the Syrian.

Charles Hedrick begins chapter 5, "A Story about a Dishonest Manager," by proposing that the parables of Jesus are designed to engage the reader, to draw him or her into the narrative's plot and action, where discoveries may be made about oneself and one's world. Readers of the stories of Jesus are always left with a complication needing resolution. Such is the case with the Parable of the Dishonest Manager (Luke 16:1–7) and its appended commentary (Luke 16:8–13). Dr. Hedrick argues that it presents readers with an unresolved complication, rather than a moral lesson. "What does it mean?" is the wrong question to put to a narrative because meaning does not innately reside in the text. Rather, meaning is the product of a particular reader's response to the text. An author decides what the text says; the reader decides what it means. It is up to the reader to ponder the story and construct a meaning.

Chapter 6, "The Revolutionary Paradigm of Grace," by Lyle Story, is an exposition of the theme of grace in the Synoptic Gospels with primary focus on the parables of Jesus. Dr. Story's thesis is that Jesus embodies and communicates grace to both sinners and righteous persons as a grand reversal and paradox of commonly held religious norms. With regard to God's grace to sinners, Story analyzes Jesus' teachings on table fellowship, acceptance without conditions, forgiveness of sins, healing, faith, repentance, love, and joy. With regard to God's grace to the righteous, Story explores Jesus' invitation to joy and acceptance, his disavowal of "scorekeeping," and his threats of judgment. In reflecting on the implications of his findings, Story asserts that moralism in the Church is a negation of grace and concludes with a stirring call for both sinners and righteous to appreciate the freedom of God to be gracious.

Veli-Matti Kärkkäinen contributes chapter 7, "Is the Origin of the Spirit Still a Theological Impasse? A Modest Ecumenical Proposal about the Derivation of the Spirit in the Trinity." Dr. Kärkkäinen explores the prospects for ecumenical rapprochement between East and West in relation to the longstanding breach over the *filioque* clause. He finds common ground between Eastern and Western Trinitarian theology in a common affirmation of consubstantiality. Calling for a more nuanced and sophisticated way of looking at the differences between the Christian East and West, Kärkkäinen grants that the Eastern critique of the *filioque* is important both ecumenically and theologically and should not be dismissed. The West did not have the right to unilaterally add *filioque*. Even though the *filioque* is not heretical, ecumenically and theologically it is unacceptable and therefore should be removed. For the sake of healing the wounds of separation, East and West ought to honor their somewhat different approaches regarding the place and role of the Spirit in the Holy Trinity, while pursuing attitudinal softening and healthy self-criticism.

In chapter 8, "Salvation according to Luke," Dr. Graham H. Twelftree offers a trenchant analysis of the motif of salvation in Luke's writings. Twelftree notes that only Luke's Gospel affords Jesus the title of "Savior." He argues that Luke's understanding of salvation was non-political. Based on a careful examination of pertinent texts in Luke-Acts, Twelftree shows that Luke depicts salvation as the experience of the powerful presence or Spirit or kingdom of God resulting in personal restoration. The meaning of salvation consists of personal restoration of relationships with God and the community through the forgiveness of sin. Nonetheless, salvation has profound sociopolitical implications, both for those who proclaim it and those who respond to it, in the political arena, the presence of the kingdom of God, and the demand for radical allegiance. Salvation involves a claim by a Savior, and the kind of loyalty to Him that causes those saved to relinquish all other allegiances.

In chapter 9, "Apostolic Advice: 1 Corinthians 7 as Deliberative Rhetoric," Charles Puskas offers a rhetorical analysis of 1 Corinthians 7, arguing that Paul employed basic tactics of persuasion that were taught and widely practiced in his own day. Puskas' thesis is that rhetorical criticism is one approach that can enable us to better understand this medium of Paul's living message. Dr. Puskas identifies three types of rhetoric: deliberative (persuasion), forensic (legal judgment), and epideictic (for spectators). He defines each and then dissects the structure of the first type—deliberative speech. He argues that Paul employed deliberative rhetoric in 1 Corinthians 7 as he addressed questions put to him by the Corinthian Christians regarding celibacy and marriage. In advising a moderate course of action that was advantageous for all parties involved, Paul's argumentation was diplomatic, reasonable, and in agreement with the advisory persuasion of deliberative rhetoric.

Section 3: The Need to Expand, Preserve, and Restore Traditions

Elaine Cleeton is the author of chapter 10, "'Behind Every Successful Man . . .': Recovering God the Mother in the Search for Subjectivity." Dr. Cleeton offers a metacognitive reflection on her search for connection, interspersed with tributes to Ruth Burgess. In sharing her intellectual memoirs, Dr. Cleeton revisits the experiences that led her away from—and back to—her origins. Along the way she studied speech pathology with Dr. Ruth Burgess. Dr. Cleeton was impressed by the manner in which Dr. Burgess not only prepared her for success in graduate school, but also combined family and work. She recalls that Dr. Burgess was adept at living between cultures—moving between Indian and U.S. ethnic identities, while managing conservative religious and contemporary professional conflicts. In a notable passage, Dr. Cleeton writes, "Making room for me in her life, as she carried on her family and professional responsibilities, she answered definitively the question regarding [a] women's place in both worlds, that there is but one world of which women are rightful inhabitants. She reached out, offering resources otherwise unavailable to me to promote my academic progress. Observing her life, I, too, would decide to combine an academic career with family."

In chapter 11, "The MissouriFind Project: A Labor of Love (And an Exercise in Patience, Perseverance, and Political Acumen)," David Brown and Steven Hinch describe a curriculum developed by a team under the direction of Dr. Ruth Burgess and supported by Southwest Missouri State University and Ozarks Public Television. MissouriFind was an inquiry-based, middle school curriculum based on Instrumental Enrichment, a pedagogical theory of cognitive intervention and enrichment developed by Reuven Feuerstein, founder and director of the International Center for the Enhancement of Learning Potential (ICELP) in Jerusalem, Israel. The main idea of Feuerstein's theory is that intelligence can be modified through mediated interventions. MissouriFind required students to demonstrate competency in their state's history and geography, as well as their public and private heritages. Drs. Brown and Hinch point out that the objective of the curriculum was for students to "find themselves in Missouri and Missouri in them." The curriculum was comprised of eighteen units divided into four student magazines. The units included a fifteen-to-eighteen minute video plus a variety of instructional materials. The results of the pilot study with a seventh-grade class were overwhelmingly positive.

In chapter 12, "Mediated Learning," Carolyn Nixon succinctly delineates Reuven Feuerstein's Cognitive Map as a method for identifying the nature of a learner's difficulty and providing the feedback necessary to move learning forward. The parameters of Feuerstein's Cognitive Map include content, modality/language, phase, cognitive operations, level of complexity, level of abstraction, and level of efficiency. Nixon argues that the Cognitive Map provides a critical resource for teacher training, helping teachers understand how to provide responsive feedback by adjusting one or more of the parameters of a learning task during real-time instructional episodes.

Thomson Mathew contributes chapter 13, "The Keralite Diaspora," an original analysis of the history and current situation of the Diaspora of Indian Pentecostalism in America. Dr. Mathew, whose roots are in the Indian Pentecostal Church, relates that his wife's grandfather, Pastor K. C. John, had close interactions with John Burgess, the father of Stan Burgess. After tracing the history of the Keralite Diaspora in America, he takes up the serious challenges facing Indian Pentecostals in Diaspora as they adapt to the new realities of the twenty-first century in India and abroad. Although Keralite Pentecostal leaders in India and the U.S. may be tempted to ignore the looming challenges of the twenty-first century and see these tensions as evidence of backsliding, Mathew avers that these issues will not just go away. He calls for a global conversation on Indian Pentecostalism in the twenty-first century. Led by the Spirit, such a conversation could lead to a reassessment of Keralite Pentecostal teachings and practices in the light of Scripture, tradition, experience, sanctified reason, and active discernment.

In chapter 14, "Strategizing in the Spirit in Time of War: The 1943 Assemblies of God Missionary Conference," Malcolm Brubaker conducts an analysis of the presentations delivered at an impromptu missionary conference convened by the Assemblies of God in 1943. The parents of Stan and Ruth Burgess were attendees at this conference. Brubaker sets the context for the conference, delineates its themes and objectives, and assesses its accomplishments. Dr. Brubaker sets out to determine whether the conference presentations made a significant contribution to the missions strategy of the Assemblies of God in the postwar period. He evaluates the nine extant addresses, covering the status of AG missions in Europe, Africa, India, Latin America, Palestine, and the Dutch East Indies (Indonesia), concluding that although the goals of the conference were not met, two important results were achieved. First, a precedent was set for future missionary conferences at which missionaries would gather for mutual encouragement and strategic planning. Second, a principle for strategic planning was established in which a balance would be struck between denominational oversight and initiative at the individual missionary level.

In chapter 15, "Baptism in the Holy Spirit: A Spiritual and Theological Journey," Peter Hocken traces four stages in the development of his understanding of baptism in the Spirit. In the first stage (1971–76), Dr. Hocken was initiated into the charismatic renewal and agreed with Father Simon Tugwell's view that the Pentecostal understanding of Spirit-baptism was unacceptable for a Catholic. In the second stage (1976–88), he affiliated with the Mother of God community and accepted the view that the same grace of baptism in the Spirit had been poured out across all the churches and was given in God's purpose as a major impulse for Christian unity. In the third stage (from 1989), as he pondered Louis Dallière's teaching on the second coming of the Lord, Dr. Hocken began to see the essentially eschatological significance of baptism in the Spirit as an ecclesial event of sovereign grace poured out on the whole church. In the fourth stage (from 2008) Dr. Hocken latched on to a distinction made by Pope John Paul II between the institutional and charismatic dimensions of the church—considered baptism in the Spirit as belonging to the charismatic dimension of the Church—and concluded that the Pentecostal outpouring of the twentieth century is to be understood as a charismatic grace to move the whole body of Christ toward the eschatological completion.

Dr. Kevin Ranaghan and Dorothy Garrity Ranaghan coauthor chapter 16, "The Ecumenical Imperative and the Catholic Charismatic Renewal." They provide a recollection by participant observers of the interconnections of Pentecostals and Catholics in the emergence and diffusion of the Catholic charismatic renewal. On the one hand, the Ranaghans see themselves as descendants of the 1906 Azusa Street Revival. On the other hand, they believe that when Catholics and others were baptized in the Holy Spirit and chose to stay within their own denominations, the Pentecostal movement as a whole took a giant leap forward. From its inception, therefore, the Catholic charismatic renewal had an ecumenical character. Because of the ecumenical history of baptism in the Spirit and spiritual gifts experienced in all the churches simultaneously, the Ranaghans argue that an ecumenical imperative and responsibility is conveyed by the Catholic charismatic renewal movement.

In chapter 17, "Looking Back on the Forward Way," Karl Luckert reflects on his academic endeavours, including the twenty years he served with Stan Burgess on the faculty of the Religious Studies department at Southwest Missouri State University and his subsequent research interests in retirement. The first portion of Luckert's chapter is a parody of the follies of academia, featuring recollections of the Supreme Order of the Golden Sloth, whose members slowly climbed the branches of the academic tree, pronouncing the solemn oath, "I will hang in there." The second portion of the chapter consists of a narrative of Dr. Luckert's research interests, including the development of a curriculum, "Road to Peace," which aimed to advance religious and intercultural understanding by taking young imams from China on bus tours across the United States. Passport cancellations and visa denials scuttled the project. Dr. Luckert also describes his interpretation of the artifacts from Neolithic temples in eastern Anatolia on a hill called Göbekli Tepe, which he visited in 2011, leading to the discovery of a hitherto unknown religion.

Taken together, these chapters present a clear picture of the company of colleagues and students with whom Stan and Ruth Burgess are carrying out their calling. Of their varied pursuits, Stan and Ruth loved teaching most; and aside from their family they love students best, whether undergraduates or candidates for advanced degrees. Their students in turn love and respect them for the master teachers and scholars they are. Through the subtle chemistry by which teachers transmit part of themselves to their students, Stan and Ruth have mediated a passion for lifelong learning and brilliant teaching to waves of students now teaching on higher education faculties across the globe. Because of the importance of the legacy left by Drs. Stan and Ruth Burgess, the coeditors are pleased to commend this special collection of essays in their honor.

BIBLIOGRAPHY

Anderson, Allan. *Spreading Fires: The Missionary Nature of Early Pentecostalism.* Maryknoll, NY: Orbis, 2007.
"Combined Minutes of the General Council of the Assemblies of God in the United States of America, Canada, and Foreign Lands, 1914–1917." *Assemblies of God Publications: Pre-WWII.* Springfield, MO: Flower Pentecostal Heritage Center, 2006.
Fichte, Johann Gottlieb. *The Vocation of the Scholar: Lectures Delivered at Jena.* Translated by William Smith. London: John Chapman, 1889.

Flokstra, Gerald J., III. "Sources for the Initial Evidence Discussion: A Bibliographic Essay." *Asian Journal of Pentecostal Theology* 2 (1999) 243–59.

Goff, James R., Jr., *Fields White Unto Harvest: Charles Parham and the Missionary Origins of Pentecostalism*. Fayetteville: University of Arkansas Press, 1988.

Guinness, Os. *The Call: Finding and Fulfilling the Central Purpose of Your Life*. Nashville: Nelson, 2003.

Hawley, Dale. "Research on Missionary Kids and Families: A Critical Review." Missions Resource Network, 2004. http://www.mrnet.org/system/files/library/critical_review_on_mks_families.pdf (accessed February 16, 2014).

McClung, Grant. "Try to Get People Saved: Azusa Street Missiology." In *Azusa Street and Beyond*, edited by Grant McClung, 1–21. Gainesville, FL: Bridge-Logos, 2006.

McGee, Gary. "Assemblies of God Mission Theology: A Historical Perspective." *International Bulletin of Missionary Research* 10 (1986) 166–70.

Owens, Robert. "The Azusa Street Revival: The Pentecostal Movement Begins in America." In *The Century of the Holy Spirit*, edited by Vinson Synan, 39–68. Nashville: Nelson, 2001.

Rance, DeLonn. "Training Pentecostal Missionaries: Getting Properly Wired—Hearing and Obeying the Voice of the Spirit." *The Journal of the European Pentecostal Theological Association* 32 (2012) 179–97.

Robeck, Cecil M., Jr. *Azusa Street Mission and Revival: The Birth of the Global Pentecostal Movement*. Nashville: Nelson, 2006.

———. "Pentecostalism and Mission: From Azusa Street to the Ends of the Earth." *Missiology* 35 (2007) 75–92.

From Mavelikara and Pune
to Springfield and Jerusalem

1

Stanley Milton Burgess and the Artifacts of Renewal

—Eric Nelson Newberg

In a tribute to Stanley M. Burgess, Pentecostal historian Gary B. McGee remarked, "Your academic accomplishments have reflected the renaissance of evangelical and Pentecostal scholarship that has occurred the last half century."[1] The 2012 president of the Society for Pentecostal Studies, Br. Jeffrey Gros, recently stated, "The contribution of Stanley Burgess to Pentecostal historical scholarship is monumental."[2] George O. Wood, General Superintendent of the General Council of the Assemblies of God, writes of Stan and Ruth Burgess: "You've had a great influence on my life, and I so appreciate the sterling contribution you have made to the kingdom of God and academia over these years. Both of you have modeled what it means to be true Christian scholars. Your contribution to the Pentecostal Movement has been enormous!"[3] These accolades raise the question of Stan Burgess's contribution to Pentecostal historical scholarship. This chapter will assess that contribution by means of a critical review of the major writings of Stan

---

1. Unpublished letter, Gary B. McGee to Dr. Stanley Burgess, April 6, 2004, in the collection of letters presented at the Religious Studies Appreciation Banquet in honor of Stan Burgess for twenty-eight years of service at Southwest Missouri State University, sponsored by the Council of Churches, Springfield, Missouri, April 17, 2004; hereafter referred to as *BAC*, an abbreviation of "Burgess Appreciation Collection."

2. Gros, Review of *Christian Peoples of the Spirit*, 277.

3. Unpublished letter, George O. Wood to Stan and Ruth Burgess, March 31, 2004, *BAC*.

Burgess. The chapter is divided into three sections: (1) a biographical sketch, (2) a review of the major findings of Burgess's published research, and (3) an assessment of Burgess's legacy.

The major contention of this chapter is that Stan Burgess has made a groundbreaking contribution to the study of the historical roots of Pentecostal spirituality. By means of his numerous articles, books, and monumental reference dictionary, Burgess has uncovered evidence of continuous charismatic spirituality throughout the history of Christianity.

BIOGRAPHICAL SKETCH

Stanley Milton Burgess was born on November 27, 1937 in Nagercoil, India, the only child of John and Bernice Burgess.[4] When Stan was born, he was considered a godchild by the Hindus.[5] From 1926 to 1950 Stan's parents served as Assemblies of God missionaries in South India in the state of Travancore (now Kerala) on the Malabar Coast.[6] In 1927 they established the Bethel Bible Institute (later College), the first permanent Assemblies of God Bible college outside the United States, for the purpose of training indigenous Indian Pentecostal leaders.[7] Life was not easy in India. According to his wife Ruth Vassar Burgess, whose parents also served in India from 1936 to 1952 under the aegis of the Assemblies of God, "Pentecostal missionaries were zealots."[8] As Stan recollects, "My father was constantly traveling. We couldn't afford a car, so he went by bicycle."[9] Eventually the elder Burgess procured an abandoned British military jeep, easing the strain of transportation. Stan says, "My mother had a difficult time living in India. She said she loved the people but hated the place."[10] Stan's earliest memories are of street vendors, spiders, snakes, and long delays in train stations. He attended international schools, at which he and his mother resided some distance away from Mavelikara, where his father worked at the Bible Institute. He recalls: "At the Hebron School in Conoor, a Christian school using

   4. For biographical facts, see Burgess's Vita in "Johann Eck and Humanism," 170–71.
   5. Interview with Ruth Vassar Burgess, February 17, 2005.
   6. Burgess and van der Maas, eds., *New International Dictionary of Pentecostal and Charismatic Movements*, 450; hereafter referred to as *NIDPCM*. The testimonies of Burgess's parents are featured in "A 'Welsh Revival' in South India," 1, 10–11. For a report on the ministry of John Burgess in India, see "Under His Shadow Among the Heathen," 13–14, 19.
   7. Burgess and McGee, "India," 122.
   8. Interview with Ruth Vassar Burgess, February 17, 2005.
   9. Interview with Stanley M. Burgess, March 8, 2005.
   10. Ibid.

the British model, I received a smattering of Latin, French, German, Spanish and Italian."[11]

The conditions of Burgess's early life can be surmised from his parents' reports to Pentecostal periodicals, which reflect discouragement over trying circumstances. In one letter, the elder Burgess writes concerning a terrible cholera epidemic: "Many deaths occur within a few hours from the time the sickness comes. A very few live for a few days. Many who ran from home got cholera where they went and died there. Who will be able to hide from God's face?"[12] A letter in *The Pentecostal Evangel* reports that "John H. Burgess writes of the wonderful opportunities and open doors in South India at this time. The workers, however, are few and inadequate to meet all the demands upon them . . . Brother Burgess also asks prayer for the safety of the Christian people as a dread plague of cholera has spread over all the southern section of that field."[13] Perhaps it was due to health hazards that Stan's mother attempted to shelter him and kept him indoors much of the time, although the stated reason was that Stan had a heart condition.[14] The confinement indoors allowed Stan to consume the books in his father's library, including Keswick "higher life" writings, which emphasized the empowerment of the Holy Spirit. He also devoted himself to practicing the piano and organ, musical skills he later employed in accompanying worship services. His position at the keyboard afforded Stan a vantage point from which to closely observe the exuberant manifestations of Pentecostal spirituality, while maintaining some degree of detachment. Perhaps his strategic location as a participant-observer laid the groundwork for Stan's vocation as an historian of Christian spirituality.

Due to poor health in the family, the Burgess family returned to the United States in 1950 when Stan was twelve. Re-entry into American culture was a disorienting experience for Stan, as is often the case with children of missionaries. Ruth Burgess describes the ordeal of itinerating from church to church during furlough, marching at General Council in Indian costumes. She says of the pressure missionary children face, "On furlough they experience cultural lag. Children absorb foreign culture. Back home, they feel out of place."[15] Stan says, "We were never like Americans of the churches in which we were submerged [during furlough]."[16] In Stan's case,

---

11. Ibid.
12. Burgess, "Travancore," 13.
13. "South India," 7.
14. Interview with Ruth Vassar Burgess, February 17, 2005.
15. Ibid.
16. Interview with Stanley M. Burgess, March 8, 2005.

his loneliness was exacerbated by further confinement. He says, "When we came back in 1950, I was stuck in the attic for one and a half years, because my mother thought I had a heart condition."[17] The Burgess family lived in an attic apartment in the Muskegon Heights, Michigan home of Stan's uncle, Ray Burgess.

Subsequently, Stan's father was serving as the pastor of the Trinity Assembly of God in Flint. Initially Stan was home-schooled until the myth of his heart condition was debunked. Then he attended Beecher High School, where he engaged in verbal jostling on the debate team. During his high school years Burgess crossed a spiritual landmark. He says, "I received the baptism of the Holy Spirit as I was playing the piano in church. The Spirit fell and I started speaking in tongues."[18] Burgess graduated from high school at the age of fifteen and then matriculated at the University of Michigan in Ann Arbor, where he earned a Bachelor of Social Studies in Education in 1958 and a MA in History in 1959. Burgess recalls that when he went to Ann Arbor, "my dad went with me to make sure I was okay. This was my mother's idea. That is how my dad got started on doing his BA and MA."[19] However, out of fear that his congregants would regard their pastor as worldly, the elder Burgess did not inform the church in Flint of his collegiate studies. This illustrates the anti-intellectualism that prevailed among Pentecostals in the past.[20]

For Stan Burgess, college was a broadening experience. He says, "For me at Ann Arbor the whole Pentecostal schema came down."[21] Specifically, he realized that he didn't agree with the trademark doctrine of the Assemblies of God, initial evidence, which held that speaking in tongues is the initial physical evidence of the baptism of the Holy Spirit. From this time onward Burgess was gravitating toward the belief that all Christians are baptized in the Spirit at the moment they are initiated into faith in Christ.

After a year of teaching at an inner city junior high school, Burgess was recruited to teach at Evangel College in Springfield, Missouri, where he served from 1959 to 1976, attaining the position of Chair of the Department of Social Studies. Burgess received ministerial credentials with the Assemblies of God in 1960, and seven years later he was ordained, at the behest of the denomination. His teaching load was heavy, usually between eighteen and twenty-two hours per semester. To make matters worse, as Stan

17. Ibid.
18. Ibid.
19. Ibid.
20. See Nañez, *Full Gospel*, 144, 151–53.
21. Interview with Stanley M. Burgess, March 8, 2005.

says, "They were never pleased with what you did."[22] Stan soon experienced friction with the Assemblies of God. With the advent of the charismatic renewal, Stan was invited to speak in Mainline Protestant churches. This caused much discomfort with the Southern Missouri District of the Assemblies of God, and in particular with Thomas Zimmerman.[23] Colleagues on the Evangel faculty were censured for views that were deemed to be unduly ecumenical. Stan says that he stayed out of trouble by focusing on the past. Ruth puts a different slant on it: "Stan was an intellectual in an anti-intellectual context. He survived because he was collegial."[24] When asked what he would do differently if he could do it over again, he says, "I would not spend seventeen years at Evangel."[25]

On the bright side, during his first year at Evangel, Stan married Ruth Lenora Vassar on February 26, 1960 in Abilene, Texas. Stan and Ruth have five children—Bradley (1961), Matthew (1971), Scott (1972), and twins David and Amanda (1974).[26] When asked to identify his most fulfilling accomplishments, Stan immediately answers, "Parenthood. My own family. And my student family."[27]

While teaching at Evangel, Burgess pursued a PhD in History at the University of Missouri in nearby Columbia. In 1971, he completed his doctorate in History, specializing in Renaissance and Reformation studies. In 1976 Burgess resigned from Evangel and accepted a faculty appointment in the History Department of Southwest Missouri State University. In 1977 Stan was named Director, Office of Grants, and in 1981 he served as Head of the Department of Religious Studies.

During his tenure at Southwest Missouri State, Burgess cultivated a rich network of colleagues in the academic world and mentored many aspiring scholars. He was also mentored, in particular, by Gerrit tenZythoff, Chair of the Religious Studies Department. Stan says, "He was more of a father to me."[28] When Gerrit was on his deathbed, Stan was there. He says, "I followed a leading to go to the hospital. They were just about to hook him up to the anesthesia for surgery on his brain. He told me he was scared. He was a man of faith. I laid my hand on him and prayed for him. I was the last one to see him alive because he never woke up from the surgery."[29]

22. Ibid.
23. Interview with Ruth Vassar Burgess, February 17, 2005.
24. Ibid.
25. Interview with Stanley M. Burgess, March 8, 2005.
26. Ruth Burgess, "My Life Story," 39–43.
27. Interview with Stanley M. Burgess, March 8, 2005.
28. Ibid.
29. Ibid.

Stan's colleagues and former students credit him with establishing the MA program in Religious Studies, organizing a Grants Office, recruiting the greatest number of MA students, amassing an impressive body of publications, bringing the Religious Studies Department into the computer age, modeling innovative pedagogical styles, exhibiting grace and compassion, and introducing many to Indian cuisine.[30]

One of the most transformative of Stan's academic ventures was a sabbatical in Jerusalem in 1986. While Stan immersed himself in the spiritual writings of Eastern Orthodox Christianity in the library of the Tantur Ecumenical Institute, Ruth was collaborating with Dr. Reuven Feuerstein at the Hadassah-Wizo-Canada Research Institute in Jerusalem. As Stan was exploring the pneumatology of the Eastern Church, Ruth was mastering Feuerstein's theory of structural cognitive modifiability. Ruth recalls a breakthrough conversation as they were walking into Bethlehem one evening, when Stan said, "Ruth, it's not fair; you're learning these things and you're not sharing them. I want to learn them. I want to know them."[31] As Ruth imparted Feuerstein's theory of mediated learning experience to Stan, his teaching style was renovated. Stan says, "We became more Jewish. I gained new approaches to thinking and learning. This is where I gained an appreciation for multiple perspectives. I went from a didactic to a dialectic style. You teach life, not material."[32]

In the spring of 2004 the Burgess's made a bold move. In order to devote the next chapter of their lives to mentoring the next generation of scholars of the renewal movement, they left Southwest Missouri State University and joined the faculty of Regent University School of Divinity, where Stan served as Distinguished Professor of Christian History and Ruth as a member of the Adjunct Faculty. Concerning Stan's transition, Charles W. Hedrick, Distinguished Professor of Religious Studies at Southwest Missouri State University, surmised, "Regent University is gaining an eminent scholar, skilled educator, and dedicated churchman. Your departure will leave a gap in the ranks of the university and department that can never be filled because of your unique perspectives, background, and experience. The department will greatly miss your professional leadership, gentle

---

30. Unpublished letters in *BAC*; Charles W. Hedrick to Dr. Stanley M. Burgess, April 8, 2004; Robert Hodgson to Dean Vinson Synan, September 5, 2003; Jim Moyer to Stanley M. Burgess, April 14, 2004; and Kathy J. Pulley to Drs. Stan and Ruth Burgess, April 7, 2004.

31. Ruth Burgess, "My Life Story," 52–53.

32. Interview with Stanley M. Burgess, March 8, 2005.

humor, and seasoned wisdom."[33] Kathy J. Pulley, Associate Vice President for Academic Affairs at Southwest Missouri State University, commented,

> Your research endeavors continue to be impressive. Not only have you been productive but your international reputation has made us all proud and the department even stronger. And, I know there is much more to come, regardless of where you live. It is hard to imagine the department without you being part of it.[34]

The credibility of the fledgling PhD program in Renewal Studies at Regent was greatly enhanced by the addition of Stan and Ruth Burgess to the faculty. Ruth's class in Research-Based Pedagogy was a major asset to the doctoral program, equipping students with Feuerstein's theory of mediated learning experience. Stan provided seasoned leadership to the doctoral program, serving as Director, modeling best practices in creative teaching, advising students in the history track, and providing opportunities for students to publish their work.

REVIEW OF BURGESS'S MAJOR PUBLICATIONS

Few realize that Stan Burgess's scholarly publications include a venture into the field of archaeology, published in 1979 by the Center of Archaeological Research at Southwest Missouri State University.[35] He collaborated with Juris Zarins on a cultural resources survey of the area surrounding the proposed Prosperity Lake Reservoir in Jasper County, Missouri. The site search conducted by Burgess "revealed the location of several important historic sites hitherto unrecorded in the study area."[36] One of the sites located by Burgess was Freedom Baptist Church, which was constructed in 1841 and stood until the 1880s. By 1907 all traces of it had disappeared. A two-acre cemetery adjacent to the church was also found. The artifacts collected in the cemetery, including flakes, scrapers, blades, choppers and projectile points, revealed that the area had been used for prehistoric occupation, thus adding to it archaeological significance.[37]

---

33. Unpublished letter, Charles W. Hedrick to Dr. Stanley M. Burgess, April 8, 2004, *BAC*.
34. Unpublished letter, Pulley to Burgesses, April 7, 2004, *BAC*.
35. Burgess and Zarins, *A Stage I Cultural Resources Assessment*.
36. Ibid., 13.
37. Ibid., 91–93, 115–16, 146–47.

At first glance this publication might appear anomalous for an intellectual historian. However, it can be seen as a metonym for Burgess's life task as an historian of renewal. He is a collector of artifacts, scholarly and otherwise. Anyone can see this by walking through the Burgess home, which is adorned with artifacts collected over the years in India, Europe, Israel, and the American heartland. Likewise, anyone familiar with Burgess's academic work knows that he has searched deep and wide to discover historical artifacts that have shed light on the roots of the Pentecostal spirituality.

In the opening words of his groundbreaking essay, "Medieval Examples of Charismatic Piety in the Roman Catholic Church," Burgess challenged the reigning paradigm of Pentecostal historiography. He writes, "Historians of Pentecostalism have devoted most of their attention to the period of apostolic outpourings and to the modern Pentecostal movement. In so doing, they have treated the intervening centuries as 'the long drought,' during which there were few evidences of the charismata, and these were hardly worth the trouble of further investigation."[38] The overall aim of Burgess's historical research was to end this drought.

As with all historians, Burgess was guided in his research by mentors, one of whom was Bernard Bresson, a colleague at Evangel College, who passed on to Burgess a wealth of secondary sources attesting to a wellspring of charismatic activity throughout history. Bresson was convinced that "whenever and wherever God found hungry hearts He met them."[39] He assured Burgess that the full story of spiritual ecstasy would never be told until someone had drunk deeply from the cup of the primary sources. This was perhaps the inspiration for Burgess's exhaustive research into the history of Christian perspectives on the Holy Spirit, to which he dedicated much of his life.

Burgess's three-volume work on historical pneumatology is a major accomplishment. It covers three sectors of Christian history—Ancient Christian traditions, Eastern Christian traditions, and Medieval Roman Catholic and Reformation traditions. Burgess's findings in each of these volumes are reviewed below.

Ancient Christian Traditions

In *The Holy Spirit: Ancient Christian Traditions*, Burgess diagnoses the condition that his research intends to correct. He writes, "While most

---

38. Burgess, "Medieval Examples of Charismatic Piety in the Roman Catholic Church," 15.

39. Bresson, *Studies in Ecstasy*, 18.

Christians have used His name in their religious practices, they have been woefully deficient in their knowledge of the Holy Spirit."[40] Prior to Burgess's work, there was but one scholarly study in English of the Holy Spirit in early Christianity, Henry B. Swete's *The Holy Spirit in the Ancient Church*, published in 1912. Burgess covered much of the same ground as Swete, yet from a different perspective. Following Bresson, Burgess built on the premise that the renewing power of the Holy Spirit did not cease after the apostolic age. Swete, on the other hand, took the position that following the New Testament period there was "a loss of both literary and spiritual power, . . . [as] the spiritual giants of the Apostolic age are succeeded by men of lower stature and poorer capacity. Nor does the fresh power of the first century altogether return to the Church in the years that follow."[41] If Burgess has an axe to grind, it is the widely accepted view that the Holy Spirit ceased His supernatural manifestations after the apostolic age. Burgess attempts to show that the historical record does not support the case for "cessationism."

For an interpretive schema, Burgess utilizes Jeffrey B. Russell's contrast between the "spirit of order" and the "spirit of prophecy."[42] Burgess begins with Russell's basic assumption: "In medieval Christianity, as in Christianity as a whole, both the prophetic spirit and the spirit of order were at work, sometimes in cooperation and sometimes in conflict."[43] Burgess argues for two general perspectives on the Holy Spirit, a "majority tradition" (the spirit of order) and a "minority tradition" (the spirit of prophecy).[44] Whereas the majority tradition conceived of the activity of the Spirit within institutionalized, ecclesiastical boundaries, the minority tradition insisted that the Spirit was at work in the prophetic movements that bubbled up on the fringes of the Church. Burgess insists that both perspectives contributed to the development of early Christian pneumatology and bore witness to manifestations of charismatic gifts.[45]

Burgess collects historical evidence showing that outbreaks of charismatic gifts occurred in a continuous pattern. Both the majority and minority traditions made significant contributions to the Church's understanding and practice of the gifts of the Holy Spirit. On the one hand, the most sensational example of the minority tradition was the Montanist movement,

40. Burgess, *The Holy Spirit: Ancient Christian Traditions*, 1.

41. Swete, *The Holy Spirit in the Ancient Church*, 3. Swete was sympathetic toward the Montanist movement, which he viewed as "beneficial, especially in the West, where tradition and convention were apt to exercise too great a control" (83).

42. Burgess, *Holy Spirit: Ancient Christian Traditions*, 1.

43. Ibid.

44. Ibid, 3.

45. Ibid., 7.

renowned for its prophetic practices as well as its illustrious convert, Tertullian. Montanus and his prophetesses claimed to be direct channels of the Holy Spirit. On the other hand, majority tradition envisioned the gifts of the Holy Spirit operating within institutional channels. Cyprian claimed that office and *charismata* were integral in that "the bishop has the sole claim to prophetic gifts."[46] The Cappadocian fathers spanned both traditions by dividing their time between holding positions of institutional leadership and withdrawing to monastic solitude. Significantly, they viewed the monk as "pneumatophor."[47]

Burgess regards the Cappadocian Fathers' conception of the Trinity as a hypostatic union as the high point of pneumatology in the patristic period.[48] He is at his best in synthesizing the thought of Basil, Gregory of Nyssa and Gregory Nazianzus. In spite of the plentiful activity of the Spirit and the theological brilliance of the Cappadocians, the Church never formulated a fully developed doctrine of the Holy Spirit for two main reasons—first, because pneumatology was collapsed into Christology, and, second, because the doctrine of the Holy Spirit was shaped episodically, as the Church responded to the challenges of particular doctrinal controversies.[49] For Burgess, the low water mark was Augustine's doctrine of the Spirit as the bond of love in the Trinity, which later fed the fires of the *filioque* controversy, an internecine debate between East and West over the procession of the Spirit.[50]

Most reviews of Burgess's first volume of the trilogy were overwhelmingly positive.[51] A notable exception was David D. Bundy's mixed review, which, along with some accolades, shorts Burgess for accepting the "older scholarly analysis," neglecting "recent studies of orthodoxy and heresy in the period," and giving "the appearance of being very uncritical."[52] Bundy suggests that Burgess should have used the functional approach to reconstruct

46. Ibid., 85.
47. Ibid., 141.
48. Ibid., 132–33.
49. Ibid., 13–14, 16, 27, 35, 52–53, 57–58, 98.
50. The Latin term *filioque*, meaning "and from the Son," was unilaterally inserted into the Nicene Creed by the Western church in the sixth century. The bone of contention was whether the Spirit proceeded from the Father alone (Eastern view), or from the Father and the Son (Western view). The theological fracture caused by this controversy contributed to the schism of the Eastern and Western churches in 1054 CE.
51. See Applegate, Review of *The Spirit and the Church: Antiquity*, 142–155; Menzies, Review of *The Spirit and the Church: Antiquity*, 30–31; Weaver, Review of *The Spirit and the Church: Antiquity*, 60–61.
52. Bundy, Review of *The Spirit and the Church: Antiquity*, 81–82.

how certain authors used their prophetic claims as an avenue for legitimizing their authority and influence in ecclesiastical power struggles.[53] Bundy's critique notwithstanding, most concurred with McGee's assessment: "Your magisterial trilogy of books on the Holy Spirit in the Christian tradition greatly surpassed earlier efforts and will remain the standard study for years to come."[54]

Eastern Christian Traditions[55]

Burgess is clearly enamored of the pneumatology of Eastern Christianity.[56] His appetite for research into the Eastern perspective on the Holy Spirit was whetted as he listened to a presentation by Athanasios F. S. Emmert at the annual meeting of the Society for Pentecostal Studies in 1972.[57] During the 1980s, Burgess spent six years digging in the rich soil of the East, culminated by his sabbatical in 1986 at the Tantur Ecumenical Institute in Jerusalem. In *The Holy Spirit: Eastern Christian Traditions*, published in 1989, Burgess avers that the Holy Spirit "has always been at the heart of Eastern Christian theology. It is not a doctrine apart, but an integral aspect of Eastern theological teaching."[58] He argues that the key to the Eastern emphasis on the Holy Spirit is found in a crucial theological contrast between the Eastern and Western churches, explaining, "In large part, the distinctiveness of oriental Christian pneumatology stems from Eastern anthropology (the doctrine of man), and the consequent soteriology (the doctrine of salvation)."[59] As Bur-

---

53. Ibid.

54. Unpublished letter, McGee to Burgess, April 6, 2004, BAC.

55. The Eastern Christian traditions encompass about forty separate churches, fourteen of which are designated as *autocephalous* (fully self-governing and independent). Most of the rest describe themselves as *autonomous* (meaning that their independence has not been recognized by the other Orthodox churches). Another group, known as Oriental Orthodoxy, is made up of the churches that disavowed the Council of Chalcedon. Jacobsen, *The World's Christians*, 19–20.

56. In this respect Burgess differs from Watkin-Jones, author of two sequels to the work of Swete. Watkin-Jones critiques the Eastern Church's theology as "unprogressive." He follows Adolf von Harnack's dictum that "the Greek Church has no history of dogma after the seven great Councils," holding that "the dogmatic development of the Eastern Church ceases with John of Damascus" (Watkin-Jones, *The Holy Spirit in the Mediaeval Church*, 15). Nevertheless, it should be noted that Watkin-Jones does give careful attention to the pneumatology of the Eastern Church in both of his studies.

57. Burgess, "Implications of Eastern Christian Pneumatology to Western Pentecostal Doctrine and Practice," 19. See Emmert, "Charismatic Developments," 28–42.

58. Burgess, *The Holy Spirit: Eastern Christian Traditions*, 1.

59. Ibid., 2.

gess sees it, on the one hand, the Western church espouses a "negative" anthropology, emphasizing the depravity of fallen humanity and the need for substitutionary atonement by Christ. For Western Christians, the stress on salvation through forgiveness subsumes pneumatology under Christology. On the other hand, the anthropology of the East is more "positive," placing a greater emphasis on the Holy Spirit. The Eastern Churches teach that the image of God in humans has been tarnished, not ruined by the Fall. God's purpose in Christ was re-creation. This happens through a process of *theosis* or "deification." For Eastern Christians, the ultimate goal of salvation is the renewal of the divine image to humankind through the work of the Holy Spirit.

Burgess thinks that several theological themes of Eastern Christianity could serve as healthy correctives to the tacit and uncritical acceptance of Western Christian pneumatology among Pentecostals. Among Burgess's favorite Eastern themes are the notions of sacred time and sacred space, and the sacramental conception that material things like water, bread and oil become vehicles of the Spirit through the prayer of *epiclesis*. Burgess cherishes two notable figures of the Eastern Church as antecedents of the Pentecostal/charismatic renewal movements: Symeon the New Theologian, who urged his followers to seek a baptism of the Spirit subsequent to water baptism, and Seraphim of Sarov, who held that the chief goal of the Christian life is the acquisition of the Holy Spirit.[60]

Bundy again offered a review. Although he quibbled with Burgess over matters of detail in the family tree of Orthodoxy, he offered this commendation: "The volume will serve pentecostal theologians, and others, with a concise accessible introduction to a part of the Christian intellectual and spiritual tradition which has rarely been discussed."[61]

We would be remiss if we did not discuss the influential paper that Burgess delivered at the Conference on Pentecostal and Charismatic Research in Europe in 1989, in which he describes how his mind was changed by his study of the pneumatology of Eastern Christianity. He goes on to offer an incisive and provocative assessment of what Pentecostals could learn from Eastern Christian pneumatology. According to Burgess, Pentecostals do not have a fully developed pneumatology; what they have is a gift theology, and a limited one at that, given its narrow focus on the ecstatic charismatic gifts. Burgess does not mince his words as he writes, "Eastern Christians have raised questions that have never even occurred to Pentecostals and have found answers which are highly suggestive to their modern cousins

---

60. Ibid., 53–62, 79–83.
61. Bundy, Review of *The Holy Spirit: Eastern Christian Traditions*, 34.

in the Spirit."[62] He criticizes Pentecostals for tacitly accepting the *filioque* clause "without ever thinking through the implications of that teaching to their own pneumatology."[63] This is indeed a telling point. He also brings Pentecostals up short for blurring the connection between holiness and the empowerment of the Spirit. He writes, "Perhaps it is time once again to expect a life of holiness and self-giving from those who claim to exercise prophetic gifts."[64] Further, he commends the Eastern doctrine of the "prophethood of all believers" as a hedge against spiritual elitism. Burgess commends the Eastern emphasis on divine aid in hard times, rather than the contemporary Western penchant for attributing material prosperity to divine approbation. He argues for a comprehensive view of the activity of the Holy Spirit and calls on scholars of the Pentecostal tradition to disabuse their minds of the misconception that Pentecostal spirituality represents an entirely new epoch in Christianity. He invites us to see God's greater design in the wider tradition of Christian spirituality.[65] The conclusion is vintage Burgess: "From this we all could have a better understanding of the larger Body of Christ, broaden our expectational vistas, and enlarge our language of spirituality. But this only can come when we pull the blinders from our eyes and stand back, observing in awe and wonder what God has done historically and continues to do for all those who hunger after him."[66]

Medieval Roman Catholic and Reformation Traditions

As the bouquet of a fine wine becomes more mellow and fragrant with age, Burgess's research on the roots of Pentecostal spirituality has matured over time. At the outset Burgess looked to Bresson as a guide; however, Bresson's *Studies in Ecstasy* was limited by an over-reliance on secondary sources.[67] Hence, in the third volume of his trilogy Burgess affirms the value of digging for "primary evidence for the outpouring of the Holy Spirit on the medieval Roman Church."[68] As he sifted through the *Acta Sanctorum*, an encyclopedic collection in sixty-eight volumes of extant monastic devotional literature, dusting off the heavy residue of hagiography, Burgess found a

62. Burgess, "Implications of Eastern Christian Pneumatology," 26.
63. Ibid.
64. Ibid.
65. Cf. Chan, *Pentecostal Theology*.
66. Burgess, "Implications of Eastern Christian Pneumatology," 27.
67. Interview with Stan Burgess, March 8, 2005.
68. Burgess, "Medieval Examples of Charismatic Piety in the Roman Catholic Church," 17.

plentiful vein of gems.[69] He writes, "I have discovered additional primary evidence of the outpouring of the Holy Spirit during the Middle Ages in the publications of certain leading religious orders."[70] He reiterates, "Finally, I re-emphasize the need for a study of the primary materials in every period of the history of Pentecostalism, even when our evidence is limited and not entirely credible."[71]

Along with his initial findings of plentiful evidence of the outpouring of the Spirit in the Western church, Burgess also reports that further discoveries would necessitate the surmounting of significant historical obstacles. The first obstacle is a bias against speaking in tongues in many academic studies of the manifestations of the Holy Spirit.[72] A case in point is Howard Watkin-Jones' superbly researched study of *The Holy Spirit in the Mediaeval Church*, which commends the experience of the Holy Spirit, yet neglects tongues-speaking and supernatural charismatic manifestations.[73] To counteract this bias, Burgess acknowledges that he would have to provide convincing primary source evidence. The second obstacle is the prevalence of hagiography in the history of Christian spirituality. Burgess saw that his research would have to be conducted with a critical and discerning eye. With that in mind, he laid out his agenda: "Special attention will be given to the question of whether those elements which we in the twentieth century regard as basic to the Pentecostal experience were present in the medieval outpourings."[74]

After years of disciplined study, Burgess unveiled the results of his research. Indeed, there were instances of speaking in tongues throughout

---

69. *Acta Sanctorum* (Acts of the Saints) is an encyclopedic text in sixty-eight folio volumes of documents examining the lives of Christian saints; the text is organized according to each saint's feast day. It begins with two January volumes, published in 1643, and ended with the *Propylaeum* to December published in 1940. The *Acta Sanctorum* has from the start been at the forefront of the critical method of scholarship. The *Acta Sanctorum* Database now makes this vast body of literature available in electronic form, providing a new level of access to these texts and enabling them to be searched quickly and efficiently for names, topics, and themes. To access the database, go to http://www.proquest.com/en-US/catalogs/databases/detail/acta.shtml (accessed January 6, 2014).

70. Ibid., 18.

71. Ibid., 26.

72. Burgess cites Cutten, *Speaking with Tongues* and Gorres, *Die Christliche Mystik*.

73. Watkin-Jones writes, "Moreover, the Early Church and the Church of the Middle Ages developed their inward experience of the Holy Spirit as well as their intellectual conceptions of Him. So this development of experience, in its very nature progressive, has added to the earlier deposits of truth valuable increments which can be traced only to the Spirit of God as their Source." *The Holy Spirit in the Mediaeval Church*, 12.

74. Burgess, "Medieval Examples of Charismatic Piety in the Roman Catholic Church," 17.

Christian history. Yet, no one from the apostolic period to the early nineteenth century had correlated tongues with the advent of life in the Spirit, except for Augustine, and he asserted that the correlation ceased with the first-century church.[75] Intermittently radical dualists had insisted on the necessity of a separate baptism of the Holy Spirit, but, by and large, no mainstream Christians were concerned with Spirit-baptism. As Burgess sees it, the magisterial Reformers were staunchly opposed to charismatic manifestations. In particular, Martin Luther was antipathetic toward Spirit-baptism. Burgess writes, "According to Luther, the Holy Spirit is given only to the anxious and distressed heart. Obviously, no one should boast of possessing the divine Spirit—as certain proud fanatics did—because even the most pious still must strive against sin."[76] Burgess drew a parallel between the radical spiritualists of Luther's age and twentieth-century Pentecostals. Both manifested a sense of social disequilibrium. As he puts it, "Eschatologically oriented, they have recognized the need for a special work of the divine spirit to empower them for service in what they perceive as the last days before the second coming of Christ."[77] Based on the scarcity of evidence for an association of Spirit baptism with charismatic manifestations, Burgess concludes, "This study demonstrates that Pentecostals, who rejoice in the novelty of their teachings and experiences, are fully justified in classifying their doctrine of initial evidence as distinctive."[78]

The crowning achievement of Burgess's research on historical pneumatology was the publication of the final volume of the trilogy, *The Holy Spirit: Medieval Roman Catholic and Reformation Traditions*. Based on case studies of notable Roman Catholic theologians, spiritual writers, and radicals, Burgess argues that the Third Person of the Trinity was overshadowed by the Second Person: "Western Christians usually were strongly Christocentric."[79] Burgess attributes this tendency to the negative anthropology of the West. "Because fallen humanity needed a savior who offered himself up for a propitiatory sacrifice, Roman Catholics emphasized Christology more than pneumatology."[80] Burgess finds the same downplaying of pneumatology in the Protestant Reformers, whose soteriology was dominated by forensic theories of justification. However, there were exceptions to the rule, especially in the fringe elements, such as the millenarians and radical dualists.

75. Burgess, "Evidence of the Spirit," 37.
76. Ibid., 27.
77. Ibid., 37.
78. Ibid., 38.
79. Burgess, *Holy Spirit: Medieval Roman Catholic and Reformation Traditions*, 2.
80. Ibid., 5.

Burgess uses a vivid metaphor to reiterate a theme from the first volume of the trilogy, stating, "Just as the waters of a great river cut and shape the landscape most noticeably along its banks, so religious innovation comes from fringe elements."[81]

In Burgess's view, one of the culprits responsible for the low pneumatology of the Western church is the *filioque* controversy. He believes that the *filioque* clause "disturbed the balance between the three persons of the Trinity and led to an inadequate understanding of the person and work of the Spirit."[82]

Another culprit was a revision in the make-up of the *charismata*. In surveying the medieval Catholic views of spiritual gifts, Burgess notes that Catholic theologians tended to conceive of spiritual gifts in terms of Isaiah 11:2 (wisdom, understanding, counsel, power, knowledge, and fear of the Lord), rather than the gift lists in the New Testament. Apparently, the *charismata* in 1 Corinthians 12 and 14 were thought to be extraordinary gifts reserved for the "saints." Some saints were known to have spoken in tongues, but more often they exercised the gifts of prophecy, healing and miracles.

Burgess discovers charismatic vitality in mainstream figures such as Gregory the Great, Bernard of Clairvaux, Bonaventure, Thomas Aquinas and Ignatius Loyola, as well as those on the margins, such as Rupert of Deutz, Joachim of Fiore, and Thomas Muntzer. Best of all, in my estimation, is the enlightening section on the prophetic gifting of the women mystics, Hildegard of Bingen, Gertrude of Helfta, Birgitta of Sweden, Catherine of Siena, Julian of Norwich, and Margery Kempe. One of the truly significant findings of this volume is that the radical Reformers showed a pronounced affinity for manifestations of *charismata*, reporting many ecstatic experiences. In his overall conclusion, Burgess returns to the interpretive schema introduced in volume one. He writes, "The entire Christian era has witnessed a continuing tension between major and minor traditions. This is the tension between what Jeffrey B. Russell describes as 'the spirit of order' and 'the spirit of prophecy'—in his opinion, one of the fundamental conflicts in medieval Christianity."[83]

In his review of Burgess's third volume on the Holy Spirit in *Gregorianum*, Gerald O'Collins observes, "An eirenic and fair-minded spirit pervades this learned book."[84] It is a tribute to Burgess's ecumenical awakening

---

81. Ibid., 6.

82. Ibid., 7.

83. Ibid., 125.

84. O'Collins, Review of *The Holy Spirit: Medieval Roman Catholic and Reformation Traditions*, 766.

that his work is highly regarded by Christian scholars of many traditions. O'Collins writes,

> This extremely clear and thoroughly researched work could happily serve for courses on the Trinity. As the first volume of Burgess's trilogy appeared in 1984, it took thirteen years before the third volume was published. They were thirteen years of further meticulous scholarship and pursuit of truth that is simply admirable.[85]

During his tenure at Regent (2003–2011), Burgess continued to publish his research and pursue ecumenical endeavors. He edited two important reference works, which enabled his students to publish entries. The first was a volume in the Routledge series of encyclopedias on Religion and Society.[86] The second was the fruit of years of participation in Pentecostal/Roman Catholic dialogue. Collaborating with Father Jim Puglisi, director of *Centro Pro Unione* in Rome, Burgess edited a volume published in Italian comprised of entries describing the contributions of Protestant luminaries in early modern and modern history.[87] In 2011 Burgess contributed a chapter to Vinson Synan's anthology of essays on Spirit-empowered Christianity in which he delivered a perceptive critique of contemporary Pentecostalism.[88] Burgess was also co-editor with Michael Palmer of the *Wiley-Blackwell Companion to Religion and Social Justice*.[89] Finally, Burgess capped his research on historical pneumatology with a collection of primary source documents representing Christian perspectives on the Holy Spirit throughout the entire Christian era.[90] Taken together, the body of work produced by Stan Burgess deserves to be regarded as an impressive and notable achievement.

THE BURGESS LEGACY

The family, friends, colleagues, and students of Stan Burgess know him to be a man with a passion for intellectual honesty. In his illuminating essay "Cutting the Taproot: The Modern Pentecostal Movement and Its Traditions," he looks back on his Pentecostal roots in order to critique past missteps and

---

85. Ibid., 767.
86. Burgess, ed., *Encyclopedia of Pentecostal and Charismatic Christianity*.
87. Burgess, ed., *Tesimoni Della Fede: Nelle Chiese Della Riforma*.
88. Burgess, "Change and Continuity," 47–54.
89. Palmer and Burgess, eds., *The Wiley-Blackwell Companion*.
90. Burgess, ed., *Christian Peoples of the Spirit*.

suggest future directions of the historiography of renewal.[91] Burgess begins by describing how early Pentecostals cut themselves away from their direct forbears, the Wesleyan-Holiness and Higher Life movements, the "taproot" of American Pentecostalism.[92] According to Burgess, the Pentecostals themselves did not set out to cut their historical taproot. Those of the Holiness and Higher Life traditions started the fight by accusing the Pentecostals of fanaticism, spiritual arrogance, and demon possession. Burgess cites R. A. Torrey's alleged vitriolic castigation of the Pentecostals as "the last vomit of Satan."[93] Persecution prompted the Pentecostals to see themselves in a contrarian light as a unique restoration movement on which the mantle of the Spirit-filled New Testament Church had uniquely fallen. Based on this self-understanding, Pentecostals harbored ambivalence concerning their historical lineage. They found their identity and distinctiveness in glossolalia, faith healing, and ecstatic worship experiences.

To show that this was not unusual, Burgess writes, "Finally, when early Pentecostals cut the taproot they were playing out one of the most recent chapters in a long run of conflicts between prophetic and institutional religion."[94] They justified their putative freedom from tradition by reasoning that tradition was a sign of spiritual deadness. Unknowingly, though, Pentecostals developed their own tradition of counter-tradition, prizing the value of being open to the leading and direction of the Spirit. However, in cutting the taproot of wider Christian traditions, Pentecostals could not see how "God had blessed Christians of all ages with waves of renewal."[95] For the first four decades of their existence, Pentecostals feared and distrusted the outside church world. Two later developments freed Pentecostals from their radical insularity: affiliation with the National Association of Evangelicals and the Charismatic Renewal. The former drew Pentecostals into common causes with the broader stream of evangelicalism; the latter involved them in fellowship and cooperative ventures with mainstream charismatics. The ongoing Roman Catholic/Pentecostal dialogue, begun in 1972, has had the same broadening effect. In a kind yet authoritative manner, Burgess urges Pentecostals to see what is happening before their very eyes. Whether they like it or not, their movement has become part of mainstream American Christianity.

91. Burgess defines "renewal" as what the Holy Spirit has done throughout the centuries of Christian history including but not limited to the Pentecostal/Charismatic movements.

92. Burgess, "Cutting the Taproot," 57.

93. Ibid., 59.

94. Ibid., 62.

95. Ibid.

Above all else, Burgess's legacy is embodied in what many refer to as "The Dictionary." In the first edition of the *Dictionary of Pentecostal and Charismatic Movements*, published in 1988, Burgess and coeditor Gary B. McGee gathered eight hundred articles from sixty scholars. The *DPCM* makes the statement that the Pentecostal and charismatic movements are international in their geographical scope, cultural makeup, and theological perspectives. The publication of the *DPCM* was a clear indication that the Pentecostal and charismatic movements were coming of age. At the time of the 1988 edition, statistician David Barrett estimated the number of participants in the Pentecostal and charismatic movements at 360,618,240, constituting 24 percent of all Christians. Barrett comments, "The sheer magnitude and diversity of the numbers involved beggar the imagination."[96] Barrett's remark touches directly on the function of the *DPCM* as a means of disseminating vital information on the epochal mass movement that had become the "third force in Christendom." But all were not pleased. Some criticized the *DPCM* because it did "not hew to classical Pentecostal doctrines," totally missed "the genius of the revival's eschatological hope," and reflected the "continuing reluctance of Pentecostal scholarship to deal effectively with inspiration and inerrancy."[97] According to Burgess, Walter Hollenweger found it wanting for giving inadequate attention to the multicultural and international diversity of Pentecostalism outside of North America. Burgess himself admits that decisions over certain entries were swayed by outside pressures.[98]

A revised and expanded edition, titled *The New International Dictionary of Pentecostal and Charismatic Movements*, coedited with Eduard van der Maas, was published in 2002. The second edition is divided into three segments—a global survey, global statistics, and the collection of biographical and topical articles. It contains one thousand entries with over five hundred illustrations and graphics covering over two thousand years of Christian history and sixty countries and regions. Barrett and Johnson's statistics are updated, estimating that Pentecostals, charismatics and neocharismatics had increased to 27.7 percent of organized global Christianity.[99] Burgess's findings from his three-volume work on the Holy Spirit in Christian history are condensed in his pithy article on the doctrine of the Holy Spirit and

---

96. Barrett, "Statistics, Global," 829.

97. Lee, Review of *Dictionary of Pentecostal and Charismatic Movements*, 30.

98. Interview with Stan Burgess, March 8, 2005.

99. Barrett and Johnson, "Global Statistics," 284. In the 2001 edition of the *World Christian Encyclopedia*, Barrett estimates the world Pentecostal population at 523.8 million and projects it to reach 811.6 million by 2025. Barrett, Johnson, and Kurian, eds., *World by Countries*, 20.

entries on Gregory Thaumaturgus, Hildegard of Bingen, Seraphim of Sarov, and Symeon the New Theologian.[100] Many articles from the first edition that catered to classical Pentecostalism are absent. Much new material relating to the current neo-charismatic movement is included.

E. Kingsley Larbi of Ghana commends the *NIDPCM* for surpassing the spatial and temporal limitations of the previous edition, but he faults the articles for still being "tilted in favor of the North American scene" with a lopsided number of contributors from the West, particularly North America.[101] This critique is well taken and should be addressed in the event of a third edition. Nonetheless, most would join Gary B. McGee in congratulating Burgess on a monumental achievement:

> *The New International Dictionary of Pentecostal and Charismatic Movements*, a milestone in the examination of contemporary religious movements, represents the vital globalization and revision of a previous landmark study. Christians of many stripes, adherents of the non-Christian religions, and non-Christians alike have benefited from your scholarship, hopefully in ways that will create better understanding and good will in our troubled world. This too is a work of the Holy Spirit.[102]

The genius of both editions of the *Dictionary* is that they take a significant step toward recording the knowledge base of global Pentecostalism.[103]

CONCLUSION

Stanley M. Burgess has played a leading role in raising the bar of historical scholarship in the Pentecostal and charismatic movements. His contributions

---

100. "Doctrine of the Holy Spirit: Ancient Fathers; Medieval Churches; Reformation Traditions," 730–69. The other entries by Burgess in *NIDPCM* are "James ('Jim') Orsen Bakker," "Epiclesis (epiklesis)," "John Wright Follette," "Hildegard of Bingen," "Gregory Thaumaturgus," "Hope Chapel," "India," "David Kent Irwin," "Thomas D. Jakes, Sr.," "Klaude Kendrick," "Joyce Meyer," "David Mohan," "Paul S. Morton, Jr.," "Neocharismatics," "Quakers (Society of Friends)," "Jerry Sandidge," "Jerry Savelle," "Seraphim of Sarov," "Signs and Wonders," "Eusebius A. Stephanou," "Warren Badenoch Straton," "Francis A. Sullivan, S. J.," "Symeon the New Theologian," "Thomas E. Trask," "Theodore Roosevelt Vassar," "Miroslav Volf," and "Thomas Fletcher Zimmerman."

101. Larbi, Review of *The New International Dictionary of Pentecostal and Charismatic Movements*, 38.

102. Unpublished letter, McGee to Burgess, April 6, 2004, *BAC*.

103. The research projects of Burgess's students in the PhD program in Renewal Studies at Regent University have benefited greatly from the knowledge base recorded in the *NIDPCM*.

to the knowledge base of the history of Pentecostal spirituality have been substantial. His trilogy has not only filled in the gaps in the non-Pentecostal studies on the Holy Spirit by Swete and Watkin-Jones, but also addressed contemporary pneumatological concerns.[104] He has expanded former conceptions of the historical roots of the Pentecostal tradition. Building upon the foundation laid by Bresson, he has documented an unbroken thread of renewal extending throughout church history. As iron sharpens iron, Burgess's dialogue with learned comrades, like Bundy, has enhanced the craft of historiography in Pentecostal studies. With a twinkle in his eye he introduced flocks of students to the riches of the pneumatology of Eastern Orthodox Christianity. The merit of Burgess's call for an ecumenical appreciation of the pneumatology of Eastern Christianity is widely recognized by scholars in the Society for Pentecostal Studies.[105] In recognition of his distinguished career, in 2011 Burgess received the Lifetime Achievement Award from the Society for Pentecostal Studies.

Most importantly, Stan Burgess should be honored for his relentless search for the trans-temporal and trans-spatial principles that characterize the ongoing work of the Holy Spirit. In the spirit of the title of this book, *Children of the Calling*, Burgess has contributed to a major shift in the calling of Pentecostal scholarship from an emphasis on missionary evangelism to a critical reevaluation of Pentecostalism in its many forms. With that in mind, I would contend that Stan Burgess's most enduring accomplishment is the unearthing of historical artifacts that document the renewing work of the Holy Spirit throughout the entire Christian era.

---

104. Burgess, *Holy Spirit: Medieval Roman Catholic and Reformation Traditions*, 8.
105. Gros, "It Seems Good to the Holy Spirit and Us," 177.

Stanley M. Burgess, 2014
Photo Credit: Burgess Archives

BIBLIOGRAPHY

Works by Stanley M. Burgess

Burgess, Stanley M. "Change and Continuity among Twentieth Century Peoples of the Spirit." In *Spirit-Empowered Christianity in the 21st Century*, edited by Vinson Synan, 47–54. Lake Mary, FL: Charisma House, 2011.
———. "Cutting the Taproot: The Modern Pentecostal Movement and Its Traditions." In *Spirit and Renewal: Essays in Honor of J. Rodman Williams*, edited by Mark W. Wilson, 56–66. Sheffield: Sheffield Academic, 1994.

———. "Evidence of the Spirit: The Ancient and Eastern Churches." In *Initial Evidence: Historical and Biblical Perspectives on the Pentecostal Doctrine of Spirit Baptism*, edited by Gary B. McGee, 3–19. Peabody, MA: Hendrickson, 1991.

———. "Evidence of the Spirit: The Medieval and Modern Western Churches." In *Initial Evidence: Historical and Biblical Perspectives on the Pentecostal Doctrine of Spirit Baptism*, edited by Gary B. McGee, 20–40. Peabody, MA: Hendrickson, 1991.

———. *The Holy Spirit: Ancient Christian Traditions*. 1984. Peabody, MA: Hendrickson, 1997.

———. *The Holy Spirit: Eastern Christian Traditions*. Peabody, MA: Hendrickson, 1989.

———. *The Holy Spirit: Medieval Roman Catholic and Reformation Traditions (Sixth-Sixteenth Centuries)*. Peabody, MA: Hendrickson, 1997.

———. "Implications of Eastern Christian Pneumatology to Western Pentecostal Doctrine and Practice." Paper presented to the Conference on Pentecostal and Charismatic Research in Europe, Rijksunivesiteit Utrecht, The Netherelands, June 28–July 1, 1989.

———. "Johann Eck and Humanism." PhD diss., University of Missouri, 1971.

———. "Medieval Examples of Charismatic Piety in the Roman Catholic Church." In *Perspectives on the New Pentecostalism*, edited by Russell P. Spittler, 14–26. Grand Rapids: Baker, 1976.

Burgess, Stanley M., ed. *The Encyclopedia of Pentecostal and Charismatic Christianity*. New York: Routledge, 2006.

———. *Reaching Beyond: Chapters in the History of Perfectionism*. Peabody, MA: Hendrickson, 1986.

Burgess, Stanley M., and Gary B. McGee, eds. *Dictionary of Pentecostal and Charismatic Movements*. Grand Rapids: Zondervan, 1988.

Burgess, Stanley M., and Michael D. Palmer, eds. *The Wiley-Blackwell Companion to Religion and Social Justice*. Malden, MA: Wiley-Blackwell, 2012.

Burgess, Stanley M., and Eduard M. van der Maas, eds. *The New International Dictionary of Pentecostal and Charismatic Movements*. Grand Rapids: Zondervan, 2002.

Burgess, Stanley M., and Juris Zarins. *A Stage I Cultural Resources Assessment of the Proposed Prosperity Lake Project Area, Jasper County, Missouri, 1978*. (Project, CAR-138). Springfield, MO: Center for Archaeological Research, Southwest Missouri State University, 1979.

Burgess, Stanley M., et al., eds. *Tesimoni della fede: nelle Chiese della riforma*. Rome: Citta Nuova, 2010.

Book Reviews of Burgess's Works

Applegate, Lloyd R. Review of *The Spirit and the Church: Antiquity*, by Stanley M. Burgess. *Journal of Religion and Psychical Research* 13 (1990) 142–55.

Bundy, David D. Review of *The Spirit and the Church: Antiquity*, by Stanley M. Burgess. *Pneuma* 7 (1985) 81–82.

———. Review of *The Holy Spirit: Eastern Christian Traditions*, by Stanley M. Burgess. *EPTA Bulletin* 9 (1990) 33–34.

Coulter, Dale M. Review of *The Holy Spirit: Medieval Roman Catholic and Reformation Traditions (Sixth-Sixteenth Centuries)*, by Stanley M. Burgess. *Journal of Pentecostal Theology* 14 (1999) 135–42.

Gros, Jeffrey. Review of *Christian Peoples of the Spirit: A Documentary History of Pentecostal Spirituality from the Early Church to the Present*, by Stanley M. Burgess. *Pneuma* 34 (2012) 277–78.

Larbi, E. Kingsley. Review of *The New International Dictionary of Pentecostal and Charismatic Movements*, edited by Stanley M. Burgess and Eduard M. van der Maas. *International Bulletin of Missionary Research* 27 (2003) 38.

Lee, Edgar R. Review of *Dictionary of Pentecostal and Charismatic Movements*, edited by Stanley M. Burgess and Gary B. McGee. *Paraclete* 23 (1989) 29–30.

Marino, Bruce R. Review of *Reaching Beyond: Chapters in the History of Perfectionism*, by Stanley M. Burgess. *Paraclete* 22 (1988) 28–29.

Menzies, William W. Review of *The Spirit and the Church: Antiquity*, by Stanley M. Burgess. *Paraclete* 22 (1988) 30–31.

———. Review of *The New International Dictionary of Pentecostal and Charismatic Movements*, rev. and exp. ed., edited by Stanley M. Burgess and Eduard M. van der Maas. *Asian Journal of Pentecostal Studies* 6 (2003) 145–47.

O'Collins, Gerald. Review of *The Holy Spirit: Medieval Roman Catholic and Reformation Traditions (Sixth-Sixteenth Centuries)*, by Stanley M. Burgess. *Gregorianum* 79 (1998) 766–67.

Pluess, J. D. Review of *The Holy Spirit: Antiquity*, by Stanley M. Burgess. *EPTA Bulletin* 5 (1986) 23–26.

Weaver, Rebecca H. Review of *The Spirit and the Church: Antiquity*, by Stanley M. Burgess. *Second Century: A Journal of Early Christian Studies* 6 (1987–88) 60–61.

Personal Collections

Burgess Appreciation Collection. A collection of letters of tribute presented at the Religious Studies Appreciation Banquet in honor of Stan Burgess for twenty-eight years of service at Southwest Missouri State University. Sponsored by the Council of Churches, Springfield, Missouri, April 17, 2004.

Burgess, Ruth L. V. "My Life Story." Idell Lewis, Storykeeper. Springfield, MO: Ethnic Life Stories Project, 2002.

Interview with Ruth Vassar Burgess, February 17, 2005, Virginia Beach, Virginia

Interview with Stanley M. Burgess, March 8, 2005, Norfolk, Virginia.

Articles Cited

Burgess, J. H. "Travancore, S. India, Swept by Terrible Plague." *The Pentecostal Evangel* 805 (July 6, 1929) 13.

Goff, James R., Jr. "Closing Out the Church Age: Pentecostals Face the Twentieth-First Century." *Pneuma* 14 (1992) 7–21.

Gros, Jeffrey. "It Seems Good to the Holy Spirit and Us: The Ecclesial Vocation of the Pentecostal Scholar." *Pneuma* 34 (2012) 167–84.

Lee, Swang-Hwan. "The Relevance of St. Basil's Pneumatology to Modern Pentecostalism." *Cyberjournal for Pentecostal Charismatic Research* (2000). http://www.pctii.org/cyberj/cyber7.html.
Lewis, Paul. "Reflections of a Hundred Years of Pentecostal Theology." *Cyberjournal for Pentecostal Charismatic Research* (2003). http://www.pctii.org/cyberj/cyber12.html.
MacIntyre, J. "The Holy Spirit in Greek Patristic Thought." *Scottish Journal of Theology* 7 (1954) 353–75.
Nestler, Erich. "Was Montanism a Heresy?" *Pneuma* 6 (1984) 67–78.
"South India." *The Pentecostal Evangel* 1137 (February 22, 1936) 7.
Stephanou, Eusebius A. "The Charismata in the Early Church Fathers." *The Greek Orthodox Theological Review* 21 (1976) 125–46.
"Under His Shadow Among the Heathen: Thousands Hear the Gospel in South India." *The Latter Rain Evangel* 25, no. 5 (February 1933) 13–14, 19.
"A 'Welsh Revival' in South India: An Interview with Brother and Sister John H. Burgess of Mavelikara, Travancore, S. India, Now on Furlough." *The Pentecostal Evangel* 949 (May 21, 1932) 1, 10–11.

Books Cited

Barrett, David B., et al., eds. *The World by Countries: Religionists, Churches Ministries.* Vol. 1 of *World Christian Encyclopedia: A Comparative Survey of Church and Religions in the Modern World.* Oxford: Oxford University Press, 2001.
Bartleman, Frank. *Azusa Street.* 1925. Reprint, Plainfield, NJ: Logos International, 1980.
Blumhofer, Edith L., et al., eds. *Pentecostal Currents in American Protestantism.* Urbana: University of Illinois Press, 1999.
Bresson, Bernard L. *Studies in Ecstasy.* New York: Vantage, 1966.
Brumback, Carl. *Suddenly . . . from Heaven: A History of the Assemblies of God.* Springfield, MO: Gospel, 1961.
Chan, Simon. *Pentecostal Theology and the Classical Spiritual Tradition.* Sheffield: Sheffield Academic, 2000.
Conn, Charles W. *Like a Mighty Army, Moves the Church of God, 1886–1955.* Cleveland, TN: Church of God, 1955.
Cutten, George B. *Speaking in Tongues.* New Haven: Yale University Press, 1927.
Emmert, Athanasios F. S. "Charismatic Developments in the Eastern Orthodox Church." In *Perspectives on the New Pentecostalism,* edited by Russell B. Spittler, 28–42. Grand Rapids: Baker, 1972.
Ensley, Eddie. *Sounds of Wonder: Speaking in Tongues in the Catholic Tradition.* New York: Paulist, 1977.
Ewart, Frank J. *The Phenomenon of Pentecost.* Hazelwood, MO: Herald, 1947.
Frodsham, Stanley H. *With Signs Following: The Story of the Pentecostal Revival in the Twentieth Century.* Springfield, MO: Gospel, 1946.
Jacobsen, Douglas. *The World's Christians: Who They Are, Where They Are, and How They Got There.* Malden, MA: Wiley-Blackwell, 2011.
Kärkkäinen, Veli-Matti. *Pneumatology: The Holy Spirit in Ecumenical, International, and Contextual Perspective.* Grand Rapids: Baker Academic, 2002.

Kendrick, Klaude. *The Promise Fulfilled: A History of the Modern Pentecostal Movement.* Springfield, MO: Gospel, 1961.

Kydd, Ronald. *Charismatic Gifts in the Early Church.* Peabody, MA: Hendrickson, 1984.

———. *Healing through the Centuries: Models for Understanding.* Peabody, MA: Hendrickson, 1998.

Lawrence, Bennet F. *The Apostolic Faith Restored* (1916). In *Three Early Pentecostal Tracts,* edited by Donald W. Dayton, 7–119. New York: Garland, 1985.

Nañez, Rick M. *Full Gospel, Fractured Minds? A Call To Use God's Gift of the Intellect.* Grand Rapids: Zondervan, 2005.

Reid, H. M. B. *The Holy Spirit and the Mystics.* London: Hodder and Stoughton, 1925.

Robeck, Cecil M., ed. *Charismatic Experiences in History.* Peabody, MA: Hendrickson, 1985.

Russell, Jeffrey B. *A History of Medieval Christianity: Prophecy and Order.* New York: Crowell, 1968.

Swete, Henry Barclay. *The Holy Spirit in the Ancient Church: A Study of Christian Teaching in the Age of the Fathers.* London: Macmillan, 1912.

Turner, William H. *Pentecost and Tongues: The Doctrine and History.* Shanghai: Shanghai Modern, 1939.

Wacker, Grant. *Heaven Below: Early Pentecostals and American Culture.* Cambridge, MA: Harvard University Press, 2001.

Watkin-Jones, Howard. *The Holy Spirit from Arminius to Wesley: A Study of Christian Teaching concerning the Holy Spirit and His Place in the Trinity in the Seventeenth and Eighteenth Centuries.* London: Epworth, 1929.

———. *The Holy Spirit in the Medieval Church: A Study of Christian Teaching concerning the Holy Spirit and His Place in the Trinity from the Post-patristic Age to the Counter-Reformation.* London: Epworth, 1922.

2

Ruth Vassar Burgess: Many Cultures, Multiple Perspectives

—Lois E. Olena

The remarkable story of Ruth Vassar Burgess must be told with the theme of heritage at its beginning and its end—a heritage that shaped the course of Ruth's life and provided for her a multitude of perspectives like a beautiful kaleidoscope for seeing, experiencing, and contributing to the world in ways characterized by grace, kindness, love of life and learning, and a strong sense of justice.[1] Ruth's was a heritage shaped by a sense of calling, purpose, and destiny both in her father's European forebears and the subsequent American journeys of her parents' families—the Vassars and the Barnetts. It was that sense of divine calling that resulted in Ruth's missionary parents—and those of then ten-year-old Stanley Milton Burgess—meeting at the Highclerc Boarding School in Kodaikanal, Tamil Nadu, South India in 1948. And the rest is history!

---

1. Though no doubt Ruth's students and family would write this chapter differently, I trust that my efforts here will provide honor to whom honor is due for a woman extraordinary in so many ways. It is rare indeed to experience such rich quality of engagement with another human being. Her gentleness and joy have calmed my spirit even as her insights have stirred my mind. Her smile has brought a refreshing grace that spurs me on to images of the woman I might be in twenty years with God's help. I look forward to cultivating my friendship with Ruth for many years to come.

PERSPECTIVES OF CHILDHOOD

European Roots and American Dreams

At the age of sixteen, Ruth's mother, Freddie ("Estelle") Barnett heard an audible voice telling her to go to India. A few years later at Southwestern Bible School in Enid, Oklahoma,[2] Ruth's father, Ted Vassar, fell head over heels for this small-statured, sparky young Texan girl. When he proposed, however, Estelle responded, "I can't marry you, I have a call to India." "I know you have a call," Ted replied, but I'm willing to follow the Scripture that says to go into all the world and preach the gospel. And I'm willing to follow you to India and help fulfill that call."[3]

Ted Vassar had a rich heritage of those willing to leave home because of faith; his French Huguenot ancestors, the LeVasseurs, fled France because of Catholic persecution, escaping to England with their lives. In 1635, John and Elizabeth LeVasseur settled in Jamestown, Virginia. Several generations later during westward expansion of the New World, the family settled in Missouri, helping Chouteau establish St. Louis in 1764. In the late 1880s, Ted's parents John and Lenora took part in the Oklahoma Land Run, settling near Tryon, Lincoln County and eventually moved to Pawhuska, Oklahoma in Osage County; there John worked as a veterinarian, and Lenora was known as a specialty seamstress. Ted and Estelle had pastored an Assemblies of God (AG) church there prior to leaving for India, and this was the town where Ruth would eventually spend a year while her parents traveled to raise missions funds.

Meanwhile, a couple hundred miles to the south in Texas, Estelle's father Tom worked in middle management for Texaco Oil Company.[4] Though the oil boom in Texas resulted in the family moving a great deal, they eventually settled in Electra, Texas where the company provided a house and company car. Bowie would be the location years later upon returning from India, where Ruth's parents would plant a new Assemblies of God church, and she would begin her educational journey. Ruth's grandmother, Ruth

---

2. Founded by P. C. Nelson, this school merged with others and eventually became Southwestern University of the Assemblies of God (SAGU) in Waxahachie, Texas. For more on P. C. Nelson, see Burke and Holder, "Daddy Nelson," 20–25.

3. Interview with Ruth Vassar Burgess, Strafford, Missouri, June 5, 2013. I conducted formal, recorded interviews with Ruth on June 5, July 8, and August 17 of 2013. Direct quotes from those interviews will pertain to the overall volume of transcribed and annotated material from the interviews with Ruth Burgess and will be cited hereafter: Interviews with Ruth Burgess, 2013.

4. Tom and his wife Ruth had four children: Johnnie Mae, Estelle, Herschel, and Mary Jo. Herschel's son is Tommy Barnett, founder of the Los Angeles Dream Center.

Elizabeth Byrd Barnett, was more overt in her feminism than Ruth's other grandmother. She was a suffragette, voted the first time she could, and drove a car before licenses were in vogue. Grandmother Barnett would prove to be an important role model for Ruth throughout her life for many reasons, but particularly as a champion of gender equity and human rights.[5]

India (1937–1942)

Before those American years, however, Ruth's story began in Pune, India where she was born in 1939. Two years prior, her parents had packed up her two-year-old brother, Bobby Jo, and traveled to Pune for their first missionary term (1937–1942). Only three months and one day after they arrived in India, however, young Bobby Jo died from being wrongly treated for malaria when in fact he had a case of appendicitis. Ruth grew up with a sense of sadness over the loss of this "'ghost brother' [seen] frequently in the ministry slides."[6] When she returned to India as an adult and went to visit Bobby's grave, Ruth found it had been vandalized by the Christian Ministers' Alliance in Pune who wanted to eventually appropriate the land to grow roses and make money. Seeing this desecration of Bobby's grave dealt a terrible blow to two values—heritage and tradition—which had become so strong by this point in Ruth's life; seeing the grave so mistreated left her feeling her "tradition had been violated and [her] heritage diminished."[7]

---

5. Ruth's new book, *Spirited Sisters*, preserves the heritage of eight women in her life. Grandmother Barnett's life story is remarkable itself, including her willingness to walk out of a comfortable status into the Pentecostal movement. One of her efforts for human rights in particular included burning her husband's KKK robe and pointed hat! The book also has recipes for each generation. "Food has always been a part of the *honey* that connects us together," Ruth recalls. This was largely because of her India upbringing. Food was always a big celebration—feasting, everyone there, sitting on the ground together, eating with one's fingers. Ruth says, "Grandmother Vassar always included her 'chickies' in making biscuits, bread, and mulberry pie, in such a loving way" (Interviews with Ruth Vassar Burgess, 2013).

6. Interviews with Ruth Vassar Burgess, 2013.

7. Idell Lewis, "My Life Story: Ruth Burgess," 3. The Ethnic Life Stories Project was the "brainchild" of Jim Mauldin of Springfield, Missouri. The project provided an opportunity for Storytellers (individuals within the Springfield community with roots in non-American cultures) to relay to Storykeepers the account of their lives, in order to appreciate the ethnic diversity present in the area. The sixty-five-page account of Ruth's story, along with many others, is available online here: Springfield-Green County Library, accessed January 20, 2014, http://thelibrary.org/lochist/els/menu.cfm. Direct link: http://thelibrary.org/lochist/els/burgess.pdf. Years later, Ruth's mentor Reuven Feuerstein would reinforce in her heart and mind "the significance of tradition and heritage [and the importance of engaging] . . . in intergenerational transmission of

Though the bereaved couple was delighted at the birth of a healthy baby when Ruth was born, their Hindu neighbors sent a messenger to console Ruth's father at the birth of a daughter instead of a son. The issue of gender inequity was a repeated theme throughout Ruth's life. When she was an adult she discovered a letter her father had sent back to the States to his mother announcing Ruth's birth; although he expressed excitement over a healthy baby he added, "But mother, I had hoped for a son."[8] In spite of that disappointment, however, Ruth soon became her father's favorite due to her ability to "carry on conversations and expand ideas very easily."[9]

"Baby Ruth" as she came to be called, lived from 1939 to 1941 in the historic city of Pune in Maharashtra, southeast of Mumbai (then Bombay); Pune was then a significant city within the British Colonial Empire. The family lived in a cantonment area, sharing a large colonial bungalow with a Scottish man named Rev. Thomas Stoddart ("Grandpa Stoddart") who ministered to English soldiers. Because Ruth had English-speaking parents and an Indian *ayah* (governess), she learned Marathi and English simultaneously.

America (1941–1947)

With the entry of the United States into World War II, the Vassars had to leave India. After returning to the States, the couple started a church in Bowie, Texas. During this time, Ruth's mother often fed tramps that would come through town; her kindness and sense of duty and calling to both earthly and heavenly service provided a strong example of faith even in times of financial struggles. That faith translated into risk-taking, something Ruth admired in both her parents and a trait she felt they had inherited from their own remarkable parents. Ruth made a public confession of her faith at age five in Bowie, at a storefront church. Later when the family returned to India, she was baptized in a tin tank on the mission compound.

Ruth's brother Teddy was born in 1943 and then her sister Helen in 1945 while the family was in Bowie. Not long after, with the end of World War II, the wheels began turning for the family's return to India. Noel Perkin, with the AG Department of Foreign Missions (DFM), had been

---

values. Unless people invest in their children and grandchildren, these wisdom principles which result in reasoned behavior will not be transmitted into the future. We have to cherish our children and encourage them to transmit our beliefs in order for them to survive" (ibid., 52).

8. Ibid., 2.
9. Ibid.

persistently writing, asking the couple to take charge of a boys' orphanage in Junnar, India that an Australian missionary, Jessie Ferguson, was turning over to the AG. The location had acreage for farming, and there was opportunity to develop a school. Estelle was thrilled; they had learned the language, had a love for the Indian people, and were ready to go. All they needed was money! At that time in the AG, raising funds for institutional social work was far more difficult than funding theological training or evangelism. Because the current AG missions culture did not prioritize social work at the time, Ruth's parents had to bear financial responsibility for the food, clothing, medicine, and educational supplies of seventy-five children and helpers at the orphanage and school.

India (1947–1952)

Driven by a sense of calling and a love for people, in 1947 Ruth's parents set their faces again toward India. They pulled Ruth out of second grade, then in Abilene, Texas,[10] boarded the *Marine Adder* from San Francisco and sailed for Bombay. The Vassars moved to Junnar—a remote village forty-five minutes north of Pune. That year was a momentous time, with the partition of India and Pakistan in August of that year. Ruth recalls that one day, when the family was visiting in Pune, a great crowd gathered. In the midst of the throng, her father lifted her high on his shoulders and asked what she saw. After the third attempt, Ruth finally blurted out, "Well, there's a man and it looks like they are carrying him on a stretcher. He hardly has any clothes on and he's bald headed. He just has a white cloth around his legs."[11] Looking at her soberly, her father instructed, "Never forget that man. His name is Mahatma Gandhi. He will be known as one of the greatest men of the twentieth century."[12]

In the midst of all the national turmoil, as well as the lack of missions support from the U.S., the family faced times of great financial struggles and yet experienced miracles of provision. Ruth recalls,

> My parents carried a heavy burden, living in a land of famine and pestilence, and being a minority culture. It was an act of faith to be there. When certain Americans sought a great quantity of

---

10. The AG church in Abilene was without a pastor and asked the Vassars to fill that post. Though the Vassars told them they were heading back to India eventually, the church asked them to just come preach for a few months before leaving for India. They stayed there from January to April 1947.

11. Lewis, "My Life Story: Ruth Burgess," 27.

12. Ibid.

> material things, while we were growing up in a culture where we lived with life's bare necessities, questions of fairness were raised in my mind. As an example, when I went to boarding school, mother took me to the shoemaker and he would draw an outline around my feet and make my shoes. Living a simple life in one's early years creates a template for later years.[13]

Each October Estelle would obtain bolts of cloth from Bombay and make articles of clothing for all the children to be sure they got something new for Christmas. Even so, Ruth would hear her parents crying at night sometimes, anxious they would not have enough. Ted was practical, though; in times of abundant harvests, he would even buy items on the black market and hide them in a brick storage building called a "go-down." Life and death were daily realities. The years of independence from Great Britain brought extreme hunger, pests, and disease. Ruth recalls that "diarrhea, sore eyes, rickets, malaria, cholera, and small pox were common maladies . . . [with] bodies being cremated on the riverbank."[14] Such troubles were reflected on the anguished faces of her Hindu neighbors.

Even with such struggles, though, the Vassars loved and were enriched by the people and their food, culture, language, and traditions. Junnar was an amazing place for a little girl who loved chameleons, beetles, bugs, and every creature! From cats to dogs, donkeys to cows, this remote part of India in the shadow of Mount Shivaniri[15] provided fertile stomping grounds and nurtured a love of animals[16] that would stay with Ruth the rest of her life.

Not long after arriving in Junnar, eight-year-old Ruth made the 1,000-mile trip south to Kodaikanal in Tamil Nadu to attend the Highclerc Boarding School (now known as Kodaikanal International School). It was there that she met ten-year-old Stan Burgess. Stan was a day student at the school and (due to a supposed heart problem) lived nearby with his mother Bernice

---

13. Ibid., 26.

14. Ibid., 5. Ruth saw her life in India as being "split between order and disorder, comfort and deprivation, and earthly and heavenly service. Independence from Great Britain's colonial reign brought social and civil unrest . . . [but w]hether at boarding school or on the plains, the adults encouraged us to remain calm, to be self-directed, and to work toward positive alternatives" (ibid., 28).

15. The compound was at the base of this mountain. In 2002, Ruth wrote *Tales from Beside Shivaniri: An Ethnographic Study Including Oral Histories from Orphans, 1947–1952*, published in India. The book resulted from interviewing fifty people who lived on the Junnar compound from 1947–1952. She integrated their stories with pictures her parents had and collaborated on their corporate history. Documenting their story fifty years later was an effort to help the orphans process any feelings of disintegration.

16. Some animal interactions were not so happy, though, such as the time her father had to kill a cheetah that had attacked a village boy!

while his father (John) taught in Travancore at the school the Burgesses had pioneered in 1927—Bethel Bible Institute, India's first Pentecostal theological institution.[17] Stan and Ruth met at a missionary prayer meeting. Ruth remembers this "active, blond haired, blue-eyed fellow"[18] playing the piano for the meeting, and not long after, "Aunt Bernice," as Stan's mom came to be called, began inviting the boarders to their lodge for tea and prayers. Stanley was happy to see them and joked around, and his mother invited Ruth to play checkers with him due to his health condition. "He was kindly and willing to share his Sugar Creek Gang books," she remembers. "I was impressed, but felt sorry that he was isolated from most of his peers."[19]

The Burgesses and Vassars became like extended family; though Stan's parents returned to the U.S. in 1950, the families kept in touch. At Kodai, occasionally the missionaries would comment how funny it would be if some of their children ended up marrying one another. One mother commented that her son Clarence should marry Ruth, but Stan's mother said she wanted *Stan* to marry her! At the time of this writing, fifty-four years later, Ruth is still delighted she chose Stan over Clarence.[20]

Kodaikanal was a "veritable paradise" in the Palni Hills. The Presbyterian Church and other supporters had established a school to "provide an American education for children of missionaries, diplomats, and other foreign workers."[21] Ruth's parents wanted to ensure that when she returned to the United States a smooth transition would be possible. The academic rigor of the school was no problem for Ruth, who was a year ahead of her peers when she returned to America after eighth grade. She found the social and cultural transitions quite difficult, though. Reflecting on the impact of cultural shifts when returning to the U.S., Ruth explains,

---

17. For more information, see Bethel Bible College, http://www.bbcpunalur.org/.
18. Lewis, "My Life Story: Ruth Burgess," 38.
19. Ibid.
20. The friendship forged between the Burgesses and the Vassars was especially strengthened in times of intense trial. In 1949, Ted and Estelle again faced the tragedy of losing a child on the mission field. Ruth's younger sister Rose Marie died in utero due to a misdiagnosis of Ruth's mother during pregnancy. Ted and Estelle were too poor to have a tombstone or even buy flowers. Stan's mother prepared a little box with Stan's baby pillow to put underneath Rose's head. Since Ted said funerals were "a man's thing," the women stayed at home while Stan and his father stood at the grave with Ted. Young Ruth and her brother Teddy felt bad for their parents, so they went around to their neighbors to ask if they could pluck flowers for little Rose's grave. Subsequent missionaries to Kodaikanal (in Alabama at the time of Rose Marie's death) denied she was ever born, an absurd accusation that stunned and grieved the Vassar family (ibid., 25–26; and Interviews with Ruth Vassar Burgess, 2013).
21. Lewis, "My Life Story: Ruth Burgess," 5.

> You look like everybody else—fair skin, blue or brown or green eyes, lighter hair—but you think differently. You understand different perspectives . . . You can't understand why some things bother your peers and why they do certain things because if only they had seen what other parts of the world do and [how they] survive, they would realize there is more than one alternative.[22]

These themes of culture and perspective would come to be a central feature of Ruth's life while she continued to process the impact not only of her parents' calling within multiple geographic and theological cultures but also her own sense of identity and purpose in the world as she became a child of the "third culture":

> Thus my European heritage underpinnings were formed, but the foundation for our family was built in the United States Midwest heartland. The intergenerational transmission of values provided authenticity for our beliefs. For example, social justice came from the French Huguenots. The Scots passed on family and kin bonds. Living respectfully with one's community was the mortar from my English heritage. It appeared the form and function of my family's home was going to be predictable. But, no. Somehow my parents heard the rhythms from a different drummer and left their homeland. These songs were not composed in major harmonies, but included minor, asynchron[ous] melodies birthed in eastern lands. Their heartbeats resounded to tabla rhythms. They responded to the Great Commission and trusted God to take care of them and their families. Little consideration was given to their earthly futures, because the artifact of time was believed to end shortly. Hence my life blended western Indian culture and Midwestern United States culture. As I synthesized these unusual bedfellows, I became a child of the "third culture."[23]

---

22. Ibid., 8.

23. Lewis, "My Life Story: Ruth Burgess," 13. "Sociologist Ruth Hill Useem coined the term 'Third Culture Kids' after spending a year on two separate occasions in India with her three children, in the early fifties. Initially they used the term 'third culture' to refer to the process of learning how to relate to another culture; in time they started to refer to children who accompany their parents into a different culture as 'Third Culture Kids.' Useem used the term 'Third Culture Kids' because TCKs integrate aspects of their birth culture (the first culture) and the new culture (the second culture), creating a unique 'third culture.'" ("What is a Third Culture Kid?," TCKid, accessed February 20, 2014, http://tckid.com/what-is-a-tck.html.) See also Pollock and Van Reken, *Third Culture Kids*.

PERSPECTIVES OF TRANSITION: AMERICA (1952–1957)

Upon returning to the United States in 1952 at the end of their second missionary term, Ted and Estelle Vassar needed to travel to raise money for the orphanage. They had seen the strong ministry potential of these young boys. Later missionaries would just take boys to the train station after they graduated from the orphanage and tell them, "Go find work," but the Vassars saw their ministry there as helping to strengthen the church in India, so they wanted to invest more fully in their futures. One young man, Benjamin Shinde, who Ruth called *tilu* ("older brother") eventually became an administrator of Southern Asia Bible College and pastor at First Assembly of God in Bangalore.[24]

To be free to travel, Ted and Estelle decided to leave their three children—Ruth, Teddy, and Helen—with Ted's mother Lenora Vassar in Pawhuska, Oklahoma, headquarters of the Osage Indian tribe—yet another cultural adventure for Ruth! Lenora had recently lost her husband and daughter to cancer and was now taking on, as Ruth notes, "these three ruffians!" Ted bought an old Victorian house in town, and Ruth began her freshman year of high school. She soon was busy making adjustments to life in the United States as a teenager. In India, whether at home or at the boarding school, they had support people to assist them, so she had not done many of the traditional chores a child would do. Her primary responsibilities had been "to act properly, read to improve my mind, to keep up with what was going on in the United States, and to be a kind person."[25]

---

24. Southern Asia Bible College has since produced more than 3000 alumni. "About Us," Southern Asia Bible College, accessed January 21, 2014, http://sabc.cgld.org/about-us/. See Burgess, "Benjamin Prasad Shinde."
Ruth takes seriously the title "brother" as applied to those young men with whom she grew up in Junnar. She goes back to India occasionally to walk out the tradition of the oldest child of the patriarch carrying on the values of that patriarch. Most recently in the spring of 2014 she sponsored a "Sister's Dinner" for 150 people, in honor of her father and to honor those in the Junnar Boys Home Association. In India, since people do not have an identity unless they are part of a group, Ruth's father established this Association for the orphans. This identity with a group has helped the young men with such practical matters as securing jobs and finding wives. Reflecting on her 2014 visit, Ruth comments, "It was a joy to see the faithful remnant from my parents' day who still love Christ and are serving Him. They are the fruit of my parents' lives. If my parents had not gone, these 150 Christians would not have been at that dinner together. They told me, 'When Daddy was here, we were never hungry, and we always had clean clothes to wear'" (Interview with Ruth Burgess, March 2, 2014). Whenever Ruth passes on, it will be the responsibility of her oldest son to go to Junnar and honor the legacy of his grandfather.

25. Lewis, "My Life Story: Ruth Burgess," 14.

All of those disciplines served her well, though she soon discovered new responsibilities and chores.

After the year of itineration, Ruth's father Ted wearied of "mixed messages" coming from the DFM and reached a turning point. After all his work, spending five-and-a-half years in India, bringing in people who tilled the land, building several granite stone edifices—a school, nursery, and a two-story dormitory for the boys—there was *still* no support base for the orphanage.[26] The funds raised during the year of deputation went back to support the DFM. Ted decided they simply could not go on this way. In addition, Teddy was having learning problems, so they decided to stay in the U.S. and not return to India. They had raised thousands of dollars for the orphanage and the work in Junnar, but with the missions department not having people grounded in theology *and* anthropology, it was a continual uphill battle.

Consequently, Ted went to the West Texas district superintendent and said he was open for a church. Specifically, he asked if they had one that was struggling. From 1954 to 1956 the family lived in Seminole, Texas. Ruth's time of cultural transplant into America of the 1950s was a time of awakening for her. She was coming face to face with strict and literal Pentecostal biblical interpretations and yet venturing out at times with her own "daring deeds . . . attempted with abandonment out on the sandy West Texas high plains."[27] As a child of many cultures as a "third culture kid," she was learning that there was more than one way of doing things; she was seeing multiple perspectives and discovering that not everything is either clearly "right" or "wrong." Coming to grips with being more liberal than her missionary parents, Ruth sometimes felt bewildered about the different forms of worship and wondered how God was in all of it. She had observed the Marathi form of worship from her childhood, the Presbyterian boarding school, and now the more stringent forms of U.S. AG Pentecostalism. Coming back to the States, the emphasis was on "Let go and let God have His

---

26. The schoolmaster at the Hindu school in town was beating the Christian boys for not bowing down to the Hindu gods. Saving the boys from this abuse fueled Ted's sense of urgency to build a school on the Junnar compound. When asked why they took the beatings, the boys responded, "Christ took so much for us; we thought we could take a little for Him." Ted wanted to build a nursery to handle the babies they received and because previously so many were dying. His motivation for building a granite boys' dorm was because the previous one had a one-foot opening between the wall and the roof, and one day a six-foot cobra was found there eating a rat! Ruth remembers her father running to get his gun to shoot the snake, and his subsequent efforts to blow up granite from the property, haul the stone, and shape it to make the dorm (Interview with Ruth Vassar Burgess, March 2, 2014).

27. Lewis, "My Life Story: Ruth Burgess," 33.

way," but Ruth reasoned, *once you do that, you lose control.* She appreciated the order the Presbyterians had at Kodaikanal and wondered, *how can it be that only one way of worshipping is right?* These thoughts had been in her mind even as an eight-year-old, and much of her life she had obeyed her parents and the church out of fear. Because fear turned into guilt, it was easier to comply. But now in her teen and early adult years, her mind was occupied with working through issues of culture, perspective, thinking, and being. In the midst of that struggle, Ruth's transition to America brought a deep loneliness for India, for the "smells of eucalyptus, snapdragons, fresh pears, and crackling firewood."[28] No longer would her mouth salivate when "smelling *dhal bhat* cooking, *bakkar* browning, or *chai* being hawked by a vendor. Gone were the long conversations since in [her] new homeland time was money and schedules were to be kept. Further enculturation was to occur as [she] transitioned into adulthood."[29]

Although Ruth's repeated migrations back and forth between India and the U.S. and then crisscrossing the Midwest made her "envious of people who have stable roots and have lived in one locale," she realized later that moving so much had given her

> courage later in life to do research projects in Israel and India and to venture away from the status quo. [She] came to understand that if [she] didn't tap into [her] distinctiveness that the male oriented power structure would not recognize what [she] did. The good ole' boys club did not recognize a thinking woman from afar. [She] wanted a fair, equitable club.[30]

All while keeping to her parents' strict rules of holiness, Ruth thrived in her high school environment both academically and socially and began to develop a love for drama. She longed to be an actor or attorney, but her mother was embarrassed, thinking both vocations inappropriate for a Pentecostal young lady and that in pursuing them, she could lose her soul. Much of the Pentecostal world at that time considered certain behaviors as "sinful," such as going to football games, because they were considered "lustful." Later, though, Ruth's brother was allowed to play football though the family could not go to watch him. Ruth reflects on the injustice of a system that "allowed the boys more freedom than it did the girls . . . somehow girls were expected to be the keepers of responsible moral behavior."[31]

28. Ibid., 34.
29. Ibid.
30. Ibid., 12.
31. Ibid., 31.

In the middle of her senior year Ruth's parents accepted a church in Levelland, Texas where because of her accelerated studies at Kodai she graduated high school in 1956 at the age of sixteen. She was an avid reader, focusing on news magazines in order to converse intelligently with her father, women's magazines in order to relate to her mother, and devotional and literary materials to strengthen her soul.

During her senior year Ruth worked as a secretary at Bob Johnson Irrigation Company and saved money for her college wardrobe. She qualified for scholarships at Vassar College, Rice University, and the University of Texas. Her father liked the idea of her going to Vassar because of the historical family connection, but her mother protested vehemently out of fear Ruth would lose her salvation at an "east coast liberal school."[32] They ended up sending Ruth to Southwestern Junior College in Waxahachie, Texas, which Ruth saw as two wasted years. She couldn't understand why people there weren't more interested in *learning and becoming*. There was a sense that a person was OK if he or she went to "three or four prayer meetings a day and observed certain dress codes."[33] This highly emotional expression of Christianity was accompanied by no desire to learn. "The teacher just read from the book. They'd say, 'The Spirit is falling!' just so they wouldn't have to take a test . . . How is this 'Christian'?"[34] Ruth recalls that this was a place with "little academic rigor, many prayers sessions, and unusual social restrictions . . . It was difficult to be there [as someone] able to outthink a lot of people who were supposed to be caring for us, so I got into a lot of mischief."[35]

Her academic abilities and her global perspectives frustrated her in less-than-vigorous environments and spurred her on to more. Her high school teachers thought she was smart, but none gave career guidance. Ruth recalls, "Through books I would cast myself into different characters and imagine that sort of life. Through daydreams I imagined myself back in India living a life for others but not knowing how to earn enough money to support my dreams."[36]

---

32. Ibid., 33.
33. Interviews with Ruth Vassar Burgess, 2013.
34. Ibid.
35. Lewis, "My Life Story: Ruth Burgess," 33.
36. Ibid.

PERSPECTIVES OF DISCOVERY: AMERICA (1958–1961)

Those dreams would soon find their path to reality when Ruth transitioned to Texas Tech University in Lubbock, which she loved for its sense of normality. Having taken classes there over the summers during her two years in Waxahachie, she had decided to transfer to Texas Tech full-time in 1958. With her strong desire to go into drama but an accompanying sense of guilt and restriction due to her mother's views of it as sinful, she longed for a way out. It soon came. Students interested in speech took a public speaking course that introduced them to speech therapy, drama, radio, emerging television, and rhetoric. She took a course with a Dr. Larson, which proved to be a turning point in her life:

> [W]e were to observe speech opportunities in different settings. One of these was the Speech and Hearing Clinic. It was here I became aware that I could use my caring and mindful ways to help others. I thought speech and hearing pathology provided a career option that would preserve my soul from damnation. When my parents agreed, I gave a big sigh of relief.[37]

Her ability to excel academically ultimately resulted in obtaining a BS in Education and Speech Therapy (and a minor in English) at Texas Tech University in Lubbock, Texas. Although she received an Associate of Arts in general studies at Southwestern, she had lost a number of credits by transferring from Southwestern. Her feeling of having wasted two years at Southwestern was now compounded by this frustrating loss. However, her father asked her, "Did you *learn* anything?" She protested, "That's not fair!" He asked her again, and she said, "Yes, I did." He said, "Well then it was not lost. I wanted you to *learn*."[38]

From Levelland, Ruth's parents moved back to Abilene, Texas[39] where they had pastored briefly in 1947 before their second missionary term began. It was to that church that Ted invited his friend John Burgess to come speak in 1959 on their way to the AG General Council in San Antonio. It was a wonderful reunion of the two families after their nine years apart. After church, Stan asked Ruth, now nineteen, out for a Coke. "As our conversation progressed he told me he had loved me since he was ten years of age and he felt it was God's will for us to marry,"[40] she reminisces. Around the

---

37. Ibid.
38. Interviews with Ruth Vassar Burgess, 2013.
39. Ruth recalls how Estelle cooked many curry dinners in Abilene, and people would drive across Texas to eat at her mother's table.
40. Lewis, "My Life Story: Ruth Burgess," 38.

dinner table Stan said to Ted, "Sir, Ruth has given her consent to marry me but I would like your permission for her hand—I mean her whole body—in marriage."[41] Amidst hearty laughter, Ted gave his permission, and the couple was married the following spring, on February 26 in Abilene First Assembly.

In the interim, Stan—now age twenty-one and with a master's degree in history from the University of Michigan—began teaching at Evangel College in Springfield, Missouri. Meanwhile, Ruth finished her last semester at Texas Tech and prepared for the wedding. Ruth remembers their wedding day as "a blur of nervous anticipation" even with representatives from India arriving "on the arms of former missionaries."[42] Stan's father performed the ceremony, and Ruth's father prayed, asking the Lord to bless the union with many children! "What?" remembers Ruth, "That wasn't what I was prepared to hear. I reached up through my veil and pinched his hand."[43]

Indeed the Lord did bless the union with children! Ruth graduated from Texas Tech in the summer of 1960 and within a month found out she was pregnant with their first child. That fall she worked as a Speech and Hearing Therapist in the Springfield Public School system, a contract she had received even before leaving Texas. It was a vigorous beginning—serving *fourteen* elementary schools and seeing over 125 children per week. Ruth taught September to December 1960, and then the district terminated her contract for 1961 because she was pregnant. John Bradley Burgess was born on Stan and Ruth's first anniversary, February 26, 1961.

Ruth describes the various journeys of their marriage.[44] The *physical* journey was like a game of paddleball—the paddle being Springfield, Missouri and the tetherball their various research-based journeys, which took them back and forth across the United States and eventually around the world. One of their first journeys took them to Michigan in 1961 so Stan could work on his doctorate. Evangel had only given Stan $500 to live on, and moving costs alone were $500, so Ruth had to get a job; they had a new baby and no money. So she took courses in speech therapy at the University of Michigan in Ann Arbor to get certified by the Michigan Education Department as a public school teacher. In addition, Ruth was awarded a scholarship at their cleft palate clinic and worked there in the afternoons. Later she served as Speech-Language Clinician for the Dearborn Township

---

41. Ibid.
42. Ibid., 39.
43. Ibid.
44. Ibid., 39–40.

in Inkster, Michigan. The newlyweds lived in Inkster, the first of their many "paddleball" journeys back and forth to Springfield, Missouri.

Their *spiritual* journey was one of coming to understand the nature of American denominational expression in contrast to the experiences of their youth in India. The focus in India had been more on mission than on expressing lack of tolerance for differences, as seemed to be the case in the U.S. Their spiritual background in India, such as their experience of attending an interdenominational boarding school, pushed them to more of an ecumenical viewpoint. Stan and Ruth were also grieved over the growing Caucasian male supremacy in the American AG that had steadily increased since the AG joined the National Association of Evangelicals in 1943. This alliance made for a "bully pulpit" over women who had received callings from God, resulting in diminishing numbers of ordained female ministers. This growing lack of full leadership opportunities made Ruth feel, "This was not the Spirit-led fellowship that moved both of my grandmothers to leave mainstream churches."[45]

Great consolation came along the way, though, from their *emotional* journey. Ruth so beautifully describes it: "our emotional journey . . . started by faith, [and] grew throughout the decades. Our love has formed us into soul mates. We continue to be distinct, yet we become more as one. Stan became more instinctive while I became more organized."[46] The next several decades would see these two soul mates support one another through the ups and downs of finishing graduate degrees, developing in their professional careers, raising five children, and growing in their faith.

PERSPECTIVES OF VOCATION: SPRINGFIELD, COLUMBIA, AND INDIA (1962–1985)

In 1962 Stan and Ruth returned to Springfield, Missouri because of Stan's work at Evangel College. Ruth had been staying home to care for Brad, but because the couple needed the money, she decided to substitute teach language in a fifth- and sixth-grade rounders program in Strafford. Ruth enjoyed the children there, but when Brad came down with dehydration early in 1963, the school would not let her take sick days to be with him, so she chose not to return. Instead, Ruth applied for her old position at Springfield Public Schools. Since the school district needed to begin a secondary program she was asked to take on the project. Then, along with Margaret Curtis, Ruth founded the Southwest Missouri Speech-Language-Hearing

45. Ibid., 40.
46. Ibid.

Association, the district's secondary speech-language program. This position began Ruth's involvement of advocacy for children with special needs[47] and also helped her support the family while Stan worked on his doctorate at the University of Missouri at Columbia ("Mizzou") and taught weekends at Evangel.

At that time, in the work she was doing, Ruth was known as a clinician. After obtaining a master's and doctorate, one would be known as a pathologist. The speech therapy field itself was young and changing all the time, depending on current pressing needs and the availability of resources to meet those needs. Vietnam veterans who had received head trauma, had voice problems, etc., needed help. They didn't have stuttering problems, but they definitely had language problems. With such a lack of speech language therapists in this new field, the government needed people trained using the national standards set by the American Speech-Language-Hearing Association. Hence, Congress allotted scholarships in this field. In 1964 while still working at Springfield Public Schools during the academic year, Ruth began her master's at Mizzou in the summers, receiving full Veterans Administration scholarships for three of the four years she was there because the government wanted students like Ruth to provide services to veterans.[48]

Eventually Stan and Ruth moved closer to Fulton, Missouri, twenty-seven miles east of Columbia, to be nearer to the university. They lived there from 1967 to 1968; Ruth continued working on her master's and was employed as a language pathologist in the Fulton Public Schools (serving three elementary schools). In 1968 she received her MA in Speech and Language Pathology.

The summer after Ruth got her master's, Evangel College *asked Stan*—interestingly enough—if his wife would be interested in teaching speech. Dr. Nona Dalan was head of the Speech Department at the time and had just received her doctorate from the University of Denver. She had also taught at Southwestern when Ruth was an undergrad, so the two had some history. Ruth served as Assistant Professor of Speech at Evangel College from 1968 to 1976. During her years teaching at Evangel, Ruth gave birth to *four children in three years* (between 1971 and 1974).

Almost exactly ten years after the birth of their first child, Ruth gave birth to their second son, Stanley Matthew ("Matt") in 1971. At the time,

---

47. Ruth recounts further details: "Public Law 94–142 . . . provided a free, public education for children with disabilities. By tying implementation to federal funds, families and children began to realize their rights in a democratic society" (ibid., 61).

48. During that year, Stan and Ruth and thirty-one others became charter members of the new Evangel Temple Christian Center, an AG church plant that began on the campus of Evangel College.

Stan was finishing his PhD and went to defend his dissertation at Columbia after Ruth got home from the hospital! One year later, Scott Vassar was born in 1972. Fortunately in 1973, just one year before their twins Heidi Amanda Elizabeth ("Mandy") and Justin David ("David") were born, Stan had begun building a new home at the "ranch" in Strafford, Missouri.[49]

Navigating varying perspectives certainly kept Ruth occupied in her busy, five-child household. For example, Ruth recounts a conversation one evening around their country kitchen table:

> The topic of conversation turned to the famine in Ethiopia. I asked each of the four children what they thought might be the solution. Quickly Amanda said, I think we should send them lots of food; we have food in storage houses that we could send. Matthew wrinkled his brow and responded, That wouldn't do much good because they would just eat the food; there would still be a famine; the problem is that Ethiopia didn't have an appropriate long-term government policy that provided for its people and without a responsible government the people will suffer. Silence descended. I prodded for Scott's opinion. Scott wrinkled his face and said, I don't want to deal with their problems. Suddenly David burst in the conversation—I think we should send them many missionaries and get their souls saved; if they are going to die anyway they might as well go to heaven. One family, four children, and four divergent responses.[50]

Decades later, Ruth and Stan take great delight in the beautiful diversity of their children and grandchildren. Brad, now a businessman in California, married Debbie DeLucia, and they had Sophia and Michael. Matt, an attorney with Walmart in Arkansas, married Jennifer Hill, and they had John Matthew ("Jack") and Mary Katherine ("M. K." or "Cake"). Scott, a surgeon specializing in urology, married Danielle DeLucia, and they had Charlotte Michaelis ("Charlie" or "Cocoa") and Clara Lucia. Mandy, a businesswoman in Virginia Beach, married Matthew Scott Levinson, and they had Vanessa Ruth Elizabeth. David, a Presbyterian minister in Missouri, married Sarah Elizabeth Knief, and they had Amelia Elizabeth, Sarah ("Sadie") Vassar, and Samuel Wesley ("Taco Bell"). Each was shaped in some way by the diverse

---

49. One year later, in 1975, Ted Vassar, who had been pastoring San Angelo First Assembly in Texas, passed away in Springfield, Missouri. No doubt he was welcomed by his beloved Savior who saw his years of selfless service in India and struggling U.S. churches and said, "Well done, thou good and faithful servant" (Interviews with Ruth Burgess, 2013).

50. Lewis, "My Life Story: Ruth Burgess," 43. For more details on the five Burgess children, see ibid., 40–43.

cultures of their "missionary kid" parents and their missionary grandparents. Each of them is a child of the calling in their own way.

When the twins Mandy and David were only two years old, Ruth began her PhD work at the University of Missouri. Her major emphasis was in speech and language therapy with supporting fields in specific learning disabilities and educational research. Dr. Charlotte Wells, Ruth's advisor and esteemed mentor, had told Ruth she was retiring in three years and warned her, "If you don't finish by then, you'll have to start over!"[51] Thus, the next three years (1976–1979) were an unbelievable whirlwind of activity and energy. Ruth's mother left Texas and came to Springfield in the fall of 1976 to stay with the family for the first year and help take care of the children so Ruth could establish residency.

Stan had decided to leave Evangel due to various issues, and Ruth was considering leaving as well. She had put in enough years to get a sabbatical, but when she went to ask for one in order to do her doctorate, the dean looked at her and said, "Looks like you'd be satisfied with one doctorate in the family." This insensitive comment was crushing to Ruth. Never taken into consideration was the fact that their family had so freely given so much for years and years at sub-pay, that their five children would not be able to go to college on the salary Stan was making, or that *she was a scholar in her own right with significant contributions to make in her field.* When she appealed the matter, she was told that her application could not be supported because she "wouldn't be happy at Evangel without her husband."[52]

---

51. Interviews with Ruth Burgess, 2013; see also Lewis, "My Life Story: Ruth Burgess," 49.

52. Interviews with Ruth Burgess, 2013. Ruth found out over the years that if people wanted to get back at Stan for some reason, they'd take a hit at Ruth. Sadly, this seemed like one of those occasions. That fall when SMSU's Dean at the College of Education called Evangel for a recommendation, the Evangel Dean—attempting to blackball her—said Ruth was "too stringent." The SMSU Dean said, "Good! That's the type I like!"

Sadly, when Stan and Ruth left Evangel, the rumor went out that they were having marital problems and on the verge of breaking up! One of Ruth's so-called friends said she couldn't be seen with them, because they were leaving and were able to get a position elsewhere in town! Jim and Twila Edwards, professors at Evangel, stood by Stan and Ruth during this difficult time. Another Evangel faculty member saw her later and asked her, "Do you feel the devil over there at SMSU?" Ruth was surprised and said, "No!" (Interviews with Ruth Burgess, 2013).

In March of 2014, Ruth was the featured speaker for Evangel's sixth annual Stanley M. Horton lectureship series. In the 2013–2014 academic year, the series was expanded to three events to feature speakers affiliated with the three schools (Evangel, AGTS, and Central Bible College) making up the newly consolidated Evangel University. Ruth's two-day presentations highlighted the untold stories of women such as Grace Ashcroft whose gifts and contributions helped to shape Evangel and then presented the nature and struggles of children of a third culture.

The week before finals in August of 1976 Ruth got a call from Dr. Bruce Turner at Southwest Missouri State University (SMSU), saying he had a job for her. Although leaving Evangel meant she would lose her tenure, she said she would love to come to SMSU but could not right then, because she was establishing residency in Columbia to do her PhD. He said he needed her background for accreditation and would make a deal—if she'd work at SMSU, he would fly her back and forth! The flight offer never panned out, but Greyhound did the trick. Thus began what would turn out to be a twenty-eight-year career at SMSU's College of Education. For the next three years this mother of five worked on her PhD and taught full-time—traveling back and forth from Springfield to Columbia.[53]

Ruth's doctoral research focused on the relationship of language and cognition. Her study involved testing the hypothesis about which model was more effective—the psychoeducational model that used standardized testing (intelligence, language, math, social—the dominant model in the U.S. during the twentieth century) or the developmental model.[54] Ruth developed a Receptive Syntax Semantics Test (RSST) to determine whether seven-year old boys could detect syntax semantics and semantic syntax errors in them. She wanted to see whether their rule behavior could hold the correct syntax or semantic message.

To answer these questions and verify her supposition, Ruth needed a pilot study, and the Greenwood Laboratory School at SMSU was a great place to do it. She did the pilot in the summer of 1978 then replicated her study in different city schools in Springfield. She discovered through her research that the Piagetian measures of intelligence or development were closer to the test she had developed. They were highly significant statistically at the .001 level. Her hypothesis supported the developmental theory more than the psychoeducational theory that was more widely accepted.

Coming back to SMSU, Ruth was *very* excited, because her doctoral committee had not fully supported her doing this innovative project. Every week she had to go in and justify her doctoral hypothesis and approach to her advisor, who had said it was not worthy and would never pass. But Ruth

---

53. One of the SMSU classes Ruth taught was in Lebanon, Missouri. Since she was traveling back and forth from Springfield to Columbia, Stan would begin the class then she would come by and finish it. Ruth found out in that class just how much some students hated people with disabilities at that time. One of her students, a regular education teacher, said disabled people should be sterilized! Ruth retorted, how would they like it if a law went out that said people making less than so much money a year should be castrated!? "They didn't give a damn about people with disabilities," Ruth exclaimed (Interviews with Ruth Burgess, 2013).

54. In the 1960s and 1970s Piaget had become more popular with his developmental or constructivist approach.

believed in it and fought for it, working hard that summer to get her advisor to accept the topic. Finally, when the dissertation showed great promise, Dr. Wells was elated. She had told her previously, "If this falls flat, you will have to start all over again!" With five kids and having gone through all she had already, Ruth felt there was no way she could do it again. But after Ruth's accomplishment, Dr. Wells said, "I wonder what you could have been if you'd had a chance."[55]

Ruth passed her written comps and orals in the first part of December 1978. According to university policy students had to wait six months before they could defend their dissertations. "If I finish it and have it typed," she pled, "will you let me graduate?" "Of course!" They said sarcastically, again not believing it would happen. It was now the end of June, and she had until August to finish. She had to write the whole dissertation in six weeks! On Sunday mornings, she would get the family ready to go to church then focus on whatever aspect of the dissertation was at hand. After church Stan would bring the kids back, they would have dinner, she would be with them in the afternoon, and then plan her classes for the week. One Saturday, due to cognitive block from all the stresses, she confessed to Stan, "I'm not going to get it done." "But you have it all in your head," he said. "You *know* what it means! You *tell me* what it means, and I'll write it down for you!" He did two or three pages that way, and that got rid of her cognitive block. Ten days later she had the rough draft. They found a typist who was able to finish the whole project in one weekend.

When Ruth went to defend, they told her she would sit behind Dr. Wells' desk to inform the committee. One of them asked her to tell them a little about herself. Ruth began speaking in Marathi, her native language from India, and they thought she was having a stroke! The audiologist thought she was speaking in tongues, another thought she was crazy and had broke down under the tension. "It was wonderful," she remembers, "it broke the tension." In 1979, the University of Missouri at Columbia awarded Ruth her PhD in Speech-Language Pathology with supporting fields of specific learning disabilities and research.[56]

Three years after completing her PhD the Burgesses took their four youngest children to India. The kids were growing up and had seemed dissatisfied with their parents' station in life. They wanted the latest things. This concerned Stan and Ruth that their children were getting so Americanized and taking on the values of its society that the children did not appreciate the heritage of their grandparents in India, who had given their lives for that

---

55. Interviews with Ruth Burgess, 2013.
56. Burgess, "Prediction of Language Abilities from Measures of Mental Maturity."

country. So they rode the rails and Indian buses from Maharashtra in the north to Kerala in the south, and finally, by the time they were in Kerala it dawned on the children. Sitting in the chapel at the Bible college there, son David looked up at a picture of his grandfather on the wall, then turned to his mother and said, "Oh, now I know why we came." Their experience back in the land of their parents' childhoods was rich and life changing.[57]

When Ruth returned to teaching at SMSU after her doctoral defense and the India trip, she had expected—given her research findings—that her colleagues would be excited. However, she was crushed to find them as unenthusiastic as they had been *prior* to her defense. Stan told her, "You can't go on being so upset. No one here is in the field you are. You've created a new field." He told her to write to the two people she admired the most, tell them about her research, and ask whether they deemed it valuable to continue or not. So she wrote Dr. Frank Benson, a neuro linguist at University of California at Los Angeles (UCLA), and Professor Reuven Feuerstein in Jerusalem, Israel.[58] Both men frankly responded that she was on the cutting edge of research and by all means to please continue. This initial connection opened the door for Ruth to eventually travel to Israel in 1986 to collaborate with Feuerstein.

Meanwhile, she wanted to replicate her doctoral study, preferably in India. During a 1982–1984 research leave, she worked with Dr. R. V. Dhongde in Pune at Deccan College, who had replicated Dr. Roger Brown's research at Harvard University. Together they studied the syntax, semantics, and pragmatics of children learning English and children learning Marathi. She traveled to India twice around her teaching schedule at SMSU[59]—once to develop a program for teachers and once to implement the research project. During this time Feuerstein kept in touch and invited her to consider applying for a sabbatical in order to come study with him at the Hadassah-WIZO-Canada Research Institute in Jerusalem. Little did she realize the transformational direction her life was about to take.

---

57. With the passing of Ruth's mother in 1980, Ruth felt more than ever the need to communicate to her children a global perspective and their remarkable heritage.

58. See Ruth's biography of Feuerstein: *Changing Brain Structure through Cross-Cultural Learning*; as well as Burgess, "Propelling the Change, Preserving Continuity."

59. Around this same time, beginning in 1983 and for thirteen summers to 1996, Ruth conducted a program between parents of children with disabilities and public school teachers called "Swim-Gym-Learn." She did the socialization and academics for about twenty-five children at Greenwood Laboratory School each summer, and her colleague Dr. Michael McCarty worked with students to develop perceptual motor skills. Ruth found great fulfillment in having a chance to apply her theories and watch the children grow. "At one point I used to teach just so I could do this program in the summers," she recalls (Interviews with Ruth Burgess, 2013).

PERSPECTIVES OF TRANSFORMATION

Sabbatical in Israel (1986)

Ruth received the sabbatical for 1986, and Stan received one concurrently to study the spirituality of Eastern Christianity. The family flew from London, England to Israel at Christmastime 1985, settling in at the Tantur Institute for Ecumenical Studies,[60] located between Jerusalem and Bethlehem. In January of 1986 Ruth met Feuerstein for the first time, beginning a remarkable mentor relationship that would continue for decades.[61]

As scholars and simply as human beings, both Stan and Ruth's lives were about to change forever. Ruth recalls: "What I was being introduced to was so different from my academic training and my growing up. As a child, emotion was OK, something I should develop. But then my academic training was all about memorizing. Those with a good memory will excel. But all of a sudden in Israel I found something entirely new."[62] In her studies with Feuerstein, Ruth was transitioning from a method of merely *imparting* to students to an "active, interactional mediation mode [which helped her design her] . . . courses around five categories: knowledge, knowledge skills, literacy, dispositions or habits of the mind, and dispositions or habits of the spirit."[63]

The Romanian-born Feuerstein had been a student of Jean Piaget and André Rey at the University of Geneva but had disagreed with Piaget's views that cognitive development proceeds according to a fixed sequence of ascending stages. Feuerstein's approach included instead the fundamental belief system that people are created in the image of God; therefore, change is possible—even in those who are cognitively challenged or culturally deprived. This view significantly impacts how a teacher views the potential of his or her students.

Upon the foundation of this belief system rested Feuerstein's theories and applied systems of Structural Cognitive Modifiability—the idea that through Reciprocal Mediated Interactional Pedagogy ("mediated

---

60. Interviews with Ruth Burgess, 2013.

61. During her sabbatical, Ruth studied with Feuerstein at the Hadassah-WIZO-Canada Research Institute in Jerusalem and at Bar Ilan University in Tel Aviv. Each Thursday Ruth would ride with Feuerstein from Jerusalem to Tel Aviv, attending a class he was teaching there. Instruction was in Hebrew, with interpretation provided for Ruth and two other English-speaking students.

62. Tantur was formed in 1960s following a rapprochement between Pope Paul VI and Patriarch Athenagoras of Constantinople in Jerusalem. See more at http://www.tantur.org.

63. Lewis, "My Life Story: Ruth Burgess," 47.

learning")—a human mediator can intervene in the thinking processes of a low functioning learner and evoke significant changes in brain structure.[64] She studied his "Content-Free" curriculum (rather than verbal or numeric) that can lead to "Cross-Content Integration." As Ruth explains,

> When a person learns how to learn, he or she can apply this to various types of cognitive content, cognitive operations, cognitive modalities, and make progress learning throughout life. Indeed through mediated learning interventions, cognitive dysfunctions can become positive cognitive functions. The person becomes capable of moving from concrete to abstract thinking and from simplistic to complex thinking encounters.[65]

Ruth immersed herself in these and other elements of Feuerstein's work[66] and began to experience transformation in the way she learned, taught, and mediated others. She began to understand that these approaches not only modify the person the mediator is working with but also modify the mediator. Her semester in Israel and subsequent visits there "changed everything," she recalls. "It changed our family dynamics. It transformed the way I taught."[67] Among other things, Ruth began to overhaul her syllabi at SMSU, integrating this entirely new perspective and adapting Feuerstein's

---

64. See Carolyn S. Nixon's chapter 12 in this present volume for a description of Feuerstein's Cognitive Map.

65. Interviews with Ruth Burgess, 2013.

66. "Feuerstein was for many years Professor of Education at Bar Ilan University in Ramat Gan, Israel. He is the founding director of the Center for Learning Enrichment in Jerusalem (ICELP). The work of the ICELP is based on Feuerstein's theory of Structural Cognitive Modifiability and his pedagogical method of Mediated Learning Experience. ICELP specializes in three applied systems: the Learning Potential Assessment Device (LPAD), Instrumental Enrichment (IE) cognitive intervention program, and Shaping Modifying Environment (See http://www.icelp.org/asp/main.asp). The major goal of ICELP's products is to provide students with cognitive tools necessary for becoming independent learners. This goal reflects a philosophical belief in human beings as open systems, who are amenable to change throughout their life spans and responsive to conditions of remediation providing that the intervention is appropriately directed to the individual's need (Feuerstein, 2000). The regular IE program includes fourteen booklets of paper-and-pencil tasks aimed at promoting analytic perception, orientation in space and time, comparisons, and classifications. Feuerstein's materials have been translated into more than twenty languages and tested in diverse cultural contexts in over forty-five countries. Remarkable results have been achieved with at risk populations, such as Holocaust survivors, the poor in Harlem, first nation Canadians, Ethiopian Jewish émigrés, and children with disabilities such as Down syndrome." Newberg, Review of *Changing Brain Structure*, 71–77.

67. Interviews with Ruth Burgess, 2013. "I found these approaches to be the most powerful human change agents I have encountered" (Lewis, "My Life Story: Ruth Burgess," 52).

ideas within her contexts. Setting goals, attaining them, and assessing them was now a new part of her life because of his influence.

Applying Feuerstein's Ideas (1988 Onward)

The years following Ruth's sabbatical were as busy as her dissertation/new parent years had been. Immediately upon entry back to the U.S., Ruth decided to put the Theory of Structural Cognitive Modifiability to the test in her research and teaching. She longed to discover why Feuerstein's theories worked so much better in Israel than in the States, and how to bring what she had learned *there* over *here*. She subsequently participated in several Feuerstein workshops, attaining the level of Master Trainer-of-Trainers in Instrumental Enrichment (IE) from the International Center for Enhancement of Learning.[68]

While working part-time at the Missouri Chest Hospital in Mount Vernon as a Speech-Language-Hearing Pathologist to help pay off debt incurred during the sabbatical, Ruth continued to teach her regular classes at SMSU and a graduate class once a week. Her graduate students were excited about her offering Feuerstein enrichment courses. She also began volunteering at the Rivendale Institute of Learning & Center for Autism in Springfield in order to test the Feuerstein theories. Rivendale was a school for children who had learning and emotional difficulties—kids the public schools had failed. But not long after experiencing mediated learning, Ruth's students began to show progress.

This was a time of willingness to try something new yet loneliness because no one else in Southwest Missouri was doing this. Here she was with the challenge of bringing something from another country and trying to explain it within the language of the people where she lived—moving them somehow from understanding to application. She read prolifically, trying to discover all she could. Before long, school districts wanted her to do inservices. She received multiple grants to do instrumental workshops and grants from the state to pay for materials.

One grant funded research to show just how many teachers she would need in order to bring about sustained change in a school district or elementary school—particularly in the small, rural districts of Southwest Missouri—so that all of the energy she had invested there could continue. Too often, she discovered, when she would help individuals from the rural areas to understand these principles and how to carry them out, either they

---

68. Ruth subsequently presented on IE in Canada, Belgium, England, Italy, Israel, India, Singapore, and the United States.

would get pushed down because people around them felt threatened, or they would become so empowered that they would move *out* of Southwest Missouri to better paying jobs in the suburbs. She discovered that to plan for success required *five* people to mediate learning or to encourage inclusion of children with disabilities into a regular classroom. However, not all could be teachers. In dealing with rural issues related to helping children and their families, one of the people involved had to be a *powerbroker in the community*. Second, the project needed a *parent* with a substantive background, one willing to get on the school board. The project also needed a *special education teacher*, a *regular teacher*, and a *counselor*. With these five people, a mediator could make a difference and bring people along for continuity.

This discovery was vital, because Ruth began to realize there was not enough of *her* to bring about change. She was speaking at conferences from Toronto to Vancouver, from Belgium to Israel. During this period she also served as a field reviewer for the Office of Education in Washington and sat on numerous state boards relating to people with disabilities in order to help them plan for the future. It was a time of intense activity trying to communicate that there were other ways of doing things—especially Feuerstein's. Research had shown he achieved sustained progress. Ruth was driven by the fact that the methods used in the U.S. at the time were not seeing sustained progress. American students were falling behind other educated or industrial nations in their ability to think critically, and things needed to change. Learning how to learn had to extend beyond the therapy or educational system—beyond direct instruction, behavior modification, or developmentalism—all of which were not working.

Although later on in her career, writing book chapters on Feuerstein and ultimately his full biography proved to be some of Ruth's most significant professional achievements,[69] much of her most personally rewarding academic contributions involved working with constituents. With each of her projects she could carry out a research project about different aspects of Feuerstein's theory. For example, she wrote the first Mellen grant in the State of Missouri to work with parents of children with disabilities. Eight Mellen mentors who were graduate students recommended by their school administrators were making changes in eight counties by empowering parents. Positive findings resulted. Then, by working with teachers through the Teachers and Innovations in Education grant in Washington, DC, Ruth was able to develop materials and train teams to support alternative intervention

---

69. Ruth currently serves on the board of the North American Feuerstein Institute. See http://icelp.info/.

strategies and help children in regular classrooms—especially those kids with disabilities.

Ruth's most significant work, then, was on the ground, striving to change people's belief systems and practice:

> I feel my life has been one of service to help others and to encourage the adoption of a positive teaching:learning (T:L) paradigm entitled mediated learning. This model (Feuerstein, 1980) requires a belief system and a value statement that all humans are capable of positive modification. The teacher-mediator has goals beyond the current sensorial situation that reach into the future. Interactive constructive activities enable learners to become capable of mental self-regulation, to engage in representational thinking, become efficient problem solvers and decision makers, and engage as effective co-mediation participants. Thus through attitudinal modifications, the mediatees (students) benefit better from the direct exposure to stimuli. They become better able to focus their minds, formulate questions, understand temporal relations, use diverse spatial relations, understand constancy and conservation, select higher-order cognitive elaborations, and communicate without impulsivity and egocentric language.[70]

To facilitate this work, Ruth applied for and received numerous grants. One was from the Missouri Department of Elementary and Secondary Education for $100,000 to develop an interactive video-computer advisement system for elementary education teacher trainees. The school said they would implement it, but after it was developed they simply stored it in boxes. After so much work to obtain financial backing, such educational disappointments proved exhausting. Ruth saw these unexpected turns as illustrating that "moral and ethical criteria were not central to decision making."[71] Her background had reinforced that one's word is as good as his or her honor, but facing these uphill battles, she found that not everyone valued honor:

> The good 'ole boy system rewards itself and uses those outside the system for its benefit. Power brokers can make and break people at the expense of moral and ethical values. I learned that democracy does not guarantee fair treatment ... One must

---

70. Lewis, "My Life Story: Ruth Burgess," 47. Ruth's later biographical writings on Feuerstein presented the theoretical aspects of his life, and she has three more manuscripts not yet published that address the practice of mediated learning. When asked what she felt have been her greatest contributions, however, it is not these writings but her "on-the-ground" efforts.

71. Ibid., 44.

remain vigilant because once the majority system is challenged, it never forgets, even though the perpetrators commit wrongs. Very few people are willing to become change makers; they feel more comfortable working within dysfunctional systems.[72]

One of those dysfunctional systems involved the interrelationship between men and women professionally. In addition to her struggles for justice in the field of education,[73] the next decade would be one of facing head-on the ever-present gender issues.

PERSPECTIVES OF JUSTICE: STRUGGLING AGAINST GENDER INEQUITY (1990S)

Ruth's nascent academic years had been a period of unrest, including second-wave feminism and the battle to pass the Equal Rights Amendment.[74] She recalls:

> Our grandmothers had earned the right to vote, but we were pressured to stay in our place. However, the boundaries encircling our traditional roles became extended. The possibilities . . . brought possibility thinking. We thought if we worked hard, thought clearly, and wore tailored, pinstriped suits we would be able to make it up the career ladder. As we were to learn later, those beliefs illustrated 'magical thinking.'[75]

Some of those hard lessons came during the 1990s, Ruth's years as Director of SMSU's Center for Research and Service.[76] She and six other female professors had formed The Women's Interest Network on campus to advocate for women's rights. One of their studies demonstrated the uneven pay and

---

72. Ibid.

73. Two decades beyond this period, Ruth would author an important piece for the cause of justice in education: Burgess, "Religion's Influence on Social Justice Practices Relating to Those with Disabilities," 575–90.

74. Ruth, Stan, and their four younger children went to Jefferson City, Missouri to march for ERA. Two of their boys were against it, and the rest of the family was for it. So off they went—booing and cheering together. The folks at Ruth's local AG church were against it. She could not imagine a woman not voting for ERA, much less a Christian! Her sorority, Delta Kappa Gamma, was also against it, so Ruth resigned from the sorority in protest.

75. Lewis, "My Life Story: Ruth Burgess," 35.

76. Ruth served as director of the Center for Research and Service from 1988–1995. See Brown and Hinch's chapter 11 in this present volume for a description of Ruth's work on The MissouriFind Project during this time. Ruth served as editor for *Missouri-Find: The Missouri Heritage-History Middle School Curriculum*, 1995.

promotion between male and female professors. However, the administration was far from ready to address issues of gender inequality, and retaliated against all seven professors in various ways.[77] Ruth's most disturbing setback was the university closing the Center for Research and Service. Injustice against women angered Ruth greatly—and still does—but in this era when these female professors had to be stronger and better[78] than the best in order to get even a modicum of the same kind of recognition as their male counterparts, her righteous anger was particularly intense. Many female professors—at SMSU prior to Ruth and her Network colleagues—had been knocked down and stayed down, but the Network was the first group that, although knocked down, got back up.[79] Although particularly intense in the 1970s-1990s, these issues continue for women today. "You can never let your guard down," Ruth advises, "You may think, *they have learned*. But they haven't learned. They've just moved into the shadow to come out again. It is a centuries-old conflict."[80]

When the Center was closed, Ruth decided to return to teaching undergraduate students preparing to be teachers—those still with stars in their eyes, who had not been beaten down by the school system. In doing this, she could bring a new theory of learning to that whole area of the State—one

---

77. One female professor got her department integrated into another and was no longer department head. Another had multiple negativisms directed to her and left due to the mistreatment. Others had to get outside legal assistance brought in, in order to obtain equal scholarships for women athletes. Ruth also recounts instances of crude behavior and speech by the male professors toward the female, even including urinating under the door of one female professor to get rid of her (Interviews with Ruth Burgess, 2013).

78. As part of the good ol' boy behavior at SMSU, some accused Ruth of being "too hard." So Ruth thought, *O.K., I need to meet you on a higher plane*. So she developed the Professional Competency Inventory Profile (PCIP), which examined the state requirements and professional organizations' expectations for what teachers should have in the area of a given course being taught. Her PCIP helped them evaluate their present level and what they wanted in a course regarding this competency. Then at the end of the course they would note what level the teacher achieved; the inventory actually documented their learning. Ruth taught this course to students preparing for their teaching degree. By this Ruth proved that no one could say she was "too hard" because she was addressing the basic competencies according to the requirements of professional organizations and State of Missouri general education requirements. She could document the whole process, and when Ruth's students took the national boards, her group scored significantly higher than the national average because of the PCIP she had designed (Interviews with Ruth Burgess, 2013).

79. These women fought, paving the way for those who would come after them. When she was going through this trial, Ruth came to the conclusion "*I'm doing it for my daughter. I'm doing it for Mandy. If I don't do it for her, she will have to*" (ibid.).

80. Ibid.

based on Feuerstein's method, and one that definitely worked.[81] She enjoyed these efforts immensely, but by the end of the 1990s she began to feel the school was using her "as a milk cow."[82] She had brought in over $2 million in grants but was grieved that the University was not distributing the money fairly. Not wanting to continue in the role of a "milk cow" any longer, not feeling well physically, and wanting to take on the task of writing Feuerstein's biography, Ruth wrote a proposal for a one-year sabbatical, which she received[83] in August 2001.

PERSPECTIVES OF SUFFERING: CANCER (2001-2002)

Although Ruth had seen great suffering as a child in India and had witnessed the suffering of people with disabilities all through her years of teaching in the U.S., her perspective on suffering was about to become even more personal. She recounts how this journey began:

> During the summer of 2001, I was feeling very tired. My physician told me that my electrocardiogram showed considerable changes from two years earlier. She was concerned about me taking a stress test for fear of a heart attack or a stroke. So I was placed on medication. During this time Stan traveled to the Philippines to teach. On the Sunday prior to his return I received communion at Antioch Methodist Church and I felt a tingling, electrical energy flow through the right side of my body.
>
> As the plane was over Alaska and Stan was returning to the United States, the stewardess awakened Stan. She asked if he was Dr. Burgess. He responded, yes. She asked, Do you have a wife who is ill? Stan gulped and murmured, Yes. He waited, anticipating some bad news. The stewardess continued, Well, I was on my relief station and I felt God wanted me to come and tell you that your wife was going to be fine; she will not die.
>
> When the plane landed . . . Stan told me what the stewardess said. I was pleased to hear the optimistic message. Then on Wednesday I had my stress test. As the cardiologist looked at the screens, he looked puzzled and asked, Why are you here? Your

---

81. In early 2001 around the time of her fortieth wedding anniversary, Ruth presented a bilingual Feuerstein Instrumental Enrichment workshop in Caserta, Italy.

82. Interviews with Ruth Burgess, 2013.

83. Despite this being a difficult time financially for the school with many people not even asking for a semester off out of fear of losing their job altogether, Ruth felt God's guidance in asking for one year. It was no small miracle in itself when she received that for which she had asked.

heart is functionally and structurally fine. We were amazed and overjoyed at the report. One month later I was diagnosed with breast cancer. Why might God heal your heart but permit you to go through surgery, chemotherapy, and psychological trauma? I don't know. But I know that I would not have made it through chemotherapy without a strong heart and that God's presence was with me through this valley of suffering.[84]

In that valley Ruth was faced with her own mortality and the looks of horror on the faces of those who loved her, realizing they might lose her. Deciding about, walking through, and recovering from treatment—many times while feeling terribly alone—were her new daily challenges. Learning how to eat, how to exercise, how to deal with altered appearance, simply how to *be* in this new world brought a perspective of suffering she had not yet known. Just as 1986 in Israel had been a watershed year for Ruth, so too was 2001— this time delineating life Before Cancer and life After Cancer.

After her recovery, Ruth conducted some workshops in St. Louis, did some writing,[85] and worked on the Feuerstein biography, but ultimately she was too weak to do it all. SMSU accepted her report, given that she had just come off of cancer treatment. She returned to her tenured post as Professor of Education and Psychology in the School of Teacher Education at SMSU, retiring two years later in 2004 in order to transition to Regent University in Virginia Beach, Virginia.

PERSPECTIVES OF PEACE: SHANTISTAN (2004–2014)

Ruth's mother had planted in her mind the idea of peace when Ruth was still a girl in the hills of South India.[86] Years later, while studying with Feuerstein in 1986, she began to wonder why, instead of emphasizing differences in one's religion or ethnological background that people did not instead focus on their commonalities. While in Israel, Ruth discovered similarities between Judaism and Christianity, realizing that one of the key connections between Feuerstein's ideas and Christianity was that both Reuven and Jesus had a Jewish mother! Both of these women had involved themselves with

---

84. Lewis, "My Life Story: Ruth Burgess," 44.

85. Burgess, "Pandita Ramabai," 1016. Ruth also wrote ten biographies for the *Testimoni della fede nelle chiese della reforma* during this time.

86. At night Ruth's mother would tuck the children in when visiting them at boarding school and say, "Pray for the peace of Jerusalem." When Ruth would ask why, Estelle would reply, "Well, the Jews are God's people." Ruth would press, "Well, aren't I a God person too?" And her mother would respond, "Oh, Ruth, you ask too many questions. Go to sleep!"

their little boys, *mediating* their learning as each young man learned critical thinking.[87] Ruth had always been one to question—a practice encouraged by her father but discouraged by her mother and many of the "church folks" throughout her life. As these ideas blossomed in her life, she began to see that through mediated learning, not only can people *learn how to learn*, but can *learn how to learn from one another* and thus work together for peace.

These ideas began to mature further in the fall of 2001, after 9-11 and Ruth's battle with cancer. But it was not until 2004, with the couple's transition to Regent University[88] that she had the necessary time to develop her *ShantiStan* concepts and begin their practical application. In Sanskrit,

---

87. "Burgess locates the genesis of Feuerstein's educational vision in the wellspring of his Orthodox Jewish background. She stresses the significance of Feuerstein's lifelong practices of rising early for prayer, rigorous compliance with kosher dietary regulations, and scrupulous attendance at Synagogue. Feuerstein grew up in a devout Orthodox Ashkenazi Jewish family and attended a yeshiva where he learned a Sephardic Hassidic rite. During the forced Jewish migrations and periodic pogroms that plagued Romania, the one cohesive element among the Jews was their religious beliefs and traditions. As a young child Reuven studied the Torah with his father everyday from 5:00 to 8:00 am. In the middle of the night the Feuerstein children were awakened by the sound of their father chanting in kabbal tones the Takun Chatzot, a prayer for the restoration of Israel. Not surprisingly, young Reuven developed into an avid Zionist. His grandfather Levy Feuerstein had bought land in Palestine, planning to emigrate there. From the age of 9, Reuven belonged to the Youth Zionist movement. At age 17 he began to work as an underground organizer for Youth Aliyah in Romania. He accepted a position [of] co-director and teacher at the School for Disturbed and Disadvantaged Children in Bucharest in 1940, simultaneously enrolling in the Teachers Seminary and later the Onescu College, all the while secretly helping Jews to prepare for emigration to Palestine. After a near arrest by the Nazis in 1944, Feuerstein fled to Palestine and began his career as pioneer educator with Youth Aliyah, working in kibbutzim with children who were survivors of the Holocaust. The educational program of Youth Aliyah was based on a "youth group" model and included study and work on the land in a youth community. The upshot of all this is that Feuerstein's career in education emerged from within the crucible of his religious and cultural heritage. A reader of Burgess' narrative could easily draw the conclusion that Feuerstein's formative educational vision was faith-based" (Newberg, Review of *Changing Brain Structure*, 2–3).

88. Upon arrival in Virginia Beach, Ruth soon discovered there was actually no teaching position for her. Later when the accreditation team required a course on communications, she was asked to develop one, called Research Based Praxis, adapting her research on learning to doctoral students. She served as an adjunct in the Regent University School of Divinity from 2004–2008. Although as always she loved interacting with her students, this was a painful time for Ruth, who for the first time in her career felt as though she was in Stan's "shadow" academically. She had always been a professional in her own right. From the first time they were introduced, the comment, "We have two PhDs for the price of one," brought Ruth significant angst. Ruth had always been respectful of Stan's life of research in religion, and he had respected her creative endeavors to understand what made humans tick. Each allowed the other the necessary personal and professional space.

Shanti means peace, and *Stan* means "land." So the central questions of this concept include: (1) how can we have a land of peace unless we share our stories;[89] (2) how do we interact with one another through mediated principles; and (3) how do our exercises in peacemaking contain the six elements of Feuerstein's Cognitive Map?

For the story or narrative portion of *ShantiStan*, Ruth selected from research thirteen peace concepts and twelve components of mediated learning. The opportunity to apply these ideas in a real-life situation soon arose when horrible riots broke out in Ahmedabad, where Ruth's sister Helen was living at the time. In the face of Hindu against Muslim violence, Helen pleaded to Ruth, "Why don't you come and do your peace thing over here? We need peace!" Ruth traveled to Gujarat, India to train a group consisting of Muslims, Hindus, and Christians in the *ShantiStan* concepts for peace. She required that elders of the religious communities select participants in the training, so they would report back to those elders.[90] For the narrative portion, each collected stories from their background. Before long in the training, they began to understand what it was about. The Muslim couple was willing to come on their motorcycle in the twilight and return in the night in a Hindu-guarded area. Not only did *ShantiStan* work with this group, but also participants in this first group replicated the experience later that summer in a high school when a group of Muslims, Hindus, and Sikhs took *ShantiStan*. Although the group had no Christians, there was a Christian on the team to teach it, so they actually had four in fusion. The Christian was so excited that he later went down to South Gujarat and taught it twice more, by himself.[91]

In working for peace through *ShantiStan*, Ruth's Indian heritage and personal faith integrate with decades of Feuerstein-influenced scholarship. In her 2008 biography of Feuerstein, the connection between his ideas and efforts toward peace ring clear—especially in a conversation between the two, when she quotes him as saying, "We must not think the Theory of Structural Cognitive Modifiability as only for children who are in need, but it must be applied to a larger audience. I claim today that all of humanity

---

89. All cultures have narratives. Some are from their heritage, some are from experiences, and some are from scientific learning.

90. The Muslim woman's uncle was in the state parliament. The Hindu girl was an attorney, and her father was an attorney. Ruth recounts, "This attorney, a leader from one of the cities, told me, when you said you were coming, I didn't believe you would. Second, I thought you would try to change my religion and you didn't. Third, I started reading what you brought, and then I realized you became my guru. You became my teacher. These barriers have been put up so that we no longer learn how to learn from each other" (Interviews with Ruth Burgess, 2013).

91. Ibid. In 2008 Ruth returned to India to field test *ShantiStan* in Ahmedabad.

is in such need to be modified."[92] Alluding to a tragedy the Feuerstein family experienced when a former ICELP psychologist was killed in a suicide bombing, Ruth asks, "How can we modify people who strap bombs to their bodies?"[93] His reply characterizes beautifully the heart of Ruth's personal and scholarly life:

> If humans can be modified, we have the need to modify beliefs and feelings. Humans can modify their hatred toward other people. Children are dying daily, and no one is reaching out to help them. Their parents have been killed. How do we help the children not to carry on the hatred to the perpetrators? Can we instill the proverb to love one's neighbor as thyself? Is it possible to appreciate cultural difference since each of us is a human being? These children need to be enhanced in their cognitive processes.[94]

Enhancing not only children but also adults in their cognitive processes in order to mediate learning and thus achieve change continued as Ruth's focus throughout her years at Regent.[95] In 2006 the Vatican invited Ruth to present a paper at the Azusa Street Centennial, taking an anthropological look at how different faiths determine reality.[96] This arrangement had come as a result of ecumenical relationships developed throughout the previous decades. During the time Stan was at SMSU, the Vatican was beginning dialogues and wanted to include him in those because of his ecumenical work. But they didn't know where he would fit. He was not AG by then, so they put him with the non-denominational group. The Centro Pro Unione (Center for Christian Unity) was responsible for conducting the reconciliation projects between Catholics and the non-denominational participants. The group met every couple years. Stan spoke at a few of the events. The application of Ruth's ideas at a Feuerstein Instrumental Enrichment in Caserta, Italy helped a non-denominational school there to be recognized by the Italian government. This helped increase Centro Pro Unione's confidence in Ruth, resulting in the invitation to present at the Vatican in 2006.

---

92. Burgess, *Changing Brain Structure*, 181.
93. Ibid., 183.
94. Ibid.
95. Burgess, "Diagnostic Approaches."
96. Burgess, "From an Anthropological Perspective, If They Exist, What Are the Epistemological Criteria for Distinguishing a Gift of the Holy Spirit from Other Paranormal Phenomena?"

CONCLUSION

Thus, the many cultures of Ruth Vassar Burgess's life provided multiple perspectives—the heritage of her childhood, the waves of transition, the adrenaline of discovery, the resolution of vocation, the hope of transformation, the struggle for justice, the surprise of suffering, and the pursuit of peace. Each perspective like a facet of a gem provides concurrent opportunities to see beauty yet feel uncertainty, to hear a clarion call yet wonder at its destination. It is through this diamond of Ruth's life that she continues to overflow into and enrich the lives of all those with whom she comes in contact—children and grandchildren, students and friends. All who stand close enough will find connection with a meaningful past and glimpse in reassuring measure a hopeful future.

Ruth Vassar Burgess, 2014
Photo Credit: Burgess Archives

BIBLIOGRAPHY

Select Works by Ruth Vassar Burgess

Burgess, Ruth Vassar. "Benjamin Prasad Shinde." In *Testimoni della fede nelle chiese della reforma*, edited by Stanley M. Burgess et al., 343–44. Rome: Citta' Nuova, 2010.

———. *Changing Brain Structure through Cross-Cultural Learning: The Life of Reuven Feuerstein.* Lewiston, NY: Mellen, 2008.

———. "Diagnostic Approaches: A Call for Theoretical and Praxis Consistency." Lecture, International Conference on Special Education: Leadership in a New Era, Exeter College, Oxford, England, 2004.

———. "Enculturation." In *Encyclopedia of Pentecostal and Charismatic Christianity*, edited by Stanley M. Burgess, 162–65. New York: Routledge, 2006.

———. "Feminism." In *Encyclopedia of Pentecostal and Charismatic Christianity*, edited by Stanley M. Burgess, 200–204. New York: Routledge, 2006.

———. "From an Anthropological Perspective, if They Exist, What Are the Epistemological Criteria for Distinguishing a Gift of the Holy Spirit from other Paranormal Phenomena?" Lecture, Azusa Street Centennial: Vatican, Rome, Italy, November 29, 2006.

———. "Pandita Ramabai: A Woman for All Seasons." *Asian Journal of Pentecostal Studies* 9 (2006) 183–98. http://www.apts.edu/aeimages//File/AJPS_PDF/06-_2_Ruth_Vassar_Burgess.pdf.

———. "Pandita Ramabai." In *The New International Dictionary of Pentecostal and Charismatic Movements*, edited by Stanley M. Burgess and Eduard M. van der Maas, 1016. Grand Rapids: Zondervan, 2002.

———. "Prediction of Language Abilities from Measures of Mental Maturity." PhD diss., University of Missouri at Columbia, 1979.

———. "Propelling the Change, Preserving Continuity: A Portrait of Reuven Feuerstein." In *Experience of Mediated Learning: An Impact of Feuerstein's Ideas in Education and Psychology.* Oxford: Elsevier Science, 2000.

———. "Religion's Influence on Social Justice Practices Relating to Those with Disabilities." In *The Wiley-Blackwell Companion to Religion and Social Justice*, edited by Michael D. Palmer and Stanley M. Burgess, 575–90. Chichester, West Sussex, UK: Blackwell, 2012.

———. *Spirited Sisters.* Portland, OR: Harper, 2014.

———. *Tales from Beside Shivaniri: An Ethnographic Study Including Oral Histories from Orphans, 1947–1952.* Ahmedabad: India, 2002.

Additional Sources Cited

"About Us." Southern Asia Bible College. http://sabc.cgld.org/about-us/.

Bethel Bible College. http://www.bbcpunalur.org/.

Burke, Bob, and Viola Holder. "Daddy Nelson." *Assemblies of God Heritage* 29 (2009) 20–25. http://ifphc.org/pdf/Heritage/2009.pdf#Page21.

Lewis, Idell. "My Life Story: Ruth Burgess" Springfield, MO: Ethnic Life Stories Project, 2002, 3. Springfield-Green County Library. http://thelibrary.org/lochist/els/burgess.pdf.

Newberg, Eric. Review of *Changing Brain Structure through Cross-Cultural Learning: The Life of Reuven Feuerstein*, by Ruth Vassar Burgess. *Journal of Christian Education: Faith Shaping Leadership, Teaching and Learning* 51 (2008) 71–77.

Pollock, David C., and Ruth E. Van Reken. *Third Culture Kids: Growing up among Worlds*. Rev. ed. Boston: Brealey, 2009.

"What Is a Third Culture Kid?" TCKid. http://tckid.com/what-is-a-tck.html.

Photos

Stanley dressed in Indian suit, Mavelikara, India, 1938

Photo Credit: Burgess Archives

Bernice, John, and Stanley Burgess, 1939

Photo Credit: Burgess Archives

Ruth Vassar, Second Grade, Bowie, Texas, 1946
Photo Credit: Burgess Archives

Ruth at Junnar Boys Orphanage, 1947

Photo Credit: Burgess Archives

Stanley M. Burgess, Beecher High School, Flint, Michigan, 1952
Photo Credit: Burgess Archives

The Sam James wedding, 1952
Joyce Holleman, Estelle Vassar, Ida James, and Ruth Vassar

Photo Credit: Burgess Archives

Ruth Vassar, High School Graduation, Levelland, TX, 1956
Photo Credit: Burgess Archives

Ruth and Stan, wedding photo, Abilene, Texas, 1960

Photo Credit: Burgess Archives

Ruth and Stan, young couple, Springfield, MO (1965)

Photo Credit: Burgess Archives

Young Burgess Family, 1970s

Photo Credit: Burgess Archives

Ruth at Junnar Boys Home, Junnar, India, 1984

Photo Credit: Burgess Archives

Ruth and Stan; Ruth presents at Exeter College, Oxford, England, 2004

Photo Credit: Burgess Archives

Stan communicating with Dr. Yakov Rand, Tel Aviv, Israel, 2006

Photo Credit: Burgess Archives

Ruth Burgess's 2006 presentation at Azusa Centennial Conference, Vatican City, Rome, Italy. Leadership Group, L-R: Dr. David Cole, President, Eugene Bible College; Dr. Stan Burgess, Distinguished Professor, Regent University, Virginia Beach, VA; Dr. Bruce Williams, o.p., faculty, Pontifical University of St. Thomas Aquinas; Dr. Ruth Burgess, Professor Emeritus, Missouri State University, Springfield, Missouri; Rev. Dr. Thomas Best, Head, World Council of Churches, Geneva, Switzerland; Father Doctor Juan Gomez, Coordinator of Ecumenical Dialogue; Rev. Dr. James Puglisi, s.a., Director of the Centro Pro Unione and the Friars of the Atonement; Dr. Charles Whitehead, Chair, International Charismatic Consultation, London, U.K.; Msgr. John Raniero Cantalamessa, ofn. cap., Preacher of the Pontifical Household; Rev. Massimo Paone, Officer Commanding, The Salvation Army, Italy; Father John Radano, Head, Christian Unity, Pontifical Council for Promoting Christian Unity

Photo Credit: Burgess Archives

Stan Burgess, St. Peter's Basilica, Rome, Italy, 2008
Photo Credit: Burgess Archives

Burgess Family, Stan and Ruth's 50th Wedding Anniversary, 2010

At the "Ranch" in Strafford: "Duke," Ruth, Stan, and "Daisy," 2013

Photo Credit: Lois E. Olena

Stan and Ruth Burgess, 2014

Photo Credit: Burgess Archives

The Quest to Understand beyond Boundaries

3

Written with the Finger of God
Divine and Human Writing in Exodus[1]

—Brian Doak

INTRODUCTION

Perhaps it is the modern obsession with communication technologies that has inspired a re-investigation of the Hebrew Bible as the product of not only the interplay between different types of communication in the ancient world (oral and written), but also the representation of writing in ancient literature. As Mogens Trolle Larsen aptly states,

---

1. *Author's note*: It is with great pleasure that I offer this essay to Stan and Ruth Burgess, whose guidance and pedagogy shaped my graduate experience at Missouri State University from 2002–2004. This essay, the first I wrote while a PhD student at Harvard University in the Fall of 2006, reminds me of the process of learning, of acclimating to a new environment, and of the excitement associated with change that the Burgesses modeled so well for me. Except for some font adjustments, I have left this essay unrevised; however, I would like to note three important books not cited below (all published after I wrote this essay) that address the question of literacy and the Bible in different ways: van der Toorn, *Scribal Culture and the Making of the Hebrew Bible*; Sanders, *The Invention of Hebrew*; and Rollston, *Writing and Literacy in the World of Ancient Israel*.

> In a situation where the general feeling seems to be that technological "progress" or "development" is rushing ahead like an express train into the night, propelled by its own internal logic and changing the world with irresistible force, it is obviously of vital interest to study other similar or parallel historical moments when new techniques for storing and disseminating knowledge, ideas and information were introduced.[2]

This search for the specifically *written* origins of a tradition, though stimulated by our own preoccupations, is not without warrant in the literary and historical depictions of writing in ancient cultures; in many languages and literatures, the act of writing is treated with a distinct sense of awe, or even dread. The knowledge of those who write is arcane, the writers are divinities or revered leaders, and their written product is a tool of creation and destruction.

The canonical and historical centrality of the book of Exodus for the religious traditions of ancient Israel only serves to emphasize the multiple and significant acts of writing perpetrated by both God and humans in that book. Indeed, arguably the central features of the Torah—the giving of the tablets of law to Moses, and the Sinai encounter in general—are surrounded by descriptions of writing. Despite the multiple examples of this important motif, there have been few concerted attempts to specifically discuss the role of writing in Exodus as a whole. Therefore my goals here are twofold:

(1) To make a detailed case for the significance of both divine and human writing in Exodus. By the end of this study, it will hopefully be clear that writing plays a decisive role in the narrative construction of Exodus and also that the memories of writing enshrined in Exodus serve to bolster the sense of power and awe attached to the Torah as a document.

(2) To explore the connection of writing and cultic acts, which are referenced together (or in close proximity to one another) in all of the critical passages (the battle with Amalek in 17:14–15, the vision of God on the mountain in 24:1–8; the "golden calf" episode in 31:18–32:35; the

---

2. Larsen, "Introduction," in *Literacy and Society*, 7. Bowman and Woolf speculate that the "enormous growth, over the past quarter-century, of interest in writing and literacy is simply the manifestation of our own society's graphocentrism, our obsession with the written word." "Literacy and Power in the Ancient World," 1. Ong speaks of entering into a type of "secondary orality" in the modern world: "Contrasts between electronic media and print have sensitized us to the earlier contrast between writing and orality. The electronic age is also an age of 'secondary orality,' the orality of telephones, radio, and television, which depends on writing and print for its existence." *Orality and Literacy*, 3.

inscribing of cultic apparel in 28:9–12, 36–38, 39:14–30). I will suggest that writing and cult may have been more intimately connected during some periods of Israel's religious activity, and that the act of writing and the products of writing are intimately involved in the search for God's physical representation on earth.

To these ends, we must first make some preliminary comments on the nature of writing in the ancient world and the secondary literature which has arisen over the past few decades regarding the complex interplay of orality and literacy in traditional societies (including ancient Israel). An examination of passages in Exodus where writing occurs will follow; wherever appropriate, we must seek to integrate the discussion of the biblical text with some ancient Near Eastern materials and with the anthropological study of writing and religion.

ORALITY AND THE POWER OF WRITING

The multitude of artistic representations of Moses and the written tablets of the Law produced since antiquity—ranging from the frescos of *Dura Europas* (third century CE; Syria), where Moses receives the Torah on a scroll instead of the traditional stone tablets, to Rembrandt van Rijn's brooding portrait of the embattled leader on the verge of smashing the Law at the foot of the mountain (1659; Gemäldegalerie, Berlin)—bear witness to the role of writing in semi- or non-literate cultures; writing is viewed with awe and suspicion, even danger, and can act as a tangible link between humans, divinity, and the very nature of reality. The historical invention and development of writing in southern Mesopotamia sometime in the late fourth millennium was, of course, much more mundane than the account of Berossus in his third-century BCE *Babyloniaca*, where humans who had previously been living "without laws just as wild animals" are granted "the knowledge of letters and sciences and crafts of all types" by a "beast named Oannes . . . from the Erythraean Sea" [i.e. Persian Gulf].[3]

Nevertheless, Berossus' description of Oannes highlights an attitude toward writing prevalent throughout nearly all ancient societies and even some modern oral cultures—writing is bestowed upon humanity by deities, and is thus inherently endued with numinous powers which transform human society. This ancient Near Eastern emphasis on the positive and civilizing origins of the craft stands in stark contrast to Plato's *Phaedrus* dialogue, which, less than a century before Berossus, famously decries the power of the written word. Plato does this by giving Socrates a short myth to tell of

3. Translation by Burstein, *The Babyloniaca of Berossus*, 155–56.

the origins of writing in Egypt: Theuth [Egyptian Thoth] creates writing and extols its virtues to the king, Thamus, who offers a series of critiques.[4] Socrates goes on to announce that it is a "great folly ... to suppose that one can transmit or acquire clear and certain knowledge of an art through the medium of writing, or that written words can do more than remind the reader of what he already knows on any given subject."[5]

Unlike with Oannes or Thoth, however, writing is not introduced to Israel in the Hebrew Bible as a general gift or cultural achievement, but rather in the highly specific terms of YHWH's socio-legal program for his people.[6] The technology is conspicuously absent from the etiological accounts in Genesis 1–11 (though compare the development of other technologies in Gen 4:20–22); the patriarchs certainly do not write, while canonically later characters like Ezra and Daniel can read and interpret with fluency. In this respect, the authors of the Bible seem to be aware of the emergence of writing at a certain time period and do not commit the blunders of anachronism that might have been possible regarding the issue of literacy.[7] Homer (or the Homeric tradition), in both the *Iliad* and *Odyssey*, is mostly aware of the issue as well, and avoids presenting us with writers in both stories.[8]

Numerous recent articles and monographs have examined the rise of literacy in antiquity and the interactions between and within oral and literate cultures, not all of which can be discussed here.[9] The result of the

---

4. As Ong points out, Thamus's objections are identical to those raised in criticism of computers: "[T]hey will rely on writing to bring things to their remembrance by external signs instead of on their own internal resources ... And as for wisdom, your pupils will have the reputation for it without the reality: they will receive a quantity of information without proper instruction, and in consequence be thought very knowledgeable when they are for the most part quite ignorant. And because they are filled with the conceit of wisdom instead of real wisdom they will be a burden to society" (Plato, *Phaedrus* 275; pp. 96–97).

5. Ibid., 97.

6. Although it is unlikely that what we have in Exodus is an "etiological" narrative for the "creation" of all writing in the world, the references to writing in Exodus do act as an etiology of writing *for Israel*, insofar as they are the first references to writing in the Bible and are presented with the mystery and divine sanction of other etiological stories (such as those throughout Genesis).

7. However, Demsky's periodization of the history of Israelite religion into "the *preliterate* patriarchal period, the *literate* Mosaic faith and the post-Exilic *Book* centered reforms of Ezra" is too extreme. Demsky, "Writing in Ancient Israel," 18.

8. The one remarkable exception occurs in the *Iliad* 6.198.99: Proteus sends Bellerophon to Lycia with "tokens / murderous signs, scratched in a folded tablet / and many of them too, enough to kill a man." The reference is possibly too cryptic to identify as writing for certain, however. See comments in Knox's introduction and notes to Fagles's translation, *The Iliad*, 21, esp. 201.

9. This interest in orality, literacy, and the rise of the book is widespread in the

last twenty or so years of intense research into writing and literacy has also helped to clarify the meaning of writing in both ancient and modern societies, and taught us not to overlook references to writing in religious texts. In his landmark study, *Orality and Literacy: The Technologizing of the World* (1982), Walter Ong made an important contribution to our understanding of the effects of writing. Ong suggested that writing is not "just another way" to convey thoughts (in addition to oral discourse), but that the act of writing actually restructures human consciousness. Although printed text seems ubiquitous around us, Ong reminds his readers of the enduring value of orality, and of the complex interplay between text and oral communication: "Orality is not an ideal, and never was . . . Yet orality is not despicable. It can produce creations beyond the reach of literates . . . Nor is orality ever completely eradicable: reading a text oralizes it. Both orality and the growth of literacy out of orality are necessary for the evolution of consciousness."[10] Ong's work, along with that of Jack Goody,[11] has been highly influential on biblical scholars who have taken up the issue of writing within the biblical texts.

Perhaps no recent work on writing and the biblical text has been as influential for understanding the textuality/orality interaction as Susan Niditch's *Oral World and Written Word* (1996). Niditch repeatedly warns against drawing an "artificial" line between oral and written expression, and has sought to understand the biblical text in terms of its "oral register," which can be explicated in terms of content pattern, formula or conventionalized patterns, and other stylistic features which can help determine the (originally) oral or written nature of a text.[12]

---

humanities as of late. For a sample of some recent (book-length) work in a variety of disciplines, see Mackay, ed., *Signs of Orality*; Worthington and Foley, eds., *Epea and Grammata. Mnemosyne, Bibliotheca Classica Batava Supplementum*; Olson and Torrance, *Literacy and Orality*; Amodio, *Writing the Oral Tradition*; Chinca, Young, and Green, eds., *Orality and Literacy in the Middle Ages*. A recent seminar at the University of Chicago reflected on the role of writing vis-à-vis empire in the ancient Near East, with collected papers in Sanders, ed., *Margins of Writing*.

For shorter studies, see Swearingen, "Oral Hermeneutics," 138–56; Gillespie, "Literacy, Orality, and the Parry-Lord 'Formula'" 147–64; Henrichs, "'Hieroi Logio' and 'Hierai Bibloi,'" 207–66; Rodgers, "Orality, Literacy, and Batak Concepts of Marriage Alliance," 433–50; Ong, "Orality, Literacy, and Medieval Textualization," 1–12.

10. Ong, *Orality and Literacy*, 171–72.

11. For a convenient summary of Goody's work, see Goody, *The Power of the Written Tradition*. Other studies have attempted to tackle the issue from the specific perspective of religious texts. For example, in *Beyond the Written Word*, Graham has focused his work not on the supposed and frequently studied dichotomy between oral and written traditions, but rather "the ongoing function of scriptural texts as oral phenomenon," 7.

12. Niditch, *Oral World and Written Word*, 10–11.

Niditch explicitly rejects a simplistic and anachronistic analysis of "literacy" in ancient Israel, noting that "'pragmatic' literacy in the pre-monarchic period probably meant 'learning enough to read a list, a name, some numbers,'"[13] and her rejection of "the romantic notion of an oral period in the history of Israel followed by the time of literacy in which Israelite literature becomes written and bookish" has important implications for our study, since Exodus narrates the putative transition from solely oral, human leadership to the presence of an "authoritative text" (i.e., the tablets).[14]

Turning more specifically to the *effects* of writing in the ancient world, it is important to note that in the ancient Near East, writing was not primarily an avenue of "self expression" for individuals, as it often is today. P. Machinist has discussed the role of writing in the service of the ancient Near Eastern empires in a manner pertinent to our discussion here. Writing does not only affect those who can read it, but the mere presence of writing can convey a sense of intimidation and even political power in the ancient world. Regarding the Assyrian inscriptions, Machinist draws our attention to factors such as the physical size of the monument, its exclusivity, and its confirmation of political hierarchies: "It was the very monumentality of the inscription . . . that communicated the monumentality of power and sovereignty—a monumentality that could be enhanced by artistic scenes and symbols that were not infrequently joined to the denotative, the inscriptional text." Thus, the text "gave to those who could read it another form of enhancement because it specified and nuanced the message of power and sovereignty not only by what it actually said, but by the sense of exclusiveness, the privilege of elite membership, it conferred on its readers."[15] R. Thomas has characterized the public inscriptions of the Athenian empire in a similar fashion. For example, the "Coinage Decree" (meant to standardize coinage and weights/measures on Athens' allies) was to be written on a stele in the polis and in front of the local mints. These decrees were "to be visible to impress on the allies the weight of Athens' authority, like a settlement

---

13. Ibid., 40. Here, Niditch follows an argument of Meyers in *Discovering Eve*, 1988.

14. Niditch, *Oral World and Written Word*, 134. Eyre and Baines make a similar point regarding writing in ancient Egypt: "Literacy was not a single invention that immediately changed the life of all who attained it . . . There are many historical gradations of literacy and changes in its potential, from being an extension or form of memory for recording and a vehicle for the display of prestige, to its eventual status as a quasi-independent means of communication (which it never achieved in Egypt)." "Interactions," 113–14.

15. Machinist, "Final Response," 295. See also the comments of Zimansky, "Writing, Writers, and Reading," 268–69, in the same volume. Niditch, *Oral World and Written Word*, 43, has observed this dynamic for the Assyrian inscriptions as well, and also cites Machinist, "Assyrians on Assyria," 101.

after a revolt, to intimidate as well as to communicate, to impress as well as to record on stone."[16]

The illiterate in a given ancient society may well have recognized writing—indeed, even today, non-literate individuals are often acutely aware of the presence of writing around them—but, as Machinist points out, "their inability to read the writing, their helplessness before it, would have communicated to them the superior authority of the rulership from which the writing came, and so, in a way complementary to those able to read, would have confirmed the hierarchy that the overall political system was founded on."[17] Although we are obviously not dealing with monumental inscriptions in Exodus (in fact, none have yet been uncovered in the Levant by any Israelite monarch), we are dealing with a textual representation of a similar kind of dynamic to that envisioned by Machinist in ancient Mesopotamia. The Tablets of the Law in Exodus are monuments of their own kind. Moses stands with the tablets, elevated above the people on Sinai; he proclaims their words to a people who, we are told, spend at least some of their time at the holy mountain cowering in fear (19:16). The written monument, over against the spoken word, conveys an autonomous sense of power and authority. "What appears . . . to be the most characteristic feature of the folklore about writing is that writing is interpreted as a physical act of power." Speaking allows us to engage in a "constant struggle to obtain and retain this power of defining the world. But if [our] conception of the world is fixed by some agency beyond my control [e.g. writing], [our] speaking has no power."[18]

A final note should be made regarding two of the more current studies in the textualization of ancient Israel: W. Schniedewind's *How the Bible Became a Book* (2004) and D. Carr's *Writing on the Tablet of the Heart* (2005).[19] The latter examines the role of literacy and writing in the process of elite "socialization" and "enculturation" in ancient Israel and the broader ancient Near East, among other things, and the way these methods evolved through the Hellenistic period. Schniedewind's work brings more to bear on the presence of writing in Exodus, since major portions of his study address

---

16. Thomas, "Literacy in Archaic and Classical Greece," 44. See also Schniedewind, *How the Bible Became a Book*, 45–47, for some examples of writing as a "projection of state power" from Ugarit.

17. Machinist, "Final Reponse," 295.

18. Holbek, "What the Illiterate Think of Writing," 192. Of course, this is partly an exaggeration, since a given culture must "decide," consciously or unconsciously, to elevate writing and the "the book" to this position of power and "autonomy."

19. Schniedewind, *How the Bible Became a Book*; Carr, *Writing on the Tablet of the Heart*.

what he calls the "numinous power of writing." In an atmosphere (such as ancient Egypt and Mesopotamia) where as little as one percent of the population could claim literacy, "writing was a guarded knowledge of political and religious elites."[20] As such, writing appeared in magical formulae, such as the Egyptian execration texts or third millennium Pyramid Texts, and can be used to affect blessings or curses on humans. The curse formula taken by the "woman with a jealous husband" in Numbers 5:16–30 is a biblical example of ritual which depends upon the "numinous" power inherent in writing, as does the census tax in Exodus 30:11–16.[21] We will return to some of these ideas at various junctures in our discussion of the divine and human writing acts in Exodus.

WRITING IN EXODUS: GOD AND MOSES, TABLET AND BOOK

Writing is described through a few key terms in Exodus.[22] *Kātab* is the default verb in the narratives and describes the generic writing act.[23] In the first-person recapitulation of the Sinai events in Deuteronomy, the act of writing is mentioned repeatedly in 4:13–5:22, as well as in 9:10, 10:2–4, 17:18, and 27:8. Deuteronomy's repeated references to the *written* nature of the laws and commandments act, whether intentionally or not, as a kind of macro-inclusio, encasing the contents of the Torah from Exodus 17 through Deuteronomy itself. With the possible exception of Daniel 5:5 (discussed below), divine writing only occurs in narrated sequence in the book of Exodus, making its appearance all the more significant in the context of the Sinai narrative.

Three other words appear to describe writing in Exodus: *ḥāraš*, *pātaḥ*, and *ḥārat*. In the writing of names upon precious stones in ch. 28, *pātaḥ* is used in the *piel* to describe the physical act of engraving upon the hard surface.[24] It appears that *ḥāraš* is basically a synonym of *pātaḥ* (when used

20. Ibid., 25.

21. Ibid., 27–34. For lack of space, we will not treat the census in Exodus 30 here, as the terminology of writing is not explicitly mentioned in the passage (though it is assumed).

22. For an insightful discussion of writing and writing materials in ancient Israel, see Lemaire, "Writing and Writing Materials," 999–1008.

23. See Exod 17:14; 24:4, 11; 32:15; 1 Kgs 11:41; 2 Kgs 23:3, etc.

24. The verb is also used this way in 1 Kgs 7:36, where the temple craftsman engraves cherubim and palm trees upon various surfaces in the temple; whether or not the phrase *wyptḥ 'l hlḥt* in this verse was meant to have any resonance with the tablets in Exodus (or vice versa) is not clear. See the slightly different description of the cherubim

in the context of writing/engraving), as in the instructions of Exod 28:11: "[Like] the work of an engraver (*ḥrš*) of stone, [like] the engravings (*ptḥ*) of a seal, you shall engrave upon the two stones the names of the sons of Israel."[25] God's own writing in 32:16 is described with a term unique in the Hebrew Bible, *ḥrwt* ("engraved"), which appears as a *qal* passive of *ḥrt* (which presumably means "engrave" or "incise"). Besides the divine finger, there are no explicit references made to writing tools in Exodus, with the possible exception of Aaron's *ḥrwt* (discussed below).[26] Isaiah 8:1 has the prophet writing *bḥrṭ 'nwš*, "with a human [normal?] engraving tool" (as if there are non-human writing tools available to the prophet which he might choose over the human tool?). Most of the writing in Exodus is enacted on hard surfaces, such as the stone tablets in chapters 32 and 34 and the cultic objects in chapters 28/39; other writing presumably occurs on a different surface (such as the *spr hbryt* in 24:7), but we are not told exactly what this might be.

17:14 Write This as a Memorial in a Book

The first injunction to write in Exodus comes at the conclusion of the battle in 17:14. Immediately after Moses/YHWH brings water from the rock at Horeb for the thirsting masses, the Israelites are attacked and experience their first battle. Joshua leads the army to victory over the Amalekites, "defeating Amalek and his people with the edge of the sword" (v. 13). Joshua's military leadership (which appears here for the first time) and the miraculous cause of victory (Moses holding up his staff on the hill above the fight, vv. 11–12) prefigure the battle scenes in the book of Joshua, where the Israelites roam from city to city eradicating various Canaanite groups (although no indication is given in chapter 17 that we have the *ḥrm* in effect, as in Josh 6:21 or 8:26).[27] After the slaughter, YHWH commands Moses to "write this

engraving (using the *ptḥ* as well) in 2 Chr 3:7.

25. All translations are my own, unless otherwise noted.

26. It is clear that *ḥrṭ* and *ḥrt* are semantically related, although Propp notes that *ḥrt* is probably not a variant or misspelling of *ḥrṭ*, as *t* and *ṭ* are "rarely if ever confused." Other roots which begin with *ḥr-* describe scratching, plowing, piercing, and digging; see Brown, Driver, and Briggs, *Brown-Driver-Briggs Hebrew and English Lexicon*, 354–61; Propp, *Exodus 19–40*, 556.

27. In fact, as Childs notes, the basic meaning of the verb *ḥlš* is "disabled" or "to weaken," indicating that the victory did not involve annihilation. Childs, *The Book of Exodus*, 311. Targum Onkelos uses *tbr*, "broke," while the Greek has "put to flight, routed." On the Greek, see Wevers, *Notes on the Greek Text of Exodus*, 270. For all references to the Targums in this chapter, see the translation and comments in Drazin, *Targum Onkelos to Exodus (based on the A. Sperber and A. Berliner editions)*.

as a memorial [or "remembrance"] (*zkrwn*) in a book (*spr*)."[28] Not only is this the first writing activity commanded in Exodus, but it is also the first act of writing depicted in the narrative of the Hebrew Bible (following the canonical story line) by any "Hebrew" or Israelite.

What is Moses to write in the document (or "scroll")? Presumably YHWH's deliverance in battle and the account of the victory are to be recorded.[29] S. Parker suspects "war adventure" stories would have been popular in early Israel, and the remarkable nature of the victory against Amalek could serve as a lesson to future generations about YHWH's provision and deliverance.[30] No indication is directly given that Moses' writing activity will be read by anyone, including Joshua; rather, Joshua will apparently *hear* the memorial account—the command for Moses is first to write, and then, "place it in the ears of Joshua" (i.e., read it to him).[31] Among the many issues in this exchange, one should notice the juxtaposition of two forms of communication—first writing, and then speaking/listening. There is no need to speculate as to whether the biblical authors believed accounts of such battles could circulate in written form or orally, since we have both writing and a verbal account narrated to Joshua.[32]

Writing is used here to permanently establish a negative recollection of the Amalekites, one that appears again in 1 Samuel 15, where Saul fails to kill Agag and thus fails to completely annihilate the group.[33] According to Fretheim, the Amalekites have "become an embodiment of evil, Pharaoh revisited, a veritable Hitlerian specter, threatening God's creational purposes."[34] In a certain sense, the very writing of this book of memorial

---

28. Idiomatic English would have us translate *spr* as "a book," without a definite article; if indeed the reference is to "the book," then we might have to assume Moses has been carrying around a logbook, etc. Houtmann, *Exodus*, 386.

29. Cassuto suggests YHWH's intention is for Moses to write about what happened in the battle and the words in v. 14, indicating Amalek's permanent erasure from the earth. Cassuto, *A Commentary on the Book of Exodus*, 206. See also Houtmann, *Exodus* 2:385–86. There is no reason to suppose, however, as does Cassuto, that the words are written on the altar mentioned in v. 14.

30. Parker, *Stories in Scripture*, 9.

31. Targum Onkelos has *wšw qdm yhwš'*, as if Joshua might read the book. Targum Onkelos seems alone in this interpretation. The reading of the book to the people in 24:7 is preserved as in the Masoretic Text, however.

32. Noth has also noticed this dual presentation, but probably draws too thick a line between Moses' act and the "clearly oral tradition" represented with Joshua. See Noth, *Exodus*, 143.

33. Cf. Mal 3:16, where the "book of remembrance" carries a *positive* connotation for the righteous.

34. Fretheim, *Exodus*, 194.

would seem to actually *preserve*, and not "utterly blot out," the memory of Amalek, as YHWH seems to intend at the end of v. 14: "for I will utterly blot out the memory (*zkr*) of Amalek from under the heavens." Note the interplay between *zkrwn* and *zkr* in the two verses (cf. Deut 25:17–19). Propp points to the possibility that *zkr* can mean "name" (compare to Akk. *zakāru*, "to speak"), in the sense of posterity (as with *šm*), and thus "Amalek will never be forgotten, but will survive only as a memory."[35]

The author here makes an additional correlation between the act of writing and the erection of an altar in 17:15 (in that the writing immediately proceeds the altar building). The association between writing and cultic functions is quite strong in Exodus and resonates throughout the latter half of the book, culminating in chapter 32. Commentators are often perplexed at the formulation in 17:15b: "Moses built an altar, and he named it 'YHWH is my banner' (*ns*)."[36] What we have here is most likely the establishment of a kind of military standard or insignia, in tandem with the altar, which stands as a "divine emblem" of YHWH. The emblem need not be written, but perhaps we are to envision the *ns* bearing YHWH's name or some other symbol. The beginning of the following verse is perhaps even more obscure: "And he said, for a hand (*yd*) on/against Yah's *ks*,[37] YHWH will do battle against Amalek from generation to generation." In light of the ambiguity, it is probably best to see *ks* in v. 16 as something similar to or connected with the "banner" or "emblem" in v. 15 (as the altar and name are related in Gen 35:7, for example).[38] The *ks* in v. 16 (and the *ns* in v. 15) may even be similar in form and function to the "Divine Weapons" (*kakkum*) and "Emblems" (*šurinnum*) referred to in Old Babylonian legal documents, where

---

35. Propp, *Exodus 1–18*, 619. Meyers notes the following: "'Reminder' and 'remembrance' are both from the root *zkr*, 'to remember,' and signify the commemorative processes of the biblical narrative." Meyers, *Exodus*, 135.

36. For another use of *ns* with this meaning, see Isa 49:22. For a detailed text critical discussion of vv. 15–16, see Childs, *The Book of Exodus*, 311–12.

37. Following Propp's translation, *Exodus 1–19*, 614. Childs, *The Book of Exodus*, 310, has "banner," while Cassuto, *A Commentary on the Book of Exodus*, 207, sees the *yd* as a "memorial pillar,"; "this altar shall be a hand . . . to the Lord's plan" (from *kss*, "count" or "reckon"). The Targumists had ample problems with this verse as well; see Drazin's comments (*Targum Onkelos to Exodus*, 178–79). The LXX calls the altar "the Lord is my refuge" and confusingly renders the first part of v. 16 as "for with a secret hand [?] the Lord fought," losing any possible nuances in the Masoretic Text connecting the two comments in vv. 15–16. See also Wevers, *Notes on the Greek Text of Exodus*, 272–73.

38. It is also possible that both words should be *ns* (banner, pole), and that the *k* and *n* were confused due to their similar shape in the Aramaic/square script; *ks* could be an abbreviated form of *ks'* (chair, throne), although this form is found nowhere else. See Propp, *Exodus 1–19*, 620.

the symbols "played a practical part in the establishing of the truth as oaths were taken in front of the god's symbol."[39] One aspect of the rituals involving an emblem (*kidinnum*) from Elam seems to have involved litigants touching the emblem, although the association of such a rite with the statement "a hand on/against the Yah's banner" is admittedly unclear.[40] YHWH's *ks* reminds the people of the deity's strength and his victory in face of their earlier complaint, and is thus similar in function to the written account (*zkrwn bspr*), an association which demonstrates the iconic role of writing and its connection with other sacred physical objects.

24:4, 12: Moses Wrote All the Words of YHWH

The acts of writing by Moses in 24:4 and the promise of future writing by YHWH himself in 24:12 serve to bracket the dazzling and highly anthropomorphic group encounter with YHWH atop Sinai in 24:9–11. The MT clearly states that Nadab, Abihu, Aaron, and the seventy elders "see God," and the context of chapter 24 itself gives us no indication that we are to somehow exclude straightforward, visual perception as at least one part of this "seeing."[41] No context is given for the speaking in the beginning of the chapter, as an unidentified "he" tells Moses to ascend the mountain after the Covenant Code in chapters 20–23. The speaker (the "he") is obviously YHWH,[42] and Moses *orally* relates "all of the words of YHWH and all the judgments" in 24:3, to which the people respond in complete affirmation (compare with Josh 24:21–22). In the next verse (24:4), Moses begins writing, and proceeds to offer a sacrifice and sprinkle the altar with blood.[43] In verse 7, Moses reads from the hitherto unmentioned "book of the covenant"

---

39. Spaey, "Emblems and Rituals," 413.

40. Ibid., 413–14.

41. The LXX, for example, attempts to mitigate the actual visual perception of the deity in 24:10–11. See Hanson, "The Treatment in the LXX of the Theme of Seeing God," 557–68.

42. Propp, *Exodus 19–40*, 292, suggests "Yahweh has been speaking to someone else [i.e., the people in chapters 20–23], but now turns to Moses personally; Noth, *Exodus*, 196, recognizes this possibility, but believes the "to Moses" in v. 1 "is evidently attached to a speech of God directed towards another audience which may now be lost from the E context."

43. Coogan claims the "earlier" passages depict God as a writer, or Moses as the scribe, as opposed to later materials (as in Deuteronomy) where a more literate population must be warned against adding or subtracting from the laws. Coogan, "Literacy in Ancient Israel," 436. This assumption seems logical in the face of the evidence for developing literacy and the powers ascribed to writing by oral cultures, but is by no means certain.

(*spr hbryt*), and the people respond again with an affirmation formula similar to the one in v. 4 (with the addition of the phrase "and we will listen" at the end). The people are then sprinkled with blood, and then Israel's leaders ascend the mountain to see God.

R. Hendel has discussed the ritual symbolism in 24:3–8, and, in dialogue with the earlier works of Robertson Smith, drawn appropriate attention to the overarching "cultural system" in which the sacrifice rituals should be viewed.[44] However, Hendel neglects to mention the act of writing in v. 4 or the book of the covenant in v. 7 as any part of this analysis. In my view, the interplay between oral commands, writing, and a "book of the covenant" demand equal consideration to the sacrificial acts in the pericope and cannot be easily disentangled from the rest of the chapter. Up until 24:4, the entire Sinai encounter (which began in chapter 19 and includes the narration of the Covenant Code in chapters 20–23) has not mentioned writing.[45] Schniedewind thinks that "the story of the revelation in Exodus 19–23 seems unaware that the Torah is text"; after all, "the Ten Commandments are prefaced by Moses' [words] saying that 'God *spoke* all these words'" in 20:1.[46]

Due to the reference 2 Kgs 23:2, 21 (and its parallel in 2 Chr 34:30), the only other places in the Hebrew Bible where the "scroll of the covenant" is mentioned, Schniedewind suggests a Deuteronomic insertion between the repetition of the peoples' responses in v. 3b and v. 7b.[47] For Schniedewind, the editorial content is marked by *Wiederaufnahme*, the repetition of a line to bridge two pieces of material or mark an editorial insertion.[48] Even if the references to writing in the chapter were added secondarily (and, based on Schniedewind's arguments, we have some reason to believe they were), we must still come to terms with their appearance in the passage vis-à-vis the spoken commands (24:3) and sacrifice. Indeed, the presentation of YHWH's words and judgments to the people is given twice, but it would

---

44. Hendel, "Sacrifice as a Cultural System," 366–90.

45. The people do experience the terror of YHWH's sounds (in voice or word?) on the mountain; compare with a fascinating study on the effects of sound and its religious connotations among the Ilahita Arapesh (New Guinea) by Tuzin et al., "Miraculous Voices," 587–88.

46. Schniedewind, *How the Bible Became a Book*, 121.

47. Ibid., 124–25. For a thoughtful analysis of the connections between the writing in Exod and 2 Kgs, see Grottanelli, "Making Room for the Written Law," 246–64.

48. Ibid., 124–25. Noth's view is still probably superior, however: "There is in any case no decisive reason for explaining the clauses about the 'words of Yahweh' as being a secondary literary addition, and thus we may assume that the obligation to the 'words of Yahweh' was a part of this covenant narrative from the beginning." Noth, *Exodus*, 198.

be incorrect to assume that the written document is necessarily elevated above the oral instructions to the people. Here, as in chapter 17, we suggest that the juxtaposition of oral and written commands (which, in the end, are probably both meant to refer to the same legal materials in chapters 20–23)[49] is intentional and gives credence to both modes of communication. The fact that the presentation first presents the oral instruction and then written reflects what was surely a pattern in the historical development of Israelite law—what was oral became written, even as the oral continued to live alongside that which is written.

During the mountaintop encounter, Moses is given only a promise regarding the two tablets: "I will give you the stone tablets with the law and the commandments which I wrote for their instruction."[50] Why can he not receive the tablets immediately? Presumably, the instructions given in chapters 25–31 will also be written somehow, and Moses must wait until the blueprint for the tabernacle and its implements is revealed. The association of divine writing on the tablets and Moses' writing in the passage serves to elevate Moses' skill and responsibility to near-divine levels, while at the same time introducing an object (the "book of the covenant") that conveys authority independent of (and even superior to) Moses.[51] With the entrance of the book, Plato's fears are realized—not only will the people be admonished by a human leader, but now also by written words which are "fixed" outside of the context of human interaction. As W. A. Graham asserts, "writing necessitates distancing of the writer from his or her readers ... Fixing a text visually objectifies its discourse as symbols on the page and makes it possible to treat it as abstract and impersonal, an object of analysis apart from the specific, always contextual situations of oral speech."[52]

---

49. The alternation between "word and commands" and "words" could reflect the desire for variation in repeated materials within narrative. This view may be simplistic, but there is a danger in going to the other extreme as well. For example, Sarna claims the "words" are those laws written in the apodictic style and unenforceable except through an individual's conscience (the Decalogue and 22:17—23:19), whereas the "commands" (21:1—22:16) "fall within the scope of the coercive power of the state and the jurisdiction of law courts." Sarna, *Exodus*, 151. Childs, on the other hand, sees a later expansion in 24:12 that "has confused the syntax"; "v. 12 has sought to combine the stone tablets which were written in the past with new teaching which were to instruct Israel in the future." He thinks the book of the covenant in chap. 24 refers generally to "the whole corpus of Sinai laws." Childs, *The Book of Exodus*, 506.

50. Contra Sarna, the tablets are not received at this time. Sarna, *Exodus*, 153. Houtman, *Exodus*, 3:298–301, seems also to imply that the tablets are received in 24:12.

51. Childs sees this dynamic most clearly in Deuteronomy 31, where the tablets are placed into the ark; "Moses will shortly die, but his formulation of the will of God [in writing] will continue" (Childs, *Introduction to the Old Testament as Scripture*, 134).

52. Graham, *Beyond the Written Word*, 15. Here, Graham also notes that the

31:18 Written with the Finger of God

Just as a highly anthropomorphic and relatively intimate depiction of the deity is an integral aspect of chapter 24, the comment involving writing in Exodus 31:18 gives a rare peak at one of God's body parts—the finger (*'ṣb'*).[53] The reference to the tablets here serves as a narrative link with chapter 24 and, among other things, helps provide a bridge to connect two narrative scenes at the mountain with the section of legal materials in between. Earlier, in Exodus 8:15, the Egyptian "magicians" (*ḥrṭmym*[54]) finally recognize Israel's divine assistance and respond to the third plague (gnats/lice) by exclaiming to Pharaoh, "It is the finger of God!" or, "It is a divine finger!"[55] The specification of the finger, as opposed to the more commonly referenced hand (*yd*), is noteworthy in light of our passage.

The deity's power to act violently through his "finger" is also illustrated in a graphic battle scene from the Baal cycle (Ugarit, thirteenth century BCE).[56] Newly armed with weapons forged by Kothar wa-Hasis, Baal strikes Yamm with the club, which apparently serves as a divine extension of Baal's own hand/fingers:

> The weapon leaps from Baal's hand,
> like a raptor from his fingers.[57]

The use of the divine finger imagery here, as sometimes in the biblical texts, is a kind of synecdoche or *pars pro toto* construction, where the finger is at least the finger but also connotes divine action and impetus. Baal's fingers are similar to the hand, but more specific, just as "raptor" (*nšr*) is more specific than "weapon." Many of the clear iconographic representations of Baal from Ugarit elsewhere in the Levant depict Baal with the famous outstretched arm, by which the viewer can see the emphasis on the striking

---

"inclination of modern hermeneuts such as Paul Ricoeur to see the written text as utterly independent of its author is an extreme but logical expression of the autonomy of the written word."

53. This incident is retold in Deut 9:10.

54. Brown, Driver, and Briggs, *The Brown-Driver-Briggs Hebrew and English Lexicon*, 355, makes an interesting connection between this term and *ḥrṭ*; the *ḥrṭm* is "one possessed of occult knowledge," i.e., the knowledge of engraving/writing.

55. Although Propp (*Exodus 19–40*, 495) translates *'lhym* as an adjective ("divine") on the basis of Exod 9:28, Ezek 1:1, 8:3, 40:2, and Job 1:16, the phrase can be accurately rendered "finger of God," which I prefer here.

56. For the following quotation from the Baal texts, I have followed the translation of Smith, found in Parker, ed., *Ugaritic Narrative Poetry*, 81–180.

57 This refrain is repeated in Col. IV.14, 16, 21, 24. Parker, *Ugaritic Narrative Poetry*, 103–4.

power of the deity and the manner in which Baal's weapon acts as an extension of the deity's own arm/fingers.[58] Baal's violent sister, Anat, later washes her own fingers, which are covered in the blood of her vanquished enemies (Col. II.32–5).

Although YHWH's hand and arm are mentioned far more often in Exodus, with conventional descriptions such as "with a strong hand"[59] or "with an outstretched arm,"[60] the fingers have their own important place in the biblical texts. The use of the finger in cultic settings and actions is significant in the Hebrew Bible and may contribute to our understanding of the connection between writing and cult. Used specifically in reference to the "forefinger" of priests, the term *ṣbʿ* appears numerous times in Leviticus chapters 4, 8, 14, and 16 in reference to the application of blood and oil to various cultic implements and humans.[61] Alternatively, fingers are invoked to describe cultic violations and misdeeds in Isa 2:8, 17:8, 59:3(?) and 58:9(?). Moreover, in Ps 8:4, the poet credits YHWH with creating the heavens, moon and stars "by the works of your fingers." N. Sarna (following Maimonides), points to finger imagery in both Psalm 8:4 and Exodus 31:18 as a way of connecting the divine writing with creation itself. Thus, "our text expresses the fundamental biblical teaching that the Ten Commandments are divine imperatives that are as much constitutive of the cosmic order as are the laws of nature."[62]

---

58. In his recent study of ancient Near Eastern iconography and the Hebrew Bible, Keel's list of illustrations contain three interesting depictions of a human's (?) or divinity's (?) index finger outstretched and pointing toward various deities and cultic objects. Keel's discussion of the stelae and seal does not attempt to explain the significance of the finger, but we can at least assume the appearance of the finger is important and notice that the finger could play an important role in divine and human artistic depictions in the Ancient Near East. Keel, *Goddess and Trees*, 66–67, 116; figs. 9, 112, and 113 (in "Figures for Part II and Appendices").

59. For the hand as marker of divine agency or power in Exodus, see 3:19, 4:13, 6:1, 13:9, 16:3; for human agency, Exod 9:35, 14:8, 35:29, 38:21. The classic study on the divine arm/hand as the deities' destructive power is Roberts, "The Hand of Yahweh," 244–51; see also Martens, "'With a Strong Hand and an Outstretched Arm': The Meaning of the Expression *byd hzqh wbzrwʿ nṭ wyh*," 123–41.

60. This particular phrase appears repeatedly throughout the Hebrew Bible, e.g., Exod 6:6; Deut 4:34, 5:15, 26:8; 2 Kgs 17:36; Ps 136:12; Jer 32:21; Ezek 20:33–34; compare with Pss 77:16, 89:11.

61. See, specifically, Lev 14:6–7, 25; 8:15; 14:16–27; 16:14, 19; also Num 19:4. In non-P texts, fingers appear in various ways that do not describe cultic activity or the divine finger as in Exod 31:18 or Deut 9:10; the significance of fingers as a sign of human contempt or arrogance, for example, is utilized in Prov 6:13, and as instruments of battle in Ps 144:1.

62. Sarna, *Exodus*, 206.

A fascinating and enigmatic recurrence of the writing finger occurs in Daniel 5:5, where a lavish royal feast is interrupted by the ominous appearance of a disembodied hand writing enigmatic words.[63] The fact that this account bears an obvious affinity with our passage in Exodus 31:18 warrants some attention. We cannot easily identify the writer in this passage, although one might assume it is an angelic figure or God himself, but "the fact that the message is written conveys a sense of finality, even of determinism."[64] After Daniel's interpretation is made in v. 25, even the king immediately accepts his fate—what is written cannot be undone. The court-tale could conceivably have served as a not-so-subtle reminder, to those "on the inside" (i.e., those who knew Torah in Daniel's audience), that the God who wrote on the tablets in Exodus can still write with the divine finger, even to decree the end of an empire.[65]

The issue in the Daniel passage highlights a dichotomy in apocalyptic literature between those who understand and those who do not; Daniel reads the words that the magicians cannot, emphasizing the well-established importance of writing during the later periods and the value of interpreting esoteric documents in the apocalyptic writings.

The larger context of the statement in Exodus 31:18 should also be considered in terms of the role of writing. In the set of instructions for the tabernacle and other cultic instruments immediately preceding 31:18 we find a repeated refrain: Moses is reminded on four occasions to have the tabernacle and its utensils built according to the "pattern" (or "structure," *tbnyt*) shown to him on the mountain in ch. 25, vv. 9 and 40.[66] It is of interest to note that Moses is specifically instructed to build according to what has been *seen* (*r'h*) on the mountain—but what does Moses see? Propp offers several pieces of evidence that lend support to the idea of the *tbnyt* as a written or drawn plan, and the Mesopotamian background for a divine temple plan is often noted in the literature.[67]

---

63. See Collins, *Daniel*, 241–55.

64. The same may be said of the "book of truth" in Dan 10:21 (ibid., 250). According to Collins, the "failure to identify the writer is a deliberate artistic device. The reader is placed in the position of the king, who knows neither where the hand came from nor what the writing says" (ibid., 246).

65. Despite the fact that the author seems to be mistaken about several historical issues relating to the Babylonian and Persian periods, chapters 1–6 still probably reflect earlier materials. For a list of these problematic historical references and a discussion of dating the material on these grounds, see ibid., 29–33. Therefore the story in chapter 5 could have applied to Jews living any time after 586 BCE.

66. Later, in 26:30 and 27:8, different sets of terms appear, with an apparently equivalent meaning. Compare with Num 8:4; 1 Chr 28:11–19; Ezek 40–42.

67. See Propp, *Exodus 19-40*, 376–77. Schniedewind believes the "simple reading"

Although separated from our account here by over a millennium, the Sumerian king Gudea's so-called "Temple Hymn" (c. 2100 BCE) provides us with an interesting correlate to the biblical tabernacle "pattern" and a divine, physical plan for the building project.[68] In a dream, Gudea (the sponsor of the hymn) sees the god Ningirsu and is instructed to rebuild the Eninnu temple complex. A woman emerges to aid in the project: "She held in her hand a stylus of shining metal, on her knees there was a tablet (with) heavenly stars" (Cyl. A, col. iv.25–26). Furthermore, a warrior appears, "who bent (his) arm holding a lapis lazuli plate on which he was setting the ground–plan of a house" (col. v.2–4).[69] However, Gudea is unable to fully comprehend the vision, and the goddess Nanše is called in to interpret. The woman with stylus is identified as Nisaba[70] (one of the patron deities of writing in the ancient Near East), and the warrior is Ninduba. Later, it is revealed that Ningirsu himself will "disclose . . . in all detail the ground-plan of his House" (col. vii.6). Unlike the "pattern" for the tabernacle in Exodus, in Gudea's account the plan is *explicitly* etched with a writing instrument (the stylus) and a divine blueprint on the lapis-lazuli plate. At the very least we can acknowledge the possibility that our authors in Exodus wanted us to understand the plans for the tabernacle as a physical object in and of themselves, or possibly even a written plan of some kind on the tablets.[71]

The reinterpretation and continued importance of the traditions represented in Exodus' intimate writing scenes appear clearly in a text like Prov 7:2–3, which reflects the growth of an important tradition linked with the Sinai scene. Notice the manner in which the commandments, law, writing, and even the fingers are closely connected, albeit with a more personalized effect than YHWH's thundering from Sinai or writing with his own "finger":

---

of 24:9—31:18 indicates the tabernacle plans, and not the legal codes, are written on the tablets described in 31:18; both are possible. These plans would also then have a parallel in the "inspired" plans for the Temple in 1 Chr 28:10–12, as well as the Mesopotamian materials. Schniedewind, *How the Bible Became a Book*, 130–31.

68. The account comes in two major parts, written on a large clay cylinder. The relevant portions for our discussion are on Cylinder A, and are conveniently translated and discussed in Edzard, *Gudea and His Dynasty*, 68–88; Jacobsen, *The Harps that Once . . . : Sumerian Poetry in Translation*, 386–444; cf. the discussion in Kramer, *The Sumerians*, 137–39. For the following portions of the text, I have used Edzard's translation.

69. Edzard, *Gudea and His Dynasty*, 72.

70. For a helpful summary of Nisaba as patroness of writing, see Michalowski, "NISABA," 575–79.

71. Nevertheless, Propp's observation seems reasonable: "[T]he text never indicates that Moses brings [a plan] down the mountain and shows it to anyone . . . one rather gets the impression that [Moses] describes [the plan] to the craftsmen by memory." *Exodus 19–40*, 377.

"Keep my commandments and live, and my Torah as the 'middle' [perhaps 'pupil,' English idiom 'apple'] of your eyes. Bind them upon your fingers; write them upon the tablet of your heart."[72]

32:15-19—34:29 The Writing Was the Writing of God

Although Exodus 32-34 contain several different references to writing, we will focus our attention on the juxtaposition between God's writing and Aaron's fashioning of the calf in chapter 32 as a way of understanding the broader role of writing throughout this group of texts. Moses' descent from the mountain ends in disaster in 32:15-20; the people, led by Aaron (or perhaps it is the other way around?), create an illegitimate image, a "molten calf," in clear violation of the command against such images earlier in 20:4. The narrator inserts a reminder (32:15-16) of the presence of the tablets—they are the "work of God," and their writing is the "writing of God." We also get a physical description of the tablets (they are written on "both sides," "front and back"), which are now called "the two tablets of the Testimony (šny lḥt h'dt)." Why the new terminology? These tablets are apparently the same ones promised in ch. 24, but the additional term 'dt has generated no small amount of discussion, which cannot all be rehearsed here.[73] B. Schwartz claims the mentioning of the 'dt (attributed to P) in 32:15 (as well as 31:18 and 34:29), in tandem with the tablets (E), is the result of an Elohistic insertion into the P tradition. Certainly, the tablets, like the 'dt (if the two can be separated, as Schwartz believes), are "material evidence" of something; in the context of the impending actions in v. 19, however, it is best to view the "two tablets of the Testimony" in continuity with the earlier tablets, and thus 'dt further intensifies the role of the tablets as the "material" covenant.[74] The overt reference to the lḥt here acts as a foreboding reminder

---

72. In a still later work, the Gospel of Luke (11:20), Jesus claims to cast out demons "by the finger of God," demonstrating the continued feasibility of the finger-as-divine-instrument motif in first-century CE Jewish thought.

73. See evaluation and bibliography in Schwartz, "The Priestly Account of the Theophany and Lawgiving at Sinai," 126-29; Propp, *Exodus 19-40*, 382-85.

74. Even if the 'dt originally stood without any reference to the tablets, we still must make sense of the fact that a) Moses was promised these tablets earlier, and b) the smashing of the tablets/'dt signifies the "symbolic" and literal breaking of the covenant on the tablets (chapters 20-23, and possibly the blueprint for the tabernacle, as discussed above). Cf. Schwartz, "The Priestly Account of the Theophany and Lawgiving at Sinai," 126. Propp's view regarding the Priestly writers preference for the term 'dt in light of its resonance with other "theme words" in P's description of the tabernacle is probably accurate and fits with our idea of the continuity of the "Testimony" within the overall tablet scheme. See Propp, *Exodus 19-40*, 385.

of God's earlier writing in 31:18, and provides a dramatic backdrop for the smashing of the tablets in 32:19.

Upon reaching the bottom of the mountain, Moses sees the revelry described in 32:6. With great anger, "he threw the tablets [down] from his hands,[75] and smashed them at the bottom of the mountain" (32:19). Commentators have amply noted the implications of this gesture; the people have broken the covenant, perhaps even irreparably (as far as YHWH is concerned in 32:10!).[76] We must be sure to emphasize the disastrous results of the smashing in light of ancient views of writing. The breaking of the words constitutes a type of "magical" act, which destroys reality itself, and not merely a "symbol" of the covenant. The Egyptian "Execration Texts" of the early second millennium apparently functioned in this way, and one could speculate as to the intended ritual significance of "object breaking" in passages like Jeremiah 19:10–13 and 28:10–16. Although the writing activity here is not directly connected to warfare as a memorial (as it was in ch. 17), it is nevertheless interesting to note the proximity of writing to a kind of inter-group religious "war" of purification, enacted in 32:26–28 by the sons of Levi against (about) three thousand men. The smashing of the tablets in the preceding narrative, when linked with the death of several thousand transgressors in the following material, demonstrates the utterly solemn and dangerous nature of the covenant written on the tablets.

In a surprising and tense exchange following Moses' confrontation with Aaron and the people, Moses places his own life in the path of the deity's rage (32:32–33): "'Now, if you will forgive their sin . . .'[77] but if not, then erase me from your book which you have written.' YHWH answered Moses, 'Whoever has sinned against me, I will erase him from my book.'" Moses seems to know about the book, and assumes his name or existence (in a favorable sense, presumably) is recorded in it. YHWH confirms that he indeed has his own book, and that erasing will take place, though not for Moses. In a study of how the illiterate view writing in various cultures, B. Holbeck notes a belief in two kinds of "heavenly writing"—writing *in*

---

75. The Masoretic Text has the singular here ("from his hand"), but the intent is clearly plural ("from his hands"), as reflected in the Greek and Targums.

76. Despite his attempts at intercession in various places, Moses becomes YHWH's rival in rashness in 32:19. In Fretheim's words, "unlike God, Moses consults with no one and gives no explanation" for his actions here. On the significance of breaking the tablets, see Cassuto, *A Commentary on the Book of Exodus*, 419; Noth, *Exodus*, 249; Childs, *The Book of Exodus*, 569; Houtman, *Exodus*, 3:613–15, etc.

77. The Greek versions expand to complete the clause; see Wevers's comment, *Notes on the Greek Text of Exodus*, 537.

heaven, and writing *from* heaven.⁷⁸ Moses has received writing from heaven in the form of the tablets, but we now learn that YHWH has been writing "in heaven" for some time. Although Sarna finds it "hard to decide whether or not the notion of heavenly books was taken literally in ancient Israel," the authors record this incident with the book and names quite seriously.⁷⁹ Indeed, the Hebrew Bible speaks of such a divine book on several other occasions, including Psalms 69:28, 139:16, and Malachi 3:16 (in the New Testament, see Phil 4:3, Rev 5:1-3; in the Qur'ān, Sūrah 57:22.)⁸⁰ Although prominent among the Dead Sea Scroll communities and other later apocalyptic groups, the idea of a "divine register" has its roots in a much earlier period in the ancient Near East.⁸¹ C. Meyers notes a prominent example from Nebuchadnezzar II, where the monarch pleads to Nabû for prosperity after restoring the Ziggurat of Borsippa; as god of scribes, Nabû was thought to have held a "heavenly writing board" and could be entreated to "write" a favorable destiny for the supplicant.⁸²

Of additional interest here is the view espoused by the deity (or at least a potentially implied view) regarding personal responsibility for sin; Moses demands that he be erased (or wiped out/ blotted out, *mḥh*) from the book, but YHWH laconically responds by asserting that only those who have committed sin against him will be erased. Later, however, YHWH promises to bring the peoples' deeds back to haunt them (32:34), and then proceeds to plague them immediately anyway (v. 35). Therefore the discussion involving the book ends on an ominous note, promising danger at an unspecified future time.

After Moses pleads to see YHWH in Exodus 33, 34:1-4, 27-29 bring us back to the writing, as the covenant with Moses and Israel (mentioned in that order, interestingly) is now directly connected with the tablets in 34:27. YHWH must replace the first set of tablets, and notes with perhaps some

78. Holbek, "What the Illiterate Think of Writing," 189.

79. Sarna, *Exodus*, 210.

80. "The appearance of many elements of these ideas in Jewish, Christian, and Muslim scripture reflects the persistence and strength of the notion of a written book as the repository of divine, suprahuman knowledge or divine, heavenly decrees. The book emerges in these traditions as a physical symbol of divine as opposed to human knowledge, and hence as a tangible symbol of authority and truth." Graham, *Beyond the Written Word*, 51.

81. For an illuminating discussion of the Mesopotamian mindset underlying such a belief, see Bottéro, *Mesopotamia: Writing, Reasoning, and the Gods*, 97-102. See also Paul, "Heavenly Tablets and the Book of Life," 345-53.

82. Meyers, *Exodus*, 261. A convenient collection of the iconographic depictions of Nabû holding the destiny tablet in one hand and stylus in the other can be found in Seidl, "NABÛ.B," 24-29.

indignation that Moses has broken these (34:1). Moses cuts out new stones (34:4) and ascends the mountain, and for yet another forty-day/forty-night interval (as in 24:18–32:19) remains with YHWH atop Sinai to receive the new tablets (34:27). Despite the grammatically ambiguous pronoun in 34:28, it is YHWH who also writes this second set of tablets, regardless of the fact that Moses is told to write something in v. 27 (possibly the book of the covenant for the second time).[83] These objects are later placed in the ark (note the harmonized account Deut 10:1–5), as 34:29 explicitly connects the *šny lḥt hʿdt* with the tablets Moses has just received and carries down from the mountain. Moses' shining face is mentioned in tandem with the carrying of the tablets, and lends authority to both Moses' divine encounter with YHWH and the objects he carries.[84] Beginning in 35:1, Moses proceeds to give the people additional (repeated) commands regarding the Sabbath and various building instructions, and we are given no indications that the words spoken are read from the tablets which seemed to play such an important role in the previous verse (34:27–29). Whether we are to assume the act of reading, or now simply see the tablets as a kind of "archival reference" is unclear.

Let us turn back, for a moment, to the heavenly writing and gold calf construction in ch. 32. Only with this description of the tablets (in tandem with the reference in 31:18) can we fully appreciate the significance of the golden calf incident and the contrast between the divine writing scene on the mountain and the events on the ground below.[85] The writing act "with the finger of God" on the *lḥt* in 31:18 and the subsequent presentation of the *lḥt* in 32:15–16 are not "redundant" or the result of "slopping editing procedures"; as Childs remarks (in reference to the chapter as a whole), a "topical scheme of contrasting scenes often dislocates the chronological sequence of

---

83. This view is despite the otherwise compelling analysis of C. Grottanelli, "Making Room for the Written Law," 253, who offers no explanation for why it must be Moses who writes the second tablets. In fact, Moses must write the tablets to sustain Grottanelli's argument relating Exod 34 to 2 Kgs 22–23. The commentators, however, are in basic agreement that YHWH is the implied subject of 34:28. See Cassuto, *A Commentary on the Book of Exodus*, 448; Childs, *The Book of Exodus*, 604; Propp, *Exodus 19–40*, 617; Houtman (*Exodus*, 3:726) sees Moses as rewriting the book of the covenant, while YHWH rewrites the Decalogue.

84. For the motif of the divinity surrounded by radiance in the Hebrew Bible, see, e.g., Ezek 1:27–28, Hab 3:4, and Ps 104:2; the classic study of this motif in light of the ancient Near Eastern materials is Mendenhall's essay, "The Mask of Yahweh," 32–68. For a related discussion, see Smith's "Near Eastern Background," 229–39. Sarna's comments (*Exodus*, 221) are also helpful.

85. Grottanelli also notices the connections between the two scenes, but his interpretation of the Exodus materials is dominated too heavily by the stories in 1 Kgs 12 and 2 Kgs 11 and 22–23. Grottanelli, "Making Room for the Written Law," 254–57.

the narrative."[86] On the other hand, this "dislocation" can also contribute to the search for narrative *continuity*, as the sharp breaks between scenes and actions invite comparison between presentations which at first glance appearing jarring and unorganized. With this in mind, it is quite plausible to view Aaron's fashioning of the calf as occurring *in the same narrative time* as the writing by God atop Sinai, and not simply in a linear sequence (i.e., first Aaron engraves, then God engraves). The author duly marks the contrasting scenes occurring on Sinai and in the camp below through the repetition of the tablets and divine writing in 31:18 and 32:15-16. *Ḥrwt* describes the writing of God engraved on the tablets, and the semantically-related *ḥrṭ* is cleverly used for Aaron's fashioning of the calf.[87] Hence, while YHWH writes (*ḥrt*) the tablets, Aaron is simultaneously "writing" (*ḥrṭ*) the calf.[88]

This comparison heightens the dramatic effect of both stories, an impression that would be partially lost without an understanding of the danger and efficacy of writing as presented throughout the book of Exodus and through the anthropological study of writing in the ancient world. The "true writing," the divine gift of tablet and written word to Moses on Sinai, is presented in parody form in the camp, where Aaron is the ringleader of an illegitimate cultic act. While the narrator would have us believe the tablets are indeed a divine gift, or even a hitherto unmentioned act of material creation akin to the events in Genesis 1-2, we are told in explicit detail about the *actual, human origin* of Aaron's "engraving." In fact, the process of creating the calf is presented in a manner reminiscent of the "idol" polemics in Isaiah 44 and Jeremiah 10: the gathering of materials (Exod 32:2-3; Isa 44:14; Jer 10:3-4); the construction of the image (Exod 32:4; Isa 44:12-13,15-17; Jer 10:9); the proclamation of worshippers (Exod 32:4, Isa 44:17), which occurs despite the fact that the people have witnessed the creation of the object (Exod 32:2-3, Isa 44:12-16,19-20). With this in mind, it is difficult

---

86. Childs, *The Book of Exodus*, 559.

87. The Greek versions heighten the comparison between Moses'/God's actions in writing and Aaron's in fashioning the tool, as the terminology they use describes a writing instrument, and God's writing is described with the exact same Greek root in v. 16. See Wevers, *Notes on the Greek Text of Exodus*, 519.

88. This connection renders the discussion of how Aaron could fashion a calf with a writing tool somewhat unnecessary, and it becomes evident that Propp (*Exodus 19-40*, 549-50) is incorrect to emend the Masoretic Text to read "bag" (*ḥryṭ*) in 32:4 (or, more precisely, to read *ḥrṭ* as a defectively spelled form of *ḥryṭ*). Cf. Gevirtz ("*ḥrṭ* in the Manufacture of the Golden Calf"), where a semantic connection between the use of *ḥrṭ* in the passage here and in Isa 8:1 is denied on the grounds that it does not makes sense to have Aaron produce an image with a stylus. In my view, the author has sacrificed this need to "make sense" to compare the tablets and the calf. To his credit, Propp (*Exodus 19-40*, 450) provides alternate ways of understanding the reference, as either a design sketched on a hard surface or a wooden image chiseled and then overlaid in gold.

to imagine Aaron's words in 32:24 ("I threw it in the fire, and out came this calf") as anything but a shrewd mockery of the idol construction process.[89]

Ultimately, then, the story in chapter 32 gives us a glimpse into the struggle to define not only the proper worship of YHWH—although that is certainly at stake—but also the true *physical representation* of YHWH and his activity in the world. This struggle does not fit into a simplistic one-to-one correlation with Jeroboam's religious program in the north during the tenth century BCE (1 Kgs 12:28), but is rooted in a real historical struggle that stands at the base of the book of Exodus itself, the struggle to define the nature of God and the proper response of the covenant people. If the tablets of the Torah serve as the correct image of God for the narrator, in contradistinction to the calf, then the authors have attempted to show that the writing and the tablets are an authentically divine creation, bestowed upon the worthy servant Moses by a God who not only creates, forgives, fights, and kills, but also a God who writes words and, in a very real sense, authors the destinies of his people through the written laws which they are to follow on the tablets.[90]

We can affirm K. van der Toorn's basic arguments about the Torah as an image of veneration in later Judaism, akin to the Mesopotamian images: both have a putatively divine origin, and both are tangible symbols of the divine presence.[91] But the story in Exodus 32 suggests the tablets were thought to function in this way at an earlier period in the tradition, at least in the tenth century BCE. Still, despite the compelling arguments in favor of a literary connection between Exodus 32 and 1 Kings 12, the struggle to define YHWH's image surely occurs earlier than Jeroboam's tenth-century actions, and we should resist the temptation to uncritically read 2 Kings 12 back into Exodus as if Exodus 32 is a desperate attempt to ground Jeroboam's "apostasy" in another period. Indeed, the stories as we now have them do present Moses' and God's authorship as a part of a "venerable," "mythological"

---

89. These points comport with Cross's view on the Mushite/Aaronid competition for the priesthood. See Cross, *Canaanite Myth and Hebrew Epic*, 198–200. Cross sees two presentations of Aaron's infidelity, the first in the beginning of chapter 32 and the second 32:26–29, where "Moses' allies are Levitical priests, confronting the idolaters, at whose head stands Aaron!" (200).

90. These views are basically in line with those of Demsky (*Writing in Ancient Israel*, 19), who writes the following regarding the prohibition of images in the Ten Commandments: "It is most instructive that this opposition to an iconographic object of veneration is expressed in the written tablets of the covenant, which themselves became the new sacred symbol and tangible sign of His presence . . . The medium of writing therefore provided the solution of the problem how to represent physically an invisible and transcendent deity."

91. Van der Toorn, "The Iconic Book," 229–48.

past, "similar to the antediluvian era which the Babylonians regarded as the Golden Age of images," but this characterization *per se* would not prevent us from attempting to understand the complex socio-religious realities of the book before the final composition of the Deuteronomistic History.[92]

28:11, 36; 39:14, 30: Engrave Signet Engravings Upon It

One additional note should be made regarding the inscribing of various cultic implements in Exodus 28 and 39. The author (and thus presumably his intended audience) seems to understand basic signet/seal technology, and the assumption that the craftsmen will be able to carry out the work assumes a certain level of literacy for the characters in the scenario envisioned by the biblical author.[93] The names and phrases (*qdš lyhwh*, "Holy to YHWH") are not mere decorative tokens. In these passages, our connection of writing and cult receives direct expression: When Aaron "bears the names" of the sons of Israel before YHWH (Exod 28:12), he carries with him the physical existence of the people into the divine presence; when Aaron wears the crown (*ṣyṣ*) of gold upon his forehead, inscribed with "Holy to YHWH," he is made ritually fit to bear the burdens of the congregation and to appear acceptable before YHWH (28:38). As Niditch correctly asserts, "more than a reminder, more than a symbol, the writing helps to remake Aaron in a visceral and real sense."[94]

CONCLUSIONS

The presence of writing in the book of Exodus must be considered not only for its contribution to the narrative as story, but also as a witness to several key socio-political issues (such as the interplay of textuality and orality in ancient Israel), for the role of writing in the history of Israel's religion, and for the struggle to define, through several centuries and editorial layers, the nature of YHWH's "true image" in the world. The presence of "the book" itself may well have served an especially important iconic role during the loss of political autonomy in the nascent Second Temple period. We certainly

---

92. Ibid., 244.

93. Carr considers the head craftsmen who are to do this engraving to possess "at least basic literacy" and concludes (after citing several other examples, e.g., Josh 18:4; 1 Sam 10:25; Isa 8:1; Num 5:23, etc.) that "writing is not confined to scribes per se but is thoroughly intertwined with social structures in the poetic and narrative worlds of the Hebrew Bible." *Writing on the Tablet of the Heart*, 118.

94. Niditch, *Oral World and Written Word*, 86.

see this dynamic represented in Nehemiah 8, for example, where the "book of the law of Moses" serves to revive national customs (vv. 14–18) in a period of social instability.

The connections between writing and the origins of the organized cult throughout Exodus should not be ignored. We may even go so far as to suggest the possibility that ritual writing played a significant role in the early forms of worship, a role that was later replaced in later periods with Torah readings and exposition in the Synagogue (a practice adopted by the early Christian church). Others have shown the viability of ritual writing in temple settings (for example, in Roman religion[95]), and certainly Numbers 5 alludes to at least one form of ritualized writing in the tabernacle. We can even discern a simple pattern of actions in the Exodus passages where writing and sacrifice occur together (17:14–16, 24:4–6, and even 32:4–6, where Aaron's "writing" is the fashioning of the calf before the sacrifice) which comports with the pattern in Numbers 5:16–31: writing immediately precedes sacrifice. Further study would need to be made into the ancient Near Eastern materials to see if there is enough evidence to sustain such a claim, however.

The authors clearly sought to fuse the sense of awe and power often connected with writing in their ancient context to the Sinai complex in such a way as to reinforce the drama and gravity of the holy encounter at the mountain. The manner in which writing is treated in Exodus would surely have been viewed favorably by later scribal cultures in the Persian period, when the process of collecting the Torah into something that would become a canon began. Indeed, the very prestige with which the physical act of writing is portrayed in Exodus at Sinai enhances—either intentionally or inadvertently—the prestige of the final textual product of the entire Sinai narrative, and, by extension, the written Hebrew Bible itself in its canonical form. Even though we will not be able to conclusively rule out the notion that the sense of awe surrounding the writing acts in Exodus (and elsewhere in the Hebrew Bible) is in fact the late *product* of an early Jewish scribal culture, the events of the Exodus narrative itself point to an older and more complex history of transmission, where the repeated emphasis on writing indicates the act was viewed as abnormal and even inherently sacred.

BIBLIOGRAPHY

Amodio, M. *Writing the Oral Tradition: Oral Poetics and Literate Culture in Medieval England.* Notre Dame: University of Notre Dame Press, 2005.

---

95. Beard, "Writing and Ritual," 114–62.

Beard, W. M. "Writing and Ritual: A Study of Diversity and Expansion in the Arval Acta." *Papers of the British School at Rome* 53 (1985) 114–62.
Berosus. *The Babyloniaca of Berosus*. Edited and translated by Stanley M. Burstein. Malibu, CA: Undena, 1978.
Bottéro, Jean. *Mesopotamia: Writing, Reasoning, and the Gods*. Translated by Zainab Bahrani and Marc Van De Mieroop. Chicago: University of Chicago Press, 1992.
Bowman, A. K., and G. Woolf. "Literacy and Power in the Ancient World." In *Literacy and Power in the Ancient World*, edited by A. K. Bownman and G. Woolf, 1–16. Cambridge: Cambridge University Press, 1994.
Brown, Francis, S. R. Driver, and Charles A. Briggs. *The Brown-Driver-Briggs Hebrew and English Lexicon*. Peabody, MA: Hendrickson, 1996.
Carr, David. *Writing on the Tablet of the Heart: Origins of Scripture and Literature*. Oxford: Oxford University Press, 2005.
Cassuto, U. *A Commentary on the Book of Exodus*. Translated by Israel Abrahams. Jerusalem: Magnes, 1967.
Childs, Brevard S. *The Book of Exodus: A Critical, Theological Commentary*. Old Testament Library. Louisville: Westminster John Knox, 1974.
———. *Introduction to the Old Testament as Scripture*. Philadelphia: Fortress, 1979.
Chinca, M., et al., eds. *Orality and Literacy in the Middle Ages: Essays on a Conjunction and Its Consequences in Honour of D. H. Green*. Utrecht Studies in Medieval Literacy. Turnhout: Brepols, 2005.
Collins, John. *Daniel*. Minneapolis: Fortress, 1993.
Coogan, Michael D. "Literacy in Ancient Israel." In *The Oxford Companion to the Bible*, edited by Bruce M. Metzger and Michael D. Coogan, 437–38. New York: Oxford University Press, 1993.
Cross, Frank Moore. *Canaanite Myth and Hebrew Epic: Essays in the History of the Religion of Israel*. Cambridge, MA: Harvard University Press, 1997.
Demsky, Aaron. "Writing in Ancient Israel. Part One: The Biblical Period." In *Mikra: Text, Translation, Reading & Interpretation of the Hebrew Bible in Ancient Judaism and Early Christianity*, edited by M. J. Mulder and H. Sysling, 2–20. Peabody, MA: Hendrickson, 2004.
Drazin, Israel. *Targum Onkelos to Exodus: An English Translation of the Text with Analysis and Commentary (Based on the A. Sperber and A. Berliner Editions)*. Hoboken, NJ: Ktav, 1990.
Edzard, Dietz Otto. *Gudea and His Dynasty*. The Royal Inscriptions of Mesopotamia: Early Periods 3/1. Toronto: University of Toronto Press, 1997.
Eyre, C., and J. Baines. "Interactions Between Orality and Literacy in Ancient Egypt." In *Literacy and Society*, edited by K. Schousboe and M. Trolle-Larsen, 91–119. Copenhagen: Akademisk, 1989.
Fretheim, Terence E. *Exodus*. Interpretation. Louisville: Knox, 1991.
Gevirtz, Stanley. "ḥrṭ in the Manufacture of the Golden Calf." *Biblica* 65 (1984) 377–81.
Gillespie, L. O. "Literacy, Orality, and the Parry-Lord 'Formula': Improvisation and the Afro-American Jazz Tradition." *International Review of the Aesthetics and Sociology of Music* 22 (1991) 147–64.
Goody, Jack. *The Power of the Written Tradition*. Washington, DC: Smithsonian Institution, 2000.
Graham, W. *Beyond the Written Word: Oral Aspects of Scripture in the History of Religion*. Cambridge: Cambridge University Press, 1987.

Grottanelli, Cristiano. "Making Room for the Written Law." *History of Religions* 33 (1994) 246–64.

Hanson, A. T. "The Treatment in the LXX of the Theme of Seeing God." In *Septuagint, Scrolls and Cognate Writings: Papers Presented to the International Symposium on the Septuagint and Its Relations to the Dead Sea Scrolls and Other Writings*, edited by G. J. Brooke and B. Lindars, 557–68. Atlanta: Scholars, 1992.

Hendel, Ronald S. "Sacrifice as a Cultural System: The Ritual Symbolism of *Exodus* 24:3–8." *Zeitschrift für die Alttestamentliche Wissenschaft* 101 (1989) 366–90.

Henrichs, A. "'Hieroi Logio' and 'Hierai Bibloi': The (Un)Written Margins of the Sacred in Ancient Greece." *Harvard Studies in Classical Philology* 101 (2003) 207–66.

Holbek, Bengt. "What the Illiterate Think of Writing." In *Literacy and Society*, edited by K. Schousboe and M. Trolle-Larsen, 183–96. Copenhagen: Akademisk, 1989.

Homer. *The Iliad*. Translated by Robert Fagles. New York: Penguin, 1990.

Houtman, Cornelis. *Exodus*. Translated by J. Rebel and S. Woudstra. 4 vols. Historical Commentary on the Old Testament. Kampen: Kok, 1993–2002.

Jacobsen, Thorkild. *The Harps that Once . . . : Sumerian Poetry in Translation*. New Haven: Yale University Press, 1987.

Keel, Othmar. *Goddess and Trees, New Moon and Yahweh: Ancient Near Eastern Art and the Hebrew Bible*. JSOTSupp 261. Sheffield: Sheffield Academic, 1998.

Kramer, Samuel Noah. *The Sumerians: Their History, Culture, and Character*. Chicago: University of Chicago Press, 1971.

Larsen, Mogens Trolle. "Introduction." In *Literacy and Society*, edited by K. Schousboe and M. Trolle Larsen, 7–13. Copenhagen: Akademisk, 1989.

Lemaire, André. "Writing and Writing Materials." In *The Anchor Bible Dictionary*, edited by David N. Freedman et al., 6:999–1008. New York: Doubleday, 1992.

Machinist, Peter. "Assyrians on Assyria in the First Millennium B.C." In *Anfänge politischen Denkens in der Antike: Die nahöstlichen Kulturen und die Griechen*, edited by K. Raaflaub, 77–104. Münich: Oldenbourg, 1993.

———. "Final Response: On the Study of the Ancients, Language, Writing, and the State." In *Margins of Writing, Origins of Cultures*, edited by S. Sanders, 291–98. Chicago: Oriental Institute of the University of Chicago, 2006.

Mackay, E. A., ed. *Signs of Orality: The Oral Tradition and its Influence in the Greek and Roman World*. Mnemosyne Supplement 188. Leiden: Brill, 1999.

Martens, Karen. "'With a Strong Hand and an Outstretched Arm': The Meaning of the Expression *byd hzqh wbzrw' nṭ wyh*." *Scandinavian Journal of the Old Testament* 15 (2001) 123–41.

Martin, H. J. *The History and Power of Writing*. Translated by Lydia G. Cochrane. Chicago: University of Chicago Press, 1994.

Mendenhall, George E. *The Tenth Generation: The Origins of the Biblical Tradition*. Baltimore: Johns Hopkins University Press, 1973.

Meyers, Carol. *Discovering Eve: Ancient Israelite Women in Context*. New York: Oxford University Press, 1988.

———. *Exodus*. New Cambridge Bible Commentary. Cambridge: Cambridge University Press, 2005.

Michalowski, Piotr. "NISABA." In *Reallexikon der Assyriologie und Vorderasiatischen Archäologie* 9 (Nab–Nuzi), edited by D. O. Edzard, 575–79. Berlin: de Gruyter, 2001.

Mulder, Martin Jan, and Harry Sysling, eds. *Mikra: Text, Translation, Reading and Interpretation of the Hebrew Bible in Ancient Judaism and Early Christianity.* Peabody, MA: Hendrickson, 2004.
Niditch, Susan. *Oral World and Written Word: Ancient Israelite Literature.* Library of Ancient Israel. Louisville: Westminster John Knox, 1996.
Noth, Martin. *Exodus.* Translated by J. S. Bowden. Philadelphia: Westminster, 1962.
Olson, D. R., and N. Torrance. *Literacy and Orality.* Cambridge: Cambridge University Press, 2004.
Ong, W. J. *Orality and Literacy: The Technologizing of the World.* 1982. Reprint, New York: Routledge, 2006.
Parker, Simon. *Stories in Scripture and Inscriptions: Comparative Studies on Narratives in Northwest Semitic Inscriptions and the Hebrew Bible.* New York: Oxford University Press, 1997.
Parker, Simon, ed. *Ugaritic Narrative Poetry.* Writings from the Ancient World 9. Atlanta: Scholars, 1997.
Paul, S. M. "Heavenly Tablets and the Book of Life." *Journal of Ancient Near Eastern Studies* 5 (1973) 345–53.
Plato. *Phaedrus and Seventh and Eighth Letters.* Translated with introductions by W. Hamilton. Middlesex, UK: Penguin, 1973.
Pomponio, F. "NABÛ.A." In *Reallexikon der Assyriologie und Vorderasiatischen Archäologie* 9 (Nab-Nuzi), edited by D. O. Edzard, 16–24. Berlin: de Gruyter, 1998.
Propp, William H. C. *Exodus 1–18: A New Translation with Introduction and Commentary.* AB 2. New York: Doubleday, 1999.
———. *Exodus 19–40: A New Translation with Introduction and Commentary.* AB 2A. New York: Doubleday, 2006.
Roberts, J. J. M. "The Hand of Yahweh." *Vetus Testamentum* 21 (1971) 244–51.
Rodgers, S. "Orality, Literacy, and Batak Concepts of Marriage Alliance." *Journal of Anthropological Research* 40 (1984) 433–50.
Rollston, Christopher A. *Writing and Literacy in the World of Ancient Israel: Epigraphic Evidence from the Iron Age.* Atlanta: SBL, 2010.
Sanders, Seth. *The Invention of Hebrew.* Traditions. Urbana: University of Illinois Press, 2009.
Sanders, Seth, ed. *Margins of Writing, Origins of Cultures.* Chicago: Oriental Institute of the University of Chicago, 2006.
Sarna, Nahum. *Exodus: The Traditional Hebrew Text with the New JPS Translation.* Philadelphia: Jewish Publication Society, 1991.
Schniedewind, William M. *How the Bible Became a Book: The Textualization of Ancient Israel.* Cambridge: Cambridge University Press, 2004.
Schwartz, Baruch. "The Priestly Account of the Theophany and Lawgiving at Sinai." In *Texts, Temples, and Traditions: A Tribute to Menahem Haran*, edited by M. V. Fox et al., 103–34. Winona Lake, IN: Eisenbrauns, 1996.
Seidl, U. "NABÛ.B." In *Reallexikon der Assyriologie und Vorderasiatischen Archäologie* 9 (Nab-Nuzi), edited by D. O. Edzard, 24–29. Berlin: de Gruyter, 1998.
Smith, Mark S. "The Near Eastern Background of Solar Language for Yahweh." *Journal of Biblical Literature* 109 (1990) 229–39.
Spaey, J. "Emblems in Rituals in the Old Babylonian Period." In *Ritual and Sacrifice in the Ancient Near East: Proceedings of the International Conference Organized by the*

Katholieke Universiteit Leuven from the 17th to the 20th of April 1991, edited by J. Quaegebeur, 411–20. Leuven: Peeters, 1994.
Swearingen, C. Jan. "Oral Hermeneutics during the Transition to Literacy: The Contemporary Debate." *Cultural Anthropology* 1 (1986) 138–56.
Thomas, R. "Literacy in Archaic and Classical Greece." In *Literacy and Power in the Ancient World*, edited by A. K. Bowman and G. Woolf, 33–50. Cambridge: Cambridge University Press, 1994.
Toorn, Karel van der. "The Iconic Book: Analogies Between the Babylonian Cult of Images and the Veneration of the Torah." In *The Image and the Book: Iconic Cults, Aniconism, and the Rise of Book Religion in Israel and the Ancient Near East*, edited by Karel van der Toorn, 229–48. Leuven: Peeters, 1997.
———. *Scribal Culture and the Making of the Hebrew Bible*. Cambridge, MA: Harvard University Press, 2007.
Tuzin, Donald F., et al. "Miraculous Voices: The Auditory Experience of Numinous Objects" (with Comments and Replies). *Current Anthropology* 25 (1984) 579–96.
Wevers, John William. *Notes on the Greek Text of Exodus*. Atlanta: Scholars, 1990.
Worthington, I., and J. M. Foley, eds. *Epea and Grammata: Oral and Written Communication in Ancient Greece*. Mnemosyne, Bibliotheca Classica Batava Supplementum. Leiden: Brill, 2001.
Zimansky, Paul. "Writing, Writers, and Reading in the Kingdom of Van." In *Margins of Writing, Origins of Cultures*, edited by S. Sanders, 257–76. Chicago: Oriental Institute of the University of Chicago, 2006.

4

The Church of the East in the Tang Dynasty (635–907 CE)

A Theological Assessment

—Paul W. Lewis

INTRODUCTION

Historically, the West has caught only fleeting glimpses into the thriving branch of Christianity that resided east of the Roman Empire, and the later Byzantine Empire. Although certain figures were known to the Western Church such as Tatian or Ephrem the Syrian, the movement, growth, and thought of this church and its Syriac liturgy remained largely unknown. Amazingly, this church moved east in its great missionary efforts eventually creating a noticeable presence in Far East Asia by the seventh to eighth centuries. While not dominant, their outreach endeavors did leave a mark in Central Asia and China. Thereby, this study will seek to fill this lacuna by focusing on the literature of this branch of Christianity in China during the Tang dynasty China (618–907 CE).[1] To more accurately portray this branch,

1. There have been many volumes over the years on the church in China, but for the Tang-Yuan Dynasties period, see Foster, *Church of the T'ang Dynasty*; Latourette,

instead of the traditional term "Nestorian,"[2] I will use the self-proclaimed phrase "Church of the East" (abbreviated COTE) to refer to this branch of Christianity.[3]

The purpose of this essay is to survey and analyze the theological positions and emphases of the Christian Chinese documents and monuments from the Tang Dynasty period of China. To fulfill its purpose, this essay will have three sections: First, a basic introduction to the Chinese literary sources of the "Xi'an Stele,"[4] the Dunhuang manuscripts, and the Luoyang

---

History of Christian Missions in China; Moule, *Christians in China Before the Year 1550*; Saeki, *Nestorian Documents and Relics*; and, more recently, Bays, *A New History of Christianity in China*; Standaert, *Handbook of Christianity in China*; Tang, *Nestorian Christianity in China*. See the harder-to-find works but with some interesting insights: Chiu, "An Historical Study of Nestorian Christianity"; Couling, *Luminous Religion*; Hickley, *First Christians in China*; Keung, *Cross and Lotus*; Young, *By Foot to China*.

2. Historically the term "Nestorian" was used for the Persian church due to their acceptance of Nestorius and his noted teachers, Diodore of Tarsus and Theodore of Mopseustia. For some, this included the dyophysite position (two natures), which became known as the "Nestorian Heresy." Since the publication of Nestorius' *The Bazaar of Heracleides*, it has been common among scholars (such as Bethune-Baker, Loofs) to state that Nestorius did not actually espouse the heresy "Nestorianism." The historic disagreements tended to be because of linguistic ambiguity (Greek vs. Syriac), Nestorius' lack in communicative ability, and a certain political dynamic between the Patriarchs in Constantinople, Alexandria, and Rome. The most articulate concise argument about the Church of the East being not "Nestorian" but in fact "Theodorian" and ultimately not dyophsite is by Brock, "The 'Nestorian' Church: A Lamentable Misnomer," 23–35. See also Baumer, "Survey of Nestorianism," 450; Braaten, "Modern Interpretations of Nestorius," 251–67; Ferreira, "Tang Christianity," 131–37 (esp. 132n6); Harvey, "Nestorianism," 644–47; Moffett, *History of Christianity in Asia*, 169–84; Sekeznyov, "Nestorius of Constantinople," 165–90; Thoppil, "Christology in the East Syriac Tradition," 154–78, esp. 159; Wickeri, "The Stone is a Mirror," 44–46; and Young, *By Foot to China*, 8–13. Note that the terms "Assyrian," "Eastern Syriac," or "Chaldean" will likewise not be used due to their historically diverse meanings.

3. Several good works in recent years have dealt with the topic of Christianity in Asia, some of the most helpful are: Baum and Winkler, *The Church of the East*; England, *The Hidden History of Christianity in Asia*; Gillman and Klimkeit, *Christians in Asia before 1500*; Moffett, *History of Christianity in Asia*; and Philip, *East of the Euphrates*, 1998. Noticeable for their drawing attention to the Asian church in their broader church histories are Irvin and Sunquist, *History of the World Christian Movement*; and Jenkins, *The Lost History of Christianity*. Especially see the seminal earlier work of Latourette, *A History of Christianity*; and his *A History of the Expansion of Christianity*, vol 2. There are two helpful compilations of essays on The Church of the East especially with essays relating to Central and East Asia: Malek, ed., *Jingjiao*; and Winkler and Tang, eds., *Hidden Treasures and Intercultural Encounters* (hereafter *Hidden Treasures*).

4. In this essay I will use "Xi'an Stele or Stone" instead of the more historically common "Nestorian Stele or Stone" in order to not imply a theological assumption relating to the materials therein. When used in these names (i.e., Xi'an Stele, Luoyang Stele), "Stele" will be capitalized; otherwise it will be in the lowercase.

monument will be offered. It is important to bear in mind that there are different "levels" of texts, ranging from the semi-official Xi'an Stele to the somewhat public funerary Luoyang Stele to the more individual Dunhuang manuscripts.[5] Second, the theological affirmations in the texts (with the levels in mind) will be summarized. Third, some theological observations, and assessments will be proposed. While the material culture of Christianity in this time period is substantial in Central Asia and China, its usage is outside the scope of this work.

THE XI'AN STELE[6] [7]

In 1625, a stele was found just outside Xi'an, China that caused a stir within the international Christian community. It purported to proclaim the official mission from *Daqin*[8] expressing the "luminous religion" (*Jingjiao* in trans-

---

5. Deeg, "Ways to Go and Not to Go," 139–41. Although we have six manuscripts/eight documents, they are only a small portion of the thirty noted to be written/translated by Jingjing (see below), beyond other Christian documents, so we need to be cautious in giving too much weight to these extant few.

6. This stele has been analyzed and discussed repeatedly since its discovery. Alexander Wylie and James Legge both made translations in the nineteenth century widely available, yet in the twentieth century translations by Drake, "Nestorian Literature," 609–14; Foster, *Church of the T'ang Dynasty*; Foster, *Nestorian Tablet and Hymn*; Moule, *Christians in China Before the Year 1550*; the important work by Saeki, *Nestorian Documents and Relics*; and Tang, *Nestorian Christianity in China*, with others, made translations even more widely accessible. Also helpful on the stele are Giles, "Notes on the Nestorian Monument at Sianfu," (1917) 93–96; (1918) 16–29; (1919) 39–49; and (1920) 15–26. For the best translation and analysis of the stele, see Pelliot, *L'inscription nestorienne de Si-ngan-fou*, ed. and supplements by Forte, 349–73. An English translation of the theological summary portion is found in Charbonnier, *Christians in China*, 25–26. All quotes in this section will be from Foster, *Nestorian Tablet and Hymn*, with page in parentheses unless otherwise notified.

7. In this essay, I will follow the basic document designations used by Saeki, *Nestorian Documents and Relics* for listing the documents. The documents will be identified in square brackets whenever they are referred to in this essay.

8. I will follow Standaert's (*Handbook of Christianity in China*, 3n4) definition and discussion of *Daqin* although there has been an ongoing discussion on what is meant by this and also another similar term *Fulin* found in the Chinese literature. For Standaert, although originally *Daqin* was used for the Eastern Roman and later the Byzantine Empire, by the time of the Tang dynasty, *Fulin* became the Byzantine Empire, and *Daqin* become more of a religious (even Christian) designation. On this see also Hirth, *China and the Roman Orient*, 283–97; Leslie and Gardiner, *Roman Empire in Chinese Sources*, xvii–xxvi, 279–83; Raguin, "China's First Evangelization," 160, 174n35; Saeki, *Nestorian Documents and Relics*, 109–12; Shiratori, "A New Attempt at the Solution of the Fu-Lin Problem," 165–329; Tang, *Nestorian Christianity in China*, 83–85; and Yule and Cordier, eds., *Cathay and the Way Thither*, 35–57. Note that there was an

literation from the traditional Chinese characters) during the Tang Dynasty. This stele chronicles the activities of the COTE in China both historically and theologically.

The discovery of the Xi'an Stele in 1625 (although some argue for a 1623 date)[9] was promoted by the Jesuits with great enthusiasm. However, for the first two centuries after its discovery, there were many who considered it to be a fraud including Voltaire.[10] By the mid-nineteenth century, the voices of the opponents of its authenticity were generally silenced. Like the date of discovery, there was also a disagreement as to where this stele was originally discovered. Was it discovered in the western outskirts of Xi'an near the monastery mentioned in the stele? Was it discovered in Zhouzhi west of Xi'an, where a *Daqin* monastery was said to be? Or was it discovered somewhere else?[11] The prevalent position is that it was found in 1625 in the outskirts of Xi'an, but there is still some dispute.

The Xi'an Stele itself is about nine feet high, over three feet wide and about a foot deep weighing about two tons. Its headstone reads, "The Tablet of the Spread of the Ta-Ch'in Illustrious Religion in China,"[12] with the iconography of a cross on a Lotus flower in a cloud. The main text of the stele, composed by Jingjing (Adam in Syriac), can be divided into three parts: a summary of the beliefs of the *Jingjiao*, a survey of the political situation of the church from the arrival of Bishop Alopen[13] in 635 to the erecting of the

---

edict in 745 that this religion would be called as coming from *Daqin* and no longer *Bosi* (Persian), which with the demise of the Sassanid Empire, and the distancing from the Persian Zoroastrianism and Manichaeism, showed great political sensitivity by the COTE's representatives; see Barrett, "Buddhism, Daoism," 45–53; Foster, *Church of the T'ang Dynasty*, 83, 87–88.

9. Those scholars who follow the 1625 date include Chiu, "Historical Study of Nestorian Christianity," 15–16; Foster, *Church of the T'ang Dynasty*, 35; Moule, *Christians in China Before the Year 1550*, 27; and more recently argued throughout Keevak, *Story of a Stele*, e.g., 5, while others follow the 1623 date, such as Moffett, *History of Christianity in Asia*, 288, 314n3; and Saeki, *Nestorian Documents and Relics*, 28–35. Others list both dates, such as Drake, "Nestorian Literature," 608–9; Gillman and Klimkeit, *Christians in Asia before 150*, 271; Latourette, *History of Christian Missions in China*, 52; Standaert, *Handbook of Christianity in China*, 15; and Wickeri, "The Stone Is a Mirror," 46.

10. Voltaire, Renan, and others saw this monument as an elaborate "Jesuit fraud" or "pious forgery," Wickeri, "The Stone Is a Mirror," 49.

11. While some say the stele was found in Zhouzhi, which is some distance West Southwest of Xi'an, others suggest it was found in Xi'an or just outside Xi'an. For a summary of positions, see Chiu, "An Historical Study of Nestorian Christianity," 2–15; and Drake, "Nestorian Monasteries," 293–340.

12. Foster, *Nestorian Tablet and Hymn*, 5. I have used Foster's "Ta-Ch'in" in this citation instead of the more commonly used Pinyin, "Daqin." I will follow the Pinyin throughout the essay, unless in a quote or title.

13. Alopen was the bishop who led the mission from the COTE to Chang'an, the

stele in 781,[14] and the expression of appreciation (a eulogy) for the benefactor of the local Christian work. The bottom and sides, written in Estrangelo Syriac with Chinese, list various priests and monks tied to *Jingjiao*.[15] In general, the stele is both a declaration of the *Jingjiao* religion and an expression of appreciation to the benefactor as well as the Tang emperors who supported the *Jingjiao* religion.

The belief system inscribed on the stele covers an array of doctrinal positions. It begins with a discussion about the nature of God including creation, Satan and sin, the coming of the Messiah (listed as part of the Trinity) and His ascension, salvation, the Scriptures, water baptism, and practices to follow (these will be discussed in more detail below). One observes traces of intercultural transmission in the inscription. For instance, the name for God, "*Alaha*" and the word for Messiah, "*Mishihe*," are Chinese transliterations of the Syriac words.[16] In addition, there are some Daoist terms such as the expression of the "*Dao*" as a term for "the way," and some notable Buddhist influence like the phrase "rowed mercy's barge,"[17] used throughout the text. Related to this are numerous allusions to the Chinese literature classics, including thirty allusions to the *Yi Jing* ("Book of Changes"), thirty allusions to *Shi Jing* ("Book of Songs"), twenty allusions to the *Chun Chiu* ("Annual of the Spring and Autumn"), one hundred allusions to historical documents, and 150 allusions to the key works called the "Four Books and Five Classics."[18] Jingjing's level of Chinese is believed by some scholars

---

capital city of the Tang Dynasty in 635 CE. Three years later in 638, an edict of toleration was given to allow Alopen and his co-workers to establish a monastery in Chang'an with twenty-one priests, and to translate and publish their beliefs in the empire. This is described on the Xi'an Stele. On Alopen, see Barat, "Aluoben, A Nestorian Missionary," 184–98; Takahashi, *Transcribed Proper Names*, 9–10; and Thompson, "Was Alopen a "Missionary?," 267–78. Although Saeki prefers to suggest that this is a translation of his name "Abraham," *Nestorian Documents and Relics*, 84–85n10, Deeg believes the name is Iranian, "Ways to Go and Not to Go," 146–48. The name Alopen also appears elsewhere in literature as Aloben, Aluoben, and Olopen, among others.

14. Or as stated in the text, "in the year of the Greeks, 1092," commonly held as 781 CE. Note that Mingana believes it should be 779 not 781 (Mingana, "Early Spread of Christianity," 329, 331–33).

15. Which followed Syriac epigraphical conventions (Hunter, "Persian Contribution to Christianity," 72).

16. Takahashi, *Transcribed Proper Names*, 8–9.

17. Foster, *Nestorian Tablet and Hymn*, 8. Hereafter a quote from the stele will be from Foster, *Nestorian Tablet and Hymn*, with only the page number in parentheses in the text unless specified otherwise.

18. Chiu, "An Historical Study of Nestorian Christianity," 107n4, citing the work of Havret. In fact, these allusions to the Daoist texts can be seen indicative of the literary milieu and not as "borrowing" or "syncreticism" (Deeg, "Ways to Go and Not to Go,"

to be of good quality literary Chinese,[19] insomuch that he apparently was sought to aid in translating a Buddhist holy book from the *Hu* language into Chinese.[20] He likewise translated thirty Christian books into Chinese (see below), perhaps even showing a Chinese education.[21] However, there are some phrases in the text that are still unclear; for instance, the section on salvation mentions the "eight conditions" and the "three constants" (7).[22] Likewise, concerning the cross in the theological section, the stele opaquely states, "He appointed the cross to determine the four quarters" (6)[23] and later, "He hung a brilliant sun which scatter the regions of darkness" (8). The obvious omission, repeatedly referred to by scholars, is a clear discussion of the cross. This omission is representative of the presence of ambiguity theologically and linguistically in the theological section of this stele. A shorter version in poetic form of this section appears later in the stele.

The second section details the historical aspects of the Church from the coming of Bishop Alopen in 635 to the erecting of the stele in 781. It starts with the Emperor Taizong and his reception of Alopen,[24] his request

---

149). See also Foster, *Church of the T'ang Dynasty*, 107.

19. Nicolini-Zani, "Past and Current Research," 41; see also Foster, *Church of the T'ang Dynasty*, 107.

20. Takakusu, "The Name 'Messiah' Found in a Buddhist Book," 589–91. Inglis suggests that the *Hu* language is Sogdian or another Persian language, "The Nestorian Share in Buddhist Translation," 12–15. Deeg sees that the quality of the Jingjing and Prajna translation to be dismissed by the emperor was evidence of Buddhist propaganda, "Ways to Go and Not to Go," 144-45. Lin wonders if Jingjing helped translate Buddhist Scripture in order to gain favor with the pro-Buddhist emperors, Lin, "General Discussion of Tang Policy," 108.

21. He may have also been born in China (Bugge, "History of Nestorian Church," 381–82). Hunter wonders if he was Chinese ("Persian Contribution to Christianity," 73 n. 8). See also Standaert, *Handbook of Christianity in China*, 25.

22. The most common understanding is that the "eight conditions" refers to the Beatitudes (e.g., Foster, *Nestorian Tablet and Hymn*, 7n2; Giles, "Notes on the Nestorian Monument at Sianfu," 12, 22) and that the "three constants" are faith, hope, and love (e.g., ibid.); however, some believe the "eight conditions" have a Buddhist interpretation (e.g., Charbonnier, *Christians in China*, 27) and that the "three constants" are the three great commandments of Matthew 22:3–40 and 7:12 found in *Didache* 1:2 (Foster, *Nestorian Tablet and Hymn*, 7), or are somewhat Manichean (for details, see Eskildsen, "Christology and Soteriology," 203; see also Giles, "Notes on the Nestorian Monument at Sianfu," 22–23), or are seen as salvation—past, present, and future (Chiu, "An Historical Study of Nestorian Christianity," 120n46).

23. The Chinese character for the Cross is "+" or in Chinese the number 10, so Moule, *Christians in China Before the Year 1550*, 35, translates it, "He set out the figure of ten," which he takes as an allusion to the cross. Certainly relating "ten" to the cross was used this way in the Yuan Dynasty (thirteenth century), but it is unclear if it is true at this point, Moule, *Christians in China Before the Year 1550*, 21.

24. Apparently previous preparations had been made, since the chancellor Fang

The Church of the East in the Tang Dynasty (635–907 CE)

for translated holy books from Alopen, his private examinations of these, and his ultimate 638 edict of official approval of this religion with the sanctioned establishment of a monastery in Chang'an.[25] The subsequent reigns of the emperors Gaozung, Xuanzong, Suzong, and Daizong are reflected in a positive light. The short description of the period of the Buddhist uprising "in the year Sheng Li," 698 CE (12) reflected the pro-Buddhist policies of the usurper Empress Wu Zetian, yet this was not portrayed positively. Later under Xuanzong, prominent monks Lohan and Jilie restored "the mysterious order and together tied up its broken meshes" (12) in Chang'an in the second mission apparently in response to the destruction caused by the Buddhist uprising.[26] Somewhat later, the very serious An Lushan Rebellion of 755–63 is referred to only indirectly as Suzong "re-established the illustrious monasteries" (13). It is noteworthy that the text does follow an obvious Deuteronomistic understanding of the imperial reign (with a clear familiarity of the OT).[27] So while the text shows the emperors in a positive light, it is only as the emperors are seen as obeying God in their support of the COTE. The following portion of the stele summarizes this section in verse. After this poetic part is the eulogy section, which notes the date of the erecting of the stele in 781, and names the Patriarch *Ning-shu* of the COTE (or in Syriac, *Hanaishu* (II) (773–780). Apparently the stele was erected after the death of the patriarch, so it is conceivable that the news had not arrived prior to the erecting (or at least the chiseling) of the stele.[28]

On the bottom and the sides of this monument, seventy names are listed in Syriac with Chinese descriptions of names and duties, with Syriac descriptions of some, including the ranks from bishop down to deacon,

---

Xuanling escorted him to the Emperor from the western part of Chang'an. Forte suggests that Alopen was part of an official envoy from Persia, which would explain the reception, "The Edict of 638 allowing the diffusion of Christianity in China," in *L'inscription nestorienne de Si-ngan-fou*, 363–67. Note also that the *Zunjing* [G] mentions two noted ministers Fang Xuanling (also noted in the Xi'an Stele as being an escort) and Wei Zheng (only mentioned here) under Taizong who presented the request for books to Alopen; Tang, *Nestorian Christianity in China*, 187n247.

25. Forte, "Edict of 638," 349–73. Note that one condition for support is that the emperor's portrait was to be on the monastery wall. This does not necessarily mean that he was to be worshiped, but rather could mean that he was to be publically seen as a benefactor.

26. Foster, *Church of the T'ang Dynasty*, 80–83.

27. Showing a familiarity of the Deuteronomistic History in the Old Testament, Tubach, "Deuteronomistic Theology in the Text of the Stele of Xi'an," 175–80.

28. Moule, *Christians in China Before the Year 1550*, 47n43; Tang, *Nestorian Christianity in China*, 18 n. 8; and Vine, *Nestorian Churches*, 132; cf. Hunter, "The Persian Contribution to Christianity in China," 74n16. This is the reason why Mingana dates the erection of the stele at 779 and not 781; see note 14.

priests, and monks.[29] The names convey religious and various ethnic provenance, such as numerous biblical names, various Syriac names (some known in Central Asia), Persian names, Syriac names of Greek or Latin origin,[30] as well as Chinese names[31] with the possibility that some of these persons may actually have been Indian.[32]

DUNHUANG DOCUMENTS[33]

Subsequent to the discovery of the Xi'an Stele in 1625 in the early part of the twentieth century, archaeologists (in a treasure-hunting sort of way) scoured Central Asia for historical finds. Two men, Aurel Stein and Paul Pelliot, came across a hidden room of eighth- to tenth-century documents in Dunhuang, Gansu province, China (formerly Chinese Turkestan).[34] Eight documents on six manuscripts that were Christian (and in some cases, had ties to the information on the Xi'an Stele) were included in this stash. Two other manuscripts formerly assumed to be a part of these documents, namely *Daqin Jingjiao Dasheng Tongzhen Guifa Zan* (Saeki's [J]) and *Daqin Jingjiao Suan Yuanben Jing* Part II, (which Saeki added to [I] below) were put forward by Kojima Osamu (thereby commonly called Kojima A and Kojima B, respectively) in the mid-twentieth century. These documents have recently been declared to be forgeries, so they will not come into this discussion.[35] Concerning the other manuscripts, the first two [noted as B,

---

29. These monks could be anchorite or cenobite monks (Hunter, "Persian Contribution to Christianity," 78, 81). As noted by Hunter, see also Vööbus, *History of Asceticism*, 106–8.

30. Black, "Syriac Inscriptions," 18–25. See also Hunter, "Persian Contribution to Christianity," 71–85; Takahashi, *Transcribed Proper Names*, 11–14.

31. Standaert, *Handbook of Christianity in China*, 23–24. Beyond this, Lee notes that the evidence of Chinese believers includes the documents being in Chinese (as well as having some Chinese monks), *Cross and Lotus*, 22. However, there may not have been many (Bays, *New History of Christianity in China*, 11; Foltz, *Religions of the Silk Road*, 72.

32. Mattan, "Missionary Enterprises," 86.

33. These are the documents that we will look at with their designation, 1. *Xuting Mishisuo Jing* [B]; 2. *Yi Shen Lun*, which has three parts, *Yu Di Er* [C], *Yitian Lun* [D], and *Shizun Bushi Lun* [E]; 3. *Daqin Jingjiao Sanwei Mengdu Zan* [F]; 4. *Zun Jing* [G]; 5. *Zhixuan Anle Jing* [H]; and 6. *Daqin Jingjiao Suan Yuanben Jing* [I].

34. On Stein, Pelliot, Albert Von Le Coq, and other "archaeologists" working in northwest China at the turn of the twentieth century, see Hopkirk, *Foreign Devils on the Silk Road*. See also Charbonnier, *Christians in China*, 52–56.

35. Lin and Rong, "Doubts Concerning the Authenticity of Two Nestorian Documents," 5–14. See also Nicolini-Zani, "Past and Current Research on Tang *Jingjiao*

The Church of the East in the Tang Dynasty (635–907 CE)

and C, D, E—C, D and E being on one manuscript] have come under some scrutiny as being questionable, but there is agreement that the original sources upon which they were based are authentic.[36] Some scholars classify these documents [B, C, D, E] as part of the translated works Alopen gave to the Emperor Taizong at his request around 635–641.[37] The third and fourth manuscripts [F, G] were the only ones with clear provenance in Dunhuang, being found by Pelliot himself in 1908 (*Pelliot chinois 3847* or *P. 3847*). The rest were acquired by private collectors.[38] The non-Alopen documents apart from *Zunjing* [G], which dates from the tenth to early eleventh centuries,[39] are thought to have come from the pen (or at least the time) of the one responsible for the Xi'an Stele text, Jingjing, and thereby appears to be from the late eighth century.[40] Jingjing (as noted above) is seen as a good writer [A, F, H], and as a very capable translator, having apparently translated thirty Christian books into Chinese [G].

The *Xuting Mishisuo Jing* [B][41] or "Book of Jesus, the Messiah"[42] can be divided into two parts. The first part is a doctrinal delineation of the Messiah, and the second is a narrative about the life of Jesus through to His death including the accompanying earthquake. Unfortunately, the rest of the manuscript is lost just after the description of the earthquake. This text shows not only great familiarity with the OT and NT in general, but also specifically with the *Didache*,[43] the Gospels of Matthew and John, and the

---

Documents," 27, who also notes that that these two forgeries are the only ones with precise dates in their texts of the early eighth century (37). The Kojima B has been reconfirmed as not part of the text because the Luoyang Stele although having the first part of the text, excludes this addition (Takahashi, *Transcribed Proper Names*, 6).

36. Deeg, "Towards a New Translation," 118; and Nicolini-Zani, "Past and Current Research," 27–29. See also Lin, Wushu, "Additional Notes," 133–42.

37. Nicolini-Zani, "Past and Current Research," 34–38, and Tang, *Nestorian Christianity in China*, 108–9. While perhaps not always the best translations (e.g., many transliteration problems), the texts certainly "show a clearly discernible Christian core" (Bays, *New History of Christianity in China*, 10).

38. Pelliot had doubts about the origins and genuineness of the other documents apart from those he personally discovered ("Christianity in Central Asia in the Middle Ages," 307).

39. Charbonnier, *Christians in China*, 58–59, and Tang, *Nestorian Christianity in China*, 116.

40. Nicolini-Zani, "Past and Current Research," 34–38, and Tang, *Nestorian Christianity in China*, 110–12, 114, 116–17.

41. On this besides the works of Drake, Saeki, and Tang, see also Lee, "A Study of a Chinese Nestorian Sutra 'Jesus Messiah,'" 46–52.

42. All title translations will follow Tang, *Nestorian Christianity in China*, 103–18, 145–200, unless notified otherwise.

43. Seah, "Nestorian Christianity," 80–81; see also Saeki, *Nestorian Documents and*

Diatessaron by Tatian (along with apparent apocryphal gospel usage).[44] Yet the text is somewhat Buddhist in terminology with strong Confucian overtones.[45] Unfortunately in the transliteration of the name for Jesus, *Yishu*, the characters used meant "scurrying rat." Happily, this transliteration was abandoned in later writings.[46]

In the *Yi Shen Lun* or "On the One God" there are three parts. In the first part, *Yu Di Er* or "Parable: Part 2" [C], the text highlights the oneness of God using parables and metaphors. In the *Yitian Lun* or "On the One Heaven" [D], God is further described, but also a contrast is made between this world and the world to come with the corresponding potential of serving God or being misled by the devil, Satan. In the *Shizun Bushi Lun* or "Sermon of the Lord, Part III" [E], there is a series of sermons based on portions from the Sermon on the Mount dealing with giving alms, prayer and judging others, while there is also a description of the death of Jesus, the resurrection story, the Great Commission, and a discussion of God's judgment.

The *Daqin Jingjiao Sanwei Mengdu Zan* or "Gloria in Excelsis Deo" [F] is a translation of a Syriac hymn[47] praising the Trinity, with both theological affirmations and doxological elements. It is written in the classic Chinese poetic style, *zan* (which is *qiyan shi*).[48]

In the *Zun Jing* or "Honored Persons and Sacred Books" [G], after an articulation of the Trinity using the Syriac transliteration for the Holy Spirit (*ruha da qudsa*), there are lists of honored persons both biblical and non-biblical, and then there is a list of important books of faith. Interestingly,

---

Relics, 153n11, 155n14, 156nn17, and 18.

44. Yao, "A Diatessaronic Reading," 153–65. See also Charbonnier, *Christians in China*, 46–47; Lee, *Cross and Lotus*, 19; Raguin, "Jesus-Messiah of Xi'an," 43.

45. Including apparent Buddhist Sanskrit words such as *arhats* and *yanluowang* for "demons" and "king of hell," respectively, and other Buddhist terms like *Fo* and *Tianzun* for God; see Charbonnier, *Christians in China*, 44; Drake, "Nestorian Literature," 680–81; Saeki, *Nestorian Documents and Relics*, 148nn4 and 6; Tang, *Nestorian Christianity in China*, 145n4, 149n30, 146n12.

46. Charbonnier, *Christians in China*, 44–45; Raguin, "Jesus-Messiah of Xi'an," 41; Seah, "Nestorian Christianity," 81.

47. The most common position on this text is that it is a Syriac hymn; e.g., Drake, "The Nestorian 'Gloria in Excelsis Deo,'" 291–300; Drake, "Nestorian Literature," 614, 741; Foster, *Church of the T'ang Dynasty*, 110; Drake, *The Nestorian Tablet*, 23–26; and Moule, *Christians in China Before the Year 1550*, 52. However, Deeg does not believe that it is a translation ("Ways to Go and Not to Go," 140–41).

48. Tang, *Nestorian Christianity in China*, 115. Note that Nicolini-Zani believes it is "an adaption of the original Syriac Liturgical text to the metrical system of the *zan*, a poetic genre" ("Past and Current Research on Tang *Jingjiao* Documents," 39).

at least three of these works are believed to be Manichean.⁴⁹ The form of this work is a diptych.⁵⁰ In an addendum (in a different hand⁵¹) to this text, it is mentioned that there were 530 *Jingjiao* books available. It is here that Jingjing's role in translating thirty books beyond the work of Alopen is mentioned (including *Daqin Jingjiao Sanwei Mengdu Zan*,[F] *Zhixuan Anle Jing*,[H] and *Daqin Jingjiao Suan Yuanben Jing* [I] from this list of Dunhuang documents⁵²) but the remainder of the five hundred had not been translated.

In the *Zhixuan Anle Jing* or "Book on Mysterious Peace and Joy" [H], there is a narrated conversation between the Messiah and his disciple (Cenwen⁵³), teaching about the way to attain peace and joy. The discussion and format are very typical of Buddhism with both Buddhist and Daoist turns of phrase.⁵⁴ It is even said to be from the Buddhist Pure Land sect perspective,⁵⁵ and appears to be written in the classic Chinese *Bianwen* Style.⁵⁶

The *Daqin Jingjiao Suan Yuanben Jing* or "Book Declaring the Origin of Origins" [I] is a short fragment that briefly describes the future where origins will be described to all. A longer version is found in the Luoyang monument as follows.

THE LUOYANG MONUMENT [K]⁵⁷

More recently in 2006, in Luoyang, the eastern capital city of the Tang Dynasty, another monument from the Tang dynasty period was found that

49. As noted by Pelliot, see Tang, *Nestorian Christianity in China*, 185–86nn225, 227, 242; see also Charbonnier, *Christians in China*, 58.

50. A diptych is a work made up of two matching tablets joined with hinges. Drake, "The Nestorian 'Gloria in Excelsis Deo,'" 295; Gillman and Klimkeit, *Christians in Asia before 1500*, 279; Saeki, *Nestorian Documents and Relics*, 277n1; Young, "Theology and Influence of Nestorian Mission," 7.

51. Drake, "The Nestorian 'Gloria in Excelsis Deo,'" 292.

52. Ibid., 296; cf. Moffett, *History of Christianity in Asia*, 319n50.

53. Possibly Simon (Saeki, *Nestorian Documents and Relics*, 305n3).

54. Tang, *Nestorian Christianity in China*, 117–18. See also Seah, "Nestorian Christianity," 80.

55. Raguin, "Jesus-Messiah of Xi'an," 46; Raguin suggests that the Christian monks met with the Buddhist Pure Land grand master, Shandao, whose temple was nearby the COTE monastery ("Jesus-Messiah of Xi'an," 46). See also Eskildsen, "Christology and Soteriology in the Chinese Nestorian Texts," 185n20; Seah, "Nestorian Christianity," 75–92.

56. Tang, *Nestorian Christianity in China*, 127–28.

57. This whole section is dependent on the only source currently available in English: Tang, "A Preliminary Study," 109–32. I will use [K] to represent this source as not

was written from a Christian perspective. It is an octagonal pillar which resembled "a Buddhist *dhāraṇi* pillar."[58] It was cut away from its base, and the surviving piece is about 85 cm high by 14 cm wide. There are six artistic expressions apart from the Chinese text, four angels and two crosses, two flying angels facing opposite each other facing the cross.[59] According to the inscription, the pillar was erected in the twelfth month of 814/5 CE and moved to another place on the sixteenth day of the third month of 829 CE. As a funerary stele, it provides a good deal of information about the beliefs of the honoree. The content of this monument is the same as [I] above, but the monument expands what would have been originally part of the text while the Dunhuang version supplies missing words for the monument.[60] This stele highlights the origins of creation and the character of the Creator and discusses the Messiah, following the Spirit, and the importance of obedience. It is notable that the monument starts with the famous *Trisagion* (or thrice holy) of the Syriac Christianity, stating, "Holy Aluohe, Holy Mighty (one), Holy [immortal] . . ."[61] Further, there seems to be multiple allusions to Isaiah, Revelation and Psalms.[62]

SUMMATION OF BELIEF[63]

This section reviews the basic *Jingjiao* beliefs highlighted in the two steles and the Dunhuang documents. In the texts, God is described as being without origin and earlier than all beginnings [A, K]. He is transcendent and the true Lord [A]. God cannot be seen, but humanity can know Him [B, F]. He is called *A-luo-he* [A, F, G, K], which is a reference to the Syriac form of the name for God, *Alaha*.[64] God created all things using His breath to make the two principles and transformed things out of darkness and emptiness [A].

---

to be confused with Saeki's [J].

58. Ibid., 109.

59. Interestingly, one cross clearly represents the Church of the East style with a flowery pattern, while one angel holds a live coal and the other angel opposite the cross holds a lotus flower (ibid.).

60. Ibid., 111.

61. Ibid., 112, 126.

62. Ibid., 112–20, 127–30, especially notes 9, 14, 15, 18, 19, 24, 41, 59, 60, 62.

63. The below summary is based upon my own paraphrase using the works of Charbonnier, Drake, Foster, Moule, Tang, along with the Chinese text; see note 6.

64. Takahashi, *Transcribed Proper Names*, 8. In Tang, *Nestorian Christiantiy in China*, 145n2, God is called "Jevah" (Jehovah?); see also Moule, *Christians in China Before the Year 1550*, 59n69; Saeki, *Nestorian Documents and Relics*, 125, 147n2; Tang, *Nestorian Christianity in China*, 145n2.

God is clearly described as part of the Triune unity [A, F, G]: noted as the Father, the *Mi-she-ho* (a Chinese transliteration of "Messiah" from Syriac), and the Holy Spirit ("pure wind" [A, F] or *ruha da qudsa*, a Syriac transliteration [G]). God is the Creator [A, C, D, I, K]; He created the first man, and made him ruler over all the creatures [A]. The first man lived in harmony and without pain, and was clean in heart without desire [A]. However, man allowed Satan (the actual transliteration is *So-tan*) to deceive him, which led to disharmony [A, D]; the man sinned [B]. The Devil with demons tempts and deceives foolish men [D].[65] Humanity, however, should fear, serve, and worship God, but only fear and serve the Emperor and parents. To worship the Emperor is idolatry, which is to be rejected [B, E].[66]

There was a distinct person of the Triune unity, the Messiah, who came and put a veil on His true majesty and became like men [A], being incarnated by the Spirit [B]. In *Daquin* [A, B, I], angels told the good news; a virgin gave birth to the Messiah.[67] A star announced this event, and Persians seeing the star came with gifts [A].[68] This Messiah started preaching at the age of five, and when He was older (the text says at age twelve), He was baptized by John, so His ministry was from age twelve to thirty-two [B].

This Messiah accomplished the old law set by the twenty-four holy ones[69] and established His new doctrine with the "pure wind" (Holy Spirit) of the Triune God so men can practice virtue and be of true faith [A]. He gave "eight conditions" in order to purify and become pure, and opened to the "three constants," for life and to destroy death [A]. He hung up (on the cross?) to break the empire of darkness [A, E], and the devil's minions were overthrown [A]. When He died, the tombs opened, and the veil in the holy place was torn in two [E]. He then "rowed mercy's barge" (8) to ascend to

---

65. Interestingly, in the text it refers to "365 sects (or kinds of men) led various ways, worn out, restless, having lost their way" [A]. [I, K] also make reference to "365 peoples from races from foreign lands."

66. Highlighted by Chang Sik Lee, "A Study of a Chinese Nestorian Sutra 'Jesus Messiah,'" 49–51.

67. Note that [B] has him born in Jerusalem in *Fulin*, but [I] has him born in Nazareth in *Daqin*, and [A] only states he was born in *Daqin*.

68. At Turpan, there is a Sogdian text describing the visit of the Magi to the baby Jesus (Baum and Winkler, *Church of the East*, 74; England, *Hidden History of Christianity in Asia*, 130).

69. The twenty-four holy ones are considered the writers of the OT; this is why the twenty-seven holy books noted below are not inclusive of the OT books. See note 72; Foster, *Church of the T'ang Dynasty*, 109n2; Leslie, "The Old Testament and Biblical Figure in Chinese Sources," 38n4. Chiu notes that Ch'ien Hsin Hsu suggests that the twenty-four refer to the number of books in the Masoretic text ("An Historical Study of Nestorian Christianity," 119n40).

the "Luminous" palace where souls are saved [A]. So the way for man to receive salvation is demonstrated as God's purpose [A, B], and the basic theology of redemption appears to be reflective of Pauline and Johannine theology.[70]

There will be a judgment for all in which every evil deed and all evil will be seen [D, E]; those who follow the Messiah will receive eternal happiness and longevity [E], but those who do not follow will be punished by living with the demons in a place of suffering [E].[71]

After His resurrection from the dead [E], the Messiah appeared to many witnesses [E]. At the completion of His work He ascended to truth [A]. After He ascended, ten days later the promise was fulfilled, and the Spirit was sent with tongues of fire appearing on each disciple [E].

In the Xi'an Stele, it mentions that the Messiah left twenty-seven holy books [A]. It has been repeatedly noted that the Syriac NT Peshitta had twenty-two books (omitting 2 and 3 John, 2 Peter, Jude, and Revelation).[72] Perhaps, the suggested twenty-seven books could reflect the Harklean and/or Philoxenian Syriac versions that were available by the early seventh century.[73] In the texts above, there are clear allusions to Leviticus and Deuteronomy [B], the Psalms [K], Isaiah [K], Matthew [B, E], the Johannine tradition [B],[74] the Book of Acts [E], and apparently the book of Revelation [I, K].[75] In [G], the works of the Gospel writers, Paul, David, and Moses are specifically mentioned, while allusions may be seen to Acts and Isaiah.[76] Also, 530 holy

---

70. Raguin, "China's First Evangelization," 175–76; Raguin, "Jesus-Messiah of Xi'an," 50.

71. It has been noted that there is only one place mentioning "eternal punishment" (Raguin, "China's First Evangelization," 179; Wickeri, "The Stone is a Mirror," 57). This is misleading since the context on the judgment is actually rather lengthy, and there is more than one document dealing with the judgment.

72. Metzger, *Text of the New Testament*, 2nd ed., 69–70; and Saeki, *Nestorian Documents and Relics*, 83n8; Vine suggests that this should come into consideration about the authenticity of the stele (*Nestorian Churches*, 133n1). It has been suggested that this reference could refer to the twenty-seven-book Syriac Old Testament (Gillman and Klimkeit, *Christians in Asia before 150*, 273); this seems unlikely since the twenty-four sages previously referred to seem to be the OT writers. See note 69.

73. Bruce, *Books and Parchments*, rev. ed., 200; McCullough, *Short History of Syriac Christianity*, 88; Metzger, *Text of the New Testament*, 70–71.

74. Raguin suggests that due to the usage of Syriac-based "Messiah" (not the Greek *Christos*), which was only found in John in the NT, and that John is listed as the foremost Gospel writer in the list in [G]. Raguin believes that this demonstrates the importance of John in the Syriac-Chinese expression of Christianity ("Jesus-Messiah of Xi'an," 41).

75. Tang's works on [I, K] highlight the role of the book of Revelation; see Tang, *Nestorian Christianity in China*.

76. Moffett, *History of Christianity in Asia*, 301.

books are mentioned, of which Jingjing only translated thirty, the rest were still in their original languages [G]. Beyond these, allusions were made to other Christian literature, such as the *Didache*, and the *Diatessaron*.

In reference to the activities of the church, the Messiah established the cleansing of the water and Spirit in order to wash away vanity for purity (i.e., baptism) [A]. The COTE representatives would strike the wood, make the sounds of charity, face toward the east for their prayers, let their beards grow as a sign of openness, and shave the crowns of their heads to demonstrate that there is no internal passion [A]. They do not own slaves showing that they do not distinguish between commoners and nobility, nor do they amass wealth [A].[77] Fasting is a part of their retreats and meditation [A]. They sing hymns seven times a day for the living and the dead, and every seven days they have a service for purifying and renewing the heart [A].[78]

In addition to the theological points summarized above, on a more historical note, it was stated that Jerusalem fell due to the lack of obedience [E]. It was also noted that from the time of the document, it has been 641 years since the Messiah's birth,[79] and all of *Fulin* (i.e., Byzantium) believes in the Messiah, but some in Persia do not [E]. In the texts, the fundamental theological issues apart from indigenous Chinese or Syriac influences (discussed below), are: 1) in [B], Jesus is portrayed as preaching by age five, being baptized by age twelve, and ministering until age thirty-two;[80] and 2) in [G], there is no clear distinction between the biblical/canonical books and other Christian books listed (i.e. the books of the Bible are compiled together in the list intermingled with other general Christian writings).

SOME THEOLOGICAL OBSERVATIONS AND ASSESSMENTS

First, one thing that stands out from the texts, immaterial if one sees a Buddhist-Daoist Christology or a contextual attempt of such,[81] the texts are

---

77. Apparently known for medicine, and social concern works (Lee, *Cross and Lotus*, 16).

78. Charbonnier noted that all of these noted practices were found among the Syriac Church monasteries (*Christians in China*, 38).

79. Foster notes that Dionysius Exiguus adjusted the calendar in the sixth century, so 641 was actually 638 (*Church of the T'ang Dynasty*, 46–47); see also Standaert, *Handbook of Christianity in China*, 5.

80. Raguin makes some suggestions as to why the ages of five and twelve are used ("China's First Evangelization," 162–63).

81. Malek, "Faces and Images," 34–36; Nicolini-Zani calls it an "indigenized theology" ("Past and Current Research," 43). Wickeri ("The Stone is a Mirror," 51–52)

all Christocentric. The Messiah is a central figure throughout the texts. The Messiah and the following of Him are directly tied to salvation, which can be seen in the primacy of Christ in both [A] and [B] and as the teacher in [H]. Perhaps, to paraphrase Philip Wickeri, these COTE representatives were witnesses to Christ, and not trying to "Christianize" China.[82]

Second, tied to the first is the variety of forms used in the proclamation of the Christian message within Tang Dynasty China. For instance, while a theological explanation of the Messiah is given in both [A] and [B], the narrative approach is also used to tell the story of Jesus. Another form used, highly valued by the Chinese, mirrors the style of Ephrem, which is the usage of poems/hymns to portray (and learn) theological truth [A, F].[83] The use of various poetic styles as well as hymnic formulations assisted the Chinese believers to engage, learn, and remember what was recited or sung. A third form of parables and analogies was frequently used for clarification and to aid the memory (e.g., seeing the landing of an arrow but not the archer as an analogy of God and Creation [C]). A fourth form, which is a common form in Buddhism, is the usage of a teacher-student dialogue [H]. For the *Jingjiao*, the significance of the techniques used flowed from the desire to make the proclamation accessible and intentionally acceptable to the Chinese audience. This could also be why the Cross is only hinted at in [A]. As Ian Gillman and Hans-Joachim Klimkeit note, "The crucifixion, and the post-Anselmic interpretations placed upon it by European Christians, remains a stumbling block for some Asians to this day. It may be that the early Nestorians had already divined this."[84]

Third, the texts show an emphasis on the practicality of belief. There is a clear presentation of the practical side of the community of faith [A] (in this case in the monastic orders). Following Christ is presented in a concrete fashion with noted prayer times and habits, personal appearance such as the growing of the beard and the shaving of the pate, no accumulation of wealth, and not owning slaves, etc., to make the Christian life demonstrably tangible. For these COTE representatives, their ethics flowed from their beliefs. As such, there was a discernible "concreteness" to their beliefs.

In conclusion, it appears that the COTE was intentional in its proclamation of the message of Christ, yet its representatives had to mediate a path

---

notes the concerns that Moffett (*History of Christianity in Asia*, 306–12) has about this Buddhist-Daoist Christology; Seah believes that this contextual movement may have impacted the effectiveness of their witness ("Nestorian Christianity," 76).

82. Wickeri, "The Stone is a Mirror," 53–54.

83. Powathil, "Early Syriac Theology," 44–45.

84. Gillman and Klimkeit, *Christians in Asia before 150*, 348n45. See also Giles, "Notes on the Nestorian Monument at Sianfu," 95.

between faithfulness to Syriac Christianity[85] and the cultural milieu[86] of the Tang dynasty and what that entails—its openness, diversity, and strong indigenous religious/philosophical perspectives. These Christians attempted to explain their beliefs in a way that the Chinese could comprehend and accept. As far as we can tell, they were the first to fully engage the Chinese to this end. Whereas some of their efforts may not be fully appreciated in the modern world, the challenges and accomplishments in this initial enterprise should be recognized, and the appropriate lessons learned by current and future generations.

Some of the missiological lessons that can come out of this study are as follows: First, the COTE used multiple ways to engage the culture. In terms of professions, we are aware of linguists, physicians, military leaders, governmental advisers, traders, as well as the noted monks traveling along the Silk Road. This breadth of professions allowed for a broader influence into the society. Second, they were open to contextualizing the message in order to proclaim the story of Jesus in the Chinese context. This included using understandable religious words (adopted from Buddhism, Daoism and Confucianism) such as the name for God, and presenting the message in an understandable form such as a Teacher-Student dialogue [H]. Third, related to the second, there seems to be sensitivity on the process of disclosure of the Christian message. The public Xi'an Stele [A] only hints at the crucifixion, but the more individual type text the "Book of Jesus, the Messiah" [B] clearly discusses the whole crucifixion. It appears that there was an intentionality to be guarded in the public declarations, but comparatively open in the more private ones that a document would tend to be. Fourth, while not in a verbatim style, there is a clear biblical foundation behind the texts and a strong undergirding of the biblical principles throughout the texts (as well as Syriac Christian perspectives). Just as identifiable is the strong awareness of the Chinese literature and religious classics. These COTE writers were fully versed in the Biblical/Syriac Christian tradition and the Chinese literature, and these did not appear to cause a dichotomy in their thinking. In the final analysis, the COTE was inventive, entrepreneurial, and creative in proclaiming the Christian message in China. Regardless of how the modern church thinks its representatives did, we can appreciate their pioneering spirit and learn from their endeavors.[87]

85. Ferreira, "Tang Christianity," 129–57.

86. For example, see on Jingjing for this aspect, Foster, *Church of the T'ang Dynasty*, 112–14.

87. I would like to thank Laura da Silva and the Assemblies of God Theological Seminary Library staff for tracking down many of the resources (including many hard to find) for this essay, and to thank Eric Newberg and Lois Olena for their helpful

BIBLIOGRAPHY

Barat, Kahar. "Aluoben, A Nestorian Missionary in 7th Century China." *Journal of Asian History* 36 (2002) 184–98.

Barrett, T. "Buddhism, Daoism and Eighth Century Chinese Term for Christianity: A Response to Recent Work by Antonio Forte and Others." In *Jingjiao: The Church of the East in China and Central Asia*, edited by Roman Malek, 45–53. Sankt Augustin: Institut Monumenta Serica, 2006.

Baum, Wilhelm, and Dietmar Winkler. *The Church of the East: A Concise History.* Translated by Miranda Henry. London: RoutledgeCurzon, 2003.

Baumer, Christoph. "Survey of Nestorianism and of Ancient Nestorian Architectural Relics in the Iranian Realm." In *Jingjiao: The Church of the East in China and Central Asia*, edited by Roman Malek, 445–74. Sankt Augustin: Institut Monumenta Serica, 2006.

Bays, Daniel. *A New History of Christianity in China.* Chickester, UK: Wiley-Blackwell, 2012.

Bethune-Baker, J. F. *Nestorius and His Teaching: A Fresh Examination of the Evidence.* Cambridge: Cambridge University Press, 1908.

Black, Matthew. "The Syriac Inscriptions on the Nestorian Monument." *Glasgow University Oriental Society Transactions* 8 (1936–37) 18–25.

Braaten, Carl. "Modern Interpretations of Nestorius." *Church History* 32 (1963) 251–67.

Brock, Sebastian. "The 'Nestorian' Church: A Lamentable Misnomer." *Bulletin of the John Rylands Library* 78 (1996) 23–35.

Bruce, F. F. *The Books and the Parchments.* Old Tappan, NJ: Revell, 1963.

Bugge, Sten. "The History of the Nestorian Church in China." *Moslem World* 24 (1934) 370–90.

Charbonnier, Jean-Pierre. *Christians in China: A.D. 600 to 2000.* Translated by M. N. L. Couve de Murville. San Francisco: Ignatius, 2007.

Chiu, Peter Chung-hang. "An Historical Study of Nestorian Christianity in the T'ang Dynasty between A.D. 635–845." PhD diss., Southwestern Baptist Theological Seminary, 1987.

Couling, C. E. *The Luminous Religion.* London: Carey, 1925.

Deeg, Max. "Towards a New Translation of the Chinese Nestorian Documents from the Tang Dynasty." In *Jingjiao: The Church of the East in China and Central Asia*, edited by Roman Malek, 115–31. Sankt Augustin: Institut Monumenta Serica, 2006.

———. "Ways to Go and Not to Go in the Contextualisation of the Jingjiao Documents of the Tang Period." In *Hidden Treasures and Intercultural Encounters: Studies on East Syriac Christianity in China and Central Asia*, edited by Dietmar W. Winkler and Li Tang, 135–52. Vienna: LIT, 2009.

Drake, F. S. "The Nestorian 'Gloria in Excelsis Deo.'" *Chinese Recorder* 66 (1935) 291–300.

———. "Nestorian Literature of the T'ang Dynasty." *Chinese Recorder* 66 (October 1935) 608–17; 66 (November 1935) 677–87; 66 (December 1935) 738–42.

———. "Nestorian Monasteries of the T'ang Dynasty and the Site of the Discovery of the Nestorian Stone." *Monumenta Serica* 2 (1936–37) 293–340.

---

editorial comments. Ultimately I would like to express my deepest appreciation and admiration to Stanley and Ruth Burgess, both who have been friends, colleagues, and mentors to my wife and me for many years.

England, John C. *The Hidden History of Christianity in Asia: The Churches of the East before 1500*. Delhi: Indian SPCK, 1998.

Eskildsen, Stephen. "Christology and Soteriology in the Chinese Nestorian Texts." In *The Chinese Face of Jesus Christ*, edited by Roman Malek, 1:181-218. Sankt Augustin: Institut Monumenta Serica/China-Zentrum, 2002.

Ferreira, Johan. "Tang Christianity: Its Syriac Origins and Character." *Jian Dao* 21 (2004) 129-57.

Foltz, Richard. *Religions of the Silk Road*. New York: St. Martin's, 1999.

Forte, Antonio. "The Edict of 638 Allowing the Diffusion of Christianity in China." In *L'inscription nestorienne de Si-ngan-fou* by Paul Pelliot, edited and supplements by Antonino Forte, 349-73. Jointly published: Kyoto: Scuola di Studi sull' Asia Orientale and Paris: Collège de France/Institut des Hautes Etudes Chinoises, 1996.

Foster, John. *The Church of the T'ang Dynasty*. London: SPCK, 1939.

———. *The Nestorian Tablet and Hymn*. London: SPCK, n.d.

Giles, Lionel. "Notes on the Nestorian Monument at Sianfu." *Bulletin of the School of Oriental and African Studies* 11 (1917) 93-96; 12 (1918) 16-29; 13 (1919) 39-49; 14 (1920) 15-26.

Gillman, Ian, and Hans-Joachim Klimkeit. *Christians in Asia before 1500*. Ann Arbor: University of Michigan Press, 1999.

Harvey, Susan Ashbrook. "Nestorianism." In *Encyclopedia of Early Christianity*, edited by Everett Ferguson, 644-47. New York: Garland, 1990.

Hickley, Dennis. *The First Christians in China*. London: China Study Project with Missio Aachen, Germany, 1980.

Hirth, F. *China and the Roman Orient*. 1885. Reprint, Chicago: Ares, 1975.

Hopkirk, Peter. *Foreign Devils on the Silk Road*. Amherst: University of Massachusetts Press, 1980.

Hunter, Erica C. D. "The Persian Contribution to Christianity in China: Reflections in the Xi'an Fu Syriac Inscriptions." In *Hidden Treasures and Intercultural Encounters: Studies on East Syriac Christianity in China and Central Asia*, edited by Dietmar W. Winkler and Li Tang, 71-85. Vienna: LIT, 2009.

Inglis, J. W. "The Nestorian Share in Buddhist Translation." *Journal of the North China Branch of the Royal Asiatic Society* 48 (1917) 12-15.

Irvin, Dale, and Scott Sunquist. *Earliest Christianity to 1453*. Vol. 1 of *History of the World Christian Movement*. Maryknoll, NY: Orbis, 2001.

Jenkins, Philip. *The Lost History of Christianity*. New York: HarperOne, 2008.

Keevak, Michael. *The Story of a Stele: China's Nestorian Monument and Its Reception in the West, 1625-1916*. Hong Kong: Hong Kong University Press, 2008.

Latourette, Kenneth Scott. *A History of Christian Missions in China*. New York: Russell & Russell, 1929.

———. *A History of Christianity*. Vol. 1. Rev. ed. Peabody, MA: Prince, 1975.

———. *A History of the Expansion of Christianity*. Vol 2. Grand Rapids: Zondervan, 1966.

Lee, Chang Sik. "A Study of a Chinese Nestorian Sutra 'Jesus Messiah.'" *Northeast Asia Journal of Theology* 13 (1974) 46-52.

Lee, Shiu Keung. *The Cross and the Lotus*. Hong Kong: Christian Study Centre on Chinese Religion and Culture, 1971.

Legge, James. *The Nestorian Monument of Hsî-an Fû in Shen-Hsî, China*. London: Trübner, 1888.

Leslie, Donald Daniel. "The Old Testament and Biblical Figure in Chinese Sources." *Sino-Judaica* 1 (1991) 37–46.
Leslie, Donald Daniel, and K. H. J. Gardiner. *The Roman Empire in Chinese Sources*. Studi Orientali 15. Rome: Bardi, 1996.
Lin, Wushu. "Additional Notes on the Authenticity of Tomioka's and Takakusu's Manuscripts." In *Jingjiao: The Church of the East in China and Central Asia*, edited by Roman Malek, 133–42. Sankt Augustin: Institut Monumenta Serica, 2006.
———. "A General Discussion of the Tang Policy toward Three Persian Religions: Manicheanism, Nestorianism, and Zoroastrianism." *China Archaeology and Art Digest* 4 (2000) 103–16.
Lin, Wushu, and Xinjiang Rong. "Doubts concerning the Authenticity of Two Nestorian Documents Unearthed at Dunhuang from the Li Collection." *China Archaeology and Art Digest* 1 (1996) 5–14.
Loofs, Friedrich. *Nestorius and His Place in the History of Christian Doctrine*. Cambridge: Cambridge University Press, 1914.
Malek, Roman. "Faces and Images of Jesus Christ in Chinese Context. Introduction." In *The Chinese Face of Jesus Christ*, edited by Roman Malek, 1:19–54. Sankt Augustin: Institut Monumenta Serica/China-Zentrum, 2002.
Malek, Roman, ed. *Jingjiao: The Church of the East in China and Central Asia*. Collectanea Serica. Sankt Augustin: Institut Monumenta Serica, 2006.
Mattan, Mar Abraham. "Missionary Enterprises of the Church of St. Thomas Christians." In *Forgotten East: Mission, Liturgy and Spirituality in the Eastern Churches*, 61–93. Satra, India: Ephrem's, 2001.
McCullough, W. Stewart. *A Short History of Syriac Christianity to the Rise of Islam*. Scholars Press General Series 4. Chico, CA: Scholars, 1982.
Metzger, Bruce M., and Bart D. Ehrman. *The Text of the New Testament: Its Transmission, Corruption, and Restoration*. 4th ed. New York: Oxford University Press, 2005.
Mingana, A. "The Early Spread of Christianity in Central Asia and the Far East: A New Document." *Bulletin of the John Rylands Library* 9 (1925) 297–367.
Moffett, Samuel. *History of Christianity in Asia*. Vol. 1, *Beginnings to 1500*. Rev. ed. San Francisco: HarperCollins, 1998.
Moule, A. C. *Christians in China Before the Year 1550*. London: SPCK, 1930.
———. *Nestorians in China: Some Corrections and Additions*. Sinological Series 1. London: China Society, 1940.
Nicolini-Zani, Matteo. "Past and Current Research on Tang *Jingjiao* Documents: A Survey." In *Jingjiao: The Church of the East in China and Central Asia*, edited by Roman Malek, 23–44. Sankt Augustin: Institut Monumenta Serica, 2006.
Palmer, Martin. *The Jesus Sutras: Rediscovering the Lost Scrolls of Taoist Christianity*. New York: Ballentine, 2001.
Pelliot, Paul. "Christianity in Central Asia in the Middle Ages." *Journal of the Royal Central Asian Society* 17 (1930) 301–21.
———. *Recherches sur les Chrétiens D'Asie Centrale et D'Extrême-Orient: II, 1: La Stèle de Si-Ngan-Fou*. Œuvres Posthumes de Paul Pelliot. Paris: La Fondation Singer-Polignac, 1984.
Philip, T. V. *East of the Euphrates: Early Christianity in Asia*. Delhi: Indian SPCK, 1998.
Powathil, Joseph. "Early Syriac Theology: Some Basic Features." In *Early Syriac Theology: An Introduction*, edited by Pauly Maniyattu, 30–53. Satna, India: Ephrem's, 2007.

Raguin, Yves. "China's First Evangelization by the 7th and 8th Century Eastern Syrian Monks: Some Problems Posted by the First Chinese Expressions of the Christian Traditions." In *The Chinese Face of Jesus Christ*, edited by Roman Malek, 159–79. Sankt Augustin: Institut Monumenta Serica/China-Zentrum, 2002.

———. "Jesus-Messiah of Xi'an." *Tripod* 74 (2002) 39–54.

Saeki, P. Y. *The Nestorian Documents and Relics in China*. Tokyo: Maruzen, 1951.

Seah, Ingram. "Nestorian Christianity and Pure Land Buddhism in T'ang China." *Taiwan Journal of Theology* 6 (1984) 75–92.

Sekeznyov, Nikolai N. "Nestorius of Constantinople: Condemnation, Suppression, Veneration, with Special Reference to the Role of His Name in East-Syriac Christianity." *Journal of Eastern Christian Studies* 62 (2010) 165–90.

Shiratori, Kurakichi. "A New Attempt at the Solution of the Fu-Lin Problem." *Memoirs of the Research Department of the Toyo Bunko* 15 (1956) 165–329.

Standaert, Nicolas. *Handbook of Christianity in China*. Vol. 1, *635–1800*. Handbook of Oriental Studies. Leiden: Brill, 2001.

Takahashi, Hidemi. *Transcribed Proper Names in Chinese Syriac Christian Documents*. Analecta Gorgiana 127. Piscataway, NJ: Gorgias, 2009.

Takakusu, Junjiro. "The Name 'Messiah' Found in a Buddhist Book: The Nestorian Missionary Adam, Presbyter, Papas of China, Translating a Buddhist Sutra." *T'oung-Pao* 7 (1896) 589–91.

Tang, Li. *A Study of the History of Nestorian Christianity in China and Its Literature in Chinese*. Frankfurt: Lang, 2002.

———. "A Preliminary Study on the Jingjiao Inscription of Luoyang: Text Analysis, Commentary and English Translation." In *Hidden Treasures and Intercultural Encounters: Studies on East Syriac Christianity in China and Central Asia*, edited by Dietmar W. Winkler and Li Tang, 109–32. Vienna: LIT, 2009.

Thompson, Glen L. "Was Alopen a 'Missionary'?" In *Hidden Treasures and Intercultural Encounters: Studies on East Syriac Christianity in China and Central Asia*, edited by Dietmar W. Winkler and Li Tang, 267–78. Vienna: LIT, 2009.

Thoppil, John. "Christology in the East Syriac Tradition." In *East Syriac Theology: An Introduction*, edited by Pauly Maniyattu, 154–78. Satna, India: Ephrem's, 2007.

Tubach, Jürgen. "Deuternomistic Theology in the Text of the Stele of Xi'an." In *Jingjiao: The Church of the East in China and Central Asia*, edited by Roman Malek, 175–80. Sankt Augustin: Institut Monumenta Serica, 2006.

Vine, Aubrey. *The Nestorian Churches*. London: Independent, 1937.

Vööbus, Arthur. *History of Asceticism in the Syrian Orient*. 3 vols. CSCO 184. Louvain: CSCO, 1958.

Wickeri, Philip. "The Stone Is a Mirror: Interpreting the Xi'an Christian Monument and Its Implications for Theology and the Study of Christianity in Asia." *Quest* 3 (2004) 37–64.

Winkler, Dietmar W., and Li Tang, eds. *Hidden Treasures and Intercultural Encounters: Studies on East Syriac Christianity in China and Central Asia*. Vienna: LIT, 2009.

Yao, Zhihua. "A Diatessaronic Reading in the Chinese Nestorian Texts." In *Hidden Treasures and Intercultural Encounters: Studies on East Syriac Christianity in China and Central Asia*, edited by Dietmar W. Winkler and Li Tang, 153–65. Vienna: LIT, 2009.

Young, John M. L. *By Foot to China*. Tokyo: Radiopress, 1984.

———. "The Theology and Influence of the Nestorian Mission to China, 635–1036." *Reformed Bulletin of Mission* 5 (1969) 1–18; 5 (1970) 1–20.

Yule, Henri, and Henri Cordier, eds. *Cathay and the Way Thither*. 4 vols. 1916. Reprint, New Delhi: Munshiram Manoharlal, 1998.

5

A Story about a Dishonest Manager
—Charles W. Hedrick

There is no general agreement among scholars as to how the parables attributed to Jesus in early Christian literature should be explained. Scholars do not even agree on how the parable is supposed to work.[1] In the scholarly literature parables are regarded as allegories, stories having a one point moral, metaphors, existential narratives, narratives constructed to encourage social reform, and simple fictions.[2] The approach taken in this study is that what scholars designate as "parables" in the Synoptic Gospels are essentially narrative—they have a beginning, middle, and end, which is the minimum essential structure for a literary unit to be considered narrative.[3] Parables, that is to say stories, work like all narrative does. They are designed to engage the reader, to draw him or her into the narrative's plot and action, where discoveries may be made about oneself and one's world.[4]

THE LIMITS OF THE STORY

The "Dishonest Steward," as the story is usually known, is generally regarded as the most unsettling narrative in the surviving brief narrative sketches

---

1. For a recent exchange among scholars on this story see Ford, "Jesus' Parable of the Dishonest Steward and America's War in Afghanistan," 3–8, with responses by Hedrick, "Sticking with the Story," 9–10; and Scott, "Is Don Corleone God?," 11–12.

2. See Hedrick, *Many Things in Parables*, 57–88.

3. Hedrick, *Parables as Poetic Fictions*, 46–50.

4. Ibid., 32–35.

(parables) attributed to Jesus of Nazareth—but it is no more so than the brief sketch of "A Man Who Wanted to Kill," which survives in the Gospel of Thomas (Saying 98).[5] Both of the protagonists in these two sketches are engaged in activity that falls outside the conventions of lawful society. To judge from the numerous interpretations (Luke 16:8–13) appended to the only surviving version of the narrative (16:1–7), the brief story posed a serious threat to the character of the Christ. Why would the Lord, Jesus Christ, select as the protagonist of the narrative "a manager" who was characterized by "unrighteousness" (16:8)? This is the main question the interpretations (16:8–13) are trying to answer in a way that will allow a positive reading of the narrative. And that same motivation, it seems, still plagues modern interpreters of this story.[6]

The primary culprit in creating this sense of discomfort interpreters have with the brief narrative sketch in Luke 16:1–8 is verse 8a, where the lord (κύριος) praised his "manager of (i.e., characterized by) unrighteousness because he acted wisely."[7] The Greek for "lord" (κύριος) in Luke 16:8a can designate either the owner (i.e., lord) of the business (16:3) or the Lord, Jesus. Scholars are divided on which figure should be understood by this word.[8]

Three observations lead me to the conclusion that the figure described in 16:8a is the Jesus character in a story told by Luke, rather than the owner of the business in a story told by Jesus.

(1) The figure described in 16:8a is not part of the dramatic action in 16:1–7. If he were, he would be speaking to his manager in first person as all the other characters in the narration do (in 16:2, 3, 5, 6, 7; cf. also 13:27; 14:24; 19:26–27). Hence a gap exists between the concluding scene of the action in 16:7 and the pronouncement about the manager in 16:8. The figure in 16:8a is described as standing outside the story looking back on the dramatic action that stopped in 16:7.[9] From this

---

5. See Hedrick, "Flawed Heroes," 4:3023–56.

6. See, for example, Scott, *Hear Then the Parable*, 255–56.

7. Reading the genitive as a genitive of quality: Funk, *A Greek Grammar of the New Testament*, para. #165.

8. Here is a random sampling of how some scholars have voted on this issue: first, that the "lord" in 16:8a is the owner of the business: Bailey, *Poet & Peasant*, 102; Scott, *Hear Then the Parable*, 258; Findlay, *Jesus and His Parables*, 82; Hultgren, *The Parables of Jesus*, 151; Blomberg, *Interpreting the Parables of Jesus*, 244; Bruce, *The Parabolic Teaching of Christ*, 366; Fitzmyer, *Gospel According to Luke*, 1097; Oesterly, *Gospel Parables*, 197; Breech, *Silence of Jesus*, 109–10. Second, that the "Lord" is Jesus: Jülicher, *Die Gleichnisreden Jesu*, 2:504; Jeremias, *Parables of Jesus*, 45–46; Smith, *Parables of the Synoptic Gospels*, 110; Klostermann and Gressman, *Das Lukasevangelium*, 525–26.

9. As Crossan put it: if the lord in 16:8a "is really Jesus himself, we are already out

different perspective he evaluates and criticizes the character of the manager from the point of view of observer, not participant. He speaks *about* the manager and his actions in third person, and not *to* the manager in first person.

(2) This judgment is in keeping with Luke's practice. The concluding summary morals (*epimythia*) in first person that Luke appends to the stories of Jesus are the voice of Luke's Jesus (Luke 11:8; 12:59; 16:9, 18:8, 14).[10] This evaluation of 16:8a fits Luke's moralistic bent, since other summary judgments appended to the stories of Jesus after the story concludes represent a saying of Luke's Jesus (8:8b-9; 12:21; 14:11, 33; 17:10; 20:15b-17).

A situation very similar to Luke 16:8a is Luke 18:6 where Luke describes Jesus as "the Lord," but has him speak the criticism of the judge in the story (who also was characterized by "unrighteousness") as direct address to an audience (18:1, "he told *them* a parable") who was listening to a story told by Jesus in a story written by Luke, rather than describe in third person what the judge had done (as was done in 16:8a), which would have created further distance between the story and the criticism. The distance between 18:1-5 and 18:6 ties 18:6 more closely with what follows (18:7-8) than with the preceding story.

(3) There are a few exceptions, but, in general, in none of the stories of Jesus are moral or ethical judgments made on either the characters in the dramatic presentation or on the actions of the characters inside the story.[11] The narrative voice of the parables is not a self-actualized narrator.[12]

In summary: there are only two possibilities to account for the identity of the speaker in Luke 16:8a. One: the speaker is the owner of the business who compliments his dishonest manager, an identification that is excluded by the argument above. Two: the speaker is Luke, the Gospel writer. On balance the "Lord" in 16:8a is the character Jesus in Luke's narrative about Jesus of Nazareth, as is also the case in 18:6. The negative assessment of the manager's actions should be attributed to the Gospel writer, Luke, who puts the words on the lips of his Jesus character.

---

of the parable and into commentary by the tradition." Crossan, "The Servant Parables of Jesus," 31.

10. See Hedrick, *Parables as Poetic Fictions*, 210-11.
11. Hedrick, *Parables as Poetic Fictions*, 58-59.
12. Ibid., 210-11.

AN ANALYSIS OF THE STORY

Thus readers are left with a brief narrative sketch that ends in 16:7 with no resolution, a situation that pertains to all of the stories of Jesus. The stories of Jesus conclude but readers are always left with a complication needing resolution.[13]

Luke 16:1b

Readers are told nothing about this man (the owner) except that he is wealthy. Readers learn in 16:5–7 that the owner's business deals in larger amounts of commodities. The term "manager" (οἰκονόμος, or *vilicus* in the Latin tradition),[14] which is also translated "steward," can refer to a slave who manages a household (see Matt 24:45, where he is not called an οἰκονόμος and Luke 12:42, where he is called οἰκονόμος) or to a free person who has charge of sizeable financial accounts (Rom 16:23).[15] In this case readers learn that he is not a slave (in 16:5–7), but has fiduciary responsibility for the owner's business accounts. An anonymous "someone" informs the owner that the manager was frittering away the substance of the business. Nothing is said about how the "someone" learned this information, or if it is perhaps gossip and hence not even true. Nothing is really said about the nature of the business, but interpreters tend to think of the οἰκονόμος as the manager of a large estate involved with farming, and the owner as, perhaps, an absentee landlord. Nevertheless, depending on the size of the estate, the responsibilities of the manager were far more extensive than simply agricultural; they involved considerable activities that may be described as executive level responsibilities.[16] Managers were also employed in various other functions in the Graeco-Roman world that were not associated with an agricultural estate.[17]

Luke 16:2

The owner summons his manager and confronts him with the anonymous accusation made against him. How the owner puts the situation to

---

13. See, for example, the story of the Unjust Judge, ibid., 187–207; and Hedrick, "An Unfinished Story about a Fig Tree," 169–92.
14. In the Roman context this figure is called *vilicus*.
15. Otto Michel, "οἰκονόμος," 5:150.
16. Aubert, *Business Managers*, 170–75.
17. Ibid., 367.

the manager suggests that he has not bothered to verify the charges made against the manager ("What is this that I hear about you?"). The question is only rhetorical, however, and is not an offer for the manager to defend himself. The owner's next statement reveals that he has apparently been fully persuaded by the anonymous accusation. He demands that the manager give an accounting of his activities as manager:[18] "For you are no longer able to manage (my business)." It seems rather clear that the manager has been peremptorily removed from his position—at least that is how the manager reads his situation (16:3). He has been given no chance to face his accuser or to defend himself, and is summarily dismissed from the owner's employ. The owner's immediate access to the manager argues against the owner being an absentee landlord, unless one assumes something not given in the story, although nevertheless quite plausible: i.e., that the owner is on a periodic trip to visit his estate.[19] But he could just as easily have lived in a nearby town, which is what Columella advised estate owners to do, since it made oversight of the estate much easier, and led to a much higher yield on the owner's investment.[20]

Luke 16:3-4

These verses are the manager's reflections said to himself—the musing of the manager upon receiving the word that his employment in the business has been terminated. The way he describes his situation after his meeting with the owner confirms that he must yet "give an account of his management of the business to the employer" (16:2), for he said to himself: "my employer is in the process of dismissing me from the management of the business" (16:3, ἀφαιρεῖται, present tense). The manager must give an account of the current state of the financial situation of the business in order to turn it over to his replacement. He reflects on what his options are after termination, which he initially sees as only two in any case, neither of which seem to him promising in the least: physical labor or begging, both of which he rejects as something he is unprepared to do. He is not strong enough to do physical labor, and as a freeman, formally having held a responsible position, he was ashamed to beg. Both of these options reveal his estimate of the desperate

---

18. "Give an account of your management" in this case must mean something like "Let's see the records of your activities as manager." And the statement seems to be the owner's attempt to assess the damage done to his business.

19. Aubert, *Business Managers*, 119–25.

20. *Res Rustica* 1.1.19–20: *Lucius Junias Moderatus Columella On Agriculture*, 1.38–39; Aubert, *Business Managers*, 126.

nature of his situation. He instead decides on a risky third course of action, which he hopes will obligate people[21] to "take him in" when he is no longer employed (16:5). That he has not shaved obligations off debts before this instance seems clear. If it were a usual thing to reduce debts, he would not have found it necessary to ponder what he should do. Had he been a slave, he would not have been free to enter into the households of others at their invitation. So if his words are taken seriously, he is not a slave, but a freeman in the service of a wealthy business owner, and had not before this moment defrauded his employer.

Luke 16:5

There is a gap between 16:4 and 16:5. Time must be allowed for the now "former" manager to muse about his situation and ponder his options, and then to proceed with his plan of contacting every single one (ἕνα ἕκαστον)[22] of the owner's debtors and arranging times for them to come to his office (προσκαλεσάμενος, summoning, inviting). So we should not conceive of the exchange between the debtors and the manager as following immediately upon the exchange between the owner and the manager, but as occurring sometime later. There is also a compression of events in 16:5-7. This kind of shady deal is best done in private, but with the compression of events the narrative might be read as putting all three persons (the manager and the two debtors) in a room at the same time on the same day immediately following the manager's interview with the owner. Such a situation is excluded by the fact that he summoned "every single one," rather than as a group. In the narrative they are treated sequentially and hence separately rather than as a group. The question that the manager puts to both debtors: "how much do you owe my employer?" and the fact that there are promissory notes to specify the amount owed in the debtors' own handwriting seems to rule out the idea that the manager has padded the bills for his own profit. The

---

21. Literally: "that they may receive me." Derrett sees in the indefinite ("they") a fourth group acting in the story: the rich man, the manager, and the general public (he overlooks the anonymous accuser). He argues that the debtors of 16:5-7 have not yet been introduced into the story, so the manager is trying to curry favor with the community for doing what God's law required of him—that is releasing the debtors from the amount of usury included in their bills. See Derrett, "Fresh Light of St Luke XVI. I," 216-17. But there is no reason why the indefinite "they" in the manager's soliloquy in 16:4 should not refer to the debtors of 16:5-7, since it was their bills he was reducing. With regard to the amount being something introduced by the manager over and above what was due to the owner: the text very carefully points out that the entire amount is owed to the owner (16:5-7: "how much do you owe my master?").

22. See Danker and Bauer, *Greek English Lexicon*, 298.

discrepancy would have been caught in the reckoning with the owner had the manager taken in less than the promissory note stated.

Luke 16:6

The first debtor owes the owner "a hundred measures of oil," or as the text says, "one hundred βάτους of oil" (a Hebrew measurement). A "bath" is a jar containing 21–23 liters, each of which equals about 5.5 gallons in today's measurements.[23] Hence the first debtor owed 550 gallons of oil. The manager tells him to write out new promissory notes (τὰ γράμματα) in the amount of fifty measures of oil—a total of about 275 gallons of oil.[24] Apparently, if the debtors sign them, these new notes will be substituted for the original promissory notes, which are then discarded. Why it should be done quickly is not clear (before the manager changes his mind? Before the debtor reports him to the owner? Before the debtors discover that he has been fired and no longer has the authority to act for the owner?). But it does convey the urgency that the manager must have felt. The manager does not tell the second debtor to act quickly (16:7), however. It is interesting that no mention is made of the debtor's tit for the manager's tat—that is to say what are the debtors expected to do for the manager. Apparently they do not even discuss what the manager expects to get out of the transaction—an omission that clearly reveals the riskiness of the manager's plan.

Luke 16:7

Then the manager puts the same question to the "other (ἑτέρῳ)." The word should be translated to "another," if there are more than two involved. The story, however, mentions only two debtors, but also says that the manager is calling on "every one of the owner's debtors" (16:5). So the reader must decide if the number of debtors propositioned by the manager is an abbreviation of a larger number.[25] One would assume that the wealthy owner of a business requiring the services of a manager of "business affairs"[26] would

---

23. Sellers "Weights and Measures," *IDB* 4:834.

24. See Jeremias, *Parables*, 184. Jeremias estimates that one hundred baths is the equivalent of about eight hundred gallons and is valued at one thousand denarii, or a little over what a common laborer would earn in three years.

25. In the longer stories of Jesus featuring a sequence there are usually more iterations than two in the sequence: the Sower, the Vineyard, the Feast, the Entrusted Money, Laborers in a Vineyard, An Injured Man on the Jericho Road.

26. White points out that it was common for large estates to employ financial

have more than two persons indebted to him. So it is possible the number of debtors stated is simply an example of the kind of thing the manager was now doing for a greater number of the owner's debtors.

The second debtor owed the owner "a hundred measures of wheat," or as the text says "one hundred κόρους of wheat (or grain)." A *koros* is a Hebrew dry measure equivalent to a *homer*, which equals 5.16 bushels; so this debtor owed about 516 bushels.[27] The manager tells him the same thing: take your promissory notes and write eighty. With this reduction in the amount of the obligation the debtor would owe, according to the new promissory notes, a little less than 413 bushels.[28] So the amounts of debt and remission in both cases are substantial. As with the debtor in 16:6, no mention is made of the debtor's tit for the manager's tat. Apparently they do not even discuss what the manager expects to get out of the transaction.

The fact that the debt owed is stated in terms of the produce of the field and orchard suggests that they may likely be tenant farmers on the owner's land, and their agreement with the owner is to pay him in produce rather than hard currency (cf. Mark 12:1–8).[29]

Summary

In brief, the story concerns a manager accused of "wasting resources" in his management of the employer's business. The reader is never told specifically what he was thought to have done. He is confronted by the owner and summarily fired. No evidence is given that the manager is guilty of what he was accused. Managers in places of great responsibility were men carefully chosen for their aptitude for management, or at least that is what the little evidence in ancient literature about managers leads one to conclude.[30] The manager, however, does not protest the owner's actions or proclaim his innocence. Instead faced with the prospect of accounting to the owner for

---

administrators (*actores*), and that the terms *actores* and *vilicus* are used as synonyms. Hence the manager in the narrative might have been a financial administrator, which is how readers see him functioning in the narrative: *Roman Farming*, 353.

27. Sellers, "Weights and Measures," *IDB* 4:835.

28. See Jeremias, *Parables*, 181. Jeremias estimates that 100 cors of wheat is the equivalent of 550 cwt. and is worth 2500 denarii, or the equivalent of a little over seven years pay for a common laborer.

29. See Aubert, *Business Managers*, 129–31; White, *Roman Farming*, 404–9.

30. See Xenophon, *Oeconomicus* 12.3–5, 11–13; 14.1–2: Xenophon, *Memorabila, Oeconomicus, Symposium, Apology*, 4:463–67, 474–75; Columella, *Res Rustica* I.8–9; XI.1: *Lucius Junius Moderatus Columella On Agriculture*, 1:82–101; *Lucius Junius Columella On Agriculture and Trees*, 3:48–69.

his service while in office, he comes up with a desperate and risky plan "to feather his nest" by defrauding his former employer. The plan involves collusion with those indebted to the business. If they will agree to defraud the owner, it will result in a significant savings to them in the amounts they must pay to the owner of the business. The manager *hopes* that this desperate action on his part will ingratiate himself with the debtors, so that when he is finally out of the job, some of his fellow conspirators will reward him with a position in their households. The narrative ends with the manager pitching his proposition to at least two of his former boss's debtors.

The reader is given very little information about the owner and nothing about the relationship between the owner and the manager. There is no evidence that the manager has actually done what he was accused of. The reader does not know if any debtors agreed to participate in the scheme to defraud their business associate, the owner of the business. The narrative ends without a resolution.[31] Did the debtors agree to the plan? When the manager was through with his accounting with the owner, did one or more of the debtors provide him shelter? At the end of the story readers are left with an image of a man engaged in what on the surface is an illegal act.

HOW DOES THE STORY WORK?

The narrative is a brief vignette about a man of influence and power who finds himself in an impossible situation. The precariousness of his situation is indicated by the only two immediate options he sees for remedying his situation—manual labor and begging. The only other option that occurs to him is both risky and as apt to fail as succeed. But it affords him a hope, nothing more or less, that if it succeeds, his personal situation will be stabilized. The plan rests on the hope that he can obligate former business associates by involving them in a high stakes illegal act. Otherwise he is on the street with no resources. Any one or all of the debtors could inform the owner of what he is attempting to do. But given the situation, it is a risk he feels he must take. Readers know nothing about his character before this moment, and nothing about his relationship with the owner—except that the owner is prone to believe the worst about him. So readers are left with the image of a powerful person who attempts to resolve his desperate situation with an illegal act.

---

31. Compare for example the following stories that end without resolution: the Unjust Judge (Luke 18:1–5); the Pharisee and the Toll Collector (Luke 18:10–13); the Fig Tree in a Vineyard (Luke 13:6–9) as discussed in Hedrick, *Parables as Poetic Fictions*, 187–207, 208–235; See also Hedrick, "An Unfinished Story," 167–92.

The story does not teach a moral lesson. It presents readers with an unresolved complication, which is to answer the question: what happened next? Do the debtors go along with the manager's plan; is it successful or not?

THE BROADER NARRATIVE CONTEXT FOR THE SITUATION REFLECTED IN THE STORY

Some commentators on the story have pointed to "the picaresque comedy" as the broader context for situating the story. In such a reading the manager turns out to be a lovable rogue "who lives by his wits"; "shallowness and not criminality is the key to his character."[32] According to Dan Via the protagonist in the story "wins the approval of his victimized employer"—by which comment Via is alluding to Luke 16:8a. And it is only Luke 16:8a that makes the narrative a picaresque comedy.[33] But we have already seen that Luke 16:8a is not part of the narrative proper; rather it is Luke's reaction to the story.

On the other hand, John Dominic Crossan has argued that regarding "Luke 16:1–7 as a 'swindler' (or trickster) tale fits [the story] into the structure proposed for such stories by Heda Jason."[34] Brandon Scott critiques Crossan in two ways: he objects that the story is not simply a trickster-dupe narrative and notes that "Crossan has confused the demands of a formal model with the actual story."[35] From my perspective a major difficulty with the identification of the story as a swindler/trickster-dupe tale is that there are no collections of these tales to compare to the story in Luke 16:1–7. The evidence offered for comparison is Jason's reconstructed model of such stories rather than specific instances of tales. As I have analyzed Luke's story above, it does not seem to fit the trickster tale; something very different is going on in the narrative, which I take to be the substance of Scott's criticism. The manager's focus is not on his former employer, but rather on his own future, or perceived lack of a future. His fraudulent act is not designed to dupe his former employer rather it is designed to secure a future for himself.

If we do not regard Luke 16:8a as the statement of the owner in the story, we are left with an open-ended story of a man finding himself in an

---

32. See Via, *The Parables*, 159–60; Scott, *Hear Then the Parable*, 263–64; and Crossan, "The Servant Parables of Jesus," 17–62.

33. Via, *The Parables*, 161.

34. Crossan, "Structuralist Analysis," 207; and Jason, *Narrative Structure of Swindler Tales*, 7.

35. Scott, *Hear Then the Parable*, 260.

impossible situation. This situation is common enough in life. People often find themselves in what they perceive as "between the rock and a hard place," and hence they will devise stratagems, risky and desperate ones, for extricating themselves. A number of these desperate plans for resolving impossible situations are found in Hebrew Bible narratives. One, for example, is the story of David and Bathsheba. In order to cover up the fact that he had "taken" (2 Sam 11:4) another man's wife and conceived a child with her (2 Sam 11:5), King David conceived what he thought was a sure and simple plan (2 Sam 11:6-8). It failed, however, for Uriah had too much integrity to enjoy the comforts of home while his troops were still engaged in battle (2 Sam 11:9-13). The failure of this "sure plan" necessitated an even more risky one. David sent Uriah back, hand-carrying a note for Joab, David's commander, with orders that Joab should put Uriah at the "forefront of the hardest fighting" and once the battle was joined Joab should withdraw the troops and leave Uriah exposed (2 Sam 11:14-15). Thus David planned to cover his indiscretion with Bathsheba by the deliberate murder of Uriah. The risky plan was successful (2 Sam 11:16-27).

Here is a second example. After successful campaigns at Jericho and Ai, a coalition of cities came together to oppose the Israelite invasion (Josh 9:1-2). The Gibeonites, however, were skeptical of the success of such a coalition, and devised a risky plan to deceive the Israelites into making a treaty with them. They sent a deputation to Joshua outfitted as if they had travelled from afar for many miles from out of the immediate area (Josh 9:3-13). At first their plan seemed successful (Josh 9:14-15). The Israelites were taken in by the deceit of the Gibeonites and they signed the treaty. The risk to the Gibeonites was that the deceit once discovered could have invalidated the treaty and the cities of the Gibeonites might have been treated as Jericho and Ai had been treated. The treaty, however, held after the deceit was discovered, even though the Israelites were unhappy with it (Josh 9:16-19). But the Gibeonites, nevertheless, were not treated as full partners but instead treated as a slave people (Josh 9:20-27). So in a sense the plan failed, or at least did not achieve all that the Gibeonites hoped that it might.

The risky or desperate plan to resolve an impossible situation appears in other narratives in Hebrew Bible; here are several others: Abraham and his wife Sarai (lying to the Pharaoh), Gen 12:10-20;[36] Jacob and Esau (selling and lying about a birthright), Gen 25:27-34; 27:5-46; Judah and Tamar (desperate plan to force a person to keep a promise), Gen 38:1-30; Judith (a risky plan to defeat the Assyrian General Holofernes), Judith 8:32-34;

---

36. The same novelistic feature appears again at Gen 20:1-18; and Gen 26:6-11.

10:11-16; 13:1-20; Saul (fearful of the Philistines Saul seeks a medium), 1 Sam 28:3-25; 31:1-13.

Jesus has actually used this novelistic feature in other narratives. For example, there is the story of a youth who makes a poor decision and finds himself in an impossible situation (Luke 15:13-16). So he devises a desperate stratagem for resolving his situation (Luke 15:17-18), expecting that his father will, if he takes him back at all, make him as a hired servant—no longer a son (15:19). And the same feature is reflected in the narrative about an absentee landlord wanting to collect the rent from those farming the land. He sent a slave[37] to collect what was due him but those in possession of the property beat him and sent him away empty handed. They treated a second slave sent by the owner in the same way—probably hoping that the property would be abandoned by the owner. The owner then devised the questionable stratagem of sending his son, hoping that "perhaps they will respect my son." But like life, sometimes desperate plans succeed (Luke 15:22-24), and sometimes they fail (Gospel of Thomas 65).

MEANING

"What does this mean?" is the wrong question to put to a narrative. For different readers will respond in many different ways to a narrative. Here is why:

> "Meaning" describes, in the final analysis, a particular reader's response to a given text. The term indicates how that particular reader responded to the narrative on the basis of his or her background, knowledge, values and experience—that is on the basis of the sum total of elements comprising the world of that particular reader. Thus "meaning" does not innately inhabit a text, where readers must search for it, but meaning is created by an interaction between a particular reader and a text. Meaning is evoked, if at all, in the reader's mind; it inevitably originates in the nexus between the text and the reader—where the reader's world intersects the text's world—for texts also have backgrounds and reflect knowledge, a sense of values, and an author's experience. Thus, an author decides what the text says, but readers decide what it means.[38]

---

37. The narrative is preserved in four versions: Mark 12:1-8//Matt 21:33-39//Luke 20:9-15//*Gospel of Thomas* 65. I am using the version in Thomas as likely the more original form. See Hedrick, *Unlocking the Secrets of the Gospel According to Thomas*, 124-25.

38. Hedrick, *Many Things in Parables*, 46-47.

Language in general is subject to many different responses, even things that seem rather clear on the surface of things. For example, here is a phrase attributed to Geoffrey Chaucer, which at first glance seems rather clear, until one is called upon to explain it: "Time and tide wait for no man." On the Internet, in a space of just a few minutes, I turned up several different explanations for the phrase:

"We can't have the impossible."[39]

"The processes of nature continue, no matter how much we would like them to stop."

"No one is so powerful that they can stop the march of time."

"Things will not wait for you when you are late."

"Nobody can stop the progression of time."

"We should act on favorable opportunities immediately, without delay."

The saying "conveys the relative impotence of man pitted against the universal forces."

Hence the first question to ask of narratives, and the parables of Jesus, in particular, is—as I have aimed at doing in the previous section—how does it work as a piece of literature?

HOW MIGHT THE STORY HAVE BEEN HEARD IN THE CONTEXT OF ISRAEL'S FICTIONS ABOUT ITSELF?

In the first part of this essay I have aimed at neutrality: I have talked about the story in language used by the story. In the initial analysis of the story, readers must use only the unambiguous information provided by the story and talk about the story using only the language of the story. Readers who go beyond these two parameters in their analysis are engaged in writing their own story. Only after a reader thoroughly understands the story as story in the context of Palestinian antiquity is one poised to consider the issue of "meaning," first in terms of the earliest auditors of the story.

To judge by the literary context in Luke and the multiple interpretations given to the narrative (Luke 16:8-13), not even the early Christians associated the story with the kingdom of God. And we have no idea how Jesus may have wanted his auditors to understand his story; all we have is the story itself with no hints embedded in the story by the storyteller as to how the story should be heard.[40] The multiple interpretations appended to

---

39. Updike, *The Centaur*, comment attributed to Cassie Caldwell in the novel, 52.

40. See the brief discussion of the history of parables interpretation in Hedrick, "Parable," *NIDB* 4:374-75.

the story clearly show that it stimulated multiple responses even in Christian antiquity.

One may, however, imagine the hypothetical responses of Jewish audiences based on a critical understanding of first-century Judaism using available literary sources contemporary with Jesus.[41] How might the story have been understood by Jewish peasants who were acculturated in Galilee and Judea in the first century? Such a criterion eliminates by definition Christian responses, since at this early period there were no Christians. Of course, there could have been as many responses as there were auditors, but I am only considering how the story may have played off against the literature that contributed to what modern scholars consider Judaism in the first century.

The Christian interpretations appended to the story (Luke 16:8–13) are later than the time of the earliest auditors, who in the main would have been Jewish rather than Christian.[42] With the exception of Luke 16:13 (which comes from Q: cf. Matt 6:24), there is no way of telling if these are traditional responses transmitted with the story in the oral period or if the substance and arrangement of all of them are to be attributed to Luke, but they at least give an insight into how some (or one, in the case of Luke) early Christians heard the story:

Luke 16:8a: Luke finds the behavior of the manager to be commendable because of his shrewdness in finding a way out of his predicament. This interpretation also tacitly approves of illegal or dishonest behavior in face of a crisis.

Luke 16:8b: this saying also commends the manager's shrewdness but subtly condemns him as a "son of this age," presumably because of dishonest behavior.

Luke 16:9: This saying is strange, but by calling on others to emulate his behavior (viz. "I tell you . . .") Luke's Jesus clearly commends the manager's shrewd use of the "mammon of unrighteousness"[43] in making "friends." I presume Luke uses the saying to commend the manager for his use of money and not because he stole it from the owner. Money is "unrighteous," and it will eventually fail, but if people use it "rightly" (i.e., for good purposes) God will receive them (assuming that the third plural is a way of

---

41. See Hedrick, *Parables as Poetic Fictions*, 113–16, 162–63, 205–7, 228–30.

42. See the discussion of Manson on the sayings: *The Sayings of Jesus as Recorded in the Gospels according to St. Matthew and St Luke Arranged with Introduction and Commentary*, 290–94, but he discusses them as independent sayings of the historical Jesus rather than as responses of Luke's Jesus to the story of the Dishonest Steward.

43. Compare Luke 18:6.

avoiding the use of a direct reference to God).⁴⁴ The saying simply ignores the manager's theft of the owner's property.

Luke 16:10-11: This saying appears to condemn the behavior of the manager. Since he evidently was not a faithful manager of his employer's possessions, he will not be entrusted with the "true [riches]."

Luke 16:13: This saying appears to condemn the manager as a lover of money, and his behavior is not at all commendable, since he has placed devotion to mammon over devotion to God.

All but the first interpretation (Luke 16:8a) find nothing commendable about the behavior of the manager.

My question, however, is how might the story have been heard by Jewish peasants who sat at the feet of Jesus a generation or two earlier than Luke? If we take seriously the assertion in Luke 16:5 that the stated debts were obligations owed to the owner of the business, then an auditor is almost forced to see the actions of the manager as theft—the manager is stealing from the owner by conspiring with the debtors to have their debts reduced. The Decalogue is quite plain in its prohibition against theft (Exod 20:15; Lev 19:11; Deut 5:19; Exod 22:1-3, 7-8), and Hebrew literature is uniform in labeling thievery as unacceptable behavior (Zech 5:3-4; Tobit 2:11-14; Prov 29:24, 30:9; Ps 50:16-18; Jer 29:26; Ezra 22:12; Hos 4:2, 7:11; Micah 6:10-11; Amos 8:5). Evaluating the actions of the manager from such a perspective would lead one to judge his actions negatively.

Some commentators have proposed that the manager in this story of Jesus should be seen as a "rogue" in the picaresque mode (see note 32). In viewing the manager as a "lovable rogue," commentators are tacitly acknowledging that he has defrauded the owner, but soften his illegal behavior in this way: "well he wasn't malicious about it, and was not actually aiming to hurt the owner, who could easily survive the loss."

The manager in the story, however, simply does not fit the characteristics of the *picaro*. In the picaresque novel⁴⁵ the *picaro* is described in "a chronicle, usually autobiographical, presenting the life story [or part of the life] of a rascal of low degree engaged in menial tasks and making his living through his wits than his industry."⁴⁶ It is true that the protagonist in the parable, like the *picaro* in the picaresque novel, is also cast in the low mimetic mode (i.e., "low degree⁴⁷"), but unlike the *picaro* the manager in the

---

44. See Manson, *Sayings of Jesus*, 293.
45. See Holman and Harmon, *Handbook to Literature*, 356-57.
46. Ibid., 356.
47. For a discussion of the fictional modes in literature see Frye, *Anatomy of Criticism*, 33-34.

story, like managers in Roman antiquity in general, is a man of considerable responsibility, power, and influence; he is scarcely engaged in "menial" tasks and does not make his living by his wits.[48] It is possible, however, that the story could have been heard as a "trickster" tale—a fired manager turning the tables on his former employer.

ANOTHER READING OF THE STORY

Without assuming information not given in the story, it raises this question: does the goal of the manager warrant the risks and the means to accomplish the goal—or, as it appears in ethical theory, do the ends justify the means? The manager was faced with the loss of livelihood, and the only two immediate options to this crisis that he sees are either becoming a common beggar or a manual laborer, neither of which he is prepared to do.[49] His dire situation, as he sees it, called for whatever action necessary to resolve his situation—even action in the extreme. He is presented as thinking that the only "reasonable" action open to him is to curry favor with his employer's debtors by fraudulently forgiving part of their debt with their complicity. In short, he takes from the rich and gives to those with less and the only thing he gets out of his Robin Hood-esque deed apparently is the hope that they might reciprocate when he finds himself on the street. It is a pretty risky plan with no certainty of success, but it was, he thought, the best decision he could make based on his situation.

Can such a deliberate illegal act ever be considered ethical or moral?[50] Here are two similar stories appearing in ancient Hebrew literature about David and Judith that also raise this question. David's story featured an end or a cause that on the surface appears negative in the abstract, and Judith's featured a cause or end that in the abstract appears commendable. David (2 Sam 11:1–27) attempted to cover up one breach of accepted community morality (rape) with another more serious act (murder), prompting the question: can it ever be considered a moral act to breach societal norms when both the end and the means are outside the law? Possibly not, but it should at least be noted that David is described as thinking it was.

The situation with Judith is not as clear. Judith was a citizen of the Israelite city of Bethulia in the hill country located above a plain where there were springs (Jdt 7:3). The Assyrian general Holofernes on the orders

---

48. Aubert, *Business Managers*, 170–71.

49. See the insightful description of the manager's precarious situation by Herzog, *Parables as Subversive Speech*, 242.

50. See the discussion of ends and means in Fletcher, *Situation Ethics*, 120–33.

of Nebuchadnezzer the Assyrian King was engaged in a war to pacify the region and if they resisted he was directed to destroy the cities that had refused to join his coalition (1:1–6, 7–12; 2:1–13); and Holofernes followed his instructions (2:14–28). The Israelites fortified their hilltop cities in preparation to resist Holofernes (4:1–5), who laid siege to the city of Bethulia with the plan of starving it into submission (7:1–32). Judith, a very devout Jewish widow (8:1–8) comes up with a desperate plan to save the city from capitulation and annihilation: her plan, simply, stated was for her to walk into Holofornes camp and kill him (8:32–34; 10:11–16)! Her plan succeeded (13:1–10). The rescue of an entire city, the preservation of their lives, and the preservation of their way of life is a commendable end, even if the means of its accomplishment must be treachery and murder. At least those who were saved thought so (13:18–20; 15:8–10).

One case had nothing to commend it as a moral act (David). The ends benefitted only David in that it covered up an immoral act, and the means breached a fundamental code of civilized society: the right to be secure in your person. The other (Judith) has a certain kind of nobility about it that even strictly law-abiding persons can appreciate. In other words under certain conditions even murder can be seen as acceptable.[51]

The manager in the story seems to fit David's situation better than Judith's. He is concerned about his own welfare rather than the welfare of others, but if Hertzog's analysis of the manager's situation is even nearly correct, then the situation concerns his personal survival, which puts an entirely different spin on the situation. According to Herzog the dismissal of the manager from the stewardship is a "death sentence."[52] And since David's story seems to establish that societal norms are at best relative, the manager may be forgiven for trying to preserve his life—and not just a standard of living.

But what does that suggest about society's rules, laws, and norms? That they only apply in non-emergency situations?

I am not arguing that this story of Jesus *teaches* that the ends justify the means, but I am arguing that the narrative is clearly open to such a reading. Because the narrator suspends judgment on the manager's actions, judgment is left up to auditors and readers. And if the narrative can legitimately be said to raise the question of "ends justify means," the question of where to draw the line is also left up to auditors and readers.

---

51. See Hedrick, "Flawed Heroes," 3052–56.

52. See Herzog's analysis of the critical situation the manager found himself in with his dismissal from the stewardship: Hertzog, *Parables as Subversive Speech*, 242.

BIBLIOGRAPHY

Ash, Harrison Boyd, ed. and trans. *Lucius Junius Moderatus Columella on Agriculture*. 3 vols. LCL 361. Cambridge, MA: Harvard University Press, 1941.

Aubert, Jean-Jacques. *Business Managers in Ancient Rome: A Social and Economic Study of Institores, 200 B. C.–A. D. 250*. Leiden: Brill, 1994.

Bailey, Kenneth E. *Poet and Peasant and Through Peasant Eyes: A Literary Cultural Approach to the Parables of Luke*. 2 vols. in 1. Grand Rapids: Eerdmans, 1976, 1980.

Blomberg, Craig L. *Interpreting the Parables of Jesus*. Downers Grove, IL: InterVarsity, 1990.

Breech, James. *The Silence of Jesus: The Authentic Voice of the Historical Man*. Philadelphia: Fortress, 1983.

Bruce, Alexander B. *The Parabolic Teaching of Christ: A Systematic and Critical Study of the Parables of our Lord*. New York: Hodder & Stoughton, 1884.

Buttrick, George Arthur, et al. *The Interpreter's Dictionary of the Bible*. 4 vols. Nashville: Abingdon, 1962.

Crossan, John Dominic. "The Servant Parables of Jesus." In *A Structuralist Approach to the Parables*, edited by Robert W. Funk, 17–62. Semeia 1. Missoula, MT: SBL, 1974.

———. "Structuralist Analysis and the Parables of Jesus: A Reply to D. O. Via, Jr." In *A Structuralist Approach to the Parables*, edited by Robert W. Funk, 192–221. Semeia 1. Missoula, MT: SBL, 1974.

Danker, Frederick William, and Walter Bauer. *A Greek-English Lexicon of the New Testament and Other Early Christian Literature*. 3rd ed. Chicago: University of Chicago Press, 2000.

Derrett, J. Duncan M. "Fresh Light on St Luke XVI I: The Parable of the Unjust Steward." *New Testament Studies* 7 (1961) 198–219.

Findlay, J. Alexander. *Jesus and His Parables*. London: Epworth, 1950.

Fitzmyer, Joseph A. *The Gospel According to Luke (X–XXIV): Introduction, Translation, and Notes*. Anchor Bible 28A. New York: Doubleday, 1985.

Fletcher, Joseph. *Situation Ethics: The New Morality*. Philadelphia: Westminster, 1966.

Ford, Richard Q. "Jesus' Parable of the Dishonest Steward and America's War in Afghanistan." *The Fourth R* 25 (2012) 3–8.

Forster, E. S., and Edward Heffner, eds. and trans. *Lucius Junius Moderatus Columella: On Agriculture and Trees*. 3 vols. LCL 408. Cambridge, MA: Harvard University Press, 1955.

Frye, Northrup. *Anatomy of Criticism: Four Essays*. Princeton: Princeton University Press, 1957.

Funk, Robert W. *A Greek Grammar of the New Testament and Other Early Christian Literature: A Translation and Revision of the Ninth-Tenth German Edition by F. Blass and A. Debrunner Incorporating Supplementary Notes of A. Debrunner*. Chicago: University of Chicago Press, 1961.

Hedrick, Charles W. "Flawed Heroes and Stories Jesus Told: The One about a Man Wanting to Kill." In *Handbook for the Study of the Historical Jesus: Individual Studies*, edited by Tom Holmén and Stanley E. Porter, 4:3021–56. Leiden: Brill, 2011.

———. *Many Things in Parables: Jesus and His Modern Critics*. Louisville: Westminster John Knox, 2004.

———. "Parable." In *The New Interpreter's Dictionary of the Bible*, edited by Katherine Doob Sakenfeld et al., 4:368–77. Nashville: Abingdon, 2009.
———. *Parables as Poetic Fictions: The Creative Voice of Jesus*. Peabody, MA: Hendrickson, 1994.
———. "Sticking with the Story: Richard Ford's Interpretation of the Dishonest Steward." *The Fourth R* 25 (2012) 9–10.
———. "An Unfinished Story about a Fig Tree in a Vineyard (Luke 13:6–9)." *Perspectives in Religious Studies* 26 (1999) 169–92.
———. *Unlocking the Secrets of the Gospel according to Thomas: A Radical Faith for a New Age*. Eugene, OR: Wipf and Stock, 2010.
Herzog, William R. *Parables as Subversive Speech: Jesus as Pedagogue of the Oppressed*. Louisville: Westminster John Knox, 1994.
Holman, C. Hugh, and William Harmon. *A Handbook to Literature*. 6th ed. New York: Macmillan, 1992.
Hultgren, Arland J. *The Parables of Jesus: A Commentary*. Grand Rapids: Eerdmans, 2000.
Jason, Heda. *The Narrative Structure of Swindler Tales*. Santa Monica, CA: Rand, 1968.
Jeremias, Joachim. *The Parables of Jesus*. Rev. ed. New York: Scribner's, 1963.
Jülicher, D. Adolf. *Die Gleichnisreden Jesu*. 2 vols. Freiburg: Mohr, 1899.
Kittel, Gerhard, and Gerhard Friedrich, eds. *Theological Dictionary of the New Testament*. Translated and edited by Geoffrey W. Bromiley. 10 vols. Grand Rapids: Eerdmans, 1964–1976.
Klostermann, Erich, and Hugo Gressman. *Das Lukasevangelium*. Tübingen: Mohr/Siebeck, 1919.
Manson, T. W. *The Sayings of Jesus as Recorded in the Gospels according to St. Matthew and St. Luke arranged with Introduction and Commentary*. London: SCM, 1949.
Marchant, E. C., and O. J. Todd. *Xenophon: Memorabila, Oeconomicus, Symposium, Apology*. 7 vols. LCL 168. Cambridge, MA: Harvard University Press, 1929.
Michel, Otto. "Οἰκονόμος." In *Theological Dictionary of the New Testament*, edited by Gerhard Kittel, translated by Geoffrey W. Bromiley, 5:149–51. Grand Rapids: Eerdmans, 1967.
Oesterly, W. O. E. *The Gospel Parables in the Light of Their Jewish Background*. London: SPCK, 1936.
Scott, Bernard Brandon. *Hear Then the Parable: A Commentary on the Parables of Jesus*. Minneapolis: Fortress, 1989.
———. "Is Don Corleone God? A Response to Richard Ford." *The Fourth R* 25 (2012) 11–12.
Sellers, Ovid R. "Weights and Measures." In *The Interpreter's Dictionary of the Bible*, edited by George A. Buttrick, 4:828–39. New York: Abingdon, 1962.
Smith, B. T. D. *The Parables of the Synoptic Gospels: A Critical Study*. Cambridge: Cambridge University Press, 1937.
Updike, John. *The Centaur*. Reprint, Greenwich, CT: Fawcett, 1963.
Via, Dan Otto, Jr. *The Parables: Their Literary and Existential Dimension*. Philadelphia: Fortress, 1967.
White, K. D. *Roman Farming*. Ithaca: Cornell University Press, 1970.

6

The Revolutionary Paradigm of Grace
—J. Lyle Story

INTRODUCTION

Paul Tournier, a noted Christian psychiatrist, expresses the paradoxical inversion of human values with the words of Jesus, followed by his own comments:

> "So the last will be first, and the first last" (Matt. 20:16). How many times I have thought about it when a man has been sobbing in my consulting room as he has given expression to disappointment with himself, his faults and failures, his despair and his feelings of inferiority! He is nearer to the Kingdom of God than I who listen to him; and I come nearer—to the Kingdom, as well as to the man—only in so far as I recognize that I am as guilty, as powerless, as inferior and as desperate as he is. Only then also can I help him, for I am delivered from all spirit of judgment, I am his companion in repentance and in waiting for grace.[1]

The Bible witnesses to a profound reversal in terms of the sinners and the righteous and the way in which God's grace comes to them.

In this chapter, *I will argue that Jesus embodies and communicates grace to both sinners and righteous persons.* Although both groups are in desperate

---

1. Tournier, *Guilt and Grace*, 112.

need, the specific messages to both groups are targeted to the pressing needs that are group-specific.

Jesus comes into the human scene as the grand reversal and paradox of commonly held religious norms. He, who is equal with God and is God, now is incarnate "in the likeness of sinful humanity" (Phil 2:6–8). He chooses people for disciples who, in and of themselves, would not amount to much—several "blue-collar" men—fishermen, tax collectors, and he is at home with immoral people and society's "low-lifers." Moreover, Jesus publicly thanks God for the reversal of human values: "I thank you, Father, Lord of heaven and earth, that you have hidden these things from the wise and understanding and revealed them to infants" (Matt 11:25). Jesus chooses many poor, weak and despised persons; he is at home with the social and religious misfits, i.e., the marginalized. In so many ways, he prefers publicly acknowledged sinners (by morality and vocation) to the "righteous." Before Jesus, there are not two clearly defined groups of people—the guilty sinners and righteous persons. Jesus only recognizes one class of persons—the guilty, which includes everyone. To the one who owns up to guilt, his word is that of grace and compassion. Religious people (then and now) have always had a difficult time believing and then admitting that God prefers the weak, the humble, the guilty, the broken, and those who live with shame. In his unbelievable grace, God receives all who are repentant in their actions, words, lifestyle, attitudes and words. His word is a word of grace and compassion, freedom, celebration, and joy. The so-called righteous (who have repressed their personal guilt) and the so-called sinners (who live with guilt and shame) can both receive genuine pardon and grace. They come to God with an open hand.

This chapter will explore illuminating texts and themes in the Gospels that Jesus highlights as he deals with both the "sinners" and the "righteous." Although all are in need of grace, he tailors his grace-message to meet the unique needs of people as "sinners" and "righteous ones."

JESUS' GRACE FOR "SINNERS"

Grace Means Table Fellowship, Involvement, and Acceptance of Sinners without Conditions

One of the repeated sneers against Jesus was that he was a "friend of tax collectors and sinners, a glutton and drunkard" (Matt 11:19; Luke 7:34). Such charges against Jesus were occasioned by very real social contact between Jesus and the "low-lifers."

In Mark 2:15–17, we find one such example in which Jesus is critiqued for his table fellowship with publicly acknowledged sinners. Mark uses the word "many" to signify a large group of tax collectors and sinners; he also desires that his readers see an implicit link between the call of one tax collector (Levi) and his table fellowship with many tax collectors and sinners. This prepares the readers for the ensuing controversy. By his call of Levi and his table fellowship with these "low-lifers," Jesus has crossed over the Jewish boundary lines, which would separate the "holy" and the "unholy." Tax collectors and sinners were not even to be taught the statutes of God, since by their vocation and lifestyle they had placed themselves outside the covenant people of God.[2] Table fellowship in Jewish practice was a sacred rite, and if entered into with "unclean" people, would thereby render one unclean (cf. Mark 7:1ff.). Table fellowship was introduced by a table blessing, which united those who ate the same bread into a holy table fellowship, a very intimate human communion. The meals Jesus shares with the religiously ostracized are "acted parables" of the kingdom of God. Joachim Jeremias says,

> In the East . . . to invite a person to a meal was an honor. It was an offer of peace, brotherhood and forgiveness; in short, sharing a table meant sharing life. In Judaism in particular, table-fellowship means fellowship before God, for the eating of a piece of broken bread by everyone who shares in the meal brings out the fact that they all have a share in the blessing which the master of the house had spoken over the unbroken bread.[3]

Table fellowship is a way of demonstrating and expressing solidarity. Jesus' radical action precipitates the accusation of Jesus' opponents to His disciples. Why did Jesus' critics accuse the disciples about Jesus and not directly deal with Jesus? Did they intend to erode the disciples' newfound loyalty to Jesus?

Jesus' response is expressed in the form of antithetical parallelism, in which he compares his needed presence with sinners with the needed presence of a physician with the sick. The words within the parentheses are certainly to be implied due to the parallelism of the lines:

Physician's presence with the sick
Those who are well	have no need	of a physician
	but	
those who are sick	(have need)	(of a physician)

---

2. See Linnemann, *Parables*, 74.
3. Jeremias, *New Testament Theology*, 115.

Jesus' presence with the sinners

the righteous	did not come to call	I
	but	
the sinners	(came to call)	(I) (Mark 2:18)

Jesus likens himself (I) to the physician who goes to the place where people are sick—where the need is genuine (real and felt). It is absurd for a person to go to medical school, internship, and set up practice, and then refuse to have dealings with the sick and diseased. It is just as absurd for Jesus to refuse to have dealings with publicly acknowledged sinners. Table fellowship and Jesus' acceptance of sinners are essential elements of his interaction and ministry with the people. His involvement with them was not to become like them in their sin but to express his role as a physician, and it is expressed in programmatic form through an "I came" (ἦλθον) statement.

This table fellowship is also expressed through the Zacchaeus story (Luke 19:1-10). Jesus is regarded as a prophet from Nazareth and is welcomed with a banquet, thrown by Zacchaeus; this feast follows Jesus' own self-invitation to Zacchaeus, the chief tax collector. His self-invitation, acceptance of the invitation, and dining with this person unleashed all kinds of religious resentment, not only from the Pharisees, but from the general population as well ("they were all grumbling" Luke 19:7). Jesus makes the unequivocal statement, "For the Son of Man came to seek and to save the lost" (19:10). With irony, Luke states that Zacchaeus was "seeking" (ἐζήτει) to see Jesus (19:3), the real seeker is Jesus who comes to seek (ζητῆσαι) the lost (19:10). Similarly, the trilogy of parables (Lost Sheep, Lost Coin and Lost Son) in Luke 15 is evoked by Jesus' table fellowship with tax collectors and sinners (15:1-2). The image of seeking is well expressed by the shepherd (15:4-7), the woman (15:8-10), the father who searches for the lost son, as well as the resentful older brother (15:11-32).

Luke frequently presents Jesus as a dinner guest hosted by others (Luke 5:29—Levi feast; 10:38—Mary and Martha; 19:5—Zacchaeus). On three separate occasions, Jesus' host is a Pharisee (7:36ff.; 11:37; 14:1). But as he sits at table among them, on each of the three occasions, Jesus directs the attention of the Pharisees away from their concerns for laws and rituals to the plight of the poor and needy, the sinful and the sick, whom the Pharisees neglect and disdain (7:39; 11:38-39; 14:1-4). Thus, even when he associates with the religious leaders, the evangelist shows the purpose of Jesus' coming to be for all humanity (2:30-32) with a ministry pointed to "the poor . . . the captives . . . the blind . . . and the oppressed" (4:18). The final commission given to the disciples embraces all of these groups, for it is to "all nations" (24:47).

The Parable of the Two Debtors is encased in the paragraph concerning the sinful woman (Luke 7:36–50). The story culminates with a proclamation of the mission of Jesus to the "outsider." Here, as elsewhere, he tampers with the religious, racial and social taboos of Jewish particularism, which assumes that God is only concerned with the Jews. A slave of a Gentile centurion is healed by Jesus' word (7:1–10). Jesus then proceeds to halt a funeral procession, touch the coffin,[4] and raise up a deceased young man, the only son of a widowed mother (7:11–17). And, as he defends the ministry of John the Baptist, Jesus is recognized to be the friend of tax collectors and sinners (7:18–35). A slave, a Gentile, a widow, tax collectors, and sinners—the unique "agenda" of Jesus' ministry to outsiders is amazing to ponder.

In terms of the immediate context of the parable, Luke has narrated the Son of Man's activity of eating and drinking contrasted with the Baptist's ascetic lifestyle, and the damning judgments pronounced on both by their critics: John is accused of possessing a demon, and Jesus is accused of being a glutton, drunkard, and friend of sinners (Luke 7:34). Jesus' practice of feasting advances into the setting for the following parable. When Jesus feasts at the home of a Pharisee, he is not critiqued for gluttony or drunkenness (v. 34). He is, however, judged for an evident lack of prophetic power, being a friend of sinners (v. 34, 39), and for his authority to pronounce the forgiveness of sins (v. 49).

As listeners and readers encounter the parables, it is made plain that God stands behind these parables in actual experience and relationship—not in mere systematic theological categories. God is portrayed in his kindness, mercy, and goodness. Jesus does not affirm that the world is basically good, but he does imply that God is a God who has planned from eternity to disclose his benevolent nature in human life. God stands behind the Parable of the Good Samaritan (Luke 10:25–37), with a vested interest in humanity—a God who comes to people on a rescue mission out of groundless compassion.[5] The Parable of the Friend at Midnight (11:5–8) is not intended to be a mere admonition on true friendship, but reveals a compassionate God who does not need to be awakened before he responds to his people when they earnestly and continually pray for the Holy Spirit (11:13).

In the ministry of Jesus, God offers humankind a new chance; indeed he is the God of the Second Chance. For through his ministry there can be a new beginning—a beginning that people are only able to make by a positive

---

4. Touching a coffin incurs one day's defilement (Num 19:21–22); by touching a corpse, Jesus would contract uncleanness for a week (Num 5:2–3; 19:11–20).

5. This does not mean that we are warranted to make the parables into extended allegories.

response to him, based on God's prior offer. God maintains the positive goal he has in view, just as the gardener maintains the vineyard and fig tree with the expectation of the final harvest. In the Parable of the Lost Sheep, God takes the initiative and does not wait for the sheep to come to its senses. The human situation is not one in which "all's well that ends well." It is just the opposite. People refuse to take the redemptive work of God seriously. The human race has already advanced to the edge of the abyss and except for the grace of God and the restraining arm of God—humankind will be lost. The Parable of the Laborers in the Vineyard (Matt 20:1–16) affirms that God has his own ways, which are contrary to human ways (Isa 55:8–9). Nonetheless, he finds a way to inspire people to participate in and to partake of his redemptive purpose in Jesus Christ.

In many ways, Jesus shows that narrow concepts and exclusive human views are much too limited for God. His desire is inclusive; God wills that all should be saved. Human egoistic thinking often conveniently classifies humankind into groups, which are restrictive in nature. But the parables of Jesus make sense only if we see a divine purpose at work in the world for all of humanity. Some parables are replete with details about the consummation and its joy. In the parables of the consummation of the age, Jesus offers the opportunity of harmonious and joyful fellowship with himself—not the sumptuousness of the meal. While people often take "sonship" and "daughtership" lightly, Jesus makes his audience aware of how far God transcends human love by offering the almost unbelievable joy of fellowship with him. Fellowship with God is not a sentimental experience or a psychological state; it is a true miracle of God's grace. Human beings are made sons and daughters of God with Christ as Lord. Humanity receives no ongoing contract with God as a Cosmic Employer. The son in the far-off country does not inherit the farm, but he is offered a home with joy and celebration. At one time, he lived a life of his choosing, but then found through various reversals that life lived recklessly and selfishly could never satisfy his soul. And so he made his way home. People can and do feel at home here on earth. Nevertheless, God's goal lies in the direction of another world that bursts the narrow boundaries of human thought and language that is limited.

Jesus intends to become the physician of the "broken" people through his table fellowship with sinners and his holistic acceptance of them without placing conditions upon them. Conversely, the Pharisees admonished the sinners to desist from sin, and they would also inflict banishment from the synagogue until the guilty persons had "cleaned up their act" and mended their ways. The social pressure against publicly acknowledged sinners was intense; it also involved economic sanctions. Through Jesus, we find his picture of God; he is not the severe judge, who is waiting for infraction so that he can exercise his judgment; rather he is the gracious Father who extends himself and grace towards people who turn themselves to him. Jesus' critics reveal their picture of God as the severe judge, when they, like the older brother in Luke 15, refuse to come in and joyfully celebrate Jesus' table fellowship with sinners. God demonstrates his unconditional grace to people through Jesus' involvement with sinners. Jesus reveals God's acceptance of sinners. Jesus becomes the physician of sinners because of his involvement and acceptance of them; thereby he reveals God's acceptance of them, without conditions, e.g., Jesus' story of the searching father does not include a probationary period for the wayward son, to prove himself (Luke 15:11–32). The lost son is met with compassion and the flurry of festive activity, to celebrate the transition from being "lost" and "dead" to "found" and "alive" (15: 32). The sinners found acceptance guaranteed to them, which is simply granted by returning home, such as the son in the far country found. By way of contrast, the older brother (Luke 15) reveals a joyless, legalistic and severe understanding of God. Surely, the older brother would have put the younger son on restriction, demanded payment of the lost money, ensuring that the son lived with the servants, put on curfew, etc. Such attitudes and expectations of the older brother clearly reveal a view of God, which is stern, harsh, demanding, exacting and legalistic. As Miroslav Volf notes, "Relationship is prior to moral rules; moral performance may *do something* to the relationship, but relationship *is not grounded* in moral performance."[6]

Grace Is Linked to the Forgiveness of Sins, Healing and Faith

Grace is not only related with table fellowship and acceptance, but embraces the forgiveness of sins, healing and faith—well expressed through numerous narratives. In Mark 2 (par.), there is a pronouncement story, which climaxes with the statement, "'But in order that you might know that the Son of Man has authority to forgive sins,' He says to the paralytic . . .'" (Mark 2:10–11). The primary thrust of the paragraph is concerned with Jesus' authority to forgive sins (four times in this paragraph—2:5, 7, 9–10), which is also expressed so emphatically in the purpose statement, "But in order that you may know that the Son of Man has *authority to forgive sins*." One of the items that stands out in this paragraph is the way that Jesus responds to the four friends; he responds to them—not to the paralytic, with something different from what they had brought their friend before Jesus. There is a cause-effect relationship between Jesus' perception of the faith of the four friends and His determination to forgive the paralytic's sins. They demolish a roof and

---

6. Volf, *Exclusion and Embrace*, 164.

bring their friend before Jesus for one reason—healing of his paralysis; initially Jesus does something different—he forgives sins. And the immediate antecedent of their faith is the persistent and dogged determination of the friends to get the paralytic before Jesus, even if it means tearing up a roof. They do not give up, even though there is no door or doorway open to them. In this context, faith is contagious and vicarious; it operates on behalf of another. Everyone anticipates the healing; Jesus publicly declares what he was doing and could do for the person; he imparts the forgiveness of sins, and then, to substantiate his authority to forgive sins, he heals the paralytic. The entire story reveals the forgiving involvement of God.

Jesus' pronouncement of forgiveness provokes the protest that Jesus is assuming the divine prerogative, "It is blasphemy! Who can forgive sins but God alone?" (Mark 2:7). The Scribes are correct; Jesus confers what God alone has the authority to confer. In the OT, there are occasions wherein forgiveness is conveyed through a prophet, "The Lord also has put away your sin" (Nathan to David in Second Sam 12:13).[7] The Jews in Jesus' day were aware of a sacrificial system wherein people performed in certain ways, responded with remorse and penitential behavior. But in Mark 2, the paralytic did not ask for forgiveness; Jesus is responding to the faith of others, and there is no prayer for the particular sins that the man might confess. Instead, Jesus simply announces and bestows the forgiveness of sins. Forgiveness is bound up here with the faith of others and healing.

Grace Is Intended to Lead to the Response of Repentance and Trust

While grace comes to sinners as an unexpected and underserved activity of God, it nonetheless is intended to evoke repentance and trust in the recipient. In the first two parables of Luke's trilogy (Luke 15), Jesus makes mention of the "sinner who repents" (15:7, 10) in his response to his critics. Similarly, with the paralytic (Mark 2:5) and the prostitute (Luke 7:48, 50), faith/trust is honored—in connection with healing and the forgiveness of sins. Jesus honors trust in him—often in connection with needs for healing and exorcism. In Matthew 11:21 (par.), Jesus upbraids the cities for rejecting him with the indictment that they failed to respond with repentance to Jesus' mighty acts of salvation. Trust in Jesus is characterized as repentance and a corresponding sense of humility. The son who returns (Luke 15:18f.) says that he is no longer worthy to be called a son, but only hopes for treatment

---

7. Cf. also Isa 44:22, "I have swept away your transgressions like a cloud" (cf. also Isa 43:25; Exod 34:6).

as a hired servant. Similarly, the centurion appeals to Jesus with a deep-seated humility, "I am not worthy to have you come under my roof; but only say the word . . ." (Matt 8:8, 10). Jesus honors this humble response in a superlative manner, "I have not found such faith even in Israel" (8:8, 10). Trust is regarded as the basic expression of repentance in that a person is no longer able to rely upon one's own possibilities, but simply to deliver oneself to the forgiveness, support, acceptance and help of Jesus. Trust is expressed through an outstretched and open hand.

What is repentance but a movement back to the God of Israel and covenant relationship and a forward movement to Jesus and his ministry, who ushers in the new age of salvation? In Luke 3, John the Baptist states that repentance for the forgiveness of sins is linked to Isaiah's message about preparing the way for universal salvation (Isa 40:3–5), which, in turn, is linked with specific decisions that people need to make: the crowd (Luke 3:10–11), the tax collectors (3:12–13), the soldiers (3:14). These acts of repentance lead to the promise that Jesus, the coming one, will baptize them in the Holy Spirit and fire (3:16). Jesus' Parable of the Wicked Tenants (Matt 21:33–46) is thoroughly grounded in Isaiah's Song of the Vineyard (compare Matt 21:33 with Isa 5:1–2), which also presses the audience to repentance, even though no such response is forthcoming (Matt 21:45–46). In other passages he directs the attention to his ministry, which ushers in the coming kingdom and also fulfills the prophecy of the OT, "something greater than the temple is here" (12:6).

There are occasions wherein sinners give expression to their repentance. For example, Zacchaeus says, "Behold, Lord, the half of my possessions I give to the poor, and if I have cheated anybody out of anything, I will pay back four times the amount" (Luke 19:8). Similarly, the prostitute in Luke 7 expresses her gratitude to Jesus in an entirely vulnerable manner without any sort of embarrassment. And Jesus says that Simon the Pharisee should recognize that her lavish demonstration is but an expression of the profound gratitude for the forgiveness of sins. In all spheres of Jesus' ministry with the "broken," Jesus accepts people and allows for changed behavior to be the outgrowth of the accepting relationship, whether it means giving up a vocation, altering social conduct, demonstrating love, following in discipleship—all of these are expressions and signs of repentance. Such responses are signs of something personal and profound that has taken root in a person's heart. Thus for example, Jesus honors the faith-response of the healed Samaritan leper and says, "your faith has saved you" (Luke 17:18). The faith-response is understood in the text to be his gratitude that must be expressed to God (18:15) and to Jesus (18:16). While the nine Jewish lepers went their way in a healed condition, the Samaritan leper has experienced real salvation, in that his healing is really incomplete unless he returns to the source of his healing and express his gratitude for what God and Jesus have done for him.

Received Grace Also Leads to Love and Joy

While grace is intended to lead to repentance and trust, it also will be followed with love and joy. A person receives grace and the forgiveness of God at the very point of turning to God as in a return home. It is an occasion of intense love and joy that must be shared (cf. the repeated theme of joy in Luke 15). At the same time, the experience of the grace and forgiveness of God must mean opening oneself up to another. There is no such thing as a privatized experience of God's grace, which makes no impact on other human relationships. By their very nature, forgiveness and grace must be shared with others. Thus, the unthinkable sin is expressed by the Parable of the Unmerciful Servant (Matt 18:23-35); the unconscionable sin is that the forgiveness by the king has had absolutely no effect on the first servant; it is as if the release of the astronomical debt has made no difference in the way that the servant treats a fellow servant; the servant does not even seem to remember that the wording of the plea of his fellow-servant was his own wording (Matt 18:26, 29). This leads Jesus to draw a comparison between the fate of the unmerciful servant and the fate of the one who withholds forgiveness from another (18:35). Indeed, the whole array of community relationships, which are noted in Matthew 18 are to be regarded against the vast backdrop of the unimaginable grace of God. We find that the person who stands aloof from others and withholds forgiveness and grace loses the very mercy and forgiveness of God; perhaps this grace was not really understood or appreciated in the first place. In the Lord's Prayer, the disciples are taught to pray, "Forgive us our debts as we also have forgiven (Matt 6:12 par.);[8] divine forgiveness must make a difference in human forgiveness. Divine grace must make a difference in terms of human grace. Goppelt says, "This correlation between God's forgiveness and forgiving one's neighbor was not a relationship of reciprocity, but a circulatory system. The circular flow between God's forgiveness and human forgiving was destroyed whenever the latter collapsed."[9] Forgiveness did not consist in simple words but the active renewal and restoration of human relationships on an ongoing basis, "I do not say to you seven times, but seventy times seven!" (Matt 18:21f.). Just as Jesus accepted others in an unconditional manner, so he enjoins an

---

8. Cf. also Mark 11:25; 5:23-24.
9. Goppelt, *Theology*, 134.

unconditional acceptance of others. It involves the personal involvement with others in intensely practical ways.

JESUS' GRACE FOR THE "RIGHTEOUS"

Jesus' grace not only reaches out to the "sinners" but to the "righteous" as well. For the people who are "publicly righteous," Jesus tailors his grace-full message to those who need to understand and appropriately respond to his person, words and works. He seeks to help his critics abandon their presuppositions and religious claims that constitute a barrier to relationship with God and others.

With Grace, Jesus Explains the Failure of the "Righteous"

At the same time that Jesus accepts society's "broken" persons, he provokes the "righteous" persons and brings their problem to a head; he creates a genuine crisis for them. In the Parable of the Searching Father, the joyous party that is held for the younger son reveals the heart of the older brother, who is working out in the field. The older brother sums up his past conduct and reveals that he really regards his relationship with his father as an employee to an employer, "Lo, these many years I have served you, and I never disobeyed your command; yet you never gave me a kid, that I might make merry with my friends" (Luke 15:29). This brother also stands aloof from his younger brother, is very angry, and refuses to go in to the celebration of joy (15:28); he distances himself from his brother through the words, "But when *this son of yours*, who has devoured your wealth through prostitutes" (15:31). He is unable to bring himself to say the words, "This brother of mine." His relationship with his father is based on performance and contract and does not reflect a genuine son-father relationship. The "righteous" are able to say, along with the rich young ruler, "all these things I have observed from my youth" (Mark 10:20). The "righteous" also pray in ways similar to the Pharisee in the Parable of the Pharisee and Publican: "Lord, I thank you that I am not like other men, robbers, evildoers, adulterers—or even like this tax collector" (Luke 18:11). Jesus' acceptance of the publicly acknowledged sinners evoked a real crisis for the "righteous." And Jesus explains the crisis and hopes for a positive response from the "righteous."

Why did this crisis develop? For Jesus, relationship to God is far different from a relationship of an employee to an employer. Such things as "score-keeping" and relative merit count for nothing. Jesus dislodges the flimsy supports and props upon which the "righteous" were basing their standing with God. The relationship that Jesus offers is that of grace, mercy and forgiveness—to a Father who only deals with his people on the basis of grace. Jesus' accepting treatment of the "sinners" is an incredible threat to personal life that is based upon performance and reward. The relative achievement and performance that one might be able to point to with pride are rendered superfluous; they mean absolutely nothing to God. God is a Father who seeks out relationship with people, which is based solely on their response to Jesus and his message of grace, mercy, forgiveness and acceptance.

In the Parable of the Workers in the Vineyard (Matt 20:1–16), Jesus informs his people that God is utterly free to extend the grace of the kingdom, while he maintains justice and order. Correspondingly, people must abandon their "work-ethic" and live in the light of God's mercy. The parable is not about business practice. Indeed if employers today were to treat their employees as the parable's householder treats his workers, they would face costly suits or undergo endless court battles. The parable, however, is about God and the utterly free way that he relates to humans who are accustomed to a system of work-payment.

The parable is closely related to its context on either side, for it is a parable of contrast. The contrast appears between the "first" and the "last." Indeed, Jesus' parable is literally surrounded by texts which affirm either "first ones will be last and last ones first" (Matt 19:30) or "the last ones will be first, and the first, last" (20:16). The contrast revealed in the reversal of positions is so unusual that it needs the reiteration, which it receives. The surprising element is the free, unmitigated, undeserved, and unencumbered grace of God that shines forth in an amazing way in the treatment of the workers by the owner of the vineyard.

The parable appears appropriately where it is—*after* the question of the "reward-obsessed" Peter (Matt 19:27) and *before* the self-seeking ambition of two other disciples who desire for themselves the choice position on the right hand and left hand of Jesus in the messianic kingdom (20:21–22). Peter's question breathes the air of the principle of recompense for self-renouncing discipleship. To be sure, faithful discipleship to Jesus will receive a just reward. Thus, Jesus' assurance to Peter of a fitting recompense for the committed service of Jesus' followers is both firm and explicit (19:28–29). Such recompense will be spelled out in still another parable, the Parable of the Talents (25:14–23) including the master's affirmation, "Well done . . ." (25:21, 23). But at the same time, disciples need to be reminded that another principle exists in the divine economy, i.e., the standard of divine grace. It is grace that defies all human standards, grace that is free of all legal norms except the law of boundless love such as the parable suggests.

It is significant that the householder makes a specific financial agreement, only with the group hired at 6:00 a.m. During the workday, there are five different groups that are hired:

Time of Hiring	Wage/Promise	Hours Worked	Work Conditions	Actual Wage
early, 6:00 a.m.	a denarius	12	heavy load and heat of the day	1 denarius
9:00 a.m.	"go into the vineyard . . . whatever is right I will give"	9		1 denarius
12:00 p.m.	he did the same	6		1 denarius
3:00 p.m.	he did the same	3		1 denarius
5:00 p.m.	"you go into the vineyard	1	cool evening breeze	1 denarius

The point of tension in the parable is created by the unusual command concerning *the order of payment*. If the workers had been paid in the order of their hiring, everybody would have gone home content—able to enjoy the evening, and nobody would be the wiser. With this novel feature, Jesus lets "the first be witnesses of the extremely generous payment of their comrades."[10]

The generosity of the householder causes the minds of the 6:00 a.m. workers to go wild with expectation. If payment is given at the rate of one denarius per hour, then they should receive at least twelve denarii. The workers who have worked for twelve hours feel a sense of double injustice. In their minds, equal wages for workers who have worked for one hour or twelve hours is unfair, and on top of that, the working conditions have been much different. The response of the householder is threefold:

(1) The owner is free to do what he wills with his money. He can be gracious, in that he possesses the full right of disposal of his property as he sees fit (Matt 20:15).

(2) Justice is maintained. As far as justice is concerned, there can be no grounds for complaint, for the owner has kept his word. Those who have worked all day received pay for a full day's work, i.e. the agreed upon denarius; grace or goodness cannot really function if it is extended at the expense of justice.

---

10. Linnemann, *Parables of Jesus*, 84.

(3) Exposure of the real motives. If there is a problem, fault, or blame, it lies with the grumbler, who has an evil eye, expressed by the owner's rhetorical question, "Is your eye evil, because I am good?" (Matt 20:15). Luther translates the question, "Is your eye cross-eyed because I am generous?"

The parable is concluded by a summary application, taking the reader back to 19:30, and thus, the parable appears to explain the saying about the first becoming last. However, it is not altogether clear how the parable emphasizes the reversal.[11] True, the first workers are paid the same as the last (1 denarius). However, the major thrust of the parable is not on the reversal from first to last or last to first, but the employer's freedom to be gracious. Thus, the clear-cut system of performance-reward is violated by the grace and freedom of God evident in the life and ministry of Jesus. He upsets the religious system and order, even the performance-reward expectation of his disciples (Matt 19:27).

In terms of life-setting and audience, the parable is clearly oriented toward the point of tension, voiced by the grumblers, echoed by Jesus' critics, even Jesus' disciples. The ones with the problem are those who are indignant and who protest the generosity of the householder.

> Jesus was minded to show them how unjustified, hateful, loveless, and unmerciful was their criticism. Such, said he, is God's goodness, and since God is so good, so am I. He vindicates the gospel against its critics . . . over and over again we hear the charge brought against Jesus that he is a companion of the despised and outcast, and are told of men to whom the gospel is an offense.[12]

Careful accounting of God's grace, tabulated with the "spread-sheets" of others, does not belong to the human domain; Jesus leads his people to reckon with a person's need to appropriate divine grace, without looking into another's "ledger." He initiates a new way of thinking about God and his freedom to order life in his sovereign and graceful way. The parable concerns God and his free grace. It challenges the reader to affirm God's freedom to be gracious without grumbling over the grace given to others who may seem to be less deserving.

Jesus makes a tremendous claim. The free and gracious activity of the employer is exemplified in Jesus. His action, reflected in the vineyard owner

---

11. Due to the interruption of the saying between the thematic concerns of chaps. 19 and 20, and the difficulty of relating the saying to the parable, Crossan assumes the saying is a Matthean addition to the parable. Crossan, *Parables*, 112.

12. Jeremias, *New Testament Theology*, 38.

is comparable to God's. The story-parable expresses the freedom of God to be gracious and good (ἀγαθός). God's grace and goodness shatters all religious barriers that people erect before God and others. Jesus' people depend upon their acceptance of God's gracious dealings and upon their willingness to allow their narrow calculations to be shattered by his grace. Thus, the parable proclaims the freedom of God in the person of Jesus to express his unmerited favor, generosity and love.

Grace Summons the "Righteous" to Attitudes of Joy and Acceptance

The trilogy of parables in Luke 15 is told to the "righteous," who critique Jesus' table fellowship with the publicly acknowledged sinners. Not only do the three parables justify Jesus' involvement with "sinners," but the parables also constitute a genuine invitation to the critics to share in the joy of the sheep that is found, the coin that is found and the son who has been found. At the end of the third parable, the father is still outside with the older brother, summoning him to "come out from the cold" and to enjoy the celebratory feast; however, the parable itself does not contain the final response of the older brother. Similarly, the Parable of the Two Debtors in Luke 7:40–47 is an invitation to repentance that means joy. Surely Jesus summons Simon and his dinner guests to adopt his open invitation; the paragraph is open-ended in that we do not learn how Simon or his guests finally responded to Jesus' words. Repentance means giving up a position of servitude in relationship with God and assuming an attitude of rejoicing, non-judgment and celebration of life. God is not interested in a relationship with people of servitude and bondage, but family relationship, celebration, joy and acceptance. Repentance means desisting from judgment and critique; the path to repentance is different from the path of the "sinner;" it means leaving behind the relative "righteousness" that has been gained. As such, this type of repentance is more difficult since there is more to leave behind. Jesus issues the invitation to joy and celebration.

Grace Summons the "Righteous" to Re-evaluate "Scorekeeping"

Jesus also beckons the "righteous" to re-evaluate their "score-keeping" mentality, and thereby exposes their real motive—"to be noticed by others." This constitutes a human reward that leaves no room for a divine reward. In Matthew 6, Jesus uses four particular examples of religious "score-keeping" or public piety (dikaiosu/nh Matt 6:1). We find a relationship of general to the particular with respect to four specific religious practices in several paragraphs:

- Generalization—"practicing piety" (6:1)
- Particular—"giving alms" (6:2-4)
- Particular—"prayer" (6:5-6)
- Particular—"praying profusely" (6:7-15)
- Particular—"fasting" (6:16-18)

The general expression "practicing piety" is followed by several particular examples that illustrate the general principle. In each instance, Jesus envisions a religious observance, which is intended to be noticed by others, informs his listeners that there will be no future reward with God, and points them to the private expressions of piety, which will be rewarded by God. For persons who keep score of their own religious performance, Jesus says they have their reward in full. The verb "have" in Matthew 6:5, is ἀπέχω, and signifies a receipt that one has received what he was after, i.e., fully paid. Thus, the verb is used to inform the "righteous" who keep score, who seek elevated religious status through their pious activity, that they have received their reward in full. There is no more to come. Only those who did these things in secret without thought of human reward and recognition—only these persons would receive reward and recognition by God. In the giving of money, the persons were to give in secret, without a left hand knowing what the right hand is doing (6:3). The term "in secret" means that the doer gives without self-consciousness. Those who find acceptance with God in the final judgment will be surprised at their reward; they will express surprise as did the sheep in the Parable of the Sheep and Goats, "Lord, when did we see you hungry and feed you, or thirsty and give you something to drink? When did we see you a stranger and invite you in, or needing clothes and clothe you? When did we see you sick or in prison and go to visit you?" (Matt 25:37-39). The sheep are utterly surprised and do not remember their acts of religious piety.

Our culture is infused with ideas of performance and reward that have been so deeply ingrained in us from childhood on:

> The early bird gets the worm. (early performance)
> No pain no gain. (disciplined performance)
> Demand your rights. (justified reward based on performance)

> There is no such thing as a free lunch. (reward comes because of performance)
> I work for what I earn. (wages are a result of performance)
> You get what you pay for. (purchases—rewards are based on paying-performance)
> People get what they deserve—nothing more nothing less.[13] (performance—reward)

And yet, this type of work ethic creeps like a vicious cancer into organized religious life then and now. If we "have the ears to hear," we soon discover in our religious life, that we do not get what we have deserved. "I deserved punishment and got forgiveness. I deserved wrath and got love. I deserved debtor's prison and got instead a clean credit history. I deserved stern lectures and crawl-on-your-knees repentance. I got a banquet—spread for me."[14]

Grace Offers a Continued Genuine Invitation with a Corresponding Threat

Even though Jesus defends his table fellowship and acceptance with society's low-lifers, he nonetheless extends a genuine invitation to the "righteous." It is important to note that the Parable of the Searching Father concludes with the father inviting the older son into the celebration of the return of the younger son. He also searches for the "righteous" son; he is outside with the older brother, pleading with him to enter the festive celebration. The celebration is incomplete without the presence of the older brother. Jesus' offer of salvation to the "righteous" is genuine and it reaches out to them as well as the publicly acknowledged sinners. At the same time, the path to salvation is still marked by repentance, although in a different form than the "sinners." Repentance for the "righteous" means an abandonment of religious pride, a performance-reward system, and a sideward look at others. The Parable of the Pharisee and the Tax Collector (Luke 18:9–14) is introduced by the explanation for why Jesus spoke the parable. He seeks to undercut "those who trusted in themselves and looked upon others with contempt" (18:9); he rejects both self-trust and the sideward glance at others.

If the invitation to the "righteous" is not received, then Jesus turns to others who will accept the invitation. Many of Jesus' sayings and parables affirm God's freedom to invite others; God is not beholden or dependent

---

13. Yancey, *Grace*, 64.
14. Ibid.

upon Israel and its leaders. Jesus says, "Many will come from east and west and sit at table with Abraham . . . in the Kingdom of Heaven" (Matt. 8:11). The invitation of others is well expressed in the Parable of the Wicked Tenants and the Parable of the Great Banquet (Luke 14:16–24) or Parable of the Marriage Feast (Matt 21:33–46). While Luke's Gospel contains a greater posture of openness to the "righteous," Matthew's Gospel reflects a polemical posture of warning and judgment for failing to appropriately respond to the gracious invitation. Matthew contains the Parable of the Two Sons (Matt 21:28–32), which is clearly polemical, "Truly I say to you, the tax collectors and prostitutes enter the Kingdom of God before you," which conveys the exclusive sense, "the tax collectors and prostitutes enter the Kingdom of God, but not you." The "righteous" have missed their chance; they are also like the guests to the wedding banquet who have murdered the messengers who came with the invitation, or murdered the vineyard owner's son (Mark 21:33–46).

IMPLICATIONS

Many people read the Bible as if it were simply a moral code, clothed with sacred authority, and in large part, an inspired book containing prohibitions and instructions that would lead us to a utopian-like existence if they are strictly followed. Consequently, religious people try to follow the biblical principles and codes, largely negative in character, and find nothing but guilt and despair or pride in their own relative "righteousness." Often the Bible is used to reinforce the ideas of the taboo and moralism. Tournier says, "Taboo is a magical prohibition: 'This is unclean, do not touch; this is forbidden, do not do it.' Taboos are prohibitions loaded with menacing dread. Moralism follows—the setting up of a rigorous code of prohibitions, a moral code . . . Religion is what you must do."[15] Thus, the rich young ruler wonders what he must *do* to inherit eternal life (Mark 10:17–22). Many of Jesus' pointed words, directed to the Pharisees deal with their external practicing of the moral code, which is based on the taboo. When people practice narrow moralism, they so easily fall into the trap of self-satisfaction with their relative righteousness, repress their conscience, or they fall into the pit of despair over their complete inability to achieve the moralistic standard. Thus, Jesus says, his critics "strain out a gnat and swallow a camel," or tithe tiny garden spices and neglect the weightier matters—justice, mercy and faithfulness (Matt 23:23).

---

15. Tournier, *Guilt and Grace*, 119.

The people whom Jesus welcomes with acceptance and affirmation are not the virtuous but the despised, not the important but the insignificant, not the "whole" but the "fragmented" and "broken," not the healthy but the sick, not those of social or religious position but the marginalized, those who are on the fringes.

The Church proclaims the grace of God and yet, moralism finds its insidious path into the life of the Church and Christian experience. Moralism is a negation of the grace of God. Down through the years of Church history, we read of various revivals and renewals that have occurred. New and fresh religious movements arise and religious orders are established (Saint Augustine, Saint Francis of Assisi, Saint Benedict, the Reformers, the Wesleys, etc.). The Spirit of God infuses people with new life and transformation. God's love is rediscovered anew and afresh and all pettiness is pushed aside. People experience the unbelievable grace of God; people are called to ministry and there is a freshness and vibrancy of faith. People feel welcomed and not judged; they experience the joy and liberty of being in Christ, they are transformed and practice genuine piety and Christian love.[16]

But with each successive revival, moralism makes its entrance and slowly creeps into the Christian life and Christian community. And moralism is the very negation of the basic principle and dynamic of grace. Rules emerge—written and unwritten codes of conduct begin to surface, prohibitions multiply. And with the entrance of moralism judgment appears. People who are unable to subscribe to certain standards feel alienated and outside of the religious loop. And then, hypocrisy begins to make its entrance into personal and community life. Hypocrisy rears its ugly head when people try to live up to this moralistic standard and cannot succeed. Thus, people begin to appear to be better than they are and begin to hide their faults and sins instead of confessing them. People pretend to be more pious than they are; this was the very sin of Ananias and Sapphira (Acts 5:1–11). With the entrance of moralism, the Spirit of God is likewise stifled. And in an effort to cling to some form of security, people cling all the more to certain principles and standards; often they become obsessed with their particular codes by which they themselves cannot live. Correspondingly, what had been a joyous encounter with God becomes constraint and legalism, obligation, fear of criticism and a picture of God as a severe judge, who is waiting for the moment to punish the one who breaks the moralistic code.

Jesus welcomes the sinners with open arms—those who do not deny their guilt, but those who confess it and are so aware of their brokenness and impotence. His grace is unconditional; his forgiveness is limitless. The

---

16. Yancey, *What's So Amazing about Grace?*, 64.

OT prophets had denounced the sins of the virtuous people and the silliness of ritual as a means of ensuring a clear conscience. "And Jesus Christ gives the final blow, by convicting of guilt the moral and scrupulous people, by proclaiming that all people are equally sinful despite all their efforts, so that not by showing off their vaunted impeccability, but by confessing their guilt, by repentance, will they find the grace which erases it."[17]

Jesus embodies, models, and teaches a grace-filled lifestyle in which he reaches out to both the "sinners" and the "righteous." In so doing, he anticipates a grace-filled response from all to his inclusive message of grace. In a paragraph from the Sermon on the Mount\Plain (Matt 5:43–48; Luke 6:27–36), Jesus underscores the truth that God is impartial in his dealings with all of humanity: "he is graceful [χρηστός] to both the ungrace-full [ἀχαρίστους] and to the evil [πονηρούς]" (Luke 6:35). Matthew's version says that God's gracious activity is impartial and goes out to both the evil and the good: "He causes the sun to shine *upon the evil and the good* [ἐπὶ πονηρούς καὶ ἀγαθούς], and he sends rain *upon the righteous and the unrighteous* [ἐπὶ δικαίους καὶ ἀδίκαιους]" (Matt 5:45). Thus, the people of God are to mirror God's gracious impartiality: "Be merciful as your heavenly father is merciful" (Luke 6:36).[18] The message of grace is so comforting for some and alarming for others. Some approach Jesus with fear and reservation, believing that God could not love them because of who they have been or what they have done. Other people approach Jesus with self-confidence and pride and trust in their relative "righteousness." Jesus meets both groups where they are in their various "life-stations;" his embodied message is both an incredible comfort and a challenging affront. But Jesus is very clear in his teaching to both groups; the lesson needs to be received and appropriated by both groups: *Appreciate the freedom of God to be gracious.*

BIBLIOGRAPHY

Crossan, John Dominic. *In Parables: The Challenge of the Historical Jesus*. New York: Harper & Row, 1973.
Goppelt, Leonard. *Theology of the New Testament*. Edited by Jürgen Roloff. Translated by John E. Alsup. Grand Rapids: Eerdmans, 1981.
Jeremias, Joachim. *New Testament Theology: The Proclamation of Jesus*. New York: Scribner, 1977.

---

17. Tournier, *Guilt and Grace*, 122.

18. Matthew's expression, "Be perfect as your heavenly father is perfect" uses the adjective "perfect" (τέλειος Matt 5:48), which is to be similarly understood as "complete/whole" with respect to God's impartial nature and impartial dealings with humanity, for the righteous and the good.

Linnemann, Eta. *Parables of Jesus: Introduction and Exposition*. London: SPCK, 1966.
Tournier, Paul. *Guilt and Grace: A Psychological Study*. New York: Harper & Row, 1982.
Volf, Miroslav. *Exclusion and Embrace: A Theological Exploration of Identity, Otherness, and Reconciliation*. Nashville: Abingdon, 1996.
Yancey, Philip. *What's So Amazing about Grace?* Grand Rapids: Zondervan, 1997.

7

Is the Origin of the Spirit Still a Theological Impasse?

A Modest Ecumenical Proposal about the Derivation of the Spirit in the Trinity

—Veli-Matti Kärkkäinen

The still continuing and unresolved ecumenical and theological problem that had a decisive effect in the split between the Christian East and West is simply this:[1] Should we continue with the (Western church's addition to the original Constantinopolitan creed) *filioque* clause, according to which the Spirit proceeds from the Father *and* the Son or return to the original formulation strongly advocated by the Christian East? Are there any prospects for rapprochement here?[2]

---

1. The standard view of the addition of the *filioque* clause is that it was first accepted by the Council of Toledo in 589 and ratified by the 809 Aachen Synod. It was incorporated in later creeds such as that of the Fourth Lateran Council in 1215 and the Council of Lyons in 1274. It is recited in liturgy throughout Western Christianity (both Catholic and Protestant).

2. This essay builds on and significantly expands the discussion of the *filioque* in my *Trinity and Revelation*, chap. 11. I also glean much material from my *Trinity: Global Perspectives*, 44–50, 56–59; "Is the Spirit Still the Dividing Line Between the Christian East and West? Revisiting an Ancient Problem of Filioque with a Hope for an

According to conventional theological wisdom, "in general, Greek theology emphasizes the divine hypostases (persons), whereas Latin theology emphasizes the divine nature."[3] In other words, it is claimed that the East begins with the threeness of the Trinity, the West with the oneness or unity.[4] While not without grounds, this kind of description is also a caricature and should be qualified.[5]

With these viewpoints in mind, this investigation proceeds in two stages. First, instead of a generic historical study, we take a focused look at the chief features of the Christian West's trinitarian formulations beginning from Augustinian theology, as well as its relation to the Eastern tradition as established by the Cappadocians, with a view to the challenges and potentials for a contemporary convergence. The second stage examines and assesses the current ecumenical proposals for rapprochement.

THE ROLE OF THE SPIRIT IN THE TRINITY IN AUGUSTINE'S VIEW

One of the continuously disputed questions that has everything to do with the resolution of the filioque problem relates to the legacy of Augustine's Trinitarian thinking.[6] More recent study sees a definite shift in the interpretation of Augustine's trinitarian theology underway. The older consensus is that because of his neo-Platonic leanings, Augustine one-sidedly put stress on the unity of the divine essence and had a hard time accounting for distinctions. That would of course mean that his approach was diametrically opposed to the Eastern view.[7] All of this has even caused some to speak of

---

Ecumenical Rapprochement," 125–42.

3. LaCugna, "Trinitarian Mystery of God," 170. LaCugna calls the Eastern view emanationist in terms of descending order from Father to Son to Spirit and finally to the world, whereas the Western can be depicted as a circle enclosing all Trinitarian members in which the whole Trinity relates to the world (170–71).

4. The classic work contrasting Eastern and Western views is Régnon, *Études de théologie positive sur la sainte Trinité*; see also Congar, *I Believe in the Holy Spirit*, 3:xv–xxi.

5. O'Collins, *Tripersonal God*, 140.

6. "It is impossible to do contemporary Trinitarian theology and not have a judgment on Augustine." Barnes, "Rereading Augustine's Theology of the Trinity," 145.

7. So, e.g., Prestige, *God in Patristic Thought*, 237; and Margerie, *Christian Trinity in History*, 110–21. One of the most vocal contemporary critics of Augustine along this line, Colin Gunton, has argued that Augustine did not correctly understand the tradition, certainly not the teaching of the Cappadocians, and ended up viewing the divine substance "behind" relations. For the Cappadocians, so this critic says, on the contrary, relations are "ontological" whereas for the Bishop of Hippo only "logical."

the "Theological Crisis of the West!"[8] Not all are convinced, however, that this is a fair reading of Augustine.[9] Two foundational problems appear in the older interpretation of Augustine, the correction of which may change our picture of the view of the Trinity held by this most influential early Western theologian. First, we know now that an unnuanced attribution to the Cappadocians—as a counterpart to the West—of either a social doctrine of the Trinity or even a consistent and authentic establishment of the threeness may be an unfounded assumption. Second, it is also a widely debated question in contemporary scholarship whether Augustine really started with the unity of the divine essence rather than with the distinctiveness of persons. Contemporary study suggests that Augustine could have built on the Cappadocians' view rather than serving as a counterexample: "Augustine begins where the Cappadocians leave off: accepting their answer to the question why not 'three gods?' he proceeds to ask 'three *what*?'"[10] The best way to look at this debate is to discern key ideas in Augustine's Trinitarian teaching.

Augustine of course affirms the tradition concerning consubstantiality as well as distinctions of the Son and Spirit.[11] Furthermore, somewhat similarly to Eastern theologians, Augustine depicts the Father as the *principium*, the primary or beginning of the deity.[12] Well known are the reflections of Augustine on the Spirit in the Trinity. He conceives of the Spirit as

---

Gunton's critique, however, as the discussion will reveal, is one-sided at its best. See *Promise of Trinitarian Theology*, 38–43. The same can be said of the opinion by Marsh, who accuses Augustine of replacing the earlier Latin emphasis on the divine monarchy of the Father with "divine substance or nature which *then* is verified in Father, Son and Holy Spirit." Marsh, *Triune God*, 132.

8. Gunton, "Augustine, the Trinity, and the Theological Crisis of the West," 33–58.

9. The most vocal critic of the alleged neoplatonic influence on Augustine is Barnes, "Rereading Augustine's Theology of the Trinity." A careful, cautious interpretation, quite critical of the old consensus, is offered by Studer, *Trinity and Incarnation*, 167–85.

10. Cary, "Historical Perspectives on Trinitarian Doctrine," 9. A helpful summary of views pro and con can be found in Olson and Hall, *The Trinity*, 44–45.

11. E.g., Augustine, *Letters* 169 (To Bishop Evodius) 2.5: "let us at the same time believe that the Son is not [the person] who is the Father, and the Father is not [the person] who is the Son, and neither the Father nor the Son is [the person] who is the Spirit of both the Father and the Son . . . [and] that these Three are equal and co-eternal, and absolutely of one nature" For the consubstantiality of the Son with the Father, see e.g., Augustine, *On the Trinity* 1.6.9; and for the Spirit with the Father and Son, see e.g., *On the Trinity* 1.6.13; 7.3.6. (All references to Augustine's works, unless otherwise mentioned, come from the standard English translation in *The Nicene and Post Nicene Fathers of the Christian Church*, Series 1, vols. 1–8, available at www.ccel.org.)

12. Augustine, *On the Trinity* 4.20.28–29. See further, Studer, *Grace of Christ and Grace of God in Augustine*, 104–5.

communion (of the Father and the Son),[13] their shared love,[14] and a gift.[15] In book 8 of *De Trinitate*, he develops his thought on the Trinity with the help of the idea of interpersonal love in terms of filiation and paternity. The Father is Lover, the Son the Beloved, and the Spirit the mutual Love that connects the two. Here of course the obvious question arises of whether this depersonalizes the Spirit: shared love can hardly be a "person."[16] My opinion is that Augustine himself hardly is guilty of depersonalization as he utilizes other metaphors that lean toward personal notions, but that in the subsequent theological tradition, Augustine's legacy was often turned into a marginalization of the personal nature of the Spirit.

For Augustine, the incarnation is a major Trinitarian event, and it shapes his view of the Trinity more fully than is often acknowledged by his interpreters.[17] He takes pains in convincing his readers that the incarnation is a unique event. For example, in expositing the Gospel story about Jesus' baptism, Augustine argues that while both the manifestation of the Spirit in the form of a dove and the Father's voice from above were temporary and symbolic, the incarnation is a permanent assumption of humanity in a real union of two natures.[18] As mentioned above, Wolfhart Pannenberg has shown convincingly that "Augustine took over the relational definition of the Trinitarian distinctions which the Cappadocians, following Athanasius, had developed. He made the point that the distinctions of the persons are conditioned by their mutual relations."[19] For Augustine the relations are eternal.[20] The Eastern idea of *perichoresis*, mutual interpenetration, is no stranger to his views.[21] At the same time, Augustine was also building on

---

13 Augustine, *On the Trinity* 5.11.12; 15.27.50. See further, Ratzinger, "The Holy Spirit as *Communio*," 325–39.

14. Augustine, *On the Trinity* 15.17.27; Augustine, *[Homilies] Tractates on the Gospel of St. John* 105.7.3.

15. Augustine, *On the Trinity* 5.12.13; 5.15.16.

16. Hilberath, "Pneumatologie," 446–47.

17. See further, Barnes, "Rereading," 154–68; Studer, *Trinity and Incarnation*, 168–85.

18. Augustine, *Letters* 169.2.5–9.

19. Pannenberg, *Systematic Theology*, 284, here refers to Augustine, *On the Trinity* 8.1. In his *Sermon on New Testament Lessons*, Augustine speaks of a distinction of persons and an inseparableness of operation (2.1–23, especially 2.15). See also *On the Trinity* 5.11.12 for an important statement about relationality in the Trinity.

20. Pannenberg, *Systematic Theology*, 1:284.

21. In *On the Trinity* (6.10.12.), Augustine says it strongly: "[I]n that highest Trinity one is as much as the three together, nor are two anything more than one. And They are infinite in themselves. So both each are in each, and all in each, and each in all, and all in all, and all are one."

the Cappadocians' idea mentioned above of the unity of the three persons in their outward works, which has the consequence that from the creaturely works we may know the divine unity.[22]

It is often claimed that the psychological analogies are key to the Trinitarian teaching in Augustine. But it has to be noted that before the Bishop of Hippo presents the psychological analogies in his *De Trinitate*, for the first seven chapters he delves into many biblical teachings and metaphors. Only in the latter part of his main work on the Trinity[23] does he employ images such as *mens/notitia/amor*—mind, mind's knowledge of itself, and the mind's love for itself—as an illustration of the Father as Being, the Son as Consciousness, and the Spirit as Love.[24] His logic is compelling: if the human mind knows love in itself, it knows God since God is love. These illustrations are of course biblically sustainable based on the idea of humanity as *imago Dei* (Gen 1:26–27). However, it is important to note that while Augustine's derivation of the Trinitarian distinctions was by and large based on the divine unity, that is not the whole picture and, at times, not even his main tactic. The psychological analogies that he suggested and developed in his work on the Trinity were simply meant to offer a very general way of linking the unity and trinity and thus creating some plausibility for trinitarian statements.[25] Furthermore, the Bishop of Hippo was aware of the limitation of the images.[26] The potential weakness of this analogy of self-presence, self-knowledge, and self-love—widely used in subsequent tradition—is that it leans toward a "monopersonal, modalistic view of God."[27] This is interesting in that in principle Augustine's analogies grow out of an interpersonal, thus communal and relational context, especially when it comes to love.

To Augustine's credit, it has to be added also that he considered the origin of the Spirit in a nuanced way. The Spirit proceeds "originally" from

---

22. Augustine, *On the Trinity* 1.4.7; 4.21.30; see further, Pannenberg, *Systematic Theology*, 1:283–84.

23. In addition to *On the Trinity* 8–15, analogies are also discussed in *[Homilies] Tractates on the Gospel of St. John* 23, as well as in *Letters* 11 and 169, among others.

24. Augustine, *On the Trinity* 8.10.14; 9.2.2. The idea of Mind, of course, has its legacy in early Christian theology beginning from the Apologists, who taught that, as the Word, the Son is the Father's thought/idea. Augustine also developed further the idea of the "vestiges of the Trinity" with the help of the tripartite constitution of the human soul, *memoria/intelligentia/voluntas*: memory, intelligence, and willing. Augustine, *On the Trinity* 9.8; 10.10.14–16; 11.10–17,18.

25. Pannenberg, *Systematic Theology*, 1:284; see also p. 287: "Augustine's psychological analogies should not be used to derive the trinity from the unity but to simply illustrate the Trinity in whom one already believes."

26. Augustine, *On the Trinity* 15.23.43.

27. O'Collins, *The Tripersonal God*, 137.

the Father and also in common from both the Father and Son, as something given by the Father.[28] In other words, he was careful in safeguarding the Father as the primary source of the Spirit[29]—an idea dear to the Christian East. And even when the Son is included in the act of procession of the Spirit, it is not from two sources but rather from a single source in order to protect the divine unity.[30] Again here, Augustine's legacy is somewhat ambiguous. On the one hand, there is no denying that Augustine's idea of the Spirit as the shared love between Father and Son and his teaching about the double procession of the Spirit helped the Christian West to ratify the *filioque* clause. On the other hand, if the West had been more sensitive to the shared tradition and to the sensibilities of the East, Augustine's idea of the procession of the Spirit from the Father through the Son, and thus in a secondary way, possibly could have helped avoid the conflict between East and West. Eastern theologians are not necessarily against the idea of the Spirit proceeding from the Father (who is the source after all) through the Son. And for Augustine, unlike so much of later Western tradition, the Spirit's derivation also from the Son did not necessarily mean inferiority in status any more than does the Son's generation from the Father (this was of course the affirmation against the Arians).[31]

THE AUGUSTINIAN HERITAGE IN RELATION TO THE CAPPADOCIANS' THEOLOGY

Now, in light of key ideas in Augustinian teaching, we can try to address at least tentatively the question of whether the Christian East and West confess the same Trinitarian faith. As repeated above, it is very important to make the distinction between Augustine's own ideas and his legacy as carried on by later (Western) tradition. Looking at Augustine's own writings, "[i]t hardly appears that Augustine had little interest in the distinctions of the persons, or that he was averse to the full import of the Incarnation."[32] Nor is it true that Augustine developed his Trinitarian theology abstractly based on analogies; he did not. He is thoroughly biblical, as a quick look, for example, in the first half of the *De Trinitate* clearly shows, let alone his biblical expositions. Nor is it right to say that—in contrast to the Cappadocians and

---

28. Augustine, *On the Trinity* 15.26.47.
29. See Augustine, *On the Trinity* 4.20.29.
30. Augustine, *On the Trinity* 5.14.
31. See further, O'Collins, *Tripersonal God*, 139.
32. Letham, *Holy Trinity In Scripture, History, Theology, and Worship*, 195.

Athanasius—Augustine neglected spirituality and salvation.[33] His focus on incarnation would itself rebut this charge. In light of these considerations, a more nuanced and sophisticated way of looking at the differences between the Christian East and West is in order.[34] I think it is best done by trying to discern the key characteristics and unique features in each without trying to artificially reconcile those or make them more dramatic than they are.

It is widely agreed that for Eastern theologians the significance of the *hypostatic* distinctions among Father, Son, and Spirit was a key concern. The East has wanted to speak of the "concrete particularity of Father, Son, and Spirit."[35] Furthermore, as is routinely noted, their theology emphasized the Father as the source of the deity. The Son and Spirit proceed from the Father from eternity. In the West, more emphasis has often been placed on the divine being/substance/essence from which the personal distinctions derive. A consequence has been an emphasis on the joint working of the three in the world.[36] Whatever the difference between the Christian East and West, each of them has faced its own challenges: for the East, it was the danger of tritheism because of the emphasis on three different *hypostaseis* and of subordinationism because of the idea of the Father as the source of divinity. Westerners have tended to be more modalistic. Moreover, Eastern theological traditions in general and Trinitarian ones in particular have been more pneumatologically oriented, whereas in the West Christology has often played the key role.

Having said all this, one also has to acknowledge that several aspects of the Augustinian tradition that were picked up by later Western tradition led to the eclipse of the Trinitarian doctrine so evident in the judgment of contemporary theologians. First, with all his stress on relationality, there is no denying that Augustine also emphasizes the divine unity and substance.[37] Therefore, there is some truth in the insistence that whereas for the

33. This is one of the theses of LaCugna's *God for Us*, 81–104.

34. Overstatements abound, and those need to be corrected: "We must acknowledge that the doctrine of the trinity in the East is an integral part of its total theological understanding. The same cannot be said for the Western formulation stemming chiefly from Augustine. Here, the doctrine is an unneeded appendage to theology." Cobb, "The Relativization of the Trinity," 5.

35. Grenz, *Rediscovering the Triune God*, 39.

36. This is the so-called Augustinian rule: the works of the Trinity *ad extra* are indivisible.

37. LaCugna's comment is an overstatement, yet contains a kernel of truth: "[Augustine's] focus on the individual apart from its personal and social relations flows directly from the ontology that begins from substance rather than person" (*God for Us*, 102). LaCugna, however, qualifies this by saying that was not Augustine's intention, yet it was picked up by his followers.

Christian East distinctions of persons (*hypostaseis*) are the key to Trinity; for Augustine the emphasis is on substance although thereby he is not neglecting relations either. Second, Augustine's idea of the Spirit as shared love between Father and Son is problematic ecumenically and biblically. In the Bible, God is love rather than the Spirit. Furthermore, Augustine's idea feeds the idea of *filioque*. Third, this analogy can hardly argue for any distinct personality of the Spirit. Fourth, while Augustine seems to handle analogies of the Trinity with care and is aware of their limitations, many of his followers elevated them to a role that easily leads away from the concrete biblical salvation history into abstract speculations. While valid in itself—based on the idea that humanity is created in the image of the Triune God—it can end up being a Trinitarian theology "from below." There are not only similarities but also differences between the Trinity and humanity.[38]

CONCLUDING REMARKS: TOWARD AN ECUMENICAL RESOLUTION

As is well known, the NT does not clarify either the interrelations of Father, Son, and Spirit, or the relation of the Spirit to Father and Son. On the one hand, Jesus says that he himself will send the Spirit (John 16:7) or that he will send the Spirit (called *Parakletos* here) who proceeds from the Father (15:26). On the other hand, Jesus prays to the Father for him to send the Spirit (14:16), and the Father will send the Spirit in Jesus' name (v. 26). Because of the lack of clarity in the biblical record as well as the rise to prominence of the Augustinian idea of the Spirit as shared love, the Christian West added the Spirit's dual procession, *filioque*. The Christian East objected vigorously to this addition claiming that it was a one-sided addition without ecumenical consultation,[39] that it compromises the monarchy of the Father as the source of divinity,[40] and that it subordinates the Spirit to Jesus with theological corollaries in ecclesiology, the doctrine of salvation, and so on.[41]

---

38. See further, Volf, "'The Trinity Is Our Social Program,'" 403–23.

39. "Can a clause deriving from one theological tradition simply be inserted in a creed deriving from another theological tradition without council?" Stylianopoulos and Heim, eds., *Spirit of Truth*, 32.

40. Ware, *The Orthodox Church*, 210–14, defends the Father's monarchy as the reason for opposing *filioque*, and critiques the Western idea of Father and Son as two independent sources of the Spirit. Ware, however, does not take into consideration the quite nuanced view of Augustine according to which the Father is the principal source while the Son is the source of the Spirit in a derivative sense (Augustine, *On the Trinity* 15.17.27).

41. Lossky has most dramatically articulated the charge of "Christomonism" against

Despite its exaggerations,[42] the Eastern critique of the *filioque* is important both ecumenically and theologically and should not be dismissed.[43] The West did not have the right to unilaterally add *filioque*.[44]

That said, in my judgment, *filioque* is not heretical even though ecumenically and theologically it is unacceptable and therefore should be removed.[45] Ecumenically and theologically it would be important for the East to be able to acknowledge the nonheretical nature of the addition—if not for other reasons, then because the biblical data is ambiguous. Furthermore, the Christian East should keep in mind the fact that with all its problems, at first the *filioque*, as mentioned above, was used in the West in support of consubstantiality, an idea shared by both traditions.[46]

While there are those who for some reason or another support the *filioque* clause,[47] there is a growing consensus among Western theologians,

---

Western theology. According to him, Christianity in the West is seen as unilaterally referring to Christ, the Spirit being an addition to the church, its ministries, and its sacraments; "The Procession of the Holy Spirit in Orthodox Trinitarian Doctrine," chap. 4 in *In the Image and Likeness of God*. See also Nissiotis, "Main Ecclesiological Problem," 31–62. All of these three objections, namely, that it was a unilateral act, that it subordinates the Son to the Spirit, and that it compromises the Father's monarchy were already presented by the most vocal critic in history, the ninth-century patriarch of Constantinople Photius in his *On the Mystagogy of the Holy Spirit*, especially 51–52, 71–72.

42. Photius insisted that the Holy Spirit proceeds from the Father *alone*, the Son having no part to play. The intention of this polemical statement was not of course to argue the total exclusion of the Son from the Spirit but to defend vigorously the monarchy of the Father as the source of the deity of both Spirit and Son. See further, Letham, *Holy Trinity*, 205.

43. For an important Orthodox statement, see Needham, "The Filioque Clause: East or West?," 142–62.

44. Peters puts it bluntly: "The insertion of *filioque* in the Western version of the Nicene Creed was an act of unwarranted authority and certainly not done in the interest of church unity." Peters, *God as Trinity*, 65.

45. Pannenberg, *Systematic Theology*, 1:319 concurs. Peters makes the brilliant point that in principle there is nothing against adding to the creeds as long as it is done in concert. Theology is an ongoing reflection, elaboration, and processing of tradition. No creed as such has to be the final word (Peters, *God as Trinity*, 66).

46. See further, Letham, *Holy Trinity*, 213.

47. Well known is the defense of *filioque* by Barth, who feared that dismissing it would mean ignoring the biblical insistence on the Spirit being the Spirit of the Son; *Church Dogmatics*, 1/1:480. Bray defends the addition with reference to the doctrine of salvation. In his opinion, the Eastern doctrine of *theosis* with its focus on pneumatology severs the relationship between Son (atonement) and Spirit. Bray, "The *Filioque* Clause in History and Theology," 142–43. While I disagree with Bray, I also commend his relating the question of the *filioque* to the Spirit, which is indeed at the heart of Eastern theology. For this, see further the comment by Stylianopoulos, "The Biblical

both Roman Catholic and Protestant, about the need to delete the addition and thus return to the original form of the creed.[48] Jürgen Moltmann for years has appealed for the removal of the addition and has suggested a more conciliatory way of putting it, namely, that the Spirit proceeds "from the Father of the Son." He wants to emphasize the biblical idea of reciprocity of Spirit and Son.[49] An alternative to *filioque*—"from the Father through the Son"—would be also acceptable to the Christian East. It would defend the monarchy of the Father (and in that sense, some kind of subordination of the Son to Father, an idea not foreign to the East) and still be ambiguous enough.[50]

I agree with Pannenberg that beyond *filioque* there is a weakness that plagues both traditions, namely, the understanding of relations mainly in terms of origins. Both East and West share that view in their own distinctive ways, the East by insisting on the role of the Father as the source and the West by making the Father primary in the deity with their idea of the proceeding of the Son from the Father and then the Spirit from both.[51] This blurs the key idea of Athanasius—the importance of which he himself hardly noticed—that relations are based on mutuality rather than origin. Another Lutheran, Ted Peters, who supports the removal of the *filioque* clause, however, remarks that the idea of the Spirit proceeding both from the Son as well as the Father also points to something valuable. It highlights relationality and communality, the Spirit being the shared love between Father and Son (and by extension, between the Triune God and the world). Furthermore, on this side of Pentecost, it reminds us of the importance of resurrection and ascension: the risen Christ in Spirit is the presence of Christ. "In this work of transcending and applying the historical event of Jesus Christ to our personal lives, we must think of the Spirit as proceeding

---

Background of the Article on the Holy Spirit in the Constantinopolitan Creed," 171. "At stake was not an abstract question but the truth of Christian salvation." For this quotation, I am indebted to Letham, *The Holy Trinity*, 203.

48. For a helpful discussion, see *Spirit of God, Spirit of Christ*, ed. Vischer. For Roman Catholic support of the removal of the *filioque* clause, see Congar, *I Believe in the Holy Spirit*, 3:80–87. In addition to Moltmann and Pannenberg, a strong defender of the Eastern view has been the Reformed. Torrance, who was instrumental in the Reformed-Orthodox dialogue. For the dialogue, see Torrance, ed., *Theological Dialogue*, 219–32. For his own views in this respect, see Torrance, *Trinitarian Perspectives*, 110–43.

49. Moltmann, *The Trinity and the Kingdom of God*, 178–79, 185–87.

50. Bobrinskoy, *Mystery of the Trinity*, 302–3. Again, my appreciation for bringing this source to my attention goes to Letham, *The Holy Trinity*, 217n64. For incisive comments, see also O'Collins, *Tripersonal God*, 139.

51. Pannenberg, *Systematic Theology*, 1:319.

from Jesus Christ."[52] Finally, Peters notes, within the divine life the Spirit indeed is the principle of relationship and unity. "The separation that takes place between Father and Son—the separation that defines Father as Father and the Son as Son—is healed by the Spirit. It is the Spirit that maintains unity in difference."[53]

Building on these insights, I believe—perhaps too naively—that a common way of formulation could be found in the beginning of the third millennium that would, on the one hand, heal the wounds of separation between the Christian East and West and, on the other hand, make it possible for each of them to honor their somewhat different approaches regarding the place and role of the Spirit in the Holy Trinity. Whether or not this happens in the near future is as much a matter of attitudinal softening and healthy self-criticism (the signs of which can already be discerned clearly in the Christian West) as of continuing to carefully revisit and reassess our trinitarian theological traditions.

BIBLIOGRAPHY

Augustine. *[Homilies] Tractates on the Gospel of St. John* 23. In vol. 7 of *The Nicene and Post-Nicene Fathers of the Christian Church*, Series 1. http://www.ccel.org/ccel/schaff/npnf107.html.

———. *Letters* 11. In vol. 1 of *The Nicene and Post-Nicene Fathers of the Christian Church*, Series 1. http://www.ccel.org/ccel/schaff/npnf101.html.

———. *Letters* 169 (To Bishop Evodius), II.5. In vol. 1 of *The Nicene and Post-Nicene Fathers of the Christian Church*, Series 1. http://www.ccel.org/ccel/schaff/npnf101.html.

———. *On the Holy Trinity*. In vol. 3 of *The Nicene and Post-Nicene Fathers of the Christian Church*, Series 1. http://www.ccel.org/ccel/schaff/npnf103.html.

———. *Sermon on New Testament Lessons: Sermon on Matthew* 3:13. In vol. 6 of *The Nicene and Post-Nicene Fathers of the Christian Church*, Series 1. http://www.ccel.org/ccel/schaff/npnf106.html.

Barnes, Michel René. "Rereading Augustine's Theology of the Trinity." In *The Trinity: An Interdisciplinary Symposium on Trinity*, edited by Stephen T. Davis et al., 145–76. Oxford: Oxford University Press, 1999.

Barth, Karl. *Church Dogmatics*. 14 vols. Edited by G. W. Bromiley and T. F. Torrance. Translated by G. T. Thomson et al. Edinburgh: T. & T. Clark, 1956.

Bobrinskoy, Boris. *The Mystery of the Trinity: Trinitarian Experience and Vision in the Biblical and Patristic Tradition*. Translated by Anthony P. Gythiel. Crestwood, NY: St. Vladimir's Seminary Press, 1999.

Bray, Gerald. "The *Filioque* Clause in History and Theology." *Tyndale Bulletin* 34 (1983) 142–43.

---

52. Peters, *God as Trinity*, 66.
53. Ibid.

Cary, Philip. "Historical Perspectives on Trinitarian Doctrine." *Religious and Theological Studies Fellowship Bulletin* (1995) 2–9.
Cobb, John B., Jr. "The Relativization of the Trinity." In *Trinity in Process: A Relational Theology of God*, edited by Joseph A. Bracken and Marjorie Hewitt Suchocki. New York: Continuum, 1997.
Congar, Yves. *I Believe in the Holy Spirit*. Translated by David Smith. 3 vols. New York: Seabury, 1982.
de Margerie, Bertrand. *The Christian Trinity in History*. Translated by Edmund J. Fordman. Petersham, MA: St. Bede's, 1982.
de Régnon, Théodore. *Études de théologie positive sur la sainte Trinité*. 3 vols. Paris: Retaux, 1892–98.
Grenz, Stanley J. *Rediscovering the Triune God: The Trinity in Contemporary Theology*. Minneapolis: Fortress, 2004.
Gunton, Colin. "Augustine, the Trinity, and the Theological Crisis of the West." *Scottish Journal of Theology* 43 (1990) 33–58.
———. *Promise of Trinitarian Theology*. 2nd ed. Edinburgh: T. & T. Clark, 1997.
Hilberath, Bernd Jochen. "Pneumatologie." In *Handbuch der Dogmatik*, edited by Theodor Schneider, 1:446–47. Düsseldorf: Patmos, 1992.
Kärkkäinen, Veli-Matti. "Is the Spirit Still the Dividing Line Between the Christian East and West? Revisiting an Ancient Problem of Filioque with a Hope for an Ecumenical Rapprochement." *Perichoresis: The Theological Journal of Emanuel University of Oradea* 9 (2011) 125–42. http://www.emanuel.ro/eng/files/Perichoresis/Perichoresis%209_2%20web.pdf.
———. *The Trinity: Global Perspectives*. Louisville: Westminster: Knox, 2007.
———. *Trinity and Revelation*. Vol. 2 of *A Constructive Christian Theology for the Pluralistic World*. Grand Rapids: Eerdmans, 2014.
LaCugna, Catherine Mowry. *God for Us: The Trinity and Christian Life*. San Francisco: HarperSanFrancisco, 1991.
———. "The Trinitarian Mystery of God." In *Systematic Theology: Roman Catholic Perspectives*, edited by Francis Schüssler Fiorenza and John P. Galvin, 1:149–92. Minneapolis: Fortress, 1991.
Letham, Robert. *The Holy Trinity: In Scripture, History, Theology, and Worship*. Phillipsburg, NJ: P. & R., 2004.
Lossky, Vladimir. "The Procession of the Holy Spirit in Orthodox Trinitarian Doctrine." In *In the Image and Likeness of God*, edited by John H. Erickson and Thomas E. Bird, 79–96. Crestwood, NY: St. Vladimir's Seminary Press, 1985.
Marsh, Thomas. *The Triune God: A Biblical, Historical, and Theological Study*. Mystic, CT: Twenty-Third, 1994.
Moltmann, Jürgen. *The Trinity and the Kingdom of God: The Doctrine of God*. Translated by Margaret Kohl. London: SCM, 1981.
Needham, Nick. "The Filioque Clause: East or West?" *Scottish Bulletin of Evangelical Theology* 15 (1997) 142–62.
Nissiotis, Nikos A. "The Main Ecclesiological Problem of the Second Vatican Council and Position of the Non-Roman Churches Facing It." *Journal of Ecumenical Studies* 6 (1965) 31–62.
O'Collins, Gerald. *The Tripersonal God: Understanding and Interpreting the Trinity*. New York: Paulist, 1999.
Olson, Roger E., and Christopher A. Hall. *The Trinity*. Grand Rapids: Eerdmans, 2002.

Pannenberg, Wolfhart. *Systematic Theology*. Vol. 1. Translated by Geoffrey W. Bromiley Grand Rapids: Eerdmans, 1991.
Peters, Ted. *God as Trinity: Relationality and Temporality in Divine Life*. Louisville: Westminster John Knox, 1993.
Photius. *On the Mystagogy of the Holy Spirit*. Astoria, NY: Studien, 1983.
Prestige, George L. *God in Patristic Thought*. London: Heinemann, 1936.
Ratzinger, Joseph. "The Holy Spirit as *Communio*: Concerning the Relationship of Pneumatology and Spirituality in Augustine." *Communio* 25 (1998) 325–39.
Studer, Basil. *The Grace of Christ and the Grace of God in Augustine of Hippo: Christocentrism or Theocentrism?* Collegeville, MN: Liturgical, 1997.
———. *Trinity and Incarnation: The Faith of the Early Church*. Translated by Matthias Westerhoff. Edited by Andrew Louth. Collegeville, MN: Liturgical, 1993.
Stylianopoulos, Theodore G. "The Biblical Background of the Article on the Holy Spirit in the Constantinopolitan Creed." In *Études Théologiques: Le IIe Concile Oecuméniqueé*, 155–73. Chambésy-Genève: Centre Orthodoxe du Patriarcat Oecuménique, 1982.
Stylianopoulos, Theodore G., and S. Mark Heim, eds. *Spirit of Truth: Ecumenical Perspectives on the Holy Spirit*. Brookline, MA: Holy Cross Orthodox, 1986.
Torrance, Thomas F., ed. *Theological Dialogue between Orthodox and Reformed Churches*. Vol. 2. Edinburgh: Scottish Academic, 1993.
———. *Trinitarian Perspectives: Toward Doctrinal Agreement*. Edinburgh: T. & T. Clark, 1994.
Vischer, Lukas, ed. *Spirit of God, Spirit of Christ: Ecumenical Reflections on the Filioque Controversy*. London: SPCK, 1981.
Volf, Miroslav. "'The Trinity Is Our Social Program': The Doctrine of the Trinity and the Shape of Social Engagement." *Modern Theology* 14 (1998) 403–23.
Ware, Kallistos. *The Orthodox Church*. New York: Penguin, 1993.

8

Salvation according to Luke
— Graham H. Twelftree

It is agreed on all sides that the motif of salvation is important in Luke's writings.[1] It is noted, for example, that the theme is prominent in his introduction to Jesus' ministry, mainly through the use and echoes of Scripture.[2] Also, the conclusions to both of Luke's volumes give a high profile to the idea of salvation (Luke 24:47; Acts 28:28). Further, among the New Testament writings, Luke's salvific vocabulary is distinctive.[3] Then, of all the

---

1. In this essay, which I dedicate with affection and fond memories to Stan and Ruth Burgess, friends and some-time fellow faculty members at the School of Divinity, Regent University, I take the opportunity to develop ideas adumbrated in Twelftree, *People of the Spirit: Exploring Luke's View of the Church*. I also thank Nick Daniels, Jimmy Schambach, and Barbara Twelftree for their help.

2. Luke 1:47 (cf. Ps 24:5; Isa 17:10; Hab 3:18); Luke 1:69 (cf., e.g., 1 Sam 2:1, 10; 2 Sam 22:3; 1 Chr 17:10, 24; Pss 18:3; 132:17; Ezek 29:31); Luke 1:71 (cf. 2 Sam 22:18; Pss 18:18; 106:10); Luke 1:77 (cf. Ps 25:18; Isa 55:7); Luke 2:30 (cf. Isa 40:5; Pss 67:3; 97:3 [LXX]); Luke 3:6 (cf. Pss 66:3 [LXX]; 97:3 [LXX]). See also Luke 2:11.

3. E.g., in his Gospel, Luke uses *apolutrōsis* ("redemption," 21:28), *diasōzein* ("to rescue," 7:3), *lutrousthai* ("to redeem," 24:21), *lutrōsis* ("ransom," 1:68; 2:38), *sōtēr* ("savior," 1:47; 2:11), *sōtēria* ("deliverance," 1:69, 71, 77; 19:9), *sōtērion* ("bringing salvation," 2:30; 3:6) and *sōzein* ("to save," 7:50; 8:12, 36, 50; [9:56 in some manuscripts; see *NTG*28]; 13:23; 17:19; 19:10; 23:37, 39), in places where there is no parallel in his sources.

In Acts, Luke uses *diasōzein* (23:24; 27:43, 44; 28:1, 4), *sōtēr* (5:31;13:23); *sōtēria* (4:12; 7:25; 13:26, 47; 16:17; 27:34), *sōtērion* (28:28) and *sōzein* (2:21, 40, 47; 4:9, 12; 11:14; 14:9; 15:1, 11; 16:30, 31; 27:20, 31).

Luke rarely drops salvific language: at Luke 8:42 (cf. Mark 5:23) a whole sentence is recast to keep the attention on Jesus and to conform to what happens later in the story; Luke 21:19 clarifies Mark 13:13; and in Luke 21:24 the interest is in a military

Gospel writers, only Luke describes salvation as God's,[4] or calls God Savior;[5] also only Luke among the synoptic Gospel writers gives Jesus the title "Savior" (Luke 2:11).[6]

Beyond acknowledging these statistics,[7] among those interested in Luke's theology little is held in common about his soteriology. For example, while I. Howard Marshall pointed out that A. R. C. Leaney took "Christ as King" to be the major emphasis of Luke, and E. Earle Ellis suggested Jesus' messiahship and mission were Luke's main interests,[8] Marshall himself went so far as to argue that, "the idea of salvation supplies the key to the theology of Luke . . . it is the central motif in Lucan theology."[9] Though it appears agreed that the universal offer of salvation found across Luke's work[10] undergirds his soteriology,[11] and that it is received by faith,[12] a major point of contention is over how the cross or death of Jesus functions in Luke's

---

siege rather than Mark's vague reference to salvation and the days of tribulation (Mark 13:19). See Twelftree, *People of the Spirit*, 45n1.

Of the synoptic writers, only Luke uses *sōtēr* ("Savior," Luke 1:47; 2:1; also see John 4:42; Acts 5:31; 13:23; and Phil 3:20 for the only use by Paul; cf. Eph 5:23). In the NT *sōtēria* ("salvation") is used eight times, once each in Luke 19:9 and Acts 4:12 (also see John 4:22; Rom 11:11; 13:11; Rev 7:10; 12:10; 19:1).

More generally, Luke uses *sōzō* ("save") eighteen times in his gospel (6:9; 7:50; 8:12, 36, 48, 50; 9:24; 13:23; 17:19; 18:26, 42; 19:10; 23:35, 37, 39) and thirteen times in Acts (2:21, 40, 47; 4:9, 12; 11:14; 14:9; 15:1, 11; 16:30, 31; 27:20, 31). Matthew uses the term fifteen times (1:21; 8:25; 9:21, 22 (2x); 10:22; 14:30; 16:25; 19:25; 24:13, 22; 27:40, 42 [2x], 49); Mark fourteen times (3:4; 5:23, 28, 34; 6:56; 8:35 [2x]; 10:26, 52; 13:13, 20; 15:30, 31 [2x]); John six times (3:17; 5:34; 10:9; 11:12; 12:27, 47); and Paul nineteen times (Rom 5:9, 10; 8:24; 9:27; 10:9, 13; 11:14, 26; 1 Cor 1:18, 21; 3:15; 5:5; 7:16 [2x]; 9:22; 10:33; 15:2; 2 Cor 2:15; 1 Thess 2:16).

4. Luke 3:6: Acts 28:28: cf. Rev 7:10; 12:10; 19:1.

5. Luke 1:47; cf. 1 Tim 1:1; 2:3; 4:10; Titus 1:3; 2:10; 3:4; 2 Pet 1:1; Jude 25.

6. Fitzmyer, *Gospel According to Luke*, 1:181. Cf. Acts 5:31; 13:23; also John 4:42; Titus 1:4; 2:13.

7. E.g., see Marshall, *Luke: Historian and Theologian*, 94-102; Bovon, *Luke the Theologian*, 276.

8. Leaney, *A Commentary on the Gospel According to St Luke*, 34-37; Ellis, *Gospel of Luke*, 10, cited by Marshall, *Luke*, 89-92.

9. Marshall, *Luke*, 92-93. Cf. Lampe, "The Holy Spirit in the Writings of Luke," 159-200. See also, e.g., Martin, "Salvation and Discipleship," 366-80.

10. Luke 2:30-32; 3:6; Acts 2:21; 11:1-18; 13:47.

11. E.g., Räisänen, "Redemption of Israel," 94-114; Green, "Salvation to the End of the Earth," 83-106.

12. Taking into account only the stories including the vocabulary of salvation, see, e.g., Luke 7:50; 8:48, 50; 17:19; 18:42; Acts 4:9; 14:9; 16:30-31. Cf. Zehnle, "Salvific Character of Jesus' Death," 420-44; Menoud, "Le salut par la foi selon le livre des Actes," 255-76.

idea of salvation.¹³ Also, the role of the Spirit in salvation is not agreed. Is the gift of the Spirit the essence or means of salvation, or *donum superadditum*, a gift subsequent to salvation?¹⁴ Moreover—related to the focus of this chapter—it is not clear what is offered in salvation. In particular it is argued by some that Luke describes salvation in terms of Jesus' healing, exorcism and forgiveness ministry,¹⁵ while others suppose that there is a socio-political dimension to salvation in Luke.¹⁶ The purpose of this chapter is to show that, while salvation is not socio-political in nature, but is the experience of the powerful presence or Spirit or kingdom of God resulting in personal restoration, for Luke salvation has profound and radical socio-political ramifications for proclaiming it and those saved by it. We will begin by examining part of the opening scene of Jesus' ministry (Luke 4:18–19) in which the socio-political nature of salvation appears most obvious, at least in English translation.¹⁷ Then, after surveying Luke's positive understanding of salvation, the final part of this essay shows that the salvation which he describes has profound socio-political implications, both for those who proclaim it and those who respond to it.

SALVATION: BENEFACTORS AND BENEFITS

Luke's public introduction to Jesus' mission takes place in the synagogue in Nazareth in an inaugural sermon following his reading from the prophet Isaiah. The text, Luke 4:18–19, taken from Isaiah 61:1, 58:6 and 61:2, can be translated thus:

> The Spirit of the Lord is upon me
> for he has anointed me.
> He has sent me to preach¹⁸ to the poor,
> to proclaim to the captives release
> and to the blind sight,
> to send away the oppressed released,

---

13. Van Zyl, "Soteriological Meaning," 533–57.

14. See the discussion by Turner, "Spirit and Salvation in Luke-Acts," 103–116.

15. E.g., Lampe, "The Holy Spirit," 159–200; Martin, "Salvation and Discipleship," 366–80; Giles, "Salvation in Lukan Theology," 10–16, 45–49 (11–12); Witherington III, "Salvation and Health in Christian Antiquity," 145–66.

16. E.g., Prior, *Jesus the Liberator*.

17. Luke 4:16–30 has received considerable attention; most recently, see Prior, *Jesus the Liberator*; and those cited by Twelftree, *People of the Spirit*, 238.

18. Despite modern translations adding the noun *euangelion* ("gospel" or "good news"), the word does not appear here in the Greek.

Salvation according to Luke   189

to proclaim the acceptable year of the Lord.[19]

Luke's readers could be expected to give special attention to this part of his narrative. The story introduces Jesus' ministry, and it carries his first public words[20] using, moreover, a combination of Scriptural texts (Isa 61:1; 58:6 and 61:2). Given that, a number of times, Luke has already identified Jesus as Savior (Luke 1:69; 2:11, cf. 30) who will bring salvation (1:71, 77; 3:6), readers can be expected to see something of the nature of salvation in this inaugural address setting out Jesus' mission.

What Luke intends to convey about salvation becomes obvious in noting the identity of the beneficiaries: the poor, the captives, the blind, and the oppressed.[21] What Luke wants his readers to understand by the term "poor" (*ptōchos*) comes into focus on noting that each time he describes Jesus' ministry to the poor Isaiah 61:1 is either quoted (Luke 4:18; 7:22) or echoed (6:20).[22] Luke's considerable interest in Isaiah[23] also suggests that his view of the poor will be informed by Isaiah. In Third Isaiah (56–66), from which all Luke's allusions to the poor come, they are not a socio-politically needy segment of the people of God, but the entire people waiting for salvation.[24] In Luke's time the same characterization of those waiting for salvation is found in the Qumran scrolls. In the Qumran *War Scroll* those who will be saved— the whole community—are called "poor" (1QM 13.13–16; cf. CD 19.9–10; also, Zech 11:11). That Luke also intends "the poor" to be read as not only the materially poor but all those needing and receiving salvation, can be seen in having Jesus address the disciples as "you who are poor" (Luke 6:20). Also, in the parable of the rich man and poor man, Lazarus, though materially poor, represents all those who receive salvation (16:19–31). The poor are, then, for Luke, not only a disadvantaged sector of society but all those waiting for and receiving salvation.[25]

That the salvation Jesus announces is for all, rather than a material disadvantaged sector of society,[26] is not overturned in describing the re-

19. Also, see Twelftree, *People of the Spirit*, 182.

20. The words of Jesus in the temptation story (Luke 4:1–13) are not addressed to the public.

21. On what follows, also see Twelftree, *People of the Spirit*, 185–86.

22. Cf. Seccombe, *Possessions and the Poor*, esp. 23–43.

23. See, esp., Luke 3:4–6; (4:18–19); 19:46; 21:26; Acts 1:8; 4:24; 7:49–50; 8:32–33; 13:34, 47; 15:18; 28:26–27.

24. See, e.g., Isa 58:4–7; 61:3; 62:4, 8. Cf. Pss 9:18; 68:10; Zech 11:7, 11.

25. Further, see Twelftree, *People of the Spirit*, 183–84.

26. So, e.g., Dussel, "The Kingdom of God and the Poor," 115–30; Cuthbertson, "The Kingdom and the Poor," 123–33.

cipients as "captives" (*aichmalōtois*, Luke 4:18). The term, only here in the New Testament, was generally used for prisoners of war (e.g., Josephus, *Ant.* 10.68). However, the Qumran scrolls refer figuratively to those implied to be captive to sin (11Q13.5–7) and the demonic (11Q13.10–15). Christians in the period also took up these metaphorical uses of "captives."[27] That Luke was probably among them is suggested by what we have seen in his use of the other key terms for the recipients of salvation in this passage.

The listed beneficiaries of salvation also include the blind. Third Isaiah, which we have already seen is particularly influential in Luke's thinking, portrays those waiting for salvation as seeking light.[28] And, in Luke's time, receiving sight remained a metaphor for salvation.[29] Luke himself, apart from the passage at hand, shows a propensity for using recovery of sight as a description of receiving salvation. In his only story of Jesus healing the blind, the person asks for salvation—"have mercy on me" (Luke 18:38)—and becomes a disciple (18:43). Also, notably, Luke can describe salvation as opening eyes and turning from darkness to light (Acts 26:18; cf. 9:8, 17–18). Therefore, for Luke to say that the announced salvation will bring sight to the blind is most probably not, primarily, notification that a physically needy sector of society will be healed, but a metaphor for salvation for all.

Luke also describes the recipients of salvation as crushed or oppressed. As with "captives," this is the only time *thrauō* is used in the New Testament. At the time the term could be used either literally[30] or metaphorically.[31] In light of his vocabulary so far, Luke probably intends the metaphorical use of "oppressed." Indeed, though he uses different terms, elsewhere he speaks of Satan binding (*deō*) a woman (Luke 13:16) or dominating or oppressing (*katadunasteuō*) people (Acts 10:38).[32]

To both the captives and the oppressed, "release" or "deliverance" (*aphesis*) is announced. Depending on the context, in Luke's world *aphesis* could mean release from legal obligations (Plutarch, *Alex.* 13.2) such as marriage or debt, or release of political and social prisoners.[33] The term could also

---

27. E.g., *T. Dan* 5.7–13; Hippolytus, *Refutation of All Heresies* 1.24.6; 10.9.3; Cyril of Jerusalem, *Procatechesis* 16.1.

28. Isa 58:10; 59:9–10; 60:1–3, 19–20; 62:1. See also Isa 42:7; cf. Luke 1:79.

29. See, esp. *Tg. Isa.* 61:1. Cf., e.g., Mark 10:46–52; John 9:1–41; Rom 2:19; 2 *Clem.* 1.6; 9.2.

30. E.g., in LXX, Exod 15:6; Num 17:11; *Pss. Sol.* 8.39; and, e.g. Diodorus Siculus, *Hist.* 20,93,2; Josephus, *Ant.* 8.390.

31. E.g., 1 Sam. (LXX) 20:34; Judith 9:10; Josephus, *J.W.* 1.323; *Barn.* 3.3 (along with Luke 4:18 also citing Isa 58:6).

32. Further, see Twelftree, *People of the Spirit*, 185–86.

33. 1 Esd 4:62; Philo, *Names* 228; Josephus, *Ant.* 12.40; 17.185.

refer to forgiveness of sin (Diodorus Siculus, *Hist.* 20.54. 2). Importantly, every other use of the noun *aphesis* in the New Testament, including by Luke, relates to forgiveness of sins.[34] Moreover, in the opening, parallel sermon in Acts, where Peter is describing the promised salvation (Acts 2:39), the "release" (*aphesis*) anticipated is explicitly said to be from sin (2:38), suggesting this is his intention in Jesus' sermon. Luke also intends the unqualified use of *aphesis* in the Nazareth sermon to encompass release from sickness that has Satanic overtones. This is suggested by the next use of the word (as a verb) for the fever that "left" (*aphēken*) Simon's mother-in-law after Jesus, described as an exorcist, "stood over her and rebuked the fever" (Luke 4:39).[35]

From the cumulative evidence of describing the recipients as poor, captive, blind, and oppressed who are released, Luke is probably neither intending to describe socio-political benefits of salvation nor that needy sectors of society are the focus of the benefits. Rather, through a cadre of metaphors, he is most likely describing salvation for all, and that it involves release from sin, sickness, and probably Satan. The expected result, then, is that salvation restores people to intended wholeness.

Luke's lack of interest, to the point of aversion, in attributing any socio-political aspects to salvation is reinforced in at least two ways. First, he has taken a radically different perspective from his Scriptures on the nature of salvation. Given Luke is very familiar with and otherwise heavily dependent on his sacred texts,[36] he has most probably deliberately formulated his perspective. In Luke's sacred writings "to save" (*sōzein*) almost always related to a military victory (e.g. [LXX] Ps 32:16–17) or an escape from danger (e.g., Gen 19:20). The result is that salvation in the Old Testament, even with reference to the future,[37] is the expression of God's powerful and tangible care for his people facing danger or an enemy. Luke, however, only twice echoes this theme.[38]

---

34. *Aphesis* (noun): seventeen times in the NT, ten of which occur in Luke-Acts; see Matt. 26:28; Mark 1:4; 3:29; Luke 1:77; 3:3; 4:18 (2x); 24:47; Acts 2:38; 5:51; 10:43; 13:38; 26:18; Eph 1:7; Col 1:14; Heb 9:22; 10:18.

35. On Luke 4:39, see Twelftree, *In the Name of Jesus*, 132 and n17.

36. See, e.g., Evans and Sanders, eds., *Luke and Scripture*; Kimball, *Jesus' Exposition of the Old Testament in Luke's Gospel*.

37. See, e.g., Isa 12:2; 33:22; Zech 9:16.

38. See Luke 1:69–71 (cf. 1 Sam 2:1, 10; 2 Sam 22:3; 1 Chr 17:24; Pss [LXX] 17:1, 4; 105:10; 131:17; Ezek 29:21), and Acts 7:25 where, conforming Moses to his portrait of Jesus as a rescuer, Luke introduces the theme (cf. Exod 2:11–25). On Acts 7:25, see Pervo, *Acts: A Commentary*, 185.

Second, Luke's deliberate non-political agenda in relation to salvation is seen early in Acts where the disciples ask the risen Jesus, "Will you at this time restore the kingdom to Israel?" (Acts 1:6). In replying that "It is not for you to know the times or periods... but you will receive power... to be my witnesses" (1:7–8), the answer is, in effect, "No!" Luke is directing his readers' attention away from any political aspirations or from thinking that Jesus had such intentions. Any political aspect of salvation is put in the indefinite future. Over against this clear non-political notion of salvation adumbrated in the Nazareth sermon, Luke sets out an equally clear alternative.

SALVATION: PERSONAL RESTORATION

The meaning of salvation and savior cannot be determined simply from the meaning of the words. The family of words Luke used to describe Jesus as Savior (*sōtēr*), and to refer to his work—"to save" (*sōzein*) and "salvation" (*sōtēria*)[39]—had a range of meanings.[40] It is the particular content Luke gives to this vocabulary that brings into view his positive understanding of salvation.

Luke's introduction to Jesus' ministry shows that the Savior (Luke 1:47) is expected to bring blessing or to look with favor on his servant (1:47–48), rescue his people from their enemies (1:69, 71), forgive their sins (1:77), and bring peace (2:11, 14), revelation and glory (2:29–32). In the more detailed body of his Gospel, the work of the Savior is described as, for example, bringing forgiveness. To the woman "who was a sinner" (7:37),[41] and who anoints his feet, Jesus says, "Your sins are forgiven" (7:48), and that it was her faith that saved her (7:50). Also, those experiencing various forms of healing can be described as saved. The man whose withered hand was restored is characterized as having his life saved rather than destroyed (6:6–10).[42] Then, the cured demonized man from the country of the Gerasenes is said to be saved (8:36). That Luke interchanges the vocabulary of salvation and healing[43] in his healing and exorcism stories reinforces his view that each is expressed in the other. Being raised from the dead is also

---

39. See n3 above.
40. See Werner Foerster and Georg Fohrer, "σώζω, κτλ," *TDNT* 7:965–1024.
41. See the discussion by Nolland, *Luke*, 1:353–54.
42. Cf. Luke 7:3; 8:48; 17:19; 18:42.
43. The verb *iaomai* ("heal") occurs in Luke 5:17; 6:18, 19; 7:7; 8:47; 9:2, 11, 42; 14:4; 17:15; 22:51; Acts 9:34; 10:38; 28:8, 27; and the verb *therapeuō* ("cure") occurs in Luke 4:23, 40; 5:15; 6:7, 18; 7:21; 8:2, 43; 9:1, 6; 10:9; 13:14; 14:3; Acts 4:14; 5:16; 8:7; 17:25; 28:9.

described as being saved (8:50). Salvation can also be equated with receiving the word (8:12) or life (9:24), and entering (18:26) and eating in the future kingdom of God (13:23), and being a son of Abraham (19:9). Moreover, in healed lepers (7:22; 17:11–19) able to rejoin society, and in using the parables of the lost sheep, the mislaid coin, and the prodigal son to describe Jesus' welcoming and eating with sinners (15:1–32), Luke draws attention to salvation as restoring relationships with God and the community.

From Acts a similar picture emerges. Salvation is being saved from this corrupt generation (Acts 2:40), and receiving forgiveness (5:31; 13:26, 38–39) and the gift of the Spirit (2:38–40, 47)—for Jews and Gentiles (11:14–15). Salvation is healing, as it was for the lame man at the Beautiful Gate (4:9–12; cf. 3:8; 14:9). Salvation is the gift of repentance;[44] it is receiving eternal life (13:46–47); and it is rescue from physical danger, as it was for Paul in the story of his shipwreck (27:20, 31, 34, 43–44).

From Luke's language, and from his description of Jesus' ministry, salvation is clearly not socio-political in terms of who benefits or what they receive. Instead, salvation is primarily removing disabling sin (that is, forgiveness) and sickness (that is, healing or exorcism) to bring personal wholeness and to enable a restored relationship with God and the community. Sometimes salvation is also bringing personal safety, in this life and the next. Since it would have been well known among his readers that Asklepiads saved individuals through healing their bodies and cities (Aelius Aristides, *Or.* 38.19), and that Asclepius, the god of healing, whose leisure it was to save individuals from sickness (39.11), was described as the savior of the whole universe (42.4; cf. Origen, *Cels* 3.3), and that Sarapis, Isis, Heracles and Zeus were also called savior,[45] Luke's description of Jesus was likely read as of a competing savior. The implications of this competing salvation become clear from other aspects of Luke's writing.

SALVATION: RADICAL RESPONSE AND IMPLICATIONS

Three aspects of Luke's description show that, although salvation may be primarily personal, it has profound socio-political implications. Readers see this in the arena in which he sets salvation, in his equating salvation with "the kingdom of God," and in the allegiance demanded in response to salvation.

    1. *The arena of salvation.* Beginning the body of his narrative, "In the days of king Herod of Judea" (Luke 1:5), Luke sets his story in the context

---

44. Acts 5:31; 11:18; cf. 11:14.
45. See Wells, *Greek Language of Healing*, 96; BDAG, "σωτήρ, ῆρος," 985.

of regional political history. Then, with the birth of Jesus taking place when Emperor Augustus issued a decree to all the world, the whole world is the political arena. Although, as we have seen, Luke's second volume denies a political agenda for the mission of the followers of Jesus (Acts 1:6-7), the mission is given a political setting (1:8). Moreover, the list of nations that soon follows in Acts (2:9-10) is probably making the same point.

The list of nations might be interpreted in light of astrological lists, lists of the Jewish Diaspora, the Table of Nations (Gen 10), or prophecies of the eschatological gathering of nations (e.g., Isa 11:11). Following the interpretive lead of Tertullian (*Adv. Jud.* 7), it has more reasonably been argued that the list is part of Luke's agenda of claiming that true power and allegiance belongs to Christ not Rome.[46] As part of their political propaganda, Roman leaders used lists of nations to celebrate military success (cf. Pliny, *Nat.* 7.98) and declare their control of the world.[47] The most notable list forms part of the *Res Gestae Divi Augusti*, which was widely distributed and known in Luke's time, and perhaps by Luke himself,[48] and begins with an assertion that Rome's power under Augustus extended over the entire inhabited world.[49] That such lists are the interpretive grid for reading Luke's list of nations as part of his strategy of claiming that universal, imperial power belongs to Jesus not to Rome is supported by other aspects of his work.

Not only, as we have just seen, does Luke's first volume have a Roman political context and his second begin by setting the scope of the mission of the church as "to the end of the earth" (Acts 1:8), also, Acts reaches its climax with Paul in Rome, the heart of the empire (28:24b-31). Further, for Luke, the gospel is for all people (Luke 2:10, 30-31; 3:6; 24:47), a point emphasized in the closing scene of his work (Acts 28:32-31).[50] In providing a global arena for his story, Luke conveys the strong impression that the salvation he describes competes with the claims of the Roman Empire. This is, as Adolf Deissmann

---

46. See Gilbert, "List of Nations," 497-529.

47. Cf., e.g., Diodorus Siculus, *Hist.* 40.4; Strabo, *Geog.* 4.3.2; Josephus, *Ant.* 15.272; Appian, *Hist. rom.* preface 1-5.

48. See Gilbert, "List of Nations," 497-529; and Gilbert, "Roman Propaganda and Christian Identity," 233-56 (247-53); followed by Penner, "Res Gestae Divi Christi," 125-73 (144).

49. See Hardy, *The Monumentum Ancyranum*; Brunt and Moore, *Res Gestae Divi Augusti*.

50. Cf. Acts 1:8; 2:14-36, 38-40. Also, see Gilbert, "List of Nations," 497-529, esp. 519.

long ago saw, "a polemical parallelism between the cult of the emperor and the cult of Christ."[51]

2. *Salvation as the kingdom of God.* After describing Jesus' good news (Luke 4:18-19) and depicting the Savior bringing salvation through casting out demons (4:31-37, 39, 41), healing the sick (4:40) and teaching (4:31-32), the first description Luke gives of this ministry of salvation is as "the good news of the kingdom of God" (4:43). Even though this kingdom is to be consummated in the future (e.g., 12:35-48; 22:16, 30), Luke has Jesus say, "The kingdom of God is among [*entos*, or within] you'" (17:21), and he describes the kingdom as present in the healings and exorcisms (7:20-22) of individuals. As equivalent to the kingdom of God, salvation is God's powerful eschatological presence bringing wholeness.

However, using the term "kingdom of God" to define salvation would have alerted Luke's readers to the idea that salvation had implications or ramifications beyond the personal. For, in both Luke's Greek world and in his Scriptures, a "kingdom" was the realm,[52] as well as the function of king.[53] In this term, then, Luke's readers would have seen him claiming for God what was the domain and activity of the emperor.

3. *The allegiance in salvation.* In Luke's Gospel, the response to salvation can be service, as in the case of Simon's mother-in-law (Luke 4:39), or glorifying God, as in the response to the raising of the dead man near Nain (7:16), or going in peace, as in the case of the sinful woman who was forgiven (7:50), or praising God as did the healed leper (17:15). It is in Luke's second volume that the broader context and radical nature of the demand involved in salvation are clearest. For example, early in Acts, on being arrested by the high priest for continuing to preach and heal, Peter and the apostles say, "We must obey God rather than any human authority" (5:29). Salvation involves an allegiance to God rather than Jewish authorities.

Luke also describes salvation as competing for an allegiance over against magic, other gods and the demonic. On Cyprus, Paul competes successfully against Elymas the magician resulting in Sergius Paulus, the

---

51. Deissmann, *Light from the Ancient East*, 342.

52. E.g., Pss (LXX) 67:33; 134:11; Tob 1:21; Bar 2:4; 1 Macc 1:6; Diodorus Siculus, *Hist.* 4.68.4; Appian, *Hist. rom.* 12.1.6.

53. E.g., (LXX), 1 Sam 15:28; 20:31; Jdth 1:1; Sir 19:8; 1 Macc 1:16; Diodorus Siculus, *Hist.* 1.43.6; Josephus, *Ant.* 13.220.

proconsul, believing (Acts 13:4–12). In Lystra, the healing of a lame man results in Paul and Barnabas barely convincing the crowd that salvation (14:9) should not be attributed to Zeus and Hermes, but to the living God to whom they should turn (14:8–18). In Philippi, Paul and Silas are arrested after exorcising a girl with "a spirit of divination" (*pneuma puthōn*, 16:16), threatening the income of her owners (16:16–24). The apostles are freed from prison by an earthquake and then are engaged in a confrontation with the magistrates who apologize to them (16:25–40). In Ephesus, after the ignominious defeat of some itinerant Jewish exorcists, believers who practiced magic burned their valuable books (19:13–20).[54] Those proclaiming and those responding to salvation declare an allegiance to God over against the gods and Rome; it is, as Luke describes the choice, a turning "from darkness to light and from the power of Satan to God" (Acts 26:18).

TO CONCLUDE . . .

According to Luke, salvation is the eschatological, powerful presence of God, ushered in by Jesus and his ministry, and proclaimed by his followers. Salvation is directed not to any needy sector of society but to all who may experience it in, for example, blessing, healing, forgiveness, or release from Satan. However, salvation is described in parallel, and in terms competing, with the emperor and other powers. In demanding an uncompromising allegiance to Christ in those saved, a fundamental threat is posed to the socio-political allegiances of society. Salvation may not have a socio-political agenda, but it involves a claim by a Savior, and a loyalty to him, that causes those saved to relinquish all other allegiances.

BIBLIOGRAPHY

Bovon, François. *Luke the Theologian: Fifty-Five Years of Research (1950–2005)*. Waco, TX: Baylor University Press, 2006.

Brunt, P. A., and John M. Moore. *Res Gestae Divi Augusti: The Achievements of the Divine Augustus*. London: Oxford University Press, 1967.

Cuthbertson, Malcolm. "The Kingdom and the Poor." *Scottish Bulletin of Evangelical Theology* 4 (1986) 123–33.

Danker, Frederick W., Walter Bauer, and William Arndt. *A Greek-English Lexicon of the New Testament and Other Early Christian Literature*. Chicago: University of Chicago Press, 2000.

---

54. Cf. Penner, "*Res Gestae Divi Christi*," 147.

Deissmann, Adolf, and Lionel R. M. Strachan. *Light from the Ancient East: The New Testament Illustrated by Recently Discovered Texts of the Graeco-Roman World.* Grand Rapids: Baker, 1978.
Dussel, Enrique. "The Kingdom of God and the Poor." *International Review of Mission* 68 (1979) 115–30.
Ellis, E. Earle, ed. *The Gospel of Luke.* New Century Bible Commentaries. London: Marshall Morgan and Scott, 1974.
Evans, Craig A., and James A. Sanders. *Luke and Scripture: The Function of Sacred Tradition in Luke-Acts.* Minneapolis: Fortress, 1993.
Fitzmyer, Joseph A. *The Gospel according to Luke: Introduction, Translation, and Notes.* Anchor Bible 28–28A. Garden City, NY: Doubleday, 1981, 1985.
Foerster, Werner, and Georg Fohrer. "σώζω, κτλ." In *Theological Dictionary of the New Testament*, edited by Gerhard Friedrich, translated by Geoffrey W. Bromiley, 7:965–1024. Grand Rapids: Eerdmans, 1971.
Gilbert, Gary. "The List of Nations in Acts 2: Roman Propaganda and the Lukan Response." *Journal of Biblical Literature* 121 (2002) 497–529.
———. "Roman Propaganda and Christian Identity in the Worldview of Luke-Acts." In *Contextualizing Acts: Lukan Narrative and Greco-Roman Discourse*, edited by Todd Penner et al., 233–56. Atlanta: SBL, 2003.
Giles, Kevin N. "Salvation in Lukan Theology." *Reformed Theological Review* 42 (1983) 10–16, 45–49.
Green, Joel B. "'Salvation to the End of the Earth' (Acts 13:47): God as Savior in the Acts of the Apostles." In *Witness to the Gospel: The Theology of Acts*, edited by I. Howard Marshall et al., 83–106. Grand Rapids: Eerdmans, 1998.
Hardy, Ernest G. *The Monumentum Ancyranum.* Oxford: Clarendon, 1923.
Kimball, Charles A. *Jesus' Exposition of the Old Testament in Luke's Gospel.* JSNT Supp94. Sheffield: Sheffield Academic, 1994.
Lampe, Geoffrey W. H. "The Holy Spirit in the Writings of Luke." In *Studies in the Gospels: Essays in Memory of R. H. Lightfoot*, edited by D. E. Nineham, 159–200. Oxford: Blackwell, 1955.
Leaney, A. R. C. *A Commentary on the Gospel according to St. Luke.* Black's New Testament Commentaries. London: Black, 1971.
Marshall, I. Howard. *Luke: Historian and Theologian.* Exeter: Paternoster, 1988.
Martin, Ralph P. "Salvation and Discipleship in Luke's Gospel." *Interpretation* 30 (1976) 366–80.
Menoud, Philippe H. "Le salut par la foi selon le livre des Actes." In *Foi et Salut selon S. Paul. (Épître aux romains 1, 16)*, edited by Markus Barth, 255–76. Rome: Institut Biblique Pontifical, 1970.
Nolland, John. *Luke.* 3 vols. Word Bible Commentary 35A, B, C. Dallas: Word, 1989.
Penner, Todd. "*Res Gestae Divi Christi*: Miracles, Early Christian Heroes, and the Discourse of Power in Acts." In *Miracle Discourse in the New Testament*, edited by Duane F. Watson, 125–73. Atlanta: SBL, 2012.
Pervo, Richard I. *Acts: A Commentary.* Hermeneia. Minneapolis: Fortress, 2009.
Prior, Michael. *Jesus the Liberator: Nazareth Liberation Theology (Luke 4.16–30).* Biblical Seminar 26. Sheffield: Sheffield Academic, 1995.
Räisänen, Heikki. "The Redemption of Israel: A Salvation-Historical Problem in Luke-Acts." In *Luke-Acts: Scandinavian Perspectives*, edited by Petri Luomanen, 94–114. Helsinki: Finnish Exegetical Society, 1991.

Seccombe, David Peter. *Possessions and the Poor in Luke-Acts*. Linz: Studien zum Neuen Testament und seiner Umwelt, 1983.
Turner, Max. "The Spirit and Salvation in Luke-Acts." In *The Holy Spirit and Christian Origins: Essays in Honor of James D. G. Dunn*, edited by Graham Stanton et al., 103–16. Grand Rapids: Eerdmans, 2004.
Twelftree, Graham H. *In the Name of Jesus: Exorcism among Early Christians*. Grand Rapids: Baker Academic, 2007.
———. *People of the Spirit: Exploring Luke's View of the Church*. London: SPCK, 2009.
Wells, Louise. *The Greek Language of Healing from Homer to New Testament Times*. Beihefte zur Zeitschrift für die neutestamentliche Wissenschaft und die Kunde der älteren Kirche 83. Berlin: de Gruyter, 1998.
Witherington, Ben, III. "Salvation and Health in Christian Antiquity: The Soteriology of Luke-Acts in Its First-Century Setting." In *Witness to the Gospel*, edited by I. Howard Marshall et al., 145–66. Grand Rapids: Eerdmans, 1998.
Zehnle, Richard. "Salvific Character of Jesus' Death in Lucan Soteriology." *Theological Studies* 30 (1969) 420–44.
Zyl, H. C. van. "The Soteriological Meaning of Jesus' Death in Luke-Acts: A Survey of Possibilities." *Verbum et Ecclesia* 23 (2002) 533–57.

9

Apostolic Advice: 1 Corinthians 7 as Deliberative Rhetoric[1]

—Charles Puskas

PROLEGOMENON

"What then is the likeness between the philosopher and the Christian, the disciple of Greece and of heaven?"[2] For a number of scholars these questions are not merely rhetorical.[3] The rhetorical question, often used by Cynics and Stoics (Arrian, *Discourses of Epictetus* 1.12; 3.22), has long been favored in argument. Even Paul is no exception here. "Where is the one who is wise? Where is the scribe? Where is the debater of this age? Has not God made foolish the wisdom of the world?" (1 Cor 1:20, NRSV). Paul would appear to be dismissing much of this rhetorical sophistry. There is another view.

---

1. This article originated as an academic paper presented to the Central States SBL Regional Meeting in the 1984 when I was an adjunct professor of New Testament at Missouri State University (then Southwest Missouri State University) of Springfield, Missouri. Congratulations, Stan and Ruth Burgess!

2. My translation of Tertullian, *Apologeticus adversos Gentes pro Christianis* 46.17, which compares the Greek sophists with Christian evangelists, ca. 197 CE. Tertullian's questions are also raised by Weima, "What Does Aristotle Have to Do with Paul?," 458 (critical of NT rhetoric); and also Church, "Rhetorical Structure & Design," 17 (an advocate).

3. See critic Anderson, *Ancient Rhetorical Theory*; and advocates Watson, *The Rhetoric of the New Testament*; and Witherington III, *New Testament Rhetoric*.

As Cicero once wrote of Plato, "it was when making fun of orators that he himself seemed to be the consummate orator."[4] The following study of 1 Corinthians 7 will suggest that Paul, too, employed basic tactics of persuasion taught and widely practiced in his own day.

Why a rhetorical analysis of 1 Corinthians 7? I have at least six reasons: 1) The audience of 1 Corinthians consists primarily of Gentiles who all reside in the city of Corinth. Corinth was located fifty miles west of Athens, the center of Greek rhetorical studies (e.g., Aristotle).[5] 2) Rhetoric and oratory were also included in the competitive events of the Isthmian games, held every other year, a few miles east of Corinth.[6] It was probably in reaction to the Corinthian fascination with rhetoric and oratory that Paul makes his deprecatory comments on wisdom and oratory in 1 Corinthians 1. 3) Although Paul describes himself as "a Hebrew born of Hebrews" (Phil 3:5), a Hebrew, Israelite, and descendant of Abraham (2 Cor 11:22)—and the author of Acts describes the apostle speaking Hebrew or Aramaic (Acts 21:40; 22:2)—Paul wrote his letters in Hellenistic Greek.

4) It is clear, for example, in 2 Corinthians chapters 10–12, how skillful Paul is in the rhetoric of persuasion.[7] Paul's stylistic techniques, such as mimesis (2 Cor 10:1), irony (10:12, "we dare not," 11:19, "being wise yourselves!"), metonymy (2 Cor 11:20, lit., "devours you" = takes your possessions), and rhetorical questions (2 Cor 11:22–23, 29) accomplish a rhetorical effect in this letter.[8] The way that Paul employs logic (*logos*), emotional appeals (*pathos*), and his own example (*ethos*) in this section that is sometimes called "the letter of tears" shows that he must have had some exposure to rhetoric (cf., Plutarch, *Mor.* 539–47). All of Paul's letters have been outlined following the guidelines of ancient rhetorical handbooks.[9] 5)

---

4. Cicero, *De Oratore* 37. Dio-Chrysostom also seeks to win over his audience by mock humility about his rhetorical skill, *Dialexis* (Discourse 42).

5. See Kennedy, "Composition and Influence of Aristotle's *Rhetoric*," 418–21.

6. Murphy-O'Connor, *St. Paul's Corinth*, 17.

7. As noted by Augustine, *de Doctrina Christiana* 4; Melanchthon, *Annotationes in Epistolas Pauli Ad Corinthios*; Bullinger, *Figures of Speech*; and Heinrici, *Der zweite Brief an die Korinther*, 436–58.

8. See Porter, "Paul of Tarsus," 576–84 (although critical of the rhetorical outlines of his letters, Porter sees in Paul's ornamental style his closest use of rhetorical technique, 578); on Paul's stylistic techniques, see also Turner, *Style: Grammar of New Testament Greek*, 80–105.

9. See Kennedy, *New Testament Interpretation*, 141–56; the survey in Murphy-O'Connor, *Paul the Letter-Writer*, 77–79; and the rhetorical outlines of each letter in Puskas and Reasoner, *The Letters of Paul*. Although my focus is on the Hellenistic forms of persuasion, there are also insights to be gained from modern rhetoric, e.g., Perelman and Olbrechts-Tyteca, *The New Rhetoric*; Andrews, *The Practice of Rhetorical Criticism*.

Paul could have acquired these speech and debate techniques in the natural course of observation and imitation (e.g., Acts 17:17-18; 19:9). However, his fluency in Hellenistic language and thought forms seem to presuppose some training in a gymnasium of Paul's Tarsus. Wherever Hellenism took root, there existed these educational institutions to transmit the Greek literary heritage for both Jews and Gentiles. The rules of rhetoric are relevant in ancient letter writing, because all ancient writing was read aloud and Paul's letters were to be read in Christian assemblies (e.g., 1 Thess 5:27).[10]

6) A sixth reason for a rhetorical analysis of 1 Corinthians 7 concerns the method itself. The full-scale commentary on Galatians by Hans Dieter Betz[11] revived interest in this method and generated much scholarly response. *The Galatians Debate*, edited by Mark Nanos, for example, devotes a section on rhetorical approaches, mostly from previously published articles.[12] Robert Jewett, *Romans* also exhibits rhetorical analysis.[13] The dean of rhetorical studies, the Classicist George Kennedy, has also published a book addressed to biblical scholars, *New Testament Interpretation through Rhetorical Criticism*.[14] Finally, the work of Margaret M. Mitchell presents a rhetorical outline of 1 Corinthians in her *Paul and the Rhetoric of Reconciliation*.[15] Despite the reluctance of some scholars to place much emphasis on the rhetorical skill of this busy, idiosyncratic, end-time oriented Jewish-Christian missionary, rhetorical analysis of the New Testament cannot be excluded for those reasons alone. Perhaps this chapter can add more clarity and credence to the method and its objectives.

According to the handbooks of Aristotle, Cicero, and Quintillian, there are three types of rhetoric: deliberative, forensic, and epideictic.

(1) Deliberative rhetoric attempts to exhort or dissuade.[16] The setting presupposed in this advisory form of persuasion is the public assembly

---

10. On the spread of Greek learning and culture, see, e.g., Hellenization in Palestine, second cent. BCE, 1 Maccabees 1-2; Philo attending Greek plays, first cent. CE, *Drunkenness* 177; *Good Person* 141; Tacitus, on the decline of oratory, 100 CE, *Dialogues de Oratibus* 19-20. For discussion of primary sources for both deliberative speeches *and* letters in Mitchell, *Paul and the Rhetoric of Persuasion*, 21-23. On specific "rhetorical epistles" (by, e.g., Demosthenes, Plutarch, Cicero, Quintillian) see Reed, "The Epistle," 187-93. See also Gavrilov, "Techniques of Reading in Classical Antiquity," 56-73.

11. Betz, *Galatians*.

12. Nanos, ed., *The Galatians Debate*, 157-98.

13. Jewett (assisted by Kotansky) *Romans*, vii-x.

14. Cited hereafter as Kennedy, *New Testament Interpretation*.

15. Mitchell, *Paul and the Rhetoric of Persuasion*, 184-86.

16. Related to deliberative rhetoric and especially the more general *paraenetic* (Gk.) or hortatory language (e.g., Rom 12-14; Gal 5-6; *Cynic Epistles*), but more forceful or intentional, is *protreptic* rhetoric. It promotes a *particular course* of action (Gk.,

where the audience must make decisions about the future. Quintillian also calls it *suasoria*. This type of rhetoric is for anyone who might need or seek advice. It concerns issues of expediency like, "Should Cato marry?" (2) Forensic rhetoric was not a personal matter in antiquity. It concerns the law courts where the audience must judge an action in the past. It is concerned with defense or accusation. For example, "Did Cato marry?" This would be an issue resulting from an accusation of bigamy or adultery. (3) Epideictic rhetoric is employed in the marketplace or amphitheatre, where the spectators must judge the art of the orator present before them. It extols common virtues and denounces common vices. For example, "Should a person marry?" dealing with the abstract ideal of marriage or celibacy.

DELIBERATIVE RHETORIC

Since 1 Corinthians 7 lies within the framework of the acknowledged "letter of questions from Corinth to Paul," it seems clear that the Corinthians are seeking *the advice of the Apostle* on the subject matter of 1 Corinthians 7. "Now concerning the matters about which you wrote" (v. 1).[17] This type of situation requesting advice, Quintilllian equates with deliberative rhetoric (*deliberativa*, or *suasoria*; Inst. Orat. 3.8.15). Paralleling the statements in 1 Cor 7:1 are the following letters by ancient scholars *responding to letters of questions* from their students: Epicurus, *Letter to Pythocles* (Diogenes Laertius, Lives 10.84–116) and Plutarch's *Letter 3, On the Tranquility of the Mind* (Mor. 464E–477F). Both are documents of advisory rhetoric on areas of concern to their students. Marriage, as we know, is a major concern of 1 Corinthians 7. The question of whether or not to marry is also cited by Quintillian as an issue of deliberative rhetoric (*Inst. Orat.* 3.5.13). Examples of deliberative rhetoric prevail on issues of public interest. In Demosthenes, *Third Philippic* (341 BCE) the famous statesman advises the Athenian assembly to unite with other Greek city states in opposing Philip of Macedon; Isocrates, *On Peace* (355 BCE) where the statesman proposes to the pub-

---

protreptein, "to urge, impel"), calling the audience to a new way of life (e.g., adopting the Cynic lifestyle, Chrysostom, *De Invidia* [*Or.* 77/78.38; LCL 385]; Crates, *Letter* 35; Arrian, *Disc. of Epictetus* 3.23). In a similar manner, Paul sought to convince or remind his readers of the truth of his gospel (e.g., Rom 1:16–17; 2:16; 16:25; 1 Cor 1:10–17; 13; Gal 1:6–9; 1 Tim 4:7b–10) and to encourage them to live according to this gospel that he preached (Rom 12–14; Gal 5–6). See Elliott and Reasoner, *Documents and Images*, 70–73; Stowers, *Letter Writing*, 91–92. The rhetoric of 1 Cor 7, however, is closer to deliberative rhetoric, and not protreptic speech, as I will show in the body of this article.

17. For a plausible reconstruction of this letter of inquiry to Paul regarding sex and marriage, see Hurd, *Origin of 1 Corinthians*, 168.

lic assembly at Athens, a policy of lasting peace between Athens and her neighbors. Isocartes, in the *Address to Philip of Macedon* (346 BCE), advises Philip on noble and honorable courses of action to undertake toward the Greek city states and the world. In the *Jewish Wars* of Josephus (90 CE), King Agrippa (*J.W.* 2:345–401) attempts to dissuade the people from going to war because if they should do so they would be in a worse situation in the future than they were presently experiencing.[18]

The English poet, John Milton, addressed the English parliament on the liberty of unlicensed printing in his *Areopagitica* (London, 1644). It is a speech that skillfully employs the Hellenistic techniques of deliberative rhetoric (e.g., Is it possible? Is it honorable? Is it expedient?) Today, most of the speeches in our law-making assemblies (e.g., on C-SPAN) are deliberative rhetoric. Here representatives advise and exhort their colleagues to make prudent and expedient legislative decisions. Most political advertisements before an election on radio and television also employ deliberative rhetoric. They attempt to advise us about making the most expedient and honorable choices at the voting booth. As we have noted, deliberative (sometimes called "political") rhetoric is concerned with what is a practical and expedient course of action for the future, both immediate and long-range future.

In deliberative rhetoric, success rests on establishing two primary motives for action: honor (Lat., *honestas*, Gk., *kalon*) and advantage (Lat., *utilitas*, Gk., *symphoron*). These points are carried out by means of "proofs," (Lat., *probatio*) based on external data (e.g., witnesses, documents, events) and internal data, which are appeals to the character of the speaker (*ethos*), the emotions of the audience (*pathos*) and finally appeals to reason (*logos*; in Aristotle, *Rhetoric* 1.2.3).

The structure of a deliberative speech consists of three major sections: 1) the *exordium* (Gk., *prooimion*), 2) main body or *proof* (*pistis*) and 3) *peroration* (*epilogos*). The structure is similar to forensic oratory except without a narration, because no one can narrate "matters to come" (Aristotle). If there is a narration it will be of matters already past as a reminder for the hearers to make better counsel about the future (Aristotle, *Rhetoric* 3.16.11).

The *exordium* is often reduced to a mere prelude to establish the appropriate mood and to secure the good will of the listener, both by praise itself and by linking that praise to the subject in question (Quintillian *Inst. Orat.* 4.1; Cicero, *De Inven.* 1.15; Aristotle *Rhetoric* 3.14).

In the main body or *proof*, the argument is formally advanced with primary reference to the motives of honor and utility with appeals to both

---

18. For other examples, see Runnalls, "The Rhetoric of Josephus," 743–45.

external data (e.g., documents, events) and internal data (i.e., *ethos, pathos,* and *logos*). The *peroration* or conclusion consists of four elements: restating one's appeal, securing the hearer's favor, amplifying one's argument and setting the hearer in an emotional frame of mind (Aristotle, *Rhet.* 3.19). Here factors alluded to in the *exordium* and adduced in the *proof* are restated a third time with all possible force. If in the *exordium* any preliminary appeal to the compassion of the judge must be made sparingly and without restraint, in the *peroration* we must give full scope to our emotions (Quintillian, *Inst. Orat.* 4.1.28; Aristotle, *Rhetoric to Alexander* 36.29ff [LCL 16]).

An issue addressed in 1 Corinthians 7 centers on *caelibatus* (Lat.): whether or not to refrain from marital relations.[19] In Corinthian culture, celibacy and some form of asceticism (Gk., *askēsis*, "strict training" in athletics, later "spiritual discipline") was observed by certain groups. First, most Cynic, Pythagorean and Neoplatonic philosophers with whom they were well acquainted, viewed celibacy as a noble and admirable lifestyle (e.g., Arrian, *Disc. of Epictetus* 3.22.77, 81; *Cynic Epistle of Diogenes* 44, against marriage and sexual relations; Philostratus, *Life of Apollonius* 1.13, "he was resolved never to wed"). Celibacy was cultivated by certain Essenes (Josephus, *J.W.* 2.119–21) and the Jewish Therapeutae in Egypt (Philo, *Contempl. Life* 2, 66–68). Abstinence was also required of certain Greco-Roman cults, such as with the Vestal Virgins of Rome and the Orphic mysteries of Greece. Second, Paul may also be responding to women prophets in Corinth (1 Cor 11:5) who are celibate (1 Cor 7:1, 5), revere wisdom (Gk., *Sophia*, 1:17; 2:1, 13: 3:19; cf. Wisd 7:7, 22; 9:17; Philo *Contempl. Life* 31), feel liberated by the Spirit (1 Cor 12:7, 11, 13; cf., Gal 3:28), and claim authority over their own bodies (7:4). The unmarried desired to remain single, and the married contemplated separating from their spouses.[20]

This embrace of celibacy at Corinth may have resulted from a genuine spiritual enthusiasm in their newfound Christian faith. With so many examples of celibate and ascetic religiosity in their culture, this manner of living was assumed to be the most appropriate way to worship Christ and live in the Spirit. Therefore, many Corinthians felt that Christian couples should

19. For Deming the context of 1 Corinthians 7 is the Cynic-Stoic debates on the advantages or disadvantages of marriage, rather than asceticism, *Paul on Marriage and Celibacy*, chap. 3. Finn, however, argues that the voluntary abstention of food, drink, sleep, wealth, and sexual activity for religious reasons (i.e., asceticism) can be found in the pagan world and Hellenistic Judaism (e.g., Philo's *Life of Moses* 2.68; *Quest.Gen.* 2.49), in *Asceticism in the Graeco-Roman World*, chaps. 1–2.

20. See discussion, 63–66, 79–83, and primary sources, 237–69, in Wire, *The Corinthian Women Prophets*. May, critical of Wire's theory, sees the main issue here as sexual immorality (Gk., *porneia*, 1 Cor 5:1; 6:13, 18; 7:2; *pornos*, 5:9–11; 6:9). May, "The Body for the Lord," 144–79.

forego marital intercourse, and those who were married should remain single to devote themselves more fully to spiritual matters. Some may have felt that divorce was necessary to preserve the spiritual life. These religious concerns are not foreign to earliest Christian teaching, since we find more rigorous (perhaps ascetic) aspects of discipleship in the "Q" logia preserved in Luke's Gospel (e.g., 14:20, 26-27; 17:27; 18:29-30; 20:34-35). Although Paul practiced celibacy (1 Cor 7:7-8),[21] his liberal advice with regard to food and drink was not very ascetic (e.g., 1 Cor 9:19-23; 10:25f, 29f; Rom 14). His views were mostly pastoral. They arose from his call to be an apostle to the nations, which he claimed was directly from the risen Christ (Gal 1; 1 Cor 15).[22] Paul also believed that he was living near the approaching end of the age (1 Cor 7:26, 29, 31; 16:22; 1 Thess 5) and was probably receptive to certain rigorous aspects of discipleship like those in the "Q" tradition (mentioned earlier).[23] As a result, Paul agreed with the Corinthian position on celibacy, with some qualifications. Apostolic advice would be needed for acting responsibly and in a way that would benefit *all* involved parties. Marriage, of course, would be recommended for those who are currently married, intend to be married, or do not have the gift of celibacy.

First Corinthians 7 is not a school exercise or a set piece written for applause. Its design is not merely extracted from handbooks. Yet it is not surprising that it should reflect the heritage of a living rhetorical tradition. Whether Paul was trained in school or acquired his talent through observation and imitation, he was a master of persuasion. It is hardly surprising

---

21. It seems unusual that Paul, a Jewish man, would remain single (e.g., Gen 2:24; Prov 18:22; Phil 3:4-5; *b. Yeb* 63). See discussion in Fee, *Corinthians*, 332-33. In the Roman world, the *lex Julia* (18 BCE) and *lex Papia* (9 CE) were established by Augustus to promote and protect the institution of marriage (for citizens of Rome). See also the marriage ideal in Rufus, "What is the Chief End of Marriage?"; see also Cohick, *Women in the World of the Earliest Christians*, 71-72. Perhaps this is why Clement of Alexandria in his reading of 1 Corinthians 9:5 concludes that Philip, *Paul,* and Peter must have all had wives, *Stromata* 3.6, also cited in Eusebius, *Eccl. Hist.* 3.30. His conclusion, however, is speculative.

22. An apostle is one who has seen the risen Lord as Paul claims to have done (1 Cor 15:8; Gal 1:15-16) although some challenged Paul's apostleship (1 Cor 9:2; 2 Cor 11). In Acts, the criterion for apostleship appears to exclude Paul (Acts 1:21-26; 15:2) although he and Barnabas are also called "apostles" (14:4, 14). Malina and Pilch see Jesus, Paul, and the other apostles all functioning as "prophetic (commissioned) change agents," *Social-Science Commentary on the Letters of Paul*, 335-37.

23. See Wimbush, *Paul the Worldly Ascetic.* "Worldly ascetics" do not withdraw from the world as do hermits or monks in desert communities, see Weber, *Protestant Ethic and Spirit of Capitalism*, where this concept is used of Protestant groups working in the modern world.

that this mastery should be grounded in the widely practiced traditions of his time.

A RHETORICAL ANALYSIS OF 1 CORINTHIANS 7

First Corinthians 7:1–40 is a complete rhetorical unit (cf., Plato, *Phaedrus* 264c). Although the previous discussion on immorality (Gk., *porneia*) in chapters 5–6 has thematic relevance, our chapter 7 is structurally separate from what precedes because of the preface: "Now concerning the matters about which you wrote" (7:1). The discourse ends at v. 40 because of the change of topic in 8:1 "Now concerning food sacrificed to idols."[24] It will be shown that the topics of 1 Corinthians 7 are thematically united and mutually related to each of its three sections, noted below, having a close literary relationship.

I have outlined the structure of 1 Corinthians 7 in the following manner: *exordium* (vv. 1–7), *proof* (vv. 8–31), and *peroration* (vv. 32–40). I will now discuss each section in order.

The main issue of 1 Corinthians 7, as I see it, is the relationship of male and female as Christians. This is a deliberative issue of civil life, because it involves the institution of marriage (Quintillian, *Inst. Orat.* 3.5.8). It concerns the practical question of what to pursue or avoid (Cicero, *Topica* 23.89) since it asks, "Should we abstain from marital relations?" These issues require an expedient course of action in the near future because married couples were abstaining from sex or separating, and unmarrieds and widows wanted to know if they could marry. The issue is also heightened by problems of sexual immorality in Corinth (*porneia*, e.g. 1 Cor 5:1, 11; 6:15–16,18).

Exordium 7:1–7

In the *exordium* of 1 Corinthians 7, it is unnecessary for Paul to secure the goodwill of his readers since he has already done it in the thanksgiving section of the letter (1:4–9, also called *proem*). In agreement with Aristotle (*Rhetoric* 3.14.21), Paul "strikes up a theme and leads into it." In the *exordium*, Paul does what is appropriate to deliberative rhetoric. First, he reaffirms what is good or noble: "it is good for a man not to have sexual relations with a woman" (1 Cor 7:1). Although the quotation raises the issue

---

24. On Paul's use of deliberative rhetoric in 1 Cor 5–16, see Puskas and Reasoner, *The Letters of Paul*, 108–13.

from a male perspective, Paul's response is more two-sided (vv. 2–5).[25] The principle in 7:1 is followed by his advice on married couples attempting to be holy (vv. 2–5). This ideal of celibacy, found in Hellenistic philosophy and apocalyptic Christianity, must be addressed in a manner that is fair to all who are concerned about it.

Second, Paul makes celibacy both practical and practicable by: 1) pointing out the advantage of following his advice (vv. 32–35) and 2) qualifying his recommendations with exception clauses (vv. 1–2, 7–9, 38, Gk., *epitherapeia*).[26] Paul is careful to reaffirm the social institution of marriage for those who do not have the gift of celibacy and would most likely be tempted with the sins of immorality (*porneia*, 7:2, 7, 9c; cf. 5:1,11; 6:18). In the *exordium*, Paul supports this point in a chiastic manner (A, B, B,' A') or male/female parallelism. Paul also considers it a violation of the marital agreement for members to separate except temporarily for religious devotion (7:4–5, 10–11, 27; cf., *m. Ketub.* 5.6–7; *m.'Eduy.* 4.10).

Third, Paul concludes by reiterating his ideal of celibacy but concedes that each person has his own gift or calling (implying that celibacy is not for everyone). By qualifying or modifying his statements, Paul is able to secure a wider hearing by softening the issue so that he does not offend any group involved in the controversy. His statements on the gift of celibacy and the mutual obligations and benefits of marriage draw both women and men, celibate and non-celibate, into the discussion.

Another characteristic of the *exordium* is to enumerate points to be developed in the *proof* and reiterated in the *peroration*.

	Topic	Exordium	Proof	Peroration
1	What is good or better	v. 1	8, 26	37–38, 40
2	Marry to avoid *porneia*	2	9, 28	36
3	Mutuality in marriage	3	14, 16	33–34, 39
4	No separation of married partners	5	10–13, 20, 24, 27a	(33–34), 39a
5	Apostolic advice/*Lord's Command*	6	8, 10, 12, 25	40

25. Bassler, "1 Corinthians," 559.

26. For a helpful list of rhetorical figures with definitions, see http://rhetfig.appspot.com/list.

6	Paul's Preference for Celibacy	7a	8, 26, 28–29, 32–35	37–38, 40
7	Each has his own gift and calling	7b	17, 20 (35)	(37) 40

Most of the above points, found in the *exordium* are amplified in the *proof*, although the *peroration* also reiterates several topics more thoroughly. Cicero mentions that the opening passage should be closely connected with the speech that follows, not as an appendage but an integral part of the whole (*De Orat.* 2.80.325). In the *exordium*, Paul appears to follow Cicero's remarks.

Proof vv. 8–31

The first three divisions are indicated by a series of datives:

> v. 8 "To the unmarried widows I say..."
> v. 10 "To the married I give charge..."
> v. 12 "To the rest I say..."

Paul's advice to the unmarrieds and widows in v. 8 repeats his preference for celibacy in the *exordium* (v. 7). His exception clause in v. 9 recalls the exception clause to marry because of *porneia* (v. 2). The advice against separation in v. 10 also recalls the advice for married couples not to deprive each other of sexual contact v. 5. The section on Christian and mixed couples continues this advice against divorce and separation (v. 12) with one exception (v. 15).

The fourth division of the *proof*, vv. 17–24, contains some important general statements on each person remaining in the social institution that God has called him or her. The subject matter of the section, permeated by amplification and reiteration is relevant to the entire chapter of the book. The fifth division, vv. 25–28, concerns the specific topic of virgins. Paul's advice is drawn from both the previous general principles (vv. 17–24) and Paul's preference for celibacy (vv. 7–8, 28).

The final division of the *proof* consists of a second set of general principles connected with the first set (vv. 29–31; cf. 17–24). The five exhortations supporting Paul's eschatological concerns actually amplify and provide a further rationale for the first set of principles: A Christian is not to be determined by his social circumstances but by his relation to Christ (17–24).

Throughout the *proof*, Paul appeals to the practicality and practicability of his position by appeals to what is good (*kalon* vv. 8, 26), exceptions to the general principle (vv. 9, 11, 15) and appeals to expediency (v. 29 "the appointed time has grown short") and advantage (v. 28, "I would spare you of that [i.e., many troubles])." These are all characteristics of deliberative rhetoric.

Peroration vv. 32–40

It appears that the conclusion begins at v. 32 and not v. 39 (as in many translations and commentaries), because the advice to the unmarried (vv. 32–35) as well as that of the widow (vv. 39–40) is reiterated. The middle section of vv. 36–38 concerns either engaged couples or celibate Christians in an arrangement of spiritual marriage without sexual relations. However, Paul's advice of preference for celibacy (vv. 28, 37–38) and his assurance that those who marry do not sin (vv. 28, 36) reiterate that which was given to the virgins in the *proof* (vv. 25–28).

In the *peroration*, Quintillian tells us, the whole torrent of eloquence and *ethos* is evident (6.1.52). Here, there are deliberative appeals to advantage (v. 32 "I want you to be free from anxieties") and benefit (v. 35a "I say this for your own benefit;" cf., 40a) and appeals to the *ethos* or character of the speaker (v. 40 "But in my judgment . . . and consider [*dokeō*] that I have the Spirit of God"). *Pathos* or emotional appeal is also conveyed in the deliberative appeals of advantage (v. 32) and benefit (v. 35).

The reiteration of previous arguments in the *peroration* is evident. The statements to the unmarried in vv. 32–35, "I want you to be free from anxieties" (v. 32; cf., Arrian, *Disc. of Epictetus* 3.22.69–72) and "I say this for your own benefit—not to lay restraint on you" (1 Cor 7:35), provide further rationales for the general principle in the *proof*: "it is better for you to remain as you are" (vv. 17–24). The explanations in vv. 32–34 concerning married and unmarried amplify the advice given to virgins in vv. 25–28.

The advice in section vv. 36–38, as mentioned, is similar to that given to virgins in vv. 25–28: Paul's preference is for celibacy, but those who marry do not sin. Those addressed here, however, are different. They are either engaged couples or a male Christian celibate providing guidance and protection to a virgin girl in a type of spiritual marriage without sexual relations.[27] The third possibility—that a father and his daughter-to-be married are addressed—seems unlikely.[28] The honorable course of action recommended

---

27. On "spiritual marriages," see in second century CE, Hermas, *Visions* 2.2.3; 9.11.3–4; Tertullian, *On Exhortation to Chastity* 12 ("take some spiritual wife!"); and modern discussion in Seboldt, "Spiritual Marriage," 103–19, 176–89.

28. For discussion of this theory and others (e.g., levirate marriage), see Fee,

here, recalls that in the *proof*: "A Christian does well when he keeps his virgin as she is" v. 37d (cf. 17–24). In the address to Christian widows (vv. 39–40), both the advice in verse 8 and the *proem* in v. 10 are both reiterated in the statement: "a wife is bound to her husband as long as he lives" (v. 39a). It concludes with Paul's repeated (vv. 7–8, 26, 28, 32ff) expression of preference: "I think she is happier if she remains as she is (a widow)" v. 40a. The *peroration* seals Paul's advice on Christian relations between males and females and his recommendation for Christians to remain in whatever social state they were in when God called them.

It appears from Paul's deliberative argument in 1 Corinthians 7 that the Corinthians, as a result of spiritual enthusiasm, felt liberated from marital obligations, were advocating social changes among men and women that they thought would enhance their spiritual status. For example, Christian couples were abstaining from sexual relations, Christians married to unbelievers were considering divorce, women prophets felt liberated from their marital obligations, unmarrieds were unsure if they should search for spouses, spiritual marriages were possibly arranged, and some couples were contemplating marriage.

These are expedient issues to be determined by the members in the immediate future (i.e., deliberative rhetoric). Paul's general advice is that all Christians should remain in the same social situation that they were when God called them. Paul advises single people remain single, married people remain married. Although he believes that the end is near, Christians still have responsibilities to each other. For the Apostle, changes in social status, whether married, divorced or single, will not affect one's spiritual relationship in the body of Christ.

CONCLUSION

First Corinthians 7, my article argues, is not polemical because few techniques of judicial rhetoric are employed. It is not *protreptic*, because Paul is not advocating some new course of action. The Apostle is *advising* them on the best course of action to take and *dissuading* them from any unwise or inappropriate actions. Both are functions of deliberative rhetoric. He is not spending time defending himself against accusations (Gal 1–4; 2 Cor 10–13) but advises them on what is sensible and expedient. It has been called "Judicious Rhetoric for a Difficult Task."[29]

Corinthians, 326–28; and Thiselton, *Corinthians*, 502–3, 594–602, and (on 1 Cor 9:5), 680–81.

29. Phrase from Wire, *Corinthian Women Prophets*, 79. "Judicious" (Fr., *judicieux*;

Paul is egalitarian regarding conjugal rights in marriage (1 Cor 7:3) and the wife having authority over the husband's body and vice versa (v. 4; cf., m. *Ketub.* 5.6; Plutarch *Mor.* 144b). Regarding Corinthian aspirations to change one's status (1 Cor 7:17–24), where Paul anticipated too much community disruption, he tended to relativize them with qualifiying statements and exception clauses (vv. 2, 7). But his words are encouraging for the slave who has become "emancipated" (Gk., *eleutheros*, v. 21).[30] All are free in the Lord (v. 22) and called to be slaves of Christ (v. 23) and not intended to be under any human master (v. 24). Paul agrees with the Corinthian concern for celibacy (as a gift for some, not all, v.7), but he relativizes the ideology of sexual abstinence for empowerment and liberation, which some women prophets may have advanced.[31] Although he agrees that celibacy can enhance Christian service (vv. 32–35), he cannot endorse the separation or divorce of married couples to accomplish this aim (vv. 5, 10–13, 20, 39).

In partial agreement with the Corinthians, Paul advises on a moderate course of action that will be advantageous for *all* parties involved. Although Paul sees the "present form of this world passing away" (v. 31) he continues to interact with the people in it. For Paul, God's empire has emerged with the crucifixion and resurrection of Christ, but he, nevertheless, discourages extreme positions that will result in unprofitable and inappropriate behavior for his communities of Christ. Paul, the end-time prophet and apostle was also a culturally-sensitive missionary and a community-building pastor.

Even though Paul regards marriage as the best safeguard against sexual immorality (*porneia*), the topic of his previous letter (1 Corinthians 5:9), and discourages divorce and separation, he encourages unmarrieds and widows to remain as they are for three reasons: 1) an expedient course of action is necessary because the time is short before the end of the age, 2) they will have the advantage of serving the Lord more fully without marital concerns and obligations, 3) because a change in social status from single to married, will have no special advantage in determining one's standing in the body of Christ. Within the ecclesial space, "there is a particular pattern of action and a particular place for everything following a cosmic order."[32]

Lat., *iudiciumas*), "exhibiting sound judgment" or "prudent," not used here in a formal forensic (or judicial) sense.

30. "But if, indeed, you have been manumitted, by all means (as a freedman) live according to (God's calling)" translation of 1 Cor 7:21 according to Bartchy, *MALLON CHRESAI: First Century Slavery*, 183; see also his outline of 1 Cor 7, 166–71. Paul's advice to make the most of one's release from slavery as an opportunity to live out God's calling also pertains to the freedwoman. See "freedmen, freedwomen," 609.

31. Wire, *Corinthian Women Prophets*, 63–64, 74–75, 93–97.

32. Økland, *Women in Their Place*, 151, on public and private spheres, 61, 141–42, 149.

Paul's directives seek to distinguish *oikos* and *ekklesia* spaces, even though the Corinthian assemblies meet in homes. They also address the struggle of establishing the roles of men and women in both private and public spheres (cf., Philo, *Spec. Leg.* 3.169; *Quaest. Gen.* 1.26).

This apostolic advice for Christians to remain as they are is practical, expedient and workable. It is practical because it is advice "in view of the impending crisis" to stay as you are for the sake of corporate-communal life. It is also expedient because of the end-time orientation of Paul and his readers and their busy missionary concerns. It is workable and practicable because Paul does not condemn those who do not have the gift of celibacy (v. 7) and discourages changing one's social position (e.g., from married to single), which is too disruptive a course of action to be advantageous. Paul's advice, as my article indicates, is both diplomatic and reasonable; there are no fiery polemics here, nor is he advocating a change of course. His advice is that which his readers could and probably would follow upon receiving the letter (although other problems would arise, e.g., 2 Cor 10–13).

Finally, we see that Paul's argumentation in 1 Corinthians 7 agrees with the advisory persuasion of deliberative rhetoric. It should not be surprising, because Paul was a missionary preacher who would use rhetoric to communicate with his audience. Both his style and structure betray marks of the preacher as we know him today and the rhetorician as he must have been known in the first century Mediterranean world. Paul, however, was not a rigid student of rhetorical handbooks but "a practitioner of the living word in the structure and thought forms of his time."[33] And rhetorical criticism is one approach that can enable us to better understand this medium of Paul's living message.

BIBLIOGRAPHY

Abbreviations for journals and book series (e.g., *NICNT, SBL*) follow those of *The SBL Handbook of Style: For Ancient Near Eastern, Biblical, and Early Christian Studies*, ed. Patrick H. Alexander et al. (Peabody, MA: Hendrickson, 1999).

Anderson, R. Dean, Jr. *Ancient Rhetorical Theory and Paul.* Rev. ed. Leuven: Peeters, 1999.

Andrews, James Robertson. *The Practice of Rhetorical Criticism.* London: Collier Macmillan, 1983.

Aristotle. *Art of Rhetoric.* Vol. 23. Translated by J. H. Freese. Loeb Classical Library 193. Cambridge, MA: Harvard University Press, 1926.

———. *Rhetorica ad Alexandrum.* Vol. 16. Translated by H. Rackham. Rev. ed. Loeb Classical Library 317. Cambridge, MA: Harvard University Press, 1926.

---

33. Church, "Rhetorical Structure and Design," 33.

Augustine. *De Doctrina Christiana*. Translated and edited by R. P. H. Green. Oxford Christian Texts. Oxford: Oxford University Press, 1995.
Bartchy, S. Scott. *MALLON CHRESAI: First-Century Slavery and the Interpretation of 1 Corinthians 7:21*. 1973. Reprint, Eugene, OR: Wipf and Stock, 2003.
Bassler, Jouette M. "1 Corinthians." In *Women's Bible Commentary*, edited by Carol A. Newsom et al., 559–60. 3rd ed. Louisville: Westminster John Knox, 2012.
Betz, Hans Dieter. *Galatians: A Commentary on Paul's Letter to the Churches in Galatia*. Hermeneia. Philadelphia: Fortress, 1979.
Bullinger, Ethelbert W. *Figures of Speech Used in the Bible: Explained and Illustrated*. 1898. Reprint, Grand Rapids: Baker, 1984.
Church, F. F. "Rhetorical Structure and Design in Paul's Letter to Philemon." *Harvard Theological Review* 71 (1978) 17–33
Cicero. *De Inventione, De Optimo Genere Oratuorum, Topica*. Vol. 2. Translated by H. M. Hubbell. Loeb Classical Library 386. Cambridge, MA: Harvard University Press, 1949.
———. *De Oratore*. Books I–II. Vol. 3. Translated by E. W. Sutton and H. Rackham. Loeb Classical Library 348. Cambridge, MA: Harvard University Press, 1942.
Clement of Alexandria. *Stromata, or The Miscellanies*. In *The Ante-Nicene Fathers: Fathers of the Second Century: Hermas, Tatian, Athenagoras, Theophilus, and Clement of Alexandria (Entire)*, edited by Alexander Roberts et al., 2:299–567. 1885. Reprint, Peabody, MA: Hendrickson, 1996.
Cohick, Lynn H. *Women in the World of the Earliest Christians: Illuminating Ancient Ways of Life*. Grand Rapids: Baker Academic, 2009.
Crates. "Letter 35." In *The Cynic Epistles: A Study Edition*, edited by Abraham J. Malherbe, 88–89. SBLSBS 12. Missoula, MT: Scholars, 1977.
Deming, Will. *Paul on Marriage and Celibacy: The Hellenistic Background of 1 Corinthians 7*. Grand Rapids: Eerdmans, 2004.
Demosthenes. *Private Orations*. Vol. 1. Translated by A. T. Murray. Loeb Classical Library 238. Cambridge, MA: Harvard University Press, 1929.
Dio Chrysostom. *De Invidia*. In *Discourses LXI–LXXX*, vol. 5. Translated by H. Lamar Crosby. Loeb Classical Library 385. Cambridge, MA: Harvard University Press, 1964.
———. *Dialexis*. In *Discourses XXXVII–LX*. Vol. 4. Translated by H. Lamar Crosby. Loeb Classical Library 376. Cambridge, MA: Harvard University Press, 1946.
Diogenes. "Epistle 44." In *The Cynic Epistles: A Study Edition*, edited by Abraham J. Malherbe, 174–75. SBLSBS 12. Missoula, MT: Scholars, 1977.
Diogenes Laertius. *Lives of Eminent Philosophers*. Vols. 1–2. Translated by R. D. Hicks. Loeb Classical Library 184–85. Cambridge, MA: Harvard University Press, 1925.
Epictetus. *Discourses*. Books III–IV. Vol. 2. Translated by W. A. Oldfather. Loeb Classical Library 218. Cambridge: Harvard University, 1928.
Eusebius. *Ecclesiastical History*. Books I–V. Vol. 1. Translated by Kirsopp Lake. Loeb Classical Library 153. Cambridge, MA: Harvard University Press, 1926.
Fee, Gordon D. *First Epistle to the Corinthians*. NICNT. Grand Rapids: Eerdmans, 1987.
Finley, M. I., and S. M. Treggiari. "freedmen, freedwomen." In *The Oxford Classical Dictionary*, edited by Simon Hornblower and Anthony Spawforth, 609. 3rd ed. New York: Oxford University Press, 1996.
Finn, Robert. *Asceticism in the Graeco-Roman World*. Cambridge: Cambridge University Press, 2009.

Gavrilov, A. K. "Techniques of Reading in Classical Antiquity." *The Classical Quarterly*, NS 47 (1997) 56–73.

Heinrici, C. F. Georg. *Der zweite Brief an die Korinther, mit einem Anhang*. 8th ed. KEK 6. Gottingen: Vandenhoeck & Ruprecht, 1900.

Hurd, John C. *The Origin of 1 Corinthians*. Macon, GA: Mercer University Press, 1983.

Isocrates. *On the Peace*. Vol. 2. Translated by George Norlin. Loeb Classical Library 229. Cambridge, MA: Harvard University Press, 1929.

———. *To Demonicus. To Philip*. Vol. 1. Translated by George Norlin. Loeb Classical Library 209. Cambridge, MA: Harvard University Press, 1929.

Jewett, Robert, assisted by Roy D. Kotansky. *Romans: A Commentary*. Hermeneia. Minneapolis, Fortress, 2007.

Josephus, *The Jewish War*. Books I–III. Vol. 2. Translated by H. St. J. Thackeray. Loeb Classical Library 203. Cambridge, MA: Harvard University Press, 1961.

Kennedy, George A. *New Testament Interpretation through Rhetorical Criticism*. Chapel Hill: University of North Carolina Press, 1984.

Malina, Bruce, and John Pilch. *Social-Science Commentary on the Letters of Paul*. Minneapolis: Fortress, 2006.

May, Alistair Scott. *"The Body for the Lord": Sex and Identity in 1 Corinthians 5–7*. London: T. & T. Clark, 2004.

Melanchthon, Philip. *Annotationes in Epistolam Pauli ad Romanos unam, et ad Corinthios duas*. 1523 Augsburg edition. DFGViewer. http://daten.digitale-sammlungen.de/~db/0002/bsb00029694/images/.

Milton, John. *Areopagitica; A Speech of John Milton for the Liberty of Unlicenc'd Printing, to the Parlament of England* (London, 1644). Dartmouth College Milton Reading Room. http://www.dartmouth.edu/~milton/reading_room/areopagitica/index.shtml.

Mitchell, Margaret M. *Paul and the Rhetoric of Persuasion*. Louisville: Westminster John Knox, 1992.

Murphy-O'Connor, Jerome. *Paul the Letter-Writer: His World, His Options, His Skills*. Collegeville, MN: Liturgical, 1995.

Musonius Rufus. "What Is the Chief End of Marriage?" Lecture 13A. In *C. Musonii Rufi: Reliquiae*, edited by Otto Hense, 67–68. Leipzig: Teubner, 1905.

Nanos, Mark, ed. *The Galatians Debate: Contemporary Issues in Rhetorical and Historical Interpretation*. Peabody, MA: Hendrickson, 2002.

Neil, Elliott, and Mark Reasoner. *Documents and Images for the Study of Paul*. Minneapolis: Fortress, 2011.

Økland, Jorunn. *Women in Their Place: Paul and the Corinthian Discourse of Gender and Sanctuary Space*. Edinburgh: T. & T. Clark, 2004.

Osiek, Carolyn. *Shepherd of Hermas: A Commentary*. Edited by Helmut Koester. Hermeneia. Minneapolis: Fortress, 1999.

Perelman, Chaim, and L. Olbrechts-Tyteca. *The New Rhetoric: A Treatise on Argumentation*. Translation by John Wilkinson and Purcell Weaver from 1958 French ed. Notre Dame: University of Notre Dame, 1969.

Philo. *Every Good Man Is Free; On the Contemplative Life*. Vol. 9. Translated by F. H. Colson. Loeb Classical Library 363. Cambridge, MA: Harvard University Press, 1941.

———. *On Abraham; On Joseph; On Moses*. Vol. 6. Translated by F. H. Colson. Loeb Classical Library 289. Cambridge, MA: Harvard University Press, 1935.

———. *Questions and Answers on Genesis*. Supplement 1. Translated by Ralph Marcus. Loeb Classical Library 380. Cambridge, MA: Harvard University Press, 1953.

Philostratus. *Life of Apollonius of Tyana*. Books I–V. Vol. 1. Edited and translated by Christopher P. Jones. Loeb Classical Library 16. Cambridge, MA: Harvard University Press, 2005.

Plutarch, *Moralia*. Vol. 6. Translated by W. C. Helmbold. Loeb Classical Library 337. Cambridge, MA: Harvard University Press, 1939.

Porter, Stanley E. "Paul of Tarsus and His Letters." In *Handbook of Classical Rhetoric in the Hellenistic Period, 330 B.C.–A.D. 400*, edited by Stanley E. Porter, 576–84. Leiden: Brill, 2001.

Puskas, Charles B. and Mark Reasoner. *The Letters of Paul: An Introduction*. Collegeville, MN: Liturgical, 2013.

Quintillian. *Institutio Oratoria*. Vols. 2–3 of 4 vols. Translated by H. E. Butler. Loeb Classical Library 124–27. Cambridge, MA: Harvard University Press, 1920–22.

Reed, Jeffrey T. "The Epistle." In *Handbook of Classical Rhetoric in the Hellenistic Period, 330 B.C.–A.D. 400*, edited by Stanley E. Porter, 171–93. Leiden: Brill, 2001.

Runnalls, D. R. "The Rhetoric of Josephus." In *Handbook of Classical Rhetoric in the Hellenistic Period, 330 B.C.–A.D. 400*, edited by Stanley Porter, 743–45. Leiden: Brill, 2001.

Seboldt, Roland H. A. "Spiritual Marriage in the Early Church: A Suggested Interpretation of 1 Cor 7:36–38." *Concordia Theological Monthly* 30 (1959) 103–119, 176–189.

Stowers, Stanley K. *Letter Writing in Greco-Roman Antiquity*. LEC 5. Philadelphia: Westminster, 1986.

Tertullianus. *Apologeticus Adversos Gentes Pro Christianis*. In *The Migne Patrologia Latina*. Vol. 1. Paris: J. P. Migne, 1844. Documenta Catholica Omnia. http://www.documentacatholicaomnia.eu/02m/0160-0220,_Tertullianus,_Apologeticus_Adversos_Gentes_Pro_Christianis,_MLT.pdf.

Tertullian. *The Apology*. In *The Ante-Nicene Fathers*, edited by Alexander Roberts et al., 3:17–55. Translated by Sidney Thelwall. Buffalo: Christian Literature, 1885.

———. "On Exhortation to Chastity." In *The Ante-Nicene Fathers: Fathers of the Third Century: Tertullian, Part Fourth; Minucius Felix; Commodian; Origen, Parts First and Second*, edited by Alexander Roberts et al., 4:50–58. Buffalo: Christian Literature, 1885.

Thiselton, Anthony C. *The First Epistle to the Corinthians*. NIGNT. Grand Rapids: Eerdmans, 2000.

Weber, Max. *The Protestant Ethic and the Spirit of Capitalism*. Translated by Talcott Parsons. Originally published as *Protestantische Ethik und der Geist des Kapitalismus* (Tübingen: Mohr/Siebeck, 1904). London: Allen & Unwin, 1930.

Weima, Jeffrey A. D. "What Does Aristotle Have to Do with Paul?" *Calvin Theological Journal* 32 (1997) 458–68.

Wimbush, Vincent. *Paul, the Worldly Ascetic: Response to the World and Self-Understanding according to 1 Corinthians 7*. Macon, GA: Mercer University Press, 1987.

Wire, Antoinette Clarke. *The Corinthian Women Prophets: A Reconstruction through Paul's Rhetoric*. Minneapolis: Fortress, 1990.

The Need to Expand, Preserve, and Restore Tradition

10

"Behind Every Successful Man...": Recovering God the Mother in the Search for Subjectivity

—Elaine R. Cleeton

This essay is framed by the twentieth-century resurgences of Pentecostalism and Feminism, against the backdrop of advanced Western marketplace capitalism. Born a Pentecostal, I was launched from my location on the margins of mid-century America by a promise that I could do anything, if I worked hard enough. The downside, that everywhere I went my honest, energetic pursuit of a purposeful life was rebuffed, elicited from my mother the bromide that "It's like that everywhere." Unwilling to give up on my dream, I persisted in my challenge of the imprisoning mental, physical, emotional, and spiritual walls of patriarchy, the State of Possession.[1] It is the purpose of this essay to recall, identify, and retrace evidence of erased humanity.

LOST MOTHER

At the age of five, I knelt down in the tenement apartment bedroom I shared with my brother, my parents at my side, and invited Jesus to come into my heart. Two years later, on a Sunday evening following my father's sermon and invitation to all who were not saved to come forward to give their lives to

---

1. Daly, *Outercourse*, 1.

the Lord, I would accept his second request, that all desiring to be filled with the Holy Spirit join him at the altar. He laid his hands on each of our heads, praying for us individually that God's Spirit would enter in, as evidenced by Saint Luke's description of tongues of fire igniting languages strange even to the speaker. Kneeling at the altar of our basement church sanctuary, the funds for building the main structure having yet to be procured, I began to speak in a beautiful language, the likes of which I had never heard. Enjoying this deep connection with the Divine One, I lay back on the floor, coming eventually to feel peace, comfort, and release from my sadness, my grief, my disappointments. Returning to the present from that sacred space, my father looked into my eyes, his face beaming with joy, happiness, and pride. This form of communication, integral to my private meditations, would decline in its significance for me until my father's funeral, fifty years later.

An emerging religious collaboration, twentieth-century Pentecostalism initially integrated by race, gender, and class, would reenergize the Protestant tradition. For what it offered spiritually, it lacked intellectually. Adherence to a literal interpretation of the King James Bible would become fodder for late-twentieth-century popularity of the "Prosperity Gospel"—with a concomitant waning of interest in the teachings of Jesus. But with growth, financial stability, and public recognition, Pentecostalism would replace the founding mother ministers with men and abandon its foundational anti-war stance; a racial fork in the road would divide the movement into the Church of God in Christ (COGIC) and the Assemblies of God (AG), moving from the margins to the center.

Its "Spirit-led" spontaneous worship would lead the liturgical embrace of end-of-the-century youth culture, drawing in young, middle-class families attempting to replicate the mythical 1950s nuclear family unit. Out of powerful mega-churches would emerge rabid, pro-gun, anti-contraception, anti-immigration, anti-civil rights, anti-affirmative action, anti-feminism, anti-gay, anti-government political conservatives poised to revoke civil rights affirming the humanity of all those outside the non-signified "universal" white male ideal. From the Protestant work ethic, fueled by delayed dreams, to the consumerist "free choice" culture,

> it's the inexplicability in straight-queer discourse of comprehending the full dimensions of the gathering darkness of the human condition—sites of bodily and cultural injury used now

"Behind Every Successful Man . . ." 221

as political opportunities for projecting all the madness of ressentiment onto an always crusading, always missionary, never grieving, never loving, reanimated world historical project of American imperialism.[2]

I recall my childhood spent reading the Bible, praying, and sharing my faith. I gradually moved away from proselytizing, believing that the power of God, when visible in our lives, pulls people toward the light. Concurrently, I became aware of my family's paltry economic circumstances. My father served young AG churches in exchange for housing and the Sunday morning offering. I experienced our material weightlessness as a sign of our having no roots, no history, no resources, and no standing in the community, leaving me to search for what I would come to experience as the shift from self-denial to unbridled material acquisition, both denying the role of the body in human subjectivity.

Privileging mind over matter, brain over body, the modern subject reflects the role of Christianity in brokering the intellectual collision of Rome, Athens, and Jerusalem:

> Represented in all its religious passion, yet philosophical subtlety, by the Trinitarian formula—God the Father, God the Son, and God the Holy Ghost, in other words, by the signifying logic of will, intelligence and affect—Christianity moved the metaphysical center of Western experience from power and reason on the outside, externally posited, to the most intimate moment of interiority, the *directly experienced* confessionality of the Christian subject . . . Henceforth the will to power would be animated by the *death of wild, instinctual behavior* and the *triumph of reactive being*. In the form of the will to power, the reduction of being human to spirit-flesh would be repeated daily as the overriding psychic reality of modernity.[3]

A loss of consciousness is replaced by mental ruminations, persistent and endless, structured as comparisons with the "not-I." Ever-present is the necessity of outpacing, outperforming, outproducing the other. The ego is unaware of itself. Its endless complaints become evidence of victimization; bullying appears on the violent end of this scale of unceasing competition.[4] The modern liberal subject emerging from that of the preceding "body of

---

2. Kroker, *Body Drift*, 59.
3. Ibid., 59–60.
4. Tolle, *A New Earth*.

Christian confessionality"[5] became the sadistic underpinning for the Western narrative of progress.

The 1960s consciousness-raising groups, inspired by *The Feminine Mystique*,[6] would identify the terrain on which I would explore my Judeo-Christian worldview, fostered by the writings of bell hooks,[7] Kate Millet, and Betty Friedan. Forced to consider the possibility that the promise of meritocracy was not working for me, I tripped over the term "misogyny," a word I had never heard. As I reconsidered work-related and personal experiences contradicting the promises of the Protestant work ethic, I began to understand that my belief in reward for hard work was founded on "a fictional terrain," that to understand its emergence and origins would necessitate "a reterritorialization that has passed through several versions of deterritorialization to posit a powerful theory of location based on contingency, history and change."[8]

How, in 1980, could this critical word have escaped my attention? I found comfort, inspiration, and company in the writings of Mary Daly guiding me to delve "deeply into the process of communication with the Self and with Others—a process which requires deep E-motion, deep Re-membering, deep Understanding,"[9] a practice producing what Rosi Braidotti describes to be "a set of narrations of my own embodied genealogy."[10] Seeking "a postmetaphysical vision of subjectivity,"[11] Braidotti calls for a departure from the supernatural realm of the father god and a recovery of the natural world of God the Mother; there is work to be done by "ecstatic speakers,"[12] "seeing," "hearing," "feeling" via connections with other humans also experiencing the violence of the Western grand narrative of progress through science.

Living without spouse or children, I moved from job to job, from career to career, free to continue my search for intimacy. A desire to know passionate human connection would exact heavy payment, even as those watching from afar would deem my life to be successful, exciting, and virtually trouble-free, having enjoyed fifty years of travel, relationships, and careers culminating with two sons and a husband. They equated my freedom

---

5. Ibid., 116.
6. Friedan, *Feminine Mystique*.
7. Gloria Watkins's *nom de plume* is bell hooks using lowercase.
8. Kaplan, "Deterritorializations," 198.
9. Daly, *Outercourse*, 3.
10. Braidotti, *Nomadic Subject*, 7.
11. Ibid.
12. Haraway, "Ecce Homo," 86.

to access and inhabit the public arena with courage to voluntarily pursue new careers—evidence of fearless self-confidence.

Those comfortably ensconced in their institutional identities, be they voluntary church bureaucrats, tenured academic functionaries, even long-standing members of Twelve-step programs, find the arrival of a nomad who learns the program, comes to speak the language, if haltingly, and seeks baptism by immersion, unsettling at best, and threatening at worst. Those holding positions of power dispose of the "other" as quickly and as neatly as possible. Those discovering the holes in the promise of reward for hard work reach for the nomad's open hands, because they have no place else to go. Renewal, resurgence, restoration—these are "four-letter" words never uttered by those who live comfortably, if not securely, behind the protective walls of status; they recognize and fear the power of engagement, of the impassioned, embodied recovering subject to be released from the prison of fear.

The nomad committed to the work of rebuilding the fragmented self as a task of "actively explicating the connections,"[13] recognizes humans of like mind; empathic curious fellow seekers offer sustenance, shelter, experience, strength, and hope. Having grown up the daughter of a Pentecostal preacher pastoring in both southern and northern small, rural, conservative villages and towns, my religious and public library/school educational experiences embraced the Victorian, gendered nuclear family ideal. As a college student in the late 1960s, longing to become a legitimate member of the professional realm, I drank in every visible detail of the academy. Having received a "call" to the mission field when I was ten, I attended Central Bible College (CBC) for one year. In search of a professional focus, my Strong Vocational Interest Test score linking me with speech pathology led my father's CBC classmate psychologist Raymond Brock to contact Professor Ruth Burgess, who would recruit me to Evangel College (now Evangel University) for the new Speech Pathology major.

Breeching the divide separating work and family, Professor Burgess brought her ten-year-old son to class one day, and to my surprise, everything proceeded according to expectation. She invited me to her home to enjoy an Indian meal served on banana leaves harvested from the tree in her back yard. Dining with the Burgesses, I learned to eat the delicious meal with my fingers. On another occasion, Professor Burgess amazed her students, by arriving to class stunningly clad and appearing in full-face make-up. Our reaction elicited a brief explanation, that following class, she would be leaving campus for a professional meeting in town. Her ability to expertly

---

13. Braidotti, *Nomadic Subjects*, 10.

navigate the terrain connecting the Holiness tradition of women's practicing extreme modesty influencing behavioral expectations of the college for women, and a modern, professional venue would serve as a guidepost for what lay ahead.

Professor Burgess's regard for my intelligence would advance my academic growth while her commitment to embracing all of her gifts and talents would indirectly foster my pursuit of living a meaningful life. I recall the day when she asked, "Elaine, what do you plan to study for your doctorate?" She was so direct, so matter of fact. I knew she was serious. But I had yet to realize that I could pursue a terminal degree. "I don't know," I replied. At best, I hoped to be invited to take my seat in the audience, never expecting to stand behind the podium.

Because of Professor Burgess's preparation, I completed the master of arts in speech pathology at the highest-ranked program in the nation. Remaining in contact, I would learn of her temporary move to Columbia, Missouri, where, with the help of her mother, she and her young children lived while she completed her doctorate. Later I would write my dissertation with my first-born strapped to my chest in a snuggly, taking care of both of us through the process. During my graduate study program in sociology, Professor Burgess opened her home to me for a research project interviewing retired AG women ministers living in Springfield, Missouri. Years later, my younger son, Will, and I would travel to Virginia to spend time with her, most memorably fishing for crabs by dropping chicken legs tied with string into the tidal pool outside her home.

Beyond preparing me for success in graduate school, Dr. Burgess embodied the nomad on the margins, combining family and work, living between cultures—moving between Indian and U.S. ethnic identities, while managing conservative religious and contemporary professional conflicts. Making room for me in her life, as she carried on her family and professional responsibilities, she answered definitively the question regarding women's place in both worlds, that there is but one world of which women are rightful inhabitants. She reached out, offering resources otherwise unavailable to me to promote my academic progress. Observing her life, I, too, would decide to combine an academic career with family. Over the years, we have traded stories of the challenges seemingly provoked by our shared commitment to excellence in the last bastion of patriarchal domination—the academy.

Offering a "postmetaphysical vision of subjectivity," Braidotti describes "woman" to be the site of multiple, complex, and potentially contradictory sets of experiences revealing "intensive interconnectedness."[14] To recover the Divine Feminine principle,[15] the elements associated with the maternal in YHWH, in Allah, in God the father, offer little comfort. Surviving vestiges of the mother preserved in the *Psalms* remain secondary to the power and authority of father-god. More satisfying is the search for evidence of the existence of the mother god in the human conscience, from which she was gradually and nearly totally exorcised over the millennia, leaving females bereft of knowledge of their bodies, their childbearing, their development of agriculture and housing, their wisdom, and their leadership.

CHALLENGING THE BINARY

To open liminal space in which connections fostering new life are formed, "women are challenged to Spin and Weave the broken connections in our Knowing, Sensing, and Feeling, becoming Alive again in our relationships to our Selves and to each Other . . . it will require Time Travel—Remembering our Future and our Past."[16] The rewriting of home and exile in Western feminist discourse, "deterritorialization,"[17] begins with the process of recovering the genealogy from the foreground permitting discovering of and embracing the reversals on which it is based.

Abandoning the doctor/patient binary, I planned a home birth. Rejecting the modern version of delivery as crisis,[18] the medical establishment became a service ready in the event of an emergency. Challenging the medical life/death binary, I considered my maternal grandmother's eleven successful home births. In the 1950s, my mother, following the trend to hospitalize childbirth, would give birth to me in hospital, in highly medicated state from which she would recover hours after I had been delivered and taken to the nursery. By the 1990s, 98 percent of all United States births would occur in hospital, where the most significant progress made subsequent to my hospital birth would be the use of multiple technologies and a soaring cesarean section rate.

While I was born under the influence of placenta-crossing drugs administered to make my mother forget the pain (a veritable 1950s "crack"

14. Braidotti, *Nomadic Subjects*.
15. Gambutas, *Language*, xxi.
16. Daly, *Outercourse*, 9.
17. Kaplan, "Deterritorializations," 187.
18. Murphy-Lawless, *Reading Birth*.

baby), I gave birth to my children at home without pharmaceuticals, without surgery, without mechanical assistance. I connected with my grandmother's birth history, finding it to be preferable to the humiliating procedures imposed on women delivering in hospital mid-century. I embraced my grandmother's experience affirming women's power and authority in childbirth. Daly observes that critical moments, often separated by time, "interact because of their subjective reality and connectedness in the consciousness of the Voyager and because of their interconnecting consequences in the world."[19] To recapture memories, insights, desire and wanting, challenging the "Acts of Exorcism of the *amnesia* inflicted by patriarchal institutions, religion in particular, by the–ologies which they engender and which in turn serve to legitimate them ... Exorcism of *amnesia* required Acts of Unforgetting ... beyond the androcratic lies about women's history."[20] In a study of women college student beliefs about the childbirth experience, students expressed terror of labor pain, believing that the process cannot be survived without anesthesia.[21]

Remembering the eleven babies my maternal grandmother, Helen, delivered at home in the early 1900s, I birthed two sons at home in 1992 and 1995. My first baby was born following eleven hours of labor. No drugs, no surgery, no high-tech monitors were needed. Family, friends, and two traditional midwives attended me. After my newborn son and I had bathed, we shared a beautiful traditional turkey dinner prepared by my mother the previous day, on a whim that would prove to be prescient of the baby's arrival.

My childhood interest in medicine would be realized as I accompanied my family members through medical crises. When my father's dementia-orchestrated demise was interrupted by a stroke, I kept my promise that he would never return to the hospital. Meeting with his physician, I argued persuasively against the hubris that my father's death could be postponed by one more visit to the Emergency Department, if not delayed indefinitely. Finally agreeing to schedule a hospice workup for my father, the doctor was surprised to learn of his immediate admission into the program; four days later, my father would die at home.

Remembering my maternal grandfather's bout with liver cancer—after two radiation treatments, he terminated therapy and returned home to resume his daily five-mile walks, to resume his visits to church members hospitalized for illness, and to live one more year of life's pleasures—I scheduled a mastectomy, and then refused cosmetic reconstruction and protease

---

19. Daly, *Outercourse*, 5.
20. Ibid, 7.
21. Cleeton, "Attitudes and Beliefs."

inhibitors, choosing to walk every day, like my grandfather, and modify my diet on behalf of living a healthy life, no matter how many or few years remain.

At the age of fourteen, my younger son, Will, was diagnosed with addictive brain disorder. Identifying and securing the recovery support he needed began with my refusing to turn him over to the criminal justice system as recommended by well-meaning family and friends. Following three months of ineffective outpatient drug treatment Will entered a residential treatment program for adolescent boys. Thirty staff members work with fifteen boys, employing family systems therapy in conjunction with Alcoholics Anonymous.

While I stayed the course, never giving up on Will, and hanging on to him until effective treatment could be secured, I ignored my emotional health. Having left the spirit-focused life of my childhood in exchange for a commitment to rationality, I no longer responded with feelings. Will urged me to pursue my healing in the rooms of Al-Anon. Today, he shares his story of experience, strength, and hope in the rooms. He would become a powerful advocate for my recovery in Al-Anon. While everything was new to me—the meetings and their ritualistic, highly-structured nature of sharing (something about cross-talk), the members wavering between the heaviness of daily life and the hope of building connections with other like-minded persons who know the ins and outs of addiction, and the complicated anonymity regulations about never saying the name of the group, the program that would not be named—it was in those rooms that I would begin the process of learning how to take care of myself by reaching out to others.

These stories do not fit the grand narrative of science—the subject is not a victim—I deliver a healthy baby without complications, my father quietly takes his last breath in the privacy of his home; the beauty of birth and the blessing of death reveal the mind/body relationship; both occur in the presence of family and friends. A room full of recovering addicts, persons of means, street-people, old and wise, young and reckless create a safe space in which to seek restoration of the mind and body connection. In each instance, professionals may assist, but never lead—never demand, never coerce, never harm. Embracing human interconnections challenges those who, having abandoned the mind/body connection, turn their life decisions over to certified "experts."

Braidotti describes a "nomadic polyglot" who seeks incongruities leading to the sites where reversals have occurred. Disturbing sedentary life, nomads discover incongruities revealing unfounded assumptions, ideologies treated as truths. Curiosity and desire to communicate can unlock doors behind which are hidden endless rows of boxes containing contradictions, stereotypes, and discriminatory practices—a veritable Indiana Jones underground repository of secrets.

Feminism feeds the voracious capitalist belly with female units excited for the chance to become part of the corporate enterprise. Supported by second wave feminism, white women enter the competitive fray, a single line of women, one behind the other, all facing in the same direction, and no one is talking. Fearing that criticism of working conditions will trigger delivery of a pink slip, women remain silent. In 1985, I earn a master's of divinity, to be ordained in the United Church of Christ. Like my mother, a licensed Assemblies of God minister, I would never pastor a United Church of Christ congregation. For the belief of many congregations, that women did not belong in the pulpit, prevailed. While serving as associate in a United Methodist Church, I was introduced to the Syracuse University women studies graduate program. Gradually, I began to take steps leading to a doctorate. Within a year, I would be accepted into the sociology graduate studies program.

Ten years later, when I began my tenure-track position, my Freire-inspired collaborative pedagogy[22] attracted the brightest majors, unintentionally challenging the reign of my senior colleagues from the top of the list of most popular professors. My colleagues accused me of criticizing their work in order to call into question incontrovertible evidence of my classroom success. While they would oppose every contract renewal, my performance outweighed their opposition, and I was tenured and promoted.

Repeatedly ambushed by insecure colleagues, I retain the belief that their vitriol will diminish.

> The subject thus is a heap of fragmented parts held together by the symbolic glue that is the attachment to, or identification with, the phallogocentric symbolic . . . I am struck by the violence of the gesture that binds a fractured self to the performative illusion of unity, mastery, self-transparence. I am amazed by the terrifying stupidity of that illusion of unity, and by its incomprehensible force.[23]

---

22. Freire, *Pedagogy*.
23. Braidotti, *Nomad Subjects*, 12.

Marginal identities evoke suspicion; belief in recovery of healthy existence provokes brutal confrontations, most of which occur when the provocateur is absent from the room. Supportive colleagues respond with confusion as to the source of enmity toward my work; the only term holding explanatory power is misogyny. While resistance to any form of change is commonplace, threats to adherence to the gender, race, and class ideals incite violent emotional, if not physical reactions.

Professor Burgess modeled resistance/insistence, being present to family, to colleagues, and to students. Inspired by her life, I accessed the public sphere while maintaining my commitment to protecting the humanity of my babies, my father, my son in recovery, and my students in the classroom. The nomad resists "collectively produced amnesia" as she preserves experiences and moments of clarity not available in the managed homocultural experiences of the sedentary. I am a nomad traveling from place to place seeking to "know" each location.

RECOVERING SUBJECTIVITY

A longing for discovery of the one universal truth to which all can and will ascribe limits each movement, including feminism. Examples of nurturing fathers and warrior mothers are so numerous, the inclination to cling to Victorian definitions of public and private spheres attests to cultural resistance to change, even when the goal is recovery of our humanity. Efforts to find the mother are thwarted by the persistent argument that we cannot afford to preserve practices of the past. Yet, while international conglomerates proclaim the establishment of the global village, border crossings enabling cultural interactions weaken the binary:

> I am arguing that nomadic consciousness is akin to what Foucault called countermemory; it is a form of resisting assimilation or homologation into dominant ways of representing the self. Feminists—or other critical intellectuals as nomadic subject—are those who have forgotten to forget injustice and symbolic poverty: their memory is activated against the stream; they enact a rebellion of subjugated knowledges.[24]

The nomad may be a keen observer, may learn multiple languages, but unable to lose a detectible accent, the newcomer is treated with suspicion, never inducted into the circle of power.

24. Ibid., 25.

Second wave feminism settles into white, middle-class comfort, a position from which even women of color resist reminders of historic racism:

> [W]hen a theory is transformed into an ideology, it begins to destroy the self and self-knowledge . . . Begun as a way to restore women's sense of reality, now it attempts to discipline real people, to remake natural beings after its own image . . . Begun as a theory of liberation, it is threatened by new theories of liberation; it builds a prison for the mind.[25]

To unseat the split mind/body binary, support for hybrid entities is required.

Speaking from the margins, hooks argues that feminist movement requires resistance to "hegemonic dominance of feminist thought" through constant interaction, questioning, and consideration of new possibilities, preventing a single theory from gaining currency, while denying its limits. "Though I criticize aspects of feminist movement as we have known it so far, a critique which is sometimes harsh and unrelenting, I do so not in an attempt to diminish feminist struggle but to enrich, to share in the work of making a liberatory ideology and a liberatory movement."[26] The work of liberation is collaboration through human connections restored, the liminal space within which human interconnections are discovered and rebuilt.

Donna Haraway describes the relationship between the fates of gender and sexuality, women, animals, plants, cyborgs, aliens; her "hybrid body" insists on recovering connections with nature, animals, plants, genders, sexualities, "Always a (feminist) theorist in and of hybridity in opposition to the 'universal sameness' of the father's (scientific) word,"[27] Haraway acknowledges the divine feminine principle, the mother God, as she is, as she was, as she is imaged to be; she gives birth to all that we know, she embraces all that is. The "closed self-referential framework of the modern scientific episteme is shattered by the power of insistent, critical questions, finally breaking apart under this pressure into its constituent elements of race, class, and gender."[28]

Finding liminal space in which to challenge patriarchal gender binary, Haraway recommends engaging science in an effort to map reality. In her primate studies, Haraway examines the relations between women, science, and capitalism. She identifies a sadistic scientific relationship with apes and monkeys, and then exploring the means by which Western science reaches this stage reveals the "complicity of the life sciences in the histories

25. Griffin, "The Way," 648.
26. hooks, *Feminist Theory*, 15.
27. Korker, *Body Drift*, 106.
28. Ibid., 109.

of colonialism and racism."[29] The "will to truth" promotes all research, regardless of its potential for imposing suffering on primates and ultimately humans as experimental subjects, who will submit to "life-extending" procedures guaranteeing unbearable chronic pain, in spite of potential diminution of quality of life and the denial of death with dignity. The crowning achievement of this nihilist project is the "production of the unmarked abstract universal, man."[30]

Liminal space in which cross-talk bridges race, gender, and cultural identities, is found in the Twelve-step rooms where individuals having experienced a restoration of mind and body share experiences of strength and hope, "opening up, through successive repetitions and mimetic strategies, spaces where alternative forms of agency can be engendered."[31] I am ready for a spiritual life finding the mother god through connections with others seeking to restore subject freedom. It is in hearing each other's stories that truth is discovered; it is in speaking life's missteps, misunderstandings, and blind spots that hope is recovered. It is in connection that suffering in isolation from shame linked with personal failures, from enraging humiliation, belittlement, and exclusion diminishes.

CONCLUSION

"Progress" relies on erasure of knowledge of the mother earth, on the lies of science serving as the ultimately unreliable foundation for the father's world. Calling upon the past and anticipating the future, access to prehistoric evidence of the mother god challenges stubborn adherence to patriarchal life/death binary. In the gray area, in the liminal space, class boundaries, professional identities, medical protocols, and zero tolerance practices and assumptions are brought into question.

The promise of progress through technology requires loss of contingency; the culture of death is not about abortion—that is a distraction from the scientific promise of putting an end to death in exchange for a willing relinquishing of living the mind/body connection. Self-absorption is not real. There is no self when there is no connection with the other. Longing to be real, desiring to know, a cry for relevance, a desire to be known, the eruption of power, the intensity of being, recovery of the divine legitimates persistent belief in its survival in the face of deadening forces.

---

29. Ibid., 111.
30. Haraway, *Primate Visions*, 233.
31. Braidotti, *Nomadic Subject*, 7.

Having left cultural insularity of my early religious experience, traveled the planet developing an understanding of social processes, I returned to my spiritual roots, in pursuit of recovery from the mind/body split, recovery of consciousness and deep self-respect:

> The feminist dream of a common language, like all dreams for a perfectly true language, of perfectly faithful name of experience, is a totalizing and imperialist one. In that sense, dialectics too is a dream language, longing to resolve contradiction. Perhaps, ironically, we can learn from our fusions with animals and machines how not to be Man, the embodiment of Western logos. From the point of view of pleasure in these potent and taboo fusions, made inevitable by the social relations of science and technology, there might indeed be a feminist science.[32]

As a child, I desired roots, history, and identity, commodities unavailable to my third-generation immigrant family, my second-generation Pentecostal assemblage; a history impacted by dependence on alcohol combined with immigrant survival techniques and working class mores denied my longing to be a member of a community built on trust, taking seriously the interests of all. I will come to understand that dominance of oppression privileges mind over body, that whatever my professional achievements and contributions, I will remain a body in the eyes of my academic peers. Sensing the reconnection of spirit, mind, and body, I feel joy, excitement, and elation. Moments of clarity sustain me as I find my way through the pain, and the healing comes:

> Coded by narratives of power yet remaining heterogeneous, local, and embodied, the body hybrid surfaces anew in a world of 'co-texts' and 'coupled structures.' A 'problematic multiplicity,' the body hybrid can only know other 'nonselves' by opening itself to new forms of reciprocal communication with all the hominds, animals, machines, aliens, zombies, and replicants of the future. In essence, if the body hybrid is not to be a copy of a master code, it must engage with the difficult heuristics of companion species. If there is no necessary immunity, there must definitely be (species) community.[33]

Full humanity can be accessible to all. Moving from forefront to background, one finds language, friends, and safe havens from which to take action contradicting professional and familial expectations. Women have

---

32. Haraway, *Simians*, 173.
33. Kroker, *Body Drift*, 133.

not lost their strength. Women have not lost their intelligence. Women have not lost their courage. However, living in the state of possession by men, of servitude to men and children, of assimilation of gendered identities, of amnesia forgetting our relationship to our earth mother, of aphasia losing the language that identifies and names our experience, of apraxia losing our motor abilities, and unmitigated boredom, this is not a natural state, and there is relief.

Archeological sites where evidence of women's full humanity can be mined, while difficult to locate, are rich repositories worthy of the attention of all who would challenge necrotic domination. For Daly, reversal means taking the claims made about masculinity and recognizing their source in the female; rationality, physical strength, decision-making, leadership, responsibility. For Braidotti, inter-cultural connections fostered by telecommunication reveal liminal space in which binary thinking is challenged. Judith Butler argues for the multidimensionality of sexuality, and Haraway for a comingling of human, species, and cyborg into the postmodern sentient being.

Professor Burgess's acts of courage combined academic rigor with a deep commitment to family, making visible the space shared by both "public" and "private" activities. The nomad's journey is sustained by those who provide shelter, conversation, temporary work—connection in its many forms. "We are still living under the sway of that aggressive male invasion and only beginning to discover our long alienation from our authentic European Heritage—gylanic, nonviolent, earth-centered culture."[34] Sitting across from my father's casket, I feel ecstatic utterings welling up in the liminal space in which connections are realized and subjectivity recovered.

BIBLIOGRAPHY

Braidotti, Rosi. *Nomadic Subjects: Embodiment and Sexual Difference in Contemporary Feminist Theory*. New York: Columbia University Press, 1994.
Butler, Judith. *Bodies That Matter: On the Discursive Limits of "Sex."* New York: Routledge, 1993.
Cleeton, Elaine. "Attitudes and Beliefs Among College Students: Results of a Single Educational Intervention." *Birth: Issues in Perinatal Care* 28 (2001) 192–201.
Daly, Mary. *Outercourse: The Be-dazzling Voyage*. San Francisco: Harper & Row, 1992.
Friedan, Betty. *The Feminine Mystique*. New York: Norton, 1974.
Freire, Paolo. *Pedagogy of the Oppressed*. New York: Continuum, 2002.
Gambutas, Marija. *The Language of the Goddess*. San Francisco: Harper & Row, 1989.
Greer, Germaine. *Sex and Destiny: The Politics of Human Fertility*. New York: Harper & Row, 1984.

34. Gambutas, *Language*, xxi.

Griffin, Susan. "The Way of All Ideology." *Signs* 7 (1982) 641–60.

Haraway, Donna. "Ecce Homo, Ain't (Ar'n't) I a Woman and Inappropriate/d Others: The Human in a Post-Humanist Landscape." In *Feminists Theorize the Political*, edited by Judith Butler and Joan Scott, 86–100. New York: Routledge, 1992.

———. *Primate Visions: Gender, Race, and Nature in the World of Modern Science*. New York: Routledge, 1989.

———. *Simians, Cyborgs, and Women: The Reinvention of Nature*. New York: Routledge, 1991.

hooks, bell. *Feminist Theory: From Margin to Center*. Boston: South End, 1984.

Kaplan, Caren. "Deterritorializations: The Rewriting of Home and Exile in Western Feminist Discourse." *Cultural Critique* 6 (1987) 187–98.

Kroker, Arthur. *Body Drift: Butler, Hayles, Haraway*. Minneapolis: University of Minnesota Press, 2012.

Millet, Kate. *Sexual Politics*. New York: Doubleday, 1970.

Murphy-Lawless, Jo. *Reading Birth and Death: A History of Obstetric Thinking*. Bloomington: Indiana University Press, 1998.

Tolle, Eckhart. *A New Earth: Awakening to Your Life's Purposes*. New York: Penguin, 2005.

11

The MissouriFind Project
A Labor of Love (And an Exercise in Patience, Perseverance, and Political Acumen)

—Steven W. Hinch and David Brown

Stephanie Reid presents her Personal History-Heritage Project for the MissouriFind pilot program at Greenwood Laboratory School in the spring of 1994.

MissouriFind was an inquiry-based, middle school curriculum funded by the Missouri Department of Elementary and Secondary Education (DESE) and the Department of Natural Resources (DNR). The curriculum was developed by a team of professionals—The MissouriFind Consortium—at Southwest Missouri State University (now known as Missouri State University) and Ozarks Public Television. The materials evolved using a collaborative model. A DESE-appointed statewide advisory board oversaw the project; while on campus, Dr. Arthur Mallory (former Southwest Missouri State University president) served as the director of the project, and Dr. Ruth Burgess, director of the Center for Research and Service, led the development of the educational content.

The Educational Component team was largely responsible for instructional design, including the infusion of critical thinking, integrating MissouriFind into the Missouri Basic Skills and Key Competencies, as well as implementing an evaluation plan. Ruth worked tirelessly in both the overall planning design and in the coordination of this team of experts. Meeting in the small, cramped conference room in the Professional Building, where the Center for Research and Service was housed, Ruth and her team usually met weekly over a period of twenty months in the planning and conceptualization phase.

Students in Dr. Roger Tipling's video production class were involved in the evaluation of the video components. Other members of the educational production group included Kay Benedict, Judy Kistler, Dawn Edgerly, Kim Meyers of Ozark Public Television, and Steve Hinch. Mr. Hinch was given the responsibility to be the lead teacher of the MissouriFind pilot in the academic year of 1993–1994. The student pilot group was the seventh grade class at the university's laboratory school, Greenwood, where Hinch was the secondary social studies teacher. He was assisted in this duty by Judy Kistler, a trained Instrumental Enrichment (I. E.) instructor. As the curriculum was being developed, both student and teacher materials were field-tested by Dr. David Brown's social studies curriculum classes.

David Brown was the instructor of a graduate course in the College of Education's Elementary Master's Program entitled Advanced Theory and Practice in Teaching the Social Studies. This course consisted of approximately eighteen students, most of whom were practicing elementary and middle school teachers in the Springfield and surrounding school districts.

The graduate students were divided into groups and each given sections of the curriculum guides, magazines, and the introductory video, which was the only one finished at the time. With the understanding that formal Missouri State History curriculum is not introduced until the fourth grade, the groups were comprised of as much of a mix of both upper and lower grade levels taught so each group could sample a comprehensive age span and compile feedback from several perspectives. They were to take these materials back to their classrooms and share them with their students to get an initial set of feedback as to "student friendliness"—format/eye appeal, readability, scope and sequence, etc.—from the eyes of lower/upper elementary/middle-level students. Later the formal evaluation of these components, including the assessment of the content was completed with the Greenwood students.

In addition to the classroom students' feedback, the graduate students provided feedback from the teachers' perspective. Both written and oral feedback was solicited and time was set aside in each class period once per week to discuss the project. Each component of the curriculum was examined. In general:

- They were asked to critique the video for its value of being the anticipatory set of each unit. Did it "hook" the students and get them excited to learn more about the unit's topic?
- Did the scope and sequence flow correctly and make sense?
- Were the student magazines a positive and viable alternative to a textbook? Might students be more likely to maintain their interest with such a "novelty?"
- Were the teacher's guides user-friendly; easy to read, provide enough information, provide sufficient and appropriate suggested resources? Could they be taught by utilizing local, readily available resources and not having to search for resources or information that was hard to find (much like a great recipe that calls for ingredients that can only be found in specialty stores)?
- Did the materials make one be proud to be a Missourian?

Additionally, some of the most important questions about this curriculum were:

- Are the teachers able to understand and confidently convey the concept of "finding oneself in Missouri and finding Missouri in each individual" to their students?
- Are the teachers able to comprehend the I. E. pedagogical theory and higher-order thinking strategies imbedded into this curriculum enough to comfortably and competently deliver the lessons?

The answers to these last two questions were extremely important to the curriculum team as both were seminal and incredibly unique to the MissouriFind curriculum. Being a native Missourian connotes a certain sense of belonging to the state, which is important; however, the act of finding oneself as an integral and compulsory part of the history, heritage, and geography of the place in which one was born—where it could not exist in its current paradigm without each individual—is quite powerful. This concept literally could not be comprehended without the skillful infusion of the tools and techniques of I. E. No other state history curriculum to the date of the inception of MissouriFind espoused this concept. It was truly extraordinary.

The feedback from the teachers was mixed but overwhelmingly positive. Not being exposed to such a curriculum and delivery was the biggest challenge, as none of them had experience with I. E. theory. In spite of this, they were able to articulate competent answers to the above questions and provided the Curriculum Component team with some reassuring and constructive criticism.

One of the first priorities in the conceptualization of the entire project was for Ruth to provide a basic training to her staff of the tenets of I. E.—a pedagogical theory of cognitive intervention and enrichment developed by Reuven Feuerstein. Feurerstein was the founder and director of the International Center for the Enhancement of Learning Potential (ICELP) in Jerusalem, Israel. For more than fifty years, Feuerstein's theories and applied systems have been implemented in both clinical and classroom settings internationally, with more than eighty countries applying his work. The idea behind this theory is that intelligence can be modified through mediated interventions. Ruth had become familiar with Feuerstein's work earlier in her career and had the opportunity to study with him in Israel during the 1980s.

This grounded theoretical approach was embedded into the MissouriFind curriculum and became a significant component of the evaluation of the program. This model, which Ruth introduced to the team, provided the framework to blend the cognitive development of the seventh grade pilot group with the rich, interdisciplinary content created for this project. Judy Kistler worked with the seventh grade Greenwood class teaching vocabulary relating to thinking, enhancing the development of cognitive skills, and showing them how to deduce relationships or patterns in other content areas through a process called "bridging."

MissouriFind, the Missouri History-Heritage Curriculum, required students to demonstrate competency in their state's history and geography, as well as their public and private heritages. Throughout the curriculum, students sought to "Find themselves in Missouri and Missouri in them." The curriculum was comprised of eighteen units divided into four student magazines. The first two magazines entitled *Missouri Beginnings: Prehistory to 1830* and *Crisis Generation: 1830 to 1865* each were comprised of five units. The last two magazines, *Missouri Modernizes: 1865–1941* and *Missouri in the*

Larger World: 1900 to the Present each housed four units. The units included a fifteen-to-eighteen minute video plus a variety of instructional materials.

Student Magazine: Example of Section 2; *Crisis Generation*. All magazines used illustrations of significant concepts and events of that time period as well as a timeline running at the bottom of the cover. Note that the "i" is embedded in the "F," thus accentuating the program's logo—"I find myself in Missouri and Missouri in me."

Throughout this undertaking, Ruth maintained an upbeat and positive attitude that was infectious. Working long hours in preparation for each of the weekly planning meetings, Ruth still had a big smile on her face as each of the members of the educational team entered the conference room for that week's update and a look at the next task at hand. If there was good news to share from the previous week's encounters with upper administration, or the oversight group in Jefferson City, Ruth would almost be giddy in her recollection of the information that she shared with us that day. Her exuberance breathed life into the gathering and made the weekly working meetings a pleasure to attend, something that cannot always be said of 3:30 p.m. meetings after a full day in the classroom.

Through this program the middle school and university students gained a deeper understanding and appreciation of their state's history and cultures. They came to recognize and identify more clearly their common heritage while being encouraged to think critically about questions posed from the past and present Missouri experience. Recognizing that most of Missouri lies outside the classroom, students were encouraged to delve into community resources, conduct interviews with extended family and community members. They visited and learned about the significance of historic preservation sites. Through this year of inquiry, students developed a portfolio of work relating to their Missouri. The overriding themes covered in this study were: land, time, economics, politics, and society.

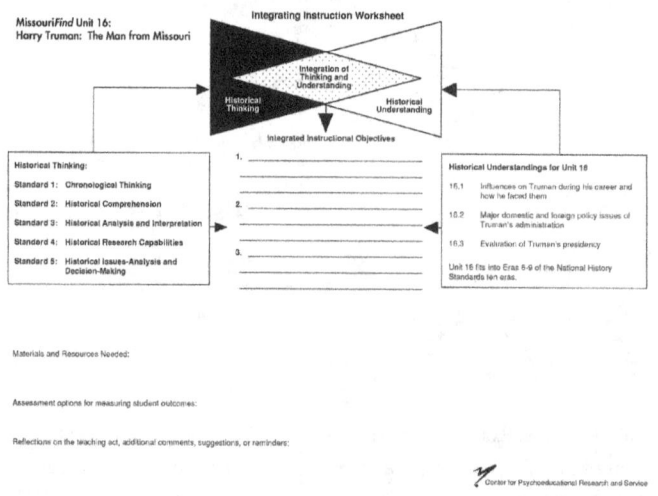

Integrating Instruction Worksheet used to align standards and instructional objectives. Example taken from Unit 16—Harry Truman: The Man from Missouri.

TAKING THE SHOW ON THE ROAD

During the month of May 1992, three focus groups were held with educators and local historical caretakers in different areas of the state to introduce MissouriFind, the Missouri History-Heritage Project and seek their contributions and collaboration. The meetings were held in Scott County, Kansas City and Independence, and in Hazelwood, a suburb north of St. Louis. MoFind personnel leading the focus groups were trained by Dr. Arlen Diamond of the SMSU Communications Department in late April.

Prior to the meetings, local educators were contacted to facilitate the focus groups by arranging the meeting location and providing additional contacts. Letters were then sent to local historians and historical preservation groups inviting them to the historical caretakers meeting, and to middle school or seventh grade social studies teachers and resource personnel inviting them to an educators' focus group. At the same time, arrangements were made at each location to introduce the project to seventh grade students in order to obtain their feedback via a Student Survey. A short video produced by Ozarks Public Television introducing the MissouriFind History-Heritage project opened each of the focus group meetings.

All focus group participants were given handouts requesting input with regard to the design of the teacher materials (themes, manuals, assessments), suggestions for videotapes (length, themes, style), and identification of existing resources. The people attending the focus groups were cooperative and generally excited about the project. There were approximately twenty individuals in attendance at each of the functions, with good feedback provided. The educators in the groups expressed a need for "this type of curriculum" but emphasized the desire to see it developed in a multidisciplinary model that ensured flexibility for the teachers to insert their own creativity and local uniqueness.

242   The Need to Expand, Preserve, and Restore Tradition

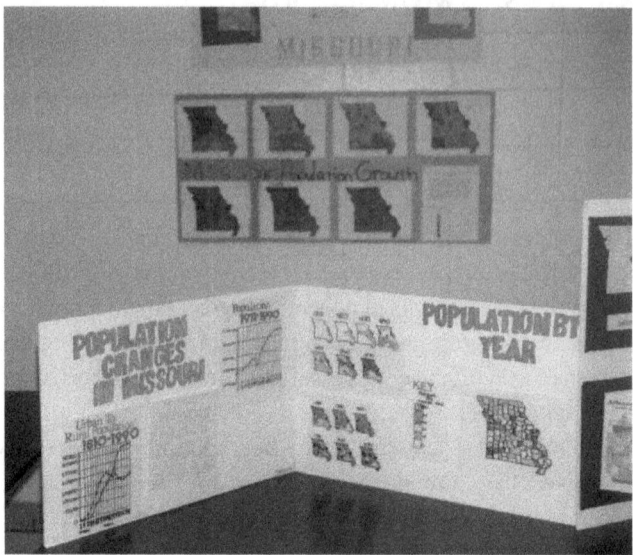

Student display of Population Growth of Missouri over time.
On display at the Greenwood PTA History Fair, April 1994.

GREENWOOD PILOT YEAR

After nearly two years of planning and preparation, MissouriFind was ready to be introduced in the classroom. Southwest Missouri State University operates the only K-12 laboratory school in the state, and was chosen as the site for the pilot study. A team teaching approach was adopted with Steve Hinch as the lead teacher and given the primary responsibility of teaching the historical content of the MissouriFind curriculum. Judy Kistler was assigned to work with Steve, with her chief responsibility to introduce and reinforce the I. E. aspect of the curriculum. Both of these individuals had been involved with the project from early in the preparation phase.

The seventh grade class in the fall of 1993 consisted of thirty students who had begun the year with a reputation for being difficult to manage. As the year unfolded, and the class matured in their emotional and intellectual development, it became apparent to the two instructors that much of this reputation was simply the fact that this was a very bright group of young people, who needed the intellectual stimulation that MissouriFind provided. By the time these students were seniors in high school this academic proficiency became evident. Over seventy-five percent of the graduating class scored above the state average on their ACT test, with four qualifying for

Bright Flight Scholarships (30 or better on the ACT). One individual, John Neely, became a National Merit Scholar Semifinalist, and another, Stephanie Reid, was recognized as a National Merit Scholar Commended student.

Besides the challenge of the particular group of students involved with the pilot, other difficulties presented themselves to the two teachers. Since some of the MissouriFind teaching materials and most of the videos were still in the development stage, the team often had only a limited time to prepare lessons. Nevertheless, they were able to integrate the curriculum components with supplemental resources from United States history classes and other social study related resources in a flexible and professional manner.

It was decided to allow for each unit of study (eighteen in all) to be covered in an approximate two-week (eight- to ten-day) period of time. Typically the video was played as an introduction to the unit in the first day. Guided inquiry techniques using cooperative-learning models usually followed up the viewing of the video. Used as an anticipatory set, the video content set the stage for later, more in-depth coverage of the major concepts that were embedded within the magazine materials. The reading material that comprised the magazines was grade-level appropriate supplemented with a wide assortment of maps, graphs, cartoons, historic photos, and other appropriate visual learning aids. The units were written in a narrative style, complete with primary-source materials such as journal entry examples and quotations. The length of each unit varied, but was in the six- to ten-page range.

Designated I. E. class periods, focusing on particular objectives or learning outcomes of the unit, were interspersed through the two-week instructional time. Early in the school year, while the students were still getting an understanding of some of the vocabulary and techniques of I. E., usually two days were set aside for these activities. The blending of the I. E. principles and the historic content of the unit would lend itself well to the culminating project or assessment activity that followed.

Early in the pilot, both Steve and Judy recognized that the seventh graders responded well to the performance-based assessments and activities, so we deliberately included these on a regular basis. Both realized that as a pilot site, we were obligated to test as many different activities as possible. The instructors found that the best work was done when students were more engaged. This occurred when the students were given the opportunity to create a product or project based on their learning of the material.

Kistler and Hinch constantly were on the lookout for guest speakers and field-trip opportunities to enhance the curriculum. In the fall of the year, while studying the "Trails In, Trails Out" unit, a ninety-five year old, one-quarter-Cherokee, one-quarter-Choctaw Chief, Russell Sage Carter, visited the class and regaled them with a wonderful assortment of Native American tales and wisdom. Visits to the Greene County Historical Museum and Wilson's Creek National Battlefield also enhanced the classes' learning of significant local historical events and resources available to the community. In the spring of the year, Judy organized an interesting and unique Architectural History Walk for the class as we investigated some of Springfield's local buildings to gain a new perspective on the place the students call home.

Student display of the Civil War Battle of Wilson's Creek, August 1861.
On display at the Greenwood PTA History Fair, April 1994.

Each unit also had a teacher's manual developed that provided the instructor with the following information:

Curriculum Overview
Introduction
Timeframe
Setting
Theme
Rationale
Unit outline
Unit Objectives
Main Ideas and Historical Content
Vocabulary and definitions
Major concepts
Information on Student Materials
Unit Teaching Plan

Video
Brief summary
Critical concepts
Preview questions
Segment summaries (with suggested questions)
Bridge from Video to Reading
Instructional objectives
Instructional Outcomes
Suggested Activities
Concept Emphasis
Skill Emphasis
Instructional Objective
Instructional Outcomes
Description—scope and sequence
Materials needed
Learning style addressed
Additional Outside Resources
Selected Supplementary Resources and Fieldtrips

As one can see from the detailed outline provided above, each unit of study was carefully designed and complete with more than enough information and ideas for a classroom teacher to implement. It was designed to be flexible, not prescriptive, but complete with enough resources to individualize instruction as needed. Many of the assessment items were authentic in nature and performance-based. Authentic assessment is a form of assessment in which students are asked to perform real-world tasks that demonstrate meaningful application of essential knowledge and skills.

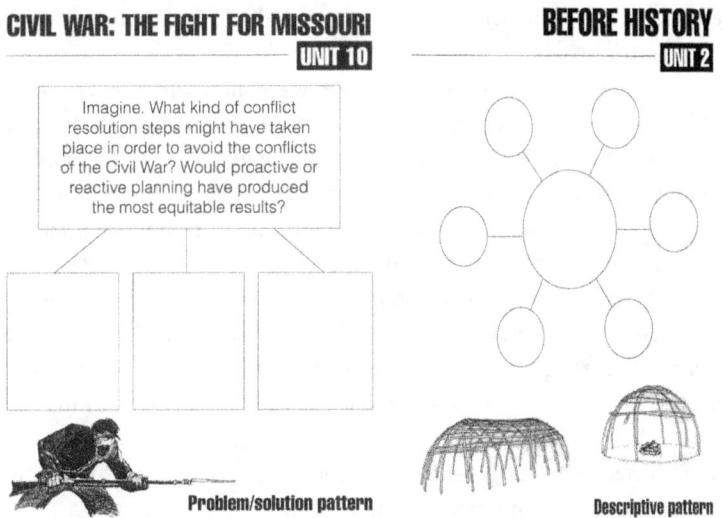

Examples of two concept maps. Concept maps were used by students to visualize the relationship between key ideas in their study of MissouriFind.

SEEING ONE'S STATE FIRSTHAND (A FEATURED CLASS ACTIVITY)

One of the more interesting projects of the MissouriFind curriculum was developed during the spring semester in the fourth magazine, *Missouri in the Larger World*. The narrative in the magazine introduced the students to the idea of taking a trip around Missouri and enjoying their own special "Missouri Heritage Soup." The project actually was created as a two-part activity. Initially the students were divided into groups, and each team was assigned a region of the state. Using the Missouri Department of Natural Resources regional designations (dividing the state into six separate geographical areas: Kansas City region, Northeast region, Central region, St. Louis region, Lakes region, and Southeast region), the teams were given the assignment of promoting their region and developing a brochure that highlighted tourism, industry, agriculture, and cultural aspects of that particular part of Missouri. The students were then to present their promotional materials to the "Department of Missouri Travel and Tourism" (a fictional governmental agency) in Jefferson City in a simulated "real world" experience. The instructors and the curriculum team were all impressed with the student's enthusiasm and energy as they gathered up information and developed some high-quality finished projects. Then, in a very professional manner, the teams presented quite convincingly their chosen region's qualities and attributes in the simulation.

This first project set the stage for the follow-up activity. Once the students had investigated their own particular region and then heard from the other groups in the simulation, they were given the individual task of developing an itinerary for a family summer vacation. The criteria for this assignment was somewhat flexible to accommodate individual interests but did require the students to include one historical site, one state park, one cultural activity, one "tourist attraction" and one "event." (This could be a festival, sporting event, community celebration, or other type of scheduled activity). The assignment also incorporated criteria such as mapping the route, plans for overnight accommodations, and other trip planning considerations. Mr. Hinch encouraged the students to give some serious thoughts to their itinerary development, to make it something that could conceivably become a reality during their summer break.

The success of this activity became apparent shortly after the start of the following school year. Stephanie Usery's mother approached me in the hall and told me the story of the family trip that summer. Mrs. Usery was very proud of her daughter, who was the chief architect and travel guide for the family excursion, using the itinerary she had developed in class that spring. Stephanie had convinced the family that her idea was a fun way to enjoy time together. Clearly she had taken a great sense of ownership in the outcome of the trip. She shared points of interest learned in MissouriFind.

Amasa Jay's Personal History-Heritage Project for the MissouriFind pilot program at Greenwood Laboratory School in the spring of 1994

CULMINATING PROJECT

In late April, a letter was sent home informing both student and parents of plans for a culminating project for MissouriFind. It was designed to provide the students an opportunity to pull together a unique set of items that individualized what their personal heritage meant to them. This was a carefully constructed assessment to allow for the students to "Find themselves in Missouri and Missouri in Them." Throughout the year, students had been exposed to heritage concepts—the meaning and value of family and community and shared historical and cultural experiences. It was our hope that each student had developed a heightened awareness of his or her own heritage and had an increased sense of responsibility to preserve it for future generations.

The letter explained to both student and parents that the display was to be a visual symbol of what was important in their own lives as a result of their increased awareness through the MissouriFind curriculum. They were asked to consider what possessions, keepsakes, and other items (such as legal documents, timelines, family trees, religious artifacts, newspaper clippings, and family pictures) illustrated and defined themselves and, possibly, their role in maintaining this identity for their children.

The instructors and the curriculum team wanted this to be an opportunity for the students to solicit the advice of their parents so encouraged the students to consider questions like, "How do you want your grandchildren to remember you?" Or, "How do you want your child to remember your parents and grandparents?" This bringing together of several generations with the student being the pivotal connection between the past and the future was at the very heart of the project and served as the essential culmination of the entire curriculum.

The results could not have been more rewarding for both instructors and students. The sense of pride and accomplishment reverberated in each of the presentations. The quality and effort exhibited by the students were apparent. Not only were stories shared with a sense of discovery and an increased self-awareness of individual time and place, but repeatedly, the students voiced a commitment and a responsibility to pass on this family heritage to future generations.

Ben Cohen's Personal History-Heritage Project for the MissouriFind pilot program at Greenwood in the spring of 1994

SOUTHWEST DISTRICT SOCIAL STUDIES TEACHERS ASSOCIATION: VOICES FROM THE PAST—OCTOBER 1995

Ruth Burgess was always on the lookout for opportunities to share MissouriFind with others and to develop partnerships with educators from around the state. When Ruth was approached by the Southwest District Social Studies Teachers Association in the summer of 1994 to present MissouriFind to their constituents, she jumped at the opportunity. The meeting was being held in Springfield that October, so it was not difficult for members of the MissouriFind team to attend. A novel idea was finally agreed upon, and it turned out to be a fun afternoon for both the presenters and the audience gathered.

The MissouriFind curriculum, especially in the four magazines' narratives, was rich in primary source materials. The team agreed to abandon the stale, dog-and-pony presentation format of sharing the story of the development of curriculum and presenting sample lesson plans. Instead, social studies teachers in attendance that day were treated to a series of oral readings from team members who used minimal props and costumes, and some rather interesting dialects and accents to "tell the stories" of some of the characters—both well-known and anonymous—from Missouri's history.

The presentation was entitled, "Voices from the Past" and included Ruth and Stan Burgess, David Brown, Judy Kistler and Steve Hinch portraying the individuals "in their own words." From George Caleb Bingham, Samuel Clemens, and Thomas Hart Benton to the plight of the mothers and daughters crossing the plains enroute to the Oregon Territory. Voices were heard loud and clear that autumn afternoon in a wonderful depiction of one of the strengths of the curriculum, its use of primary documents.

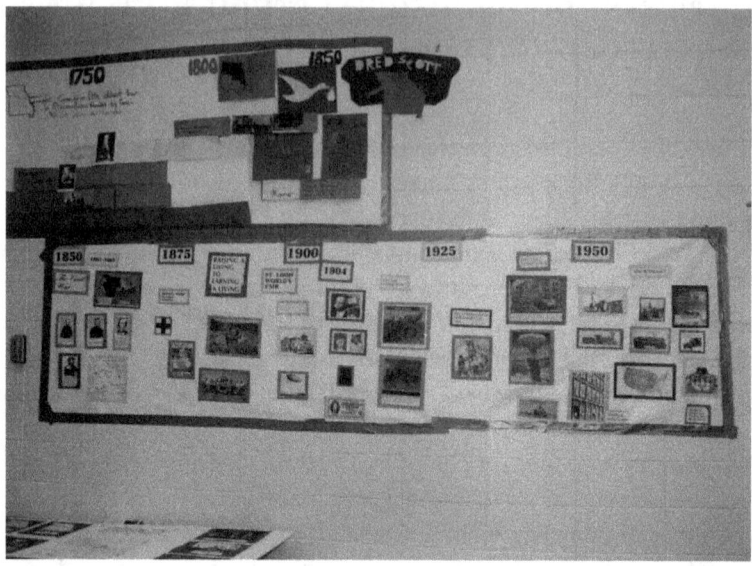

MissouriFind Timeline: An on-going student-produced timeline of major events in Missouri's history. On display at the Greenwood PTA History Fair, April 1994.

FOLLOW-UP INTERVIEWS—SPRING 1995

The year after the pilot study was completed, Ruth Burgess arranged to bring back several of the students who had participated in the curriculum. Nearing the end of their eighth grade year, these students spent the afternoon at the Greene County Historical Museum and then went out to the National Cemetery, with an Ozarks Public Television film crew who were developing a promotional video on the MissouriFind project. After the filming was over, the students convened in the Greenwood Library to participate in an interview conducted by their MissouriFind instructor, Mr. Steve Hinch.

Dr. Ruth Burgess was interested in documenting a follow-up with the students on the internalization of the main precepts of the program, specifically identifying evidence of a fuller realization of self and an increased sense of valuing commonalities and differences in others. Ruth was intrigued about how the cognitive and affective insights of these young adolescents might be developing a year past MissouriFind.

Review of the transcripts from that interview, as well as an edited video included in the promotional video, revealed a significant recollection of various activities in which the student had earlier engaged. But more importantly, a realization of the impact of the program on the student's personal development was evident in their thoughtful comments. Maia Gill, a young girl who had invited the class to her *Bat Mitsvah* ceremony, recalled the significance of sharing her cultural identity with the rest of her peers and how that had provided a more profound experience for her as a result. The *Bat Mitsvah* signifies the female reaching the age of twelve years old, becoming recognized by Jewish tradition as having the same rights as an adult, and becoming morally and ethically responsible for her decisions and actions.

Edgar Galanes, originally from Puerto Rico, added that his understanding of different cultures was expanded "really big" as a result of this experience as well as some of the other activities he was involved with in the program. He also added that, for the first time, he recognized the things he missed about the culture in which he had grown up. Edgar addressed the absence felt from past experiences with which he no longer had a direct connection—such things as the merengue music and communal parties. These were cultural identities he now recognized as significant pieces of himself, and he was concerned he might lose them. They might, as he put it, just "fall off a cliff."

Another major theme that was obvious in the responses from the student group was the recognition of the importance to preserve their stories and legacies for future generations. Jennifer Byrd stated, "before this class I never realized the importance of my heritage, but I found it *is* important for me, even at my age, to do this because my grandparents will not be around forever." Shayla Wirth added, "I think this class made our family come kind of closer together because we had to talk about how each of us were related so I could do the project. Then I found out more about how we were related to this big family out there."

NCSS CONFERENCE FALL 1994

David Brown and Steve Hinch represented the MissouriFind project at the National Council for the Social Studies (NCSS) annual conference in Phoenix, Arizona in November of 1994. For the conference seminar, Drs. Brown and Hinch prepared a series of activities designed to engage the attendees in an interactive look at some of the curricular items in the program. The two lesson ideas shared at the conference were a Civil War Memories activity and a Community Decision Making activity. The first lesson, Civil War Memories, used four primary source documents (letters, diary entries, and a military directive) to give different perspectives of the war and its impact. In addition, the activity included a journalist group. They developed questions to ask the "actors" of the four groups in a "Meet the Press" format. The intent was to present to the conference attendees the richness of the content of MissouriFind using the primary source documents and the inquiry-based active engagement of students involved with the lesson design.

The second activity shared that day was a problem-solving lesson that put groups of students in conflicting roles. Their task was to attempt to reach consensus on a controversial issue facing their community. The scenario had the student groups look at the possibility of a hazardous waste-dump site being constructed on the outskirts of their town. The groups had to analyze the benefits and costs involved to reach a consensus. The activity taught the students the need to analyze multiple perspectives, propose alternative solutions and seek group consensus in decision making. Although the audience was small, those in attendance were enthusiastic about the approach that the MissouriFind curriculum was taking and were supportive and encouraging of its success.

Many of the ideas formulated in the MissouriFind design had been first introduced to the team from an earlier conference attended by Steve Hinch and Bob Flanders. Dr. Flanders had been an important contributor in the development and writing of the student magazines in the beginning of the project; he was a member of the History Department at Southwest Missouri State University and editor of Ozark Watch, a regional journal that focused on the history and culture of the Ozark Highland area of Missouri and Arkansas. Flanders and Hinch went out to Salt Lake City, Utah to participate in the Utah Heritage Conference in the summer of 1992. The purpose of the trip was to gather information, ideas, and contacts that could be used in creating an interactive, inquiry-based curriculum that could be implemented at the middle-school level. Both of the team members brought back a rich array of ideas that could be adapted to meet the needs of our group as it was beginning to create the curriculum.

PUTTING THE COGNITIVE INTO EDUCATION: CALGARY CONFERENCE, SUMMER 1999

Fast forward to 1999. The students in the pilot group that participated in the MissouriFind curriculum as seventh graders were now seniors in high school getting ready for graduation. Ruth Burgess contacted Steve Hinch, still the social studies teacher at Greenwood, to see if he would be willing to assist in a follow-up longitudinal study of the student participants from six years earlier. The International Association for Cognitive Education was hosting its Seventh International Conference in late June of 1999. Ruth thought this event would be a good venue to showcase the long-term lasting impact on these students' construction of both personal and public heritages.

Ruth's husband, Dr. Stan Burgess, assisted in the development of the survey administered by Hinch to the graduating seniors at Greenwood that spring. The survey consisted of twenty opinion-based responses to various aspects of the goals of the curriculum. The students were asked to respond in a five-point Likert rating scale; ranging from "highly impacted me positively" to "highly impacted me negatively." The opinion statements were carefully constructed to identify three major goals of the curriculum: the first goal being evidence of personal growth; second, an increased awareness of public history; and third, an increased awareness of private heritage. The survey concluded with five open-ended responses to gather a narrative element for the study.

The conference was to be held in Calgary, Alberta, Canada during the last four days of June. The theme for the conference that year was "Putting the Cognitive into Education." Ruth submitted the abstract for the presentation earlier that spring and had summarized its focus as a chronology of the changes the cohort of students underwent as they began to realize a fuller sense of self and come to value commonalities and differences in others. Cognitive and affective insights blended as these young adolescents, from varied cultures and stations in life, began to express their insights while constructing both a personal and public heritage.

After collecting the data from the graduating seniors, Ruth and her colleagues began to analyze the information gathered and put the finishing touches on the presentation entitled, "Voices in Reflection: Developing a Sense of Self and Value for Others." The results were revealing, indicating that the overall effectiveness of the curriculum not only was internalized by the pilot group five years after participating in the curriculum but also was extremely pervasive in the three areas of concentration targeted. Noteworthy areas of growth and development identified in the survey included:

A. Personal Growth

   1. Working collaboratively with others; 76 percent of the students indicated this attribute as "highly positive impact" or "positive impact"—overall Likert average of 4.04/5.00

   2. Experiencing a variety of teaching approaches; 76 percent of the students indicated this attribute as "highly positive impact" or "positive impact"—overall Likert average of 4.08/5.00

   3. Explaining reasoning and identifying information to support decisions; 68 percent of the students indicated this attribute as "highly

positive impact" or "positive impact"—overall Likert average of 3.76/5.00

4. Examining problems and proposing solutions from multiple perspectives; 72 percent of the students indicated this attribute as "highly positive impact" or "positive impact"—overall Likert average of 3.96/5.00

B. Public History

1. Using tools of social science inquiry (maps, documents, artifacts); 68 percent of the students indicated this attribute as "highly positive impact" or "positive impact"—overall Likert average of 3.92/5.00

C. Personal Heritage

1. Identifying my place within Missouri (location, heritage, and history); 60 percent of the students indicated this attribute as "highly positive impact" or "positive impact"—overall Likert average of 4.04/5.00

During the presentation, held at the University of Calgary, the research team was able to reinforce the overall lasting impact of this program on the graduating seniors. Areas described included the sense of community established during this very significant transition period of middle school and its lasting impact on this group five years later. The pronounced ability developed self-confidence as thinkers and problem-solvers allowed for continued success throughout their high school experience. Another area noted by the research presenters was the class's ability to communicate both written and orally as signified by the fact that one-third of the seniors earned a level of distinguished (highest score possible) in their senior exhibition graduation requirement (a rigorous, multi-faceted project that includes a research component, public speaking and oral defense of the research findings) at Greenwood Laboratory School.

Even though the original format of the MissouriFind was never implemented as the official Missouri State History curriculum, the legacy evolving from its creation will always live on in fond memories by its creators and the students involved in the pilot. It was an honor and a pleasure to have had the opportunity to work so closely with Ruth Burgess on this amazing, groundbreaking curriculum design. It is probably safe to say that most of us had never worked on a project of this magnitude and certainly had not worked under the direction of anyone like Ruth. Her acumen and enthusiasm for this project were contagious; we couldn't wait to come to meetings to hear what she had to say and what we were going to work on next. Her years of studying under Feuerstein and implementing his principles of higher order thinking helped us all conceive a state history curriculum more holistic in nature and one that puts the students into situations that encourage ownership and metacognitive activity in what it takes to be a Missourian. With supporting videos and student magazines, not textbooks, most had never seen anything like it. It was a curricular structure born well before its time.

12

Feuerstein's Cognitive Map:
A Conceptual Framework for Analyzing Learning Tasks and Providing Effective Feedback

—Carolyn S. Nixon

[EPI]Where am I going?
How am I going there?
Where to next?

—John Hattie[/EPI]

For decades, educational researchers have conducted studies to determine the effectiveness of particular teaching strategies. Most recently, John Hattie's book *Visible Learning for Teachers* brings together fifteen years of evidence-based research to provide insight regarding teaching practices that have the greatest impact on student learning. The most significant of Hattie's findings is the impact of feedback on student performance. His research indicates that, "the average effect size [for feedback] is 0.79, which is twice the average of all other schooling effects."[1] Until we fully understand how

---

1. Hattie, *Visible Learning*, 118.

to define and operationalize these findings into pre-service and in-service training programs for teachers, students cannot benefit from the research. Creating a conceptual framework for how to analyze different parameters of a learning task and provide exactly the feedback a student needs is vital; done effectively, this sets the stage and holds the promise of promoting cognitive growth (i.e., learning) of the student.

Hattie advocates that, "teachers need to concentrate on what students do, say, make, or write, and modify their theories about students in light of these observations (or this evidence). Feedback from such evaluation is what teachers need to seek so they can then modify their instruction."[2] This is a crucial premise of effective instruction and learning. According to Jane Pollock, noted author on the topic of feedback, "The best way that a school can provide for a student to learn and use feedback strategies is for the teacher to make teaching changes to incorporate feedback throughout instruction."[3] Teachers should be equipped to provide feedback that "indicates what students can currently do and what they need to do in order to achieve a target curricular aim or master an en route building block related to that aim."[4] Considering that student growth may be proportional to the amount and type of feedback received and feedback that is most effective occurs during instruction, it makes sense that teachers need to have a framework for analyzing the possible ways a learning task can present difficulties for students.

Reuven Feuerstein's Cognitive Map "permits teachers to analyze the characteristics of the task responsible for the failure of the child."[5] In line with this reasoning, Feuerstein states, "It makes a difference to know whether the child failed because of an inadequate input, elaboration, or output process, or a combination of these. Being able to determine the source of his failures enables us to attack its source."[6] By using the dimensions of Feuerstein's Cognitive Map as a guide, teachers can identify the nature of the child's difficulty and provide the feedback necessary to move learning forward. Parameters of Feuerstein's Cognitive Map include content, modality/language, phase, cognitive operations, level of complexity, level of abstraction, and level of efficiency.[7]

The first parameter of the cognitive map is content. Even the most thoughtfully and carefully crafted learning task may be ineffective because

---

2. Hattie, 116.
3. Pollock, *Feedback*, 5.
4. Popham, *Transformative Assessment*, 114.
5. Feuerstein, Rand, and Rynders, *Don't Accept Me as I Am*, 205.
6. Feuerstein et al., *Instrumental Enrichment*, 205.
7. Ibid., 105–10.

a student is simply not equipped to deal with the specific content of the lesson. Students may lack background and experiential knowledge needed to access the new content at the level required. There may be specific deficits in the educational underpinnings needed to master the new concepts presented. In summary, student competence is "directly related to each subject's experiential, cultural, and educational background."[8] Content is a major factor of concern in constructing assessment items for educational testing. Teachers need to be cognizant of the fact that the content itself can pose a barrier to student understanding.

The second parameter of the Cognitive Map is modality or language. How the content is presented for the child's perception is another dimension for consideration. Is it verbal, pictorial, numerical, figural, symbolic, graphic, or some combination of these? A student may be quite proficient with content in one modality but fall short when the same content is presented in a different modality. For example, many math teachers lament the fact that students are able to solve computation problems involving numbers and yet struggle with the same content when presented in the verbal modality as word problems.

Phase is a third dimension of Feuerstein's Cognitive Map. "The mental act can be broadly divided into three phases: *input, elaboration,* and *output.*"[9] Any learning task involves perception of stimuli; this is the input phase. Once the stimulus is perceived, the mind must act or work with it in some way. This may involve classification, categorization, analysis, or synthesis; all these cognitive activities are examples of elaboration. The third phase is output; this is the expression of learning. What is the product that signifies cognitive growth? How is the learning communicated? Although these three phases are very closely interrelated, a particular student may experience difficulty in any one or more of these phases due to the nature of the learning task. A student may fail because of inappropriate or inefficient data gathering/input, inappropriate or inefficient thinking processes/elaboration, or an inability to express solutions adequately/output.[10]

Cognitive operations, the fourth dimension of the Cognitive Map, requires a deep understanding of what is required in the elaboration phase of a learning task. According to Feuerstein, "operations may range from the simple recognition and identification of objects to more complex activities such as classification, seriation, logical multiplication, and the like."[11] The

---

8. Feuerstein, Rand, and Rynders, *Don't Accept Me as I Am*, 269.
9. Ibid.
10. Feuerstein et al., *Instrumental Enrichment*, 108.
11. Ibid., 106.

more complex cognitive operations, such as deductive, inductive, and analogical reasoning, require recognition of relationships and relationships between relationships; these are much more complex elaboration tasks than simple recognition and identification of objects. Consideration of the cognitive requirements of a learning task is critical; instruction may require several steps in order for students to build the capacity for elaboration skills needed to complete the task.

The fifth dimension of Feuerstein's Cognitive Map is level of complexity. Complexity is defined as "the quantity and quality of units of information necessary to produce a given mental act."[12] Quantity, of course, refers to the number of units of information in the task; quality refers to the degree of novelty or familiarity of the units. This dimension bears some relationship to the first dimension of content in that background experience plays a critical role in one's ability to deal with cognitive demands of a given learning task. In today's assessment world, application and performance tasks are good examples of highly complex cognitive tasks. Students are required to deal with multiple sources and pieces of information to solve a problem or create a product. Successful completion of the task may require several steps completed in a more or less specific manner.

Level of abstraction, the sixth parameter of the cognitive map, refers to "the distance between the given mental act and the object or event on which it operates."[13] The task at hand may involve, at the most basic level, working with concrete objects. At a more advanced level, the task may involve some representational form of objects such as pictures. At the highest level of the abstraction hierarchy, students may be asked to perform tasks involving hypothetical objects that have no direct relationship to real objects or events. Jerome Bruner defined these three levels of abstraction as enactive, iconic, and symbolic. The "first stage of representation is *enactive*, suggesting the role of physical objects in learning. The second level is *iconic*, referring to pictorial and graphic representations. Finally, the *symbolic* level involves using words, numerals, and other symbols to represent ideas, objects, and actions."[14] One should recognize here the close relationship between the modality, or language, of the content and level of abstraction of the learning task.

The final element of Feuerstein's Cognitive Map is level of efficiency. "The mental act can also be described and analyzed according to the degree and level of efficiency with which it is produced. As a criterion for efficiency,

---

12. Ibid., 109.
13. Ibid.
14. Kennedy and Tipps, *Guiding Children's Learning of Mathematics*, 50.

one may use the rapidity-precision complex and/or the amount of effort . . . exerted by the individual in his production of a particular act."[15] Several factors contribute to the level of efficiency with which one can complete a task. Unfamiliar content and/or lack of experience with a process have a negative impact on the level of efficiency in task performance. Familiarity with the content itself has a positive impact on efficiency. In addition, repetition of a process contributes to increased efficiency with less expenditure of effort. According to Judy Willis, noted neurologist and classroom teacher, "The more one repeats an action or recalls the information, the more dendrites sprout to connect new memories to old, and the more efficient the brain becomes in its ability to retrieve that memory or repeat that action."[16]

Feuerstein's Cognitive Map provides a conceptual framework for how to analyze different parameters of a learning task and provide the responsive feedback when a student experiences difficulty. It "plays a critical role in the construction of material . . . and the interpretation of a subject's performance."[17] The Cognitive Map provides a systematic means of analyzing a learning task. "It provides four layers of analysis: the content or subject matter of the task; the modality of language of the task; the level of abstraction, novelty, and complexity of the task; and the cognitive operations required by the task."[18] Teacher training using the seven parameters of Feuerstein's Cognitive Map as a conceptual framework for determining causes of student errors or confusion is a promising application of John Hattie's research. Helping teachers understand how to provide responsive feedback by adjusting one or more of the parameters of a learning task during real-time instructional episodes is a critical factor in meeting the needs of individual learners.

---

15. Feuerstein et al., *Instrumental Enrichment*, 109–110.
16. Willis, *Research-based Strategies*, 8.
17. Feuerstein, Rand, and Rynders, *Don't Accept Me as I Am*, 270.
18. Mentis, Bernstein, and Mentis, *Mediated Learning*, 197.

Reuven Feuerstein, 1997

BIBLIOGRAPHY

Feuerstein, Reuven, Ya'acov Rand, and John E. Rynders. *Don't Accept Me as I Am: Helping "Retarded" People to Excel.* New York: Plenum, 1988.

Feuerstein, Reuven, in collaboration with Ya'acov Rand, Mildred Hoffman, and Ronald Miller. *Instrumental Enrichment: An Intervention Program for Cognitive Modifiability.* Glenview, IL: Scott, Foresman, 1980.

Hattie, John. *Visible Learning for Teachers: Maximizing Impact on Learning.* London: Routledge, 2012.

Kennedy, Leonard M., and Steven Tipps. *Guiding Children's Learning of Mathematics.* 6th ed. Belmont, CA: Wadsworth, 1991.

Mentis, M. T., Marilyn J. Bernstein, and Martene Mentis. *Mediated Learning: Teaching, Tasks, and Tools to Unlock Cognitive Potential.* 2nd ed. Thousand Oaks, CA: Corwin, 2008.

Pollock, Jane E. *Feedback: The Hinge That Joins Teaching and Learning.* Thousand Oaks, CA: Corwin, 2012.

Popham, W. James. *Transformative Assessment.* Alexandria, VA: Association for Supervision and Curriculum Development, 2008.

Willis, Judy. *Research-Based Strategies to Ignite Student Learning: Insights from a Neurologist and Classroom Teacher.* Alexandria, VA: Association for Supervision and Curriculum Development, 2006.

13

The Keralite Diaspora
—Thomson K. Mathew

Indian Pentecostalism, which flourished in India's southwestern state of Kerala during the twentieth century, enjoys a significant global presence in the twenty-first century. The phenomenal growth of this wing of the global Pentecostal/charismatic movement is accompanied by growing pains and adjustment challenges. These challenges manifest themselves in leadership issues, generational conflicts, and challenges within the expatriate churches. The future growth and well-being of this branch of Christendom will require a deep understanding of its history and careful analysis of these issues. This chapter contains the reflections of a Keralite theological educator in North America who is a participant observer of Indian Pentecostalism.

BACKGROUND

Kerala, the modern state on the coast of the Arabian Sea, was formed by the merging of Travancore, Cochin, and Malabar regions of pre-independent India; it claims a Christian heritage dating back to St. Thomas. The apostle came to India in AD 57, according to Eusebius, witnessing to the natives and planting several churches.[1] (One of these churches in Niranam was my grandfather's home church prior to his embracing the Pentecostal message.) Indian Christians claim an even earlier date of St. Thomas' arrival—AD 52.[2]

---

1. Burgess, "Development and Growth," 122.
2. S. Mathew, *Kerala Penthecosthu Charithram*, 36.

Flourishing communities of Mar Thoma Syrian Christians and Assyrian Christians in Kerala were joined by Roman Catholics in the seventeenth century.[3] Known for its beautiful shoreline and breeze-loving coconut trees, Kerala enjoyed a continuous Christian presence for twenty centuries. Ancient trade routes and modern missionary movements impacted this densely populated small Indian state and its spiritual history.

PRE-PENTECOSTAL REVIVALS

India had experienced major revivals before the twentieth-century Pentecostal awakening.[4] Several pre-Pentecostal revivals of the nineteenth century preceding North American Pentecostalism by several decades were characterized by the charismatic gifts of the Holy Spirit. These revivals with their indigenous leadership had significant impact on Kerala Christians. According to several sources, notable among these pre-Pentecostal revivals was the awakening of 1860 in Tirunelveli, Tamil Nadu, under John Christian Arulappen, an Anglican catechist trained by western missionaries.[5] This revival included speaking in tongues, interpretation of tongues, prophecy, and other "Pentecostal" manifestations. It had tremendous evangelistic impact that surprised and disoriented the traditional missionaries. This revival particularly touched the Christian Missionary Society (CMS) congregations and the Syrian Church of Malabar in Kerala.[6]

The pre-Pentecostal revivals in India took indigenous form with Indian leadership, Indian music, and a rejection of the caste system. Glossolalia became an issue of contention in these revivals. The western missionaries who were supportive at the beginning of the revivals later questioned many of its features, including unauthorized leadership, unfulfilled prophetic predictions, and unordained clergy.[7]

The nineteenth century ended in India with various mission agencies calling for special intercessory prayer for the conversion of the country. As if that prayer was being answered, a special awakening began in India in 1905.[8] Influenced by Wesleyan Holiness and Higher Life teachings from the West, this revival sought "power from on high" to fulfill the Great Commission.

---

3. Burgess, "Development and Growth," 122.

4. S. Mathew, *Kerala Penthecosthu Charithram*, 38–39; McGee, "Pentecostal and Pentecostal-like Movements," 118–122.

5. McGee, "Pentecostal and Pentecostal-like Movements,"118.

6. Ibid., 119.

7. Ibid.

8. S. Mathew, *Kerala Penthecosthu Charithram*, 32.

Revivals broke out in the Khassia Hills in the northeast of India and Pandita Ramabai's Mukti Mission in South India.[9] This awakening touched all the major Christian missionary movements in India, in anticipation of the twentieth-century Pentecostal movement.

PENTECOST IN INDIA

Gary B. McGee notes that Pentecostalism in India was positively different from that of the Azusa version, especially in terms of the function of glossolalia.[10] Tongues were not seen in India as the initial physical evidence of the baptism of the Holy Spirit or as a means of communication in the mission field. Pioneer missionary Minnie F. Abram's writings testify to this. However, ultimately Indian Pentecostalism adopted the tongues-as-evidence view. Many traditional missionaries in India received the baptism of the Holy Spirit, but due to their own reasons, most of them stayed with their sending agencies; and soon new Pentecostal missionaries began to arrive. George E. Berg who returned to India in 1908 was the first among them.[11] Formerly he was a missionary connected with the Church of God (Holiness). He went back to America, received the baptism in the Holy Spirit at Azusa, and returned to India.

Although Indian Pentecostalism traces its origins to northern India, it took real roots in the south, aided by the sacrificial services of a new generation of Pentecostal missionaries. For instance, George Berg centered his work in Bangalore. Mary Weems Chapman, the first Assemblies of God (AG) missionary to South India, settled in Madras. The revival-ready Keralites invited her to Travancore. She visited Kerala and ministered there until, finally, she made Trivandrum, capital of Kerala, her home. Together with Spencer May, another AG missionary from Britain, she published the first Pentecostal magazine in the Malayalam language, the *Penthecosthu Kahalam* (Pentecostal Trumpet). This was an influential periodical.[12]

PENTECOSTALISM IN KERALA

Robert F. Cook is considered a great pioneer of Pentecostalism in Kerala.[13] Baptized in the Spirit at Azusa in 1908, Cook arrived in India in 1913 as

9. McGee, "Pentecostal and Pentecostal-like Movements," 120.
10. Ibid., 121.
11. Ibid., 122.
12. S. Mathew, *Kerala Penthecosthu Charithram*, 79; McGee, "Pentecostal and Pentecostal-like Movements," 122.
13. S. Mathew, *Kerala Penthecosthu Charithram*, 49.

an independent missionary. He joined the AG and began to work at Kottarakara, Travancore. He later moved to Chengannur and founded the Mt. Zion Bible Institute there in 1927. (He claimed an earlier date [1922] based on some classes he taught at his house.) Cook was joined by a young Indian pastor, K. E. Abraham. Leaving the AG in 1929, they worked together independently in Kerala until parting their ways in 1930. Abraham later founded the Indian Pentecostal Church (IPC), which has become the largest indigenous Pentecostal denomination in India.[14] In 1936, Cook joined the Church of God (Cleveland) and brought the congregations he planted in Kerala under its jurisdiction.[15]

John H. Burgess was another missionary who had a tremendous impact on the future of Pentecostalism in Kerala. Commissioned as an AG missionary to India in 1926, the young Burgess served in Kerala for twenty-five years, ministering in Chengannur, Quilon (Kollam), Mavelikara, and Punalur.[16] Burgess was a visionary who saw the need for strategic leadership development of local Pentecostals. A strong believer in indigenous leadership development, Burgess founded the first AG institution for ministerial training outside the United States in Mavelikara, Kerala (my native place), in 1927. Bethel Bible School (now College) moved from Mavelikara to Punalur in 1949.[17] Burgess had a significant impact particularly on Mavelikara in personally significant ways to this writer. My wife's grandfather, Pastor K. C. John, had close interactions with Burgess. When I met Burgess at a gathering in Oklahoma City in 1977, he talked about Pastor K. C. John and sang a Malayalam song he remembered singing together with K. C. John. My great uncle, Pastor G. Samuel, later became the district pastor of Mavelikara district of the AG and my father, Pastor K. T. Mathew, served as the district minister of the Indian Pentecostal Church in Mavelikara West District until his death in 2002! Thanks to Burgess's foresight, today the AG in Kerala is governed by well-trained Indian leaders.

K. E. Abraham came from a prominent Syrian Christian family. He was training to be an orthodox minister, but was filled with the Holy Spirit on April 22, 1923.[18] He was an outstanding leader blessed with very capable associates. He built a vital indigenous movement in a nation that was yearning for freedom from colonialism: the IPC, now known all over the world as a beacon of Indian Pentecostalism. However, the IPC's development was

14. Hedlund, "Indigenous Churches," 781.
15. K. E. Abraham, *Yesukristhuvinte Eliya Dassan K. E. Abraham*, 180.
16. S. Mathew, *Kerala Penthecosthu Charithram*, 110.
17. Burgess and van der Maas, *New International Dictionary of Pentecostal and Charismatic Movements*, 122.
18. K. E. Abraham, *Yesukristhuvinte Eliya Dassan K. E. Abraham*, 67.

not without problems and splits. A major split in the IPC gave birth to the Sharon Fellowship Church in 1953, led by P. J. Thomas in Tiruvalla. His brother, P. J. Daniel, broke away with another group of churches.[19]

Pentecostalism grew fast in Kerala in spite of the oppositions it encountered in its early days from society and traditional churches. Pioneer Pentecostals paid a high price for their faith. Historic churches were not open to the Pentecostal message as many of the early Pentecostals were from Mar Thoma and Orthodox traditions. Spirit-filled people were routinely excommunicated from these churches, but opposition only propelled Keralite Pentecostals to spread their message across the state and beyond.[20] Many Keralite missionaries went to the other states of India. Some traveled to bear witness outside India. Pastor K. J. Samuel's biography, for instance, describes his experiences as a Pentecostal missionary in Pakistan during the India-Pakistan partition.[21]

As a very educated (thanks to the educational institutions built by missionaries and the culture of learning in Kerala) people living in an undeveloped area, Keralites were forced to go to the northern cities of India for employment. Pentecostal believers took their faith with them to these cities and towns and started churches and ministries in these areas. This trend has continued to this day, and now Keralites are engaged in missionary work in North India in significant ways.[22] There are Keralite Pentecostals all across India today. They also have a great number of converts. The modern charismatic movement has increased the number of Spirit-filled believers in India and enhanced the Holy Spirit movement in the nation.[23] Charismatic churches are called new generation churches in Kerala. These groups are growing fast both in Kerala and outside.[24]

KERALITE PENTECOSTAL DIASPORA

Keralite Pentecostals were missionaries from the beginning. Their travels were not limited to other Indian states or Asian nations. As early as 1936, they began to travel to Europe and the United States with their dynamic

19. Ibid., 386–391.
20. Ibid., 133.
21. Paul, *Jwalichu Prakashicha Villakku*, 19–23.
22. Burgess and van der Maas, *New International Dictionary of Pentecostal and Charismatic Movements*, 125.
23. Barrett, "The Worldwide Holy Spirit Renewal," 406.
24. Burgess and van der Maas, *New International Dictionary of Pentecostal and Charismatic Movements*, 123.

message and powerful testimonies.[25] Initial travels were in response to invitations by western missionaries and their sending bodies. Pastor K. E. Abraham, with his associate George Varghese, visited America during his third international trip in 1948, his first one being a trip to Sweden.[26] It took him thirty-two days to reach New York from Colombo, Ceylon (now Sri Lanka). By then another Keralite, P. J. Thomas, who later founded Sharon Fellowship Church, was already in America finishing his theological studies. Previously trained in ministry in Australia, Thomas earned a master's degree from Wheaton College in Chicago and returned to India in 1952.[27] Assemblies of God leaders A. C. Samuel and C. Kochummen visited the United States in 1947.[28] The leader of the Church of God, T. M. Varghese, visited America in 1952.[29]

K. E. Abraham's first foreign trip was to Sweden and other European nations in 1936. He was accompanied by K. C. Cherian. His second trip was with K. C. Cherian and P. M. Samuel in 1947. Due to an asthma attack triggered by the extreme cold weather in Europe, Abraham returned to India. P. M. Samuel followed him to India, but K. C. Cherian kept the planned schedule, visited England, and proceeded to America. He met Abraham in America in 1948.[30]

The first wave of Keralite young people came to America to study theology, encouraged and supported by the earlier visitors. They attended Bible colleges in New York, Chicago, and other cities in the United States. P. J. Thomas was the most encouraging of potential ministers to come to America because upon his return to Kerala, he realized that leadership development was a must, and a college education in Kerala was not easily available to Pentecostal youth who were generally from economically poor backgrounds. In an interview with P. S. Philip, P. M. Samuel, who later became the noted apostle to Andhra Pradesh, said that he assisted almost 400 students to come to America and Canada.[31] Many of the early arrivals returned to India and engaged in ministry, but others stayed in the U.S., especially after the new immigration laws were passed in the U.S., which gave permanent residency provisions to Asian Indians.

25. K. E. Abraham, *Yesukristhuvinte Eliya Dassan K. E. Abraham*, 266.
26. Ibid., 379.
27. Philip, "Kudiyetta Charithram," 35.
28. Ibid.
29. Ibid.
30. Ibid.
31. Ibid.

Another societal situation in America played a significant role in the expansion of Keralite Pentecostal Diaspora in the United States. This was the acute shortage of nurses in America and the decision to bring foreign nurses to meet the shortage.[32] It is believed that E. Stanley Jones, the well-known missionary to India, was influential in opening the American nursing field to Indian nurses. The first group of Indian nurses came on exchange visas. They were expected to return to India when their contracts expired. As the exchange program was replaced with the immigrant program based on the new immigration laws, the Indian nurses began to settle in the United States. Many of these nurses were Keralite Pentecostals trained in North Indian hospitals. They brought their husbands and children to America. Meanwhile, the bachelors who came to study theology joined the young immigrant nurses to form Keralite Pentecostal families in America.

The first organized Pentecostal prayer meeting of Keralites in America began among the immigrant nurses.[33] It is believed that a prayer meeting held for Keralite nurses in the New York/New Jersey area led by Pastor C. M. Varghese was the first such gathering. According to P. S. Philip who interviewed C. M. Varghese in 1991, the first prayer meeting began in a nurses' residence auditorium in October 1967.[34] Some of the spouses of the nurses also attended this meeting.

The first Keralite Pentecostal church, called India Pentecostal Assembly, was organized in New York City.[35] Achoy Mathews, M. S. Samuel, Thomas Pushpamangalam, John C. Samuel, Abraham Samuel, P. G. Mathew and A. C. John were involved in this church. The first meeting of this church took place in Manhattan on February 18, 1968. This church organized a Keralite Pentecostal convention in New York City during April 11 to 14, 1968. According to K. E. Abraham's autobiography, he and associate George Varghese were the speakers at that convention. This was during Abraham's ninth foreign trip.[36]

After a season of inactivity, by 1970 the India Christian Assembly needed a new beginning.[37] Pastors M. S. Samuel and Oommen Abraham led this effort. Oommen Abraham, K. E. Abraham's elder son, was educated in America from 1956 to 1964. He had returned to India to lead a ministry in Bangalore. He came back to America in 1970 and with M. S. Samuel restart-

32. Ibid., 36.
33. Ibid.
34. Ibid.
35. A. Mathews, "Founding of the First Keralite Church," 129.
36. K. E. Abraham, *Yesukristhuvinte Eliya Dassan K. E. Abraham*, 496.
37. Karackal, "Malayali Penthecosthu Sabhakalude Charithram," 53.

ed the India Christian Assembly, beginning worship services in Brooklyn in November 1970. In 1971, this church moved to the United Nations Church Center to accommodate the growing congregation.[38]

The resurrection of the India Christian Assembly in New York was the beginning of the growth of Keralite Pentecostal churches in America. The 1970s and 1980s witnessed the exponential growth of the Keralite Pentecostal immigrant population in America as the early arrivals sponsored their loved ones to come to America using the family reunification provisions of the immigration laws. These Malayalis (people from Kerala who speak Malayalam) settled in the major cities across the country. New York, Chicago, Atlanta, various cities in tropical Florida, Houston, Dallas, and Los Angeles had the major concentration of Pentecostal Keralites. Churches began to be organized in all these cities, and through splits, schisms, and due to genuine needs the number of these churches multiplied within these cities.

The 1970s and 1980s witnessed not only the migration of Malayalis to America, but a similar inflow of Keralites also took place in Canada.[39] During the same period, a great number of Keralites were finding skilled and unskilled labor opportunities in the Middle Eastern nations, particularly the United Arab Emirates.[40] The oil boom in the Middle East created unprecedented opportunities for Keralites, especially for well-educated Keralites. Thus Keralites became the largest group of Indians working in the Middle East. Many of these Malayalis were Pentecostals. They established churches everywhere they went—both open and underground congregations. Even Saudi Arabia had Malayalis gathering behind closed doors within soundproofed apartments! Since Middle Eastern countries did not allow naturalization, Keralites in the Middle East kept closer ties with Kerala, building homes in Kerala and sending their children to attend colleges in India.[41]

As petro dollars flowed to India, Pentecostal pastors flowed to the Middle East, pastoring congregations and doing itinerant ministries. The hardships of life in the Middle Eastern deserts opened people to the good news and produced many Indian converts to Pentecostalism. The Kuwait wars only increased the growth and influence of Keralite Pentecostals in the Middle East.

Keralite pastors visiting the Middle Eastern countries extended their visits to America. They visited churches and families across the United States, raising funds for projects in India and establishing jurisdiction over

38. Ibid.
39. Ibid., 63.
40. S. Mathew, *Kerala Penthecosthu Charithram*, 416.
41. Ibid., 415–16.

the young American congregations, many of whom were originally established as independent groups.

PENTECOSTAL CONFERENCES

Until 1983, there was no national gathering of Keralite Pentecostals in America. Several Pentecostal leaders in America discussed the need for such a gathering, but Oommen Abraham, who by then was a permanent resident and pastor in Dallas, called the first such conference in Oklahoma City in the summer of 1983.[42] About 300 people attended this gathering, mostly from Oklahoma and Texas. This small gathering, later named the Pentecostal Conference of North American Keralites (PCNAK) became a large and influential conference. Beginning with the first meeting in Oklahoma City, this writer preached at most of the first twenty conferences. Other immigrant speakers addressing especially the younger generation called American Born Keralites (ABKs) were Eazhamkulam Samkutty of Louisiana State University and Dr. Thomas Luiskutty, formerly of Oral Roberts University. Some of the PCNAK conferences attracted more than 7000 Keralite Pentecostals. Since its modest beginnings in 1983, annual PCNAK conferences were held in cities across the continent from Houston to Toronto.[43]

The PCNAK began with the hope of creating interdenominational cooperation with lesser degrees of denominational spirit among Keralite Pentecostals. This hope was realized to a great extent in the earlier conferences, but the visiting denominational leaders would not have this. Their headquarters in Kerala established affiliations and expected loyalties from American congregations.[44] Local churches initially organized by multi-denominational Pentecostals were split along the lines of members' former denominations in Kerala. It was not long before denominations developed their own conferences, taking energy to some degree from the PCNAK interdenominational conferences.[45]

---

42. Thumbamon, "Oklahoma Muthal Toronto Vare," 42.
43. Ibid., 44.
44. T. Mathew, "The Future of Keralite Pentecostals in North America," 157.
45. Kurien, "North American Church of God (India) Fellowship—Oru Thirinju Nottam," 17.

DENOMINATIONS

The denominational Pentecostal churches of Malayalis have experienced great growth in America. The twenty-fifth year *Souvenir* of PCNAK published in 2007 gives a status report on these churches. According to this source, there are about fifty Keralite Pentecostal churches in New York alone. Forty-six New York churches are listed with the names of pastors.[46] Thirteen churches in New Jersey are listed. Thirteen churches are also listed for Philadelphia.[47] The history of several churches in Michigan is included in the souvenir.[48] Twelve churches are listed for Illinois. Long lists of churches are given for Oklahoma, Florida, and Texas. Churches are also listed for Massachusetts, Michigan, Ohio, Tennessee, Georgia, North Carolina, South Carolina, Alabama, Kentucky, Virginia, Maryland, Delaware, Colorado, Washington, Oregon, Arizona, and California. The stories of several Canadian churches are also included in this publication.[49]

According to available sources, many of the American Keralite churches ceased to exist or merged with others to create the current churches.[50] Many of them experienced splits along multiple lines. However, generally speaking, the Keralite churches have thrived in North America. There are also several regional organizations and youth networks among these churches giving impetus for continuing growth. Pentecostal Youth Fellowship of New York (PYFA), Pentecostal Youth Fellowship of New York and New Jersey (PYF), Pentecostal Youth Conference of Dallas (PYCD), Pentecostal Young People's Association (PYPA), the youth wing of the IPC denomination, Central Florida Christian Fellowship (CF), Pentecostal Youth Fellowship of Florida (PYFF), and Georgia Youth Fellowship (GYF) are examples of this.[51]

As in India, prominent among the American Keralite Pentecostal denominations is the Indian Pentecostal Church (IPC). The IPC churches in the United States are divided into three regions (Eastern, Midwestern, and Western) with representation given to these regions at the General Council of the denomination headquartered in Kumbanad, Kerala. Pastor K. E. Abraham's grandson, Valson Abraham, is the general secretary of the denomination. Currently he resides in Los Angeles and heads the India Gospel Outreach (IGO), a church planting organization with a goal of establishing

---

46. Karackal, "Malayali Penthecosthu Sabhakalude Charithram," 54–55.
47. Ibid., 55.
48. Ibid., 50–63.
49. Ibid., 63.
50. Ibid., 50–63.
51. Ebenezer, ed. *Pentecostal Conference of North American Keralites*, 83–95.

an IPC church in every pin (zip) code of India.[52] Other strong denominations among Keralites in the U.S. include the Church of God (Cleveland, TN), the Assemblies of God (AG), Sharon Fellowship, New India Church of God, and Pentecostal Maranatha Gospel Church (PMG). There are no known formal networks of independent Keralite churches in America.

SUNDAY SCHOOLS

Keralite Pentecostals in North America have paid special attention to their children's spiritual formation. Sunday Schools of North American Keralites (SSNAK) headed by Joy Abraham and Susil Mathew, a graduate of Oral Roberts University, and Thomas Idiculla have produced customized curriculum materials, taking the Indian immigrant experience and concerns into account.[53] This writer has been a voluntary consultant to this association, contributing curriculum reviews and conducting teacher training sessions.

LITERATURE MINISTRY

Literature ministry has remained vital to Keralite Pentecostals both in India and abroad. Starting with pioneer missionary Minnie Abram, Pentecostals have used literature to spread their message. All Keralite denominations have their own magazines. North American Keralites have supported native periodicals to be kept informed of their native churches and ministries. Eventually, several Malayalam periodicals sprang up in the United States in the form of souvenirs, magazines, and weekly newspapers. Malayalam periodicals gave prominence to news about Pentecostal conferences and events. Prominent among these was *Kerala Express* published from Chicago (K. E. Eapen, chief editor) by a well-known Keralite family there. *Maranatha Voice* is another periodical with strong Chicago connections. Notable periodicals appear from New York and Houston. Pentecostal periodicals in Kerala also run news of their brethren in the Middle East, Europe, and North America. News about Keralite Pentecostals in Australia started appearing in Malayalam periodicals in recent years.

Editors of Keralite Pentecostal periodicals began to attend American Pentecostal conferences as early as 1980s. The *Good News* (V. M. Mathew, founding editor, C. V. Mathew, current chief editor, no relation to each other

---

52. India Gospel Outreach, accessed February 7, 2013, http://www.indiago.org/About-IGO.html.

53. Joseph, "Sunday School Ministry in North America," 81–82.

or the writer), the first interdenominational Pentecostal weekly with the expressed purpose of promoting unity among Pentecostals, led the way. Other periodicals linking Pentecostals in Kerala with the Diaspora include *Sworgeeya Dwoni* (Echoes of Heaven, Finny P. Mathew, editor), *Kristhava Chintha* (Christian Thought, K. N. Russell, chief editor), *Maruppacha* (Oasis, Achenkunju Elanthoor, chief editor), *Hallelujah* (Samkutty Chacko, chief editor), *Sankeerthanam* (Psalms, Vijoy Skaria, chief editor), and *Believers' Journal* (Samkutty Mathew, chief editor). Most of these periodicals are now available online and this has enhanced their circulation and impact.

A Keralite Pentecostal Writers' Forum (KPWF) was formed at the PCNAK conference held at Syracuse, NY in 1993.[54] Eazhamkulam Samkutty was the first president of the KPWF, and this writer was the recipient of its first writers' award. This organization is very active with chapters in the major cities of the United States, encouraging Keralite writers. Initially, Malayalam writers were the focus of KPWF's work. Currently, it is promoting Pentecostal writing both in English and Malayalam. Separate awards are given annually to the best writers in each language. Award ceremonies are held in conjunction with the PCNAK conferences.

LANGUAGE OF WORSHIP

Language of worship has been a major issue in Keralite churches in America. Initially all churches worshipped in Malayalam. As the first generation of ABKs became adolescents, the use of English increased. Preaching was often translated into English or Malayalam. The percentage of English increased as the ABKs reached adulthood. Some churches resisted the move to English, which caused many young people to leave Keralite churches to worship at non-Keralite Pentecostal or charismatic churches in their local communities. This writer knows of at least two Indian pastors who tried to study this phenomenon in their Doctor of Ministry applied research projects. Most of the Keralite Pentecostal churches are bilingual today, some using translation and others having separate services based on language used. All the PCNAK conferences have parallel sessions in English and Malayalam since 1988. E. Samkutty preached, and this writer led the communion service at the first separate English language session held at the PCNAK conference at Patterson College in New Jersey in 1987.[55]

---

54. Samuel, "Kerala Pentecostal Writers' Forum," 103–6.

55. M. Abraham, "The Origin, Evolution, and Development of PCNAK Youth Conferences," 47.

On a positive note, the congregations that held on to the Malayalam language have young people who are able to understand spoken Malayalam. Most of the ABKs cannot read or write Malayalam. Early adopters of the English language raised monolingual Keralites. Proponents of the early transition have regretted this particular outcome.

Keralite Pentecostals in Diaspora have done well to keep their faith. They have also succeeded in passing on their faith to a new generation born and raised in America. Their churches are growing well and multiplying. But Keralite Pentecostals in India and abroad are facing many real problems as they adapt to the new realities of the twenty-first century in India and abroad.

TWENTY-FIRST-CENTURY CHALLENGES

What confronts Indian Pentecostalism is not unique. All movements evolve and transform. In fact, sociologists are able to predict the development of people movements, religious and others. They say that movements and institutions are on a predictable track to decay unless proper interventions take place in a timely fashion. While proper interventions can extend the life of a human organization, they cannot forever prevent decay.

Normally, transformations of this sort happen in a generational way and changes are associated with changing generations. The North American charismatic movement is one example of this. Generational changes and several institutional changes are taking place simultaneously within the American charismatic movement. The passing of Oral Roberts, the transitions at Oral Roberts University, and the decline of the International Charismatic Bible Ministries (ICBM) conferences are clear evidences. Hopefully, American charismatics are well equipped to adapt to changes. The challenge to adapt is taking place in different dimensions of Keralite Pentecostalism. A keen analysis of the origin and development of the Indian Pentecostal movement in its context is required to understand and address these challenges. The following is a brief outline of such an analysis.

RURAL VS. URBAN

Indian Pentecostalism was a rural movement. Although Indian cities witnessed the growth of Pentecostalism in the later twentieth century, its roots were in the rural areas of Kerala and other parts of India. The work in major urban areas of India was due to the mobility of educated Keralites to the larger cities for employment. Most of the world's population now lives in urban centers. This is increasingly true of Keralites. However, Keralite Pentecostalism's cultural trappings are still rural, and its growth in urban areas requires significant adjustments.

LOCAL VS. GLOBAL

Pentecostalism of the early twentieth century in Kerala certainly had global influence. Many Indian Pentecostal practices have their roots in western Pentecostalism. These can be traced to colonialism and the western missionary enterprise. Pentecostalism as experienced by local people, however, was of local cultural flavor. For example, Pentecostal worship was characteristically Indian. Early Pentecostal worship music was eastern, not western. For a contrast, one may look at the Church of South India with its Anglican connections and the churches of South Korea with its American tunes. Their order of worship and the music used in worship are clearly western. Korean language and music, for example, took a very back seat in the Korean Christian churches. This was not the case among Pentecostals in India. Globalization of early Keralite Pentecostals ended with the western way of greeting people (shake hands, saying "Praise the Lord,") and the rest was local. This was the case in and out of Kerala.

Only a few Pentecostal leaders traveled outside India in those days. What people knew about the United States, Sweden, or England was based on mostly their word of testimony. This is not the case today. India is a leader in a globalized flat world. Communication is instant. Even rural people in India have access to television and multimedia. They know how Korean or American people dress, sing, and worship. No wonder Indian Pentecostalism finds it difficult to enforce strictly traditional lifestyle, worship, and spiritual practices.

POOR VS. RICH

Wealth has increased in India and abroad since the beginning of modern Pentecostalism. Many Keralite Pentecostals are wealthy in the new global world. Expatriates live well and bring money and foreign customs back to Kerala. In the past, Pentecostalism generally belonged to people on the wrong side of the tracks economically. This is no longer the case. Indian Pentecostals in general have experienced a social lift. They have gained high education and higher income in India and abroad. Poor people's Pentecostalism of the twentieth century is now being challenged to adapt to the needs and wants of the well off. The poor are still with us, but Pentecostals are no longer the socially marginalized. Pentecostalism of the masses now must cater to the elite also. This forces rethinking of doctrines and practices. What Pentecostal teachings were strictly doctrinal positions? What were expressions, at least partially, of social location and economic necessity?

POST-COLONIALISM VS. TRUE INDEPENDENCE

India was in the final stages of her struggle for independence when twentieth-century Pentecostalism took roots in Kerala. A loincloth-clad Mahatma Gandhi was the symbol of freedom and the power of powerlessness. Simplicity was not just a Pentecostal virtue, it was an Indian value symbolized by Gandhi way before Mother Teresa. Indigenization was more than a missiological concept—it was a statement. It is interesting to notice in this context that the Keralite Pentecostals who maintained foreign headquarters did not enjoy the growth of those who indigenized. Indian cultural Pentecostal practices were influenced by post-colonial reactions in the second half of the twentieth century. The twenty-first century is seeing a new day. India is a major emerging economy and is respected as the largest democracy in the world that never had a cultural revolution or military coup. The self-understanding of India and Indians has changed. Religious rules and regulations conforming to colonial thinking and post-colonial reactions are now being questioned. At obvious and subliminal levels, Keralite Pentecostalism is challenged to adjust to this reality.

THAT WORLD VS. THIS ONE

Indian Pentecostal theology of the twentieth century was highly otherworldly. Much of the preaching was about the second coming and the world to come. Most moving songs were about the meeting in the air. Social concerns were not well expressed as part of faith. Politics were taboo. That is not the case anymore. Politicians are on Pentecostal convention platforms. Social involvement and charitable work are taken seriously. Preaching about the world to come has been replaced, at least in some segments, with material prosperity and blessings. The air-conditioned world here is not too bad after all. Indian Pentecostalism finds itself at the crossroads. It needs to find a way to be true to its past, faithful to its biblical commitments, and relevant in its present global context.

MEGAPHONE VS. MULTIMEDIA

Technology has revolutionized the world and the Pentecostals. Open-air meetings used handheld megaphones in the past. Today Indian Pentecostals have everything from PowerPoint to *Powervision* television.[56] Sunday school teaching and pastors' seminars cannot be the same anymore. The minimum skills requirement of pastors has moved up but is not often matched by pastoral candidates. The increase in life expectancy has brought together multi-generations in the congregations. Spiritual needs are not the same within the same congregation, even in the native place. How much tradition must be preserved? How much technology must be allowed in church? What is the role of multimedia in evangelism?

ORTHODOX VS. HOLINESS

Prominent leaders of the earlier Indian Pentecostal movement were members of the historic Orthodox churches of Kerala. Some of them were on their way to becoming Orthodox priests when they encountered the Pentecostal message and experience. In their historical location, they were under pressure not only to be Indian in citizenship and non-Hindu in appearance, but also to differentiate themselves and their teachings from Orthodox traditions and non-charismatic Brethren teachings about the Holy Spirit.[57] They also had to incorporate the competitive Brethren/Holiness concept of separation from the world. Input from some culturally naïve missionaries did not make things any easier. Definitions of holiness and expressions of the same remain unresolved in the twenty-first century, especially within the Diaspora.

NATIVES VS. EXPATRIATES

If Pentecostalism's adjustment problem is serious within India, it is much more complicated in the expatriate churches and fellowships, especially in North America. Language issues, first generation immigrant mentality, generational differences in needs and tastes and educational levels of members all have complicated the issues in the West. Pressure from the local culture, especially on young people, has intensified the challenges.

---

56 Power Vision, accessed February 5, 2013, http://www.powervisiontv.com/aboutus.php.

57 S. Mathew, *Kerala Penthecosthu Charithram*, 87–94.

U.S.-EDUCATED CLERGY VS. IMPORTED PASTORS

Unlike other Asian immigrant groups, Keralites seem to prefer pastors who were trained in India to U.S.-educated ministers. American seminaries are producing a noticeable number of Asian American graduates, but decision makers in American Keralite churches still do not give them opportunities to serve, especially as senior pastors. Pastors well trained in Bible in India are not in a position to minister to ABKs with the depth and contextual understanding they require. This has caused much distress in many congregations. Although U.S.-educated ministers are now being hired as youth ministers, senior pastorates are still reserved for immigrant pastors who received their ministerial training in India.[58]

A POSSIBLE RESPONSE

Keralite Pentecostals of the twenty-first century who proudly claim the St. Thomas tradition can learn from the Apostles Peter and Paul who had to deal with this type of issue in their own generation. Handling the cultural needs and distinctiveness of the Gentile Christians was a mega problem in the early church. The first church fight was about this matter. How much of the Jewish law should gentile Christians keep? This issue could have sabotaged the growing Pentecostal church in Acts, but Peter made the right but difficult decision and persuaded the Jerusalem church council to endorse it. That is why Christianity is big among the Gentiles today. (Imagine the size and shape of Christianity today if Peter had insisted that only Jews could become Christians!) Paul had to deal with similar issues. He also was open to the Holy Spirit in this regard and allowed his followers to contextualize the uncompromising gospel. He required strict adherence to essential doctrines, but recommended tolerance in nonessential matters and love in all things. This is what is needed again.

Keralite Pentecostal leaders in India and the United States may be tempted to ignore the looming challenges of the twenty-first century. They may prefer keeping a business as usual attitude or seeing these challenges simply as evidence of backsliding. The truth is that these issues will not just go away. What might help instead is a global conversation on Indian Pentecostalism in the twenty-first century. Led by the Spirit, such a conversation may lead to an examination of Keralite Pentecostal teachings and practices in the light of Scripture, tradition, experience, sanctified reason, and active discernment. As a result, the Holy Spirit may break religious and

---

58. T. Mathew, "American Keralite Churches," 1.

cultural bondages that prevent God's people from living Spirit-led lives and empower Keralite Pentecostals in India and abroad to fulfill God's purposes for their lives more fully in the twenty-first century.

BIBLIOGRAPHY

Abraham, K. E. *Yesukristhuvinte Eliya Daasan* [A Humble Servant of Jesus Christ: Autobiography of Pastor K. E. Abraham]. Kumbanad, Kerala: K. E. Abraham Foundation, 1983.

Abraham, Mathews. "The Origin, Evolution, and Development of PCNAK Youth Conferences." In *Pentecostal Conference of North American Keralites (PCNAK) Silver Jubilee Souvenir*, edited by Oommen Ebenezer, 47–49. Orlando: PCNAK, 2007.

Barrett, David. "The Worldwide Holy Spirit Renewal." In *The Century of the Holy Spirit*, edited by Vinson Synan, 381–414. Nashville: Nelson, 2001.

Burgess, Stanley M., and Eduard M. van der Maas, eds. *The New International Dictionary of Pentecostal and Charismatic Movements*. Rev. ed. Grand Rapids: Zondervan, 2002.

Ebenezer, Oommen, ed. *Smaranika 1983–2007: Pentecostal Conference of North American Keralites (PCNAK) Jubilee Souvenir*. Orlando: PCNAK, 2007.

Hedlund, R. E. "Indigenous Churches." In *The New International Dictionary of Pentecostal and Charismatic Movements*, edited by Stanley M. Burgess and Eduard M. van der Maas, 779–84. Rev. ed. Grand Rapids: Zondervan, 2002.

India Gospel Outreach. http://www.indiago.org/About-IGO.html (accessed May 13, 2013).

Joseph, Joy. "Sunday School Ministry in North America." In *Pentecostal Conference of North American Keralites (PCNAK) Silver Jubilee Souvenir*, edited by Oommen Ebenezer, 81–82. Orlando: PCNAK, 2007.

Karackal, Shaji. "Malayali Penthecosthu Sabhakalude Charithram" [The History of the Malayali Pentecostal Churches]. In *Pentecostal Conference of North American Keralites (PCNAK) Silver Jubilee Souvenir*, edited by Oommen Ebenezer, 50–63. Orlando: PCNAK, 2007.

Kurien, P. P. "North American Church of God (India) Fellowship—Oru Thirinju Nottam" [North American Church of God (India) Fellowship—A Review]. In *NACOG Crystal Jubilee Souvenir*, edited by Johnson Zachariah, 17–24. Dallas: NACOG, 1995–2010.

McGee, Gary B. "Pentecostal and Pentecostal-like Movements (1860–1910)." In *The New International Dictionary of Pentecostal and Charismatic Movements*, edited by Stanley M. Burgess and Eduard M. van der Maas, 118–22. Rev. ed. Grand Rapids: Zondervan, 2002.

Mathew, Saju. *Kerala Penthecosthu Charithram* [History of Pentecostalism in Kerala]. 2nd ed. Kottayam, Kerala: Good News, 2007.

Mathew, Thomson K. "American Keralite Churches Must Hire Theology Graduates of U.S. Schools." Agape Partners International. http://agapepartners.org/articles/51/1/American-Keralite-Churches-Must-Hire-Theology-Graduates-of-US-Schools/Page1.html (accessed May 13, 2013).

———. "The Future of Keralite Pentecostals in North America." In *Pentecostal Conference of North American Keralites (PCNAK) Silver Jubilee Souvenir*, edited by Oommen Ebenezer, 157. Orlando: PCNAK, 2007.

Mathews, Achoy. "Founding of the First Keralite Church." In *Pentecostal Conference of North American Keralites (PCNAK) Silver Jubilee Souvenir*, edited by Oommen Ebenezer, 127–29. Orlando: PCNAK, 2007.

Paul, Mathews. *Jwolichu Prakashicha Vilakku—Pastor K. J. Samuel* [A Lamp that Shined Brightly—Pastor K. J. Samuel]. Mumbai: Suvartha, 1997.

Philip, P. S. "Kudiyetta Charithram" [The History of Immigration]. In *Pentecostal Conference of North American Keralites (PCNAK) Silver Jubilee Souvenir*, edited by Oommen Ebenezer, 34–37. Orlando: PCNAK, 2007.

Power Vision. http://www.powervisiontv.com/aboutus.php (accessed May 13, 2013).

Samuel, Sam T. "Kerala Pentecostal Writers' Forum." In *Pentecostal Conference of North American Keralites (PCNAK) Silver Jubilee Souvenir*, edited by Oommen Ebenezer, 103–6. Orlando: PCNAK, 2007.

Thumbamon, Joy. "Oklahoma Muthal Toronto Vare" [From Oklahoma to Toronto]. In *Pentecostal Conference of North American Keralites (PCNAK) Silver Jubilee Souvenir*, edited by Oommen Ebenezer, 41–46. Orlando: PCNAK, 2007.

Zacharaiah, Johnson, ed. *Smaranika 1995-2010: Crystal Jubilee Souvenir*. North American Church of God (India) Fellowship, 2010.

14

Strategizing in the Spirit in Time of War
The 1943 Assemblies of God Missionary Conference

—Malcolm R. Brubaker

Special missionary convention at Central Bible Institute, March 1943[1]
Photo Credit: Flower Pentecostal Heritage Center

1. Note: Photo was used in the *Pentecostal Evangel*, April 10, 1943, 1 and *Heritage* (1992) 21. Identified Names of those in the picture: Front (L-R) Fred Vogler, Alice F. Stewart, Helen Gustavson, Beatrice D. Hildbrand, Thelma V. Hildebrand, Ada Bolton,

A little girl's face is tucked in the second row of a group photograph of Assemblies of God (AG) missionaries and missions executives.[2] On her left sits her mother, with her father behind them both in the next row. To his right is the little girl's future father-in-law. The girl is Ruth Vassar Burgess, daughter of Ted and Estelle Vassar, directors of the Junnar Boys' Orphanage and School, Junnar, West India. The future father-in-law is John H. Burgess, founder of Bethel Bible School, Mavelikara, South India, whose son is Stanley M. Burgess.

The Vassar and Burgess families were some of the many AG missionaries forced by World War Two to return to the United States. Noel Perkin, AG national missions secretary, had invited them and others on furlough to a missionary conference in March 1943 for a time of reporting on the current state of AG missionary work and reflecting on future initiatives after conflict ceased. Other mission agencies convened similar gatherings for strategizing. The China Inland Mission prepared its postwar plans for returning.[3] One Christian and Missionary Alliance writer prepared a business-modeled plan for its China work once hostilities ceased.[4] The war caused every mission agency to evaluate what to do, including the AG denomination.

By 1943 war across the globe had constricted AG missionary efforts. The Second Sino-Japanese War begun in 1937 had been impacting the work in Korea and China. Since 1939 the war in Europe had limited AG missions work there. After the attack on Pearl Harbor much of East Asia closed with a number of AG personnel interned in camps in China, the Philippines, and even Japan itself.[5]

Edith Osgood, Grace P. Nicholson, Ruth E. Johnson, Mary E. Martin, Florence M. Smith, Jennie Wilson, Elise Simmons, Louise Hackert, Elizabeth Maynard, and Eunice Princic. 2nd row (L-R) Noel Perkin, Henrietta Tieleman, Lula Bell Hough, Laura K. Kritz, Sunshine Ball, Alice E. Luce, Marguerite Flint, Gladys Ketcham, Kathryn Long, Martha Kucera, Ellen Esler, Mildred Ginn, Ruth Vassar (daughter) and Estelle Vassar, Hattie Hacker, Anna Helmbrecht, and Marjory Mahaney. 3rd row (L-R) Ida L. Beck, Nettie Juergensen, Eva M. Carlson, Dorothy M. Boyse, Hilda Reffke, Howard Osgood, Leonard G. Bolton, Gladys E. Short, Kenneth Short, J. J. Mueller, John H. Burgess, Ted R. Vassar, William E. Davis, and Clarence T. Maloney. 4th row (L-R) Paul L. Kitch, Vivan L. Smith, W. Lloyd Shirer, Norman H. Barth, Nicholas Nikoloff, Gustave Kinderman, Arthur E. Wilson, Alfred A. Blakeney, Harry G. Downey, A. John Princic, and Lawrence O. McKinney. Back row (L-R) W. I. Evans, Joseph P. Wannenmacher, J. Roswell Flower, and E. S. Williams.

2. Perkin, "Onward to Victory," 1, 6.
3. Osgood, "Thoughts on the Evangelization of China," 16–18.
4. Bechtel, "Postwar Missionary Plans," 424–25.
5. See Warner, *Heritage* 11 (1991–1992) for articles about World War Two experiences of AG missionaries and pastors.

Several examples of the war's impact can be illustrated with the North India District Council (NIDC) of the AG. In 1941 this missionary field organization had planned its annual conference for Calcutta but shifted its location due to that city's newly imposed black-out ordinances.[6] In February of 1942 Maynard Ketcham, NIDC superintendent, counseled his members to hold steady but would not forbid any of the men who wanted to send home their wives and children.[7] In August 1942 the AG Foreign Missions Department (DFM) sent $12,000 to the NIDC for distribution to those missionaries who decided to leave India.[8] A month later Perkin's monthly letter for September quoted a letter from India that remarked that the Methodists had been told to remain in the field and not to evacuate.[9] But by year's end Ketcham reported that thirty-one members were in the United States, leaving forty to carry on the work.[10]

Perkin reported to the September 1943 General Council of the AG that there were a total of 403 missionaries and ministers under appointment for foreign service.[11] Of that number, 245 were still abroad serving in forty-one of fifty-one "missionary fronts." That would have left about 158 AG missionaries in the United States. Perkin decided to turn this negative matter into an opportunity for reflection on the present state of AG mission work as well as how to most effectively advance the work once military conflict ceased. In his February 1943 monthly letter to all missionaries, Perkin wrote:

> We are looking forward to the special missionary conference called for this coming month and wish that all our missionaries could be with us. We are hoping that those who do attend may assist in special committees to draw up recommendations to guide us in a progressive program for the development of the work as a whole.[12]

J. J. Mueller, Assistant Missionary Secretary and former North India missionary, mentioned this same matter in a letter to the current NIDC secretary, John Lewis: "Next month we will have a gathering of the representatives of the different mission fields who are now on furlough. Several days will be

---

6. Bryant to Schoonmaker, May 29, 1941.
7. Ketcham to NIDC Members, February 4, 1942.
8. Ketcham to NIDC Executive Committee, August 17, 1942.
9. Perkin to "Beloved Co-workers," September 30, 1942.
10. Ketcham, "NIDC Chairman's Report 1941–1942."
11. Perkin, "Missions Department Report," 44–52.
12. Perkin to "Beloved Co-worker," February 27, 1943.

given to the reading of papers by those selected from each field and discussion of the post-war policies."[13]

The outcomes of the impromptu convention of 1943 were significant on three counts; the conference: (1) inspired AG church and missions executives to set goals for personnel (500 new missionaries) and for financial support (five million dollars in cash); (2) stimulated the AG to think strategically with a view of the whole rather than relying on individual missionary initiative; and (3) anticipated AG mission programs that Perkin developed in the 1950s.[14]

THE REPORTS OF THE MARCH 1943 CONFERENCE

During March 16–18, fifty-eight missionaries from eighteen countries along with AG national executives met at the chapel of Central Bible Institute to hear eleven reports from selected presenters.[15] Copies of seven of the reports are available, and two other presenters' papers are summarized in *Pentecostal Evangel* articles (the material of two presenters has not been preserved: Mary Martin of Liberia and Lloyd McKinney of Malay States and South China). Did these reports meet Perkin's aims for the conference? Were they strategic in the sense of offering specific recommendations, or were they merely taken up with anecdotal stories illustrating AG missions work in various fields? These questions will guide the following summaries of the nine existing addresses.

Europe (Presentation 1)

Nicolas Nikoloff's twenty-eight-page report on Europe was the longest in length. The first five pages dealt with an eschatological question of great import to Pentecostals: If Christ's return was imminent, why should there be any concern about long-range planning? His answer: "No, I am not going to dress in a white robe and climb Pike's Peak there to await the return of the Lord! On the contrary, I shall be busy doing the work of the Lord as though He will come after a thousand years."[16] The next eleven pages surveyed Pentecostal efforts in Russia, the Baltic states, Poland, Romania,

---

13. Mueller to Lewis, February 26, 1943.

14. See the foundational works of McGee, *This Gospel*, 165–68; *Miracles, Missions, & American Pentecostalism*, 170; and "Pentecostals and Their Strategies for Global Missions," 203–24.

15. Perkin, "Onward to Victory," 1.

16. Nikoloff, "Missionary Conference: Report on Europe," 5.

Bulgaria (his native land), Greece, Yugoslavia, Czechoslovakia, Hungary, Austria, Germany, France, Italy, Belgium, Portugal, and Spain.[17] Interestingly, though the AG would appoint G. Kinderman as a "field secretary" in 1943, the AG had no official missionaries and only four "ordained ministers in foreign lands" with a European assignment (two in Greece, one in Poland, and one in Germany).[18] Nikoloff closed his paper with a statement of support for empowering the national workers and some practical suggestions for a post-war plan of missionary work: send short-term experienced pastors to Europe, establish a Bible school in Central Europe, and provide humanitarian assistance to an expected needy continent after the war.

West Africa (Presentation 2)

By 1943 the AG had ninety-three missionaries organized in nine African fields (Belgian Congo, Egypt, Gold Coast [Ghana], Ivory Coast, Liberia, Nigeria, Sierra Leone, South Africa, and Tanganyika). A. E. Wilson's "Report on West Africa" focused primarily on Upper Ivory Coast and its Mossi people.[19] His view of missions was fairly conventional with mission stations as centers of evangelism to surrounding areas. He had recently opened Central Bible School for training national leaders. However, Wilson did advocate for a central missions treasury from which to draw missionaries' salaries rather than the itineration system as followed in the AG. That suggestion may have led in part to the financial goals of the conference (see below). Wilson also recognized the need to care for the health of missionaries by shortening their terms where climate was demanding.

China (Presentation 3)

Howard C. Osgood spoke about China and represented forty-seven AG missionaries scattered in five regions (North, Northwest, South, Southwest, and Manchuria). His tightly written and organized talk formulated specific strategies for expanding the Christian gospel (particularly in Yunnan Province): (1) cooperate with other evangelical groups such as the China Inland Mission; (2) unify all Pentecostal groups under a common name in China—"The Association Called of God;" (3) organize a Bible school for

17. This chapter will use 1943 political boundaries and names unless contemporary usage is needed for clarification.

18. All numbers of missionaries at the time of this conference come from the 1943 "Ministers Directory."

19. Wilson, "Report on West Africa," 3–14.

Southwest China where there was a good start among tribal peoples, but initiate new efforts among the majority Chinese population; and (4) establish strategic locations for church-planting teams of eight missionaries.[20] A variety of workers were needed: evangelists, secretaries, school teachers for missionary children, nurses, and Bible school instructors. His broad view was that 200 new missionaries and a field secretary would be needed after the war and organized around the three cultural and linguistic regions of Peking, Canton, and Kunming. His paper also addressed the eschatological question whether Christians should bother about planning for the future in light of Christ's imminent return. He said that should Jesus tarry, his coming Christian people must prepare now for future missionary efforts, declaring, "And if so, then all Fundamental peoples, in America and England at least, ought to awake now to sudden action and prepare to hurl into the conflict against evil all their resources, so that the gospel may be carried quickly and thoroughly throughout the world."[21]

India (Presentations 4 and 5)

AG missionaries in British India were divided into two areas: sixty-four missionaries in North India, twenty-two in South India and Ceylon.[22] C. T. Maloney gave the formal paper on South India, "Report on South India and Ceylon," and A. A. Blakeney presented the paper on North India, "The Full Gospel in North India." Maloney's report focused on four features of the South India District Council (SIDC): (1) four primary language groups divide this region; (2) the Malayalam language district is the most advanced in terms of missionary involvement (twelve AG missionaries), a well-established Bible school run by John Burgess, and over thirty local churches; (3) SIDC missionaries rent homes with no missionary compounds; and (4) "all the work throughout our field is evangelistic and with no institutional work."[23] Maloney did not point out that a major advantage of Pentecostal work in South India was that there were many nominal Christians who were drawn to the vitality and dynamism of Pentecostal churches.[24]

---

20. Osgood, "Thoughts on the Evangelization of China," 5–12.
21. Ibid., 4.
22. See more on North India in my doctoral dissertation, "Evolving Models of Missions," 290–93.
23. Maloney, "Report on South India and Ceylon," 12.
24. This fact was first brought to my attention by Ruth Burgess in a telephone call, February 19, 2009. See also Bergunder, *South Indian Pentecostal Movement*, 239.

Blakeney's paper spent several pages giving a proper contextualization of AG work in North India. Pentecostal work began around 1908 on the United Province-Nepal border—likely referring to the early stations of Will Norton, Lillian Denney, and Minnie Abrams' Bezaleel Evangelistic Mission work. Defending the mission station approach in North India, he cited the caste system that made conversions difficult and the precedent of previous Protestant mission stations as models:

> By the compound system I mean that method of gathering the Indian Christians together in a community on the mission property, with the missionaries in full charge, and for the most part, entirely responsible for their financial support, spiritual training and education. As Pentecostal missionaries, after seeing the great contrast between the district Christians [referring to Christians living in villages and towns among the general Hindu and Muslim populations], we seemed naturally to decide on the former as our policy. It surely was the better of the two. You can easily see that this was not exactly the New Testament method. But let any who feel to criticize at this long range remember that India has been considered by many who have visited various other foreign fields, the most difficult country on earth in which to carry on according to New Testament methods. Then, too, we had the older denominations before us as examples and we felt in those days that we needed humbly to learn from them.[25]

Evidently, Blakeney was convinced that a mission station strategy was contextually a better fit for North India even if it did not correspond to New Testament methods.

In terms of future prospects, Blakeney saw several changes that gave him hope: (1) an increase in a liberal education with Western ideas of religious toleration, (2) India's potential economic importance as seen in it becoming "the arsenal of the East during this war," (3) a sense of self-worth and capability among national workers who increasingly expected respect at all levels, and (4) the planting of churches in the North by "our Indian Pentecostal brethren from South India."[26] Hence, Blakeney made four proposals: First, he called for the AG to cooperate with the independent Pentecostals who were bringing "vision and faith." Second, he commended a focus on the cities where short-term Bible schools for workers could train more national workers. Third, he proposed that the AG recruit more married missionary couples who are well-educated and some even with agricultural know-

---

25. Blakeney, "The Full Gospel in North India," 14–15.
26. Ibid., 16–23.

how would be helpful. Finally, Blakeney advised the AG to evaluate which mission stations were currently not occupied and should be closed with the money spent elsewhere on more productive areas. He was a bit unsure of the maturity of the national churches at that moment to become independent but had appreciation for the Bible schools at Hardoi (women) and Laheria Sarai (men) and the work they were doing.

One of the side benefits of this conference was the potential for field-level gatherings. Blakeney and Marguerite Flint called together the six NIDC missionaries present to address their own specific issues and strategies.[27] The group's recommendations parallel the same emphases as those found in Blakeney's report.

Latin America and Palestine (Presentations 6 and 7)

The reports on Latin America by John L. Franklin and on Palestine by Ida Beck are not extant as given at the March 1943 conference but subsequently appeared in abridged form in the *Pentecostal Evangel*; Franklin's report centered on Central America but was representative of 126 AG missionaries spread out over sixteen nations of the Caribbean islands, Central and South America, as well as Hispanic ministries in the United States.[28] He noted there had been increasing freedom to evangelize and church plant in Catholic majority countries with good results. Following indigenous methods, missionaries like Ralph Williams in Central America had raised up churches in a number of these countries with their own leadership and organization. There was a good Bible institute in El Salvador. He saw the immediate need for twenty-five new couples for such ministries as evangelization work in Cuba, a Bible school in Guatemala, and gospel and Bible literature distribution. In closing, he appealed, "LET'S OCCUPY LATIN AMERICA FOR THE GOSPEL. NOW!" (emphasis his).[29]

Beck's report was one of two given by a woman.[30] At that time there were seven AG missionaries in Palestine—six women and one man.[31] She noted the irony of sending missionaries to the homeland of Christianity. Since Muslim and Jewish peoples were highly resistant to the gospel (persons who became Christian were quickly ostracized socially and economi-

27. "Copy: Recommendations of the North India Committee," AGWM Archives.
28. Franklin, "Latin America Calling," 1, 8–9.
29. Ibid., 9.
30. Beck, "Problems and Opportunities in Palestine," 10–11.
31. For a larger picture of Pentecostal efforts in Palestine, see Newberg, *Pentecostal Mission in Palestine*; and Gannon, "The Shifting Romance with Israel."

cally), AG work in Palestine was primarily among Arabic Christians from the Catholic and Orthodox faiths. She noted that though the number of women missionaries made ministry to children a primary activity, there was a need for a Bible school and properly educated missionaries to train national believers.

Nigeria and Dutch East Indies (Presentations 8 and 9)

Two presenters' papers have not been officially identified as such, but they wrote articles in the *Pentecostal Evangel* that likely resemble their conference reports; one by Lloyd Shirer appeared in January 1943 and dealt with the usefulness of gospel literature in the West African context.[32] His twenty-two years of ministry had been most effective when printed Bibles and gospel literature were available. Shirer reported that co-laborers in Nigeria—Everett and Dorothy Phillips, Rex Jackson, and Elmer Frink—were "having a glorious harvest" that "began through that literature that was printed in Springfield."[33] The article was spiced with missionary anecdotes to illustrate that point.

The second *PE* article that likely represents what a presenter gave in conference is one written by Kenneth G. Short and covered ministry in Borneo, Dutch East Indies (Indonesia).[34] The Dutch East Indies was made up of thousands of islands stretched over 3,000 miles of ocean with over sixty million people. Christianity had arrived with Roman Catholic missionaries in the 1500s followed by German Lutheran and Dutch societies. Short regarded these latter groups as largely "modernistic" in their theology. However, Christian and Missionary Alliance people were doing a good work and used a seaplane to transport its workers around the chain of islands. Short came to Borneo in 1936 and with his wife were only two of four AG missionaries in the Dutch East Indies. He had developed a burden to reach inland tribal peoples. The healing of a blind girl opened one village to the gospel and led to numerous conversions. There were also some positive areas in more heavily populated regions such as Java where indigenous churches had sprung up. Their leaders were poorly educated but could become the basis of a strong Pentecostal work. Short had recognized the need for a Bible school, but the war interrupted its implementation; also, he saw that there was potential church growth among the Chinese immigrants to these islands. After the war Short envisioned that five new couples could

32. Shirer, "The Power of Gospel Literature in Africa," 1–2, 5–7.
33. Ibid., 7.
34. Short, "Proving God in Borneo," 2–3, 8–9.

be used to set up a central headquarters to run a reception center for new missionaries, a rest home on the field, and a literature center. His thoughts for training national workers had shifted from having one central location to utilizing small, short-term Bible schools that would enable students to maintain ministry in their respective cultures and environments.

THEMES OF THE REPORTS

These 1943 AG missions conference papers evidence a missiological understanding of a changing world. Four common themes reflect this awareness. First, there was an awareness of a need for an indigenous-focused missiology even where conditions in places such as North India and Palestine had made progress difficult toward that ideal.[35] Alice Luce was present at this conference, and it had been her 1921 three-part *Pentecostal Evangel* series, "Paul's Missionary Methods," that introduced Roland Allen's ideas of self-supporting, self-governing, and self-propagating churches.[36] That model had been followed by Luce, H. C. Ball, Ralph Williams, and Melvin Hodges in Latin America where church planting had produced strong national leadership, as was seen in J. L. Franklin's paper.

Second, in 1943 the open fields for continuing missionary work were sub-Sahara Africa and Latin America. The African reports were glowing with optimistic opportunities for expanded AG missions there. As noted, Latin America had become a success story already by 1943. Transportation to and from these places could be difficult but possible during the war years. By the end of 1943 there were thirty-six people approved for AG missionary work.[37] Of that number twenty-nine had declared Latin America and three sub-Sahara Africa as their missions field (four were undeclared).

Third, the speakers consistently spoke of the value of establishing Bible schools to train national workers for evangelism and church planting.[38] Some such as Ida Beck and Nicholas Nikoloff expressed the need to establish these types of schools in their fields; others such as Clarence Maloney and John L. Franklin reported the effectiveness of schools already in existence.

---

35. In 1933 the executive committee of the NIDC recommended to its members that they read Roland Allen's works which had influenced Alice Luce's AG missiology. See Mueller, "Minutes of the NIDC Executive Committee Meeting at Rupaidiha."

36. Luce, "Paul's Missionary Methods," *PE* (January 8, 1921) 6–7; (January 22, 1921) 6, 11; (February 5, 1921) 6–7.

37. No author, "Wishing You A Happy, *Missionary* New Year!," 8–9.

38. For a broad view of Pentecostal Bible school training, see Wilson, "Bible Institutes, Colleges, Universities."

The fourth feature of the presentations was indeed an attempt to "strategize in the Spirit." Perkin's purpose for the conference was to share reports and to think how to move forward after military hostilities would cease. Reports by Osgood, Nikoloff, Short, Franklin, Blakeney, and Wilson gave both general and specific recommendations for their respective fields. Osgood, in particular, noted how his own vision of China expanded from one valley in Yunnan Province to the entire country and beyond:

> Then, on the way to America from Yunnan this last time, I began to visualize the whole of China and affectionately to meditate on plans for her evangelization, on a larger scale than we as Assemblies of God have ever attempted it. And now, after several months here at Central Bible Institute, while mingling with students who have calls to all parts of the world, I have been led to think just a bit in terms of evangelizing the globe.[39]

Suggested strategies included the role of Bible schools as noted above, allocation of more personnel to expand and strengthen current numbers of missionaries, re-location of missionaries to key cities central to reaching surrounding regions, and communication with the AG home constituency so as to enlarge the amount of missionary giving.

However, all this planning was regarded as secondary to the direction and enablement of the Holy Spirit. Robert W. Cummings, North India missionary, reminded the 1943 General Council that such strategic thinking could become merely a human endeavor and be worthless if the Holy Spirit's touch was left out.[40] His comments show the tension inherent between the "Spirit" and the "strategy" in a Pentecostal organization like the AG.[41]

GOALS SET BY THE CONFERENCE: AN ASSESSMENT

Just prior to the conference Perkin had written, "The war is not an unmixed evil in that it has forced us in many places to rethink our policies and plan more definitely for the establishment of the native church in each land."[42] At the end of the conference or soon after the national executive missionary

---

39. Osgood, "Thoughts on the Evangelization of China," 3.

40. Cummings, "Christ's Living Ministry," 6–7, 12.

41. This is seen in such titles about AG missions such as Wilson, *Strategy of the Spirit*.

42. Perkin to "Our Missionaries Abroad."

committee set six goals.⁴³ The following section describes and evaluates whether these targets were reached.

First goal: select field secretaries over major regions to administer and advise missionaries as well as be promoters of these fields in the United States. By year's end two men were approved by the general presbytery: H. C. Ball for Latin America and H. B. Garlock for Africa.⁴⁴ In subsequent years other field secretaries such as Howard C. Osgood for China and Robert Cummings for India were appointed.⁴⁵

Second goal: recruit five hundred new missionaries ready by war's end. Figures for all AG missionaries as reported at two-year intervals show no large spike in numbers but a general increase toward that goal: 1943 (441 missionaries), 1945 (488), 1947 (641), 1949 (731), 1951 (700) 1953 (905), and 1955 (1047).⁴⁶ That goal took twelve years to reach. Setting a number was easier than implementing a workable plan to reach that goal.

Third goal: raise an advance fund of five million dollars so that qualified people could be immediately sent to the field without having to spend one to two years of itineration. Two months after the conference there was a small sidebar in a *Pentecostal Evangel* page with the wartime caption, "The Mission Field Needs You! We must advance!"⁴⁷ At the September 1943 General Council in Springfield, Missouri, the missionary service ended with 700 people coming forward, thereby signifying that they were open to the missionary call.⁴⁸ This appeal had the merit of rushing newly recruited missionaries to the field as soon as possible, but the downside to this approach was that missionaries recruited would eventually need to gain long-term support while on the field and on furloughs. Ketcham, North India missionary and Asia regional secretary, observed this flaw in several couples who came to India.⁴⁹ One couple did not last a full term due to illness; the other eventually gained support and later transferred to missions work in the Philippines.⁵⁰

---

43. Perkin publicly announced these goals at the Twentieth General Council, "The Diary of a Delegate to the General Council," 2–3, 9. See also Perkin, "Missionary Department Report," 43–47.

44. Editorial announcement in *PE* (June 5, 1943) 10, and "Introducing New Members of Our Missionary Department Staff," *PE* (November 27, 1943) 10.

45. McGee, *This Gospel Must Be Preached*, 172–73.

46. Figures compiled by Kathleen Bird from General Council Ministers and Missionary directories and General Council minutes available at www.iFPHC.org.

47. *PE* (May 29, 1943) 7.

48. No author, "Missionary Service at General Council," 11.

49. Ketcham, Recorded audio interview with Gary B. McGee, July 13, 1983.

50. No author, "Keeping Up to Date," 9; and "Missionaries by Country: North India."

Fourth goal: appoint advisory committees to offer counsel to various fields. One such committee for Europe was formed of missionaries and ministers such as Joseph Wannenmacher, Hungarian-born AG pastor in Milwaukee. He had attended the March conference due to his short-term evangelistic ministry in Eastern Europe. At the September General Council missionary service he described the situation in Europe.[51] In a 1965 historical review of the April 1943 missionary conference, Perkin did not mention this goal. Presumably the omission was because this goal was never realized to any degree beyond the short-lived European committee.[52]

Fifth goal: provide additional training of missionary candidates and missionaries home on furlough. The rigors of climate, non-Christian religions, and foreign customs needed to be communicated to prospective and even current missionaries. Robert and Mildred Cummings were asked to remain at Central Bible Institute and teach additional missiological classes on such cross-cultural challenges.[53] The benefits of missionaries coming together to receive training led to another conference in June 1948 when over one hundred missionaries came together at Central Bible Institute for seminars and reports.[54]

Sixth goal: organize regional missionary conventions to promote and publicize AG missionary work. In the fall of 1943 Kenneth Short, home from the Dutch East Indies due to the war, took on the editorial role of producing a quarterly report, "Missionary Challenge."[55] In addition, he was asked to plan and lead regional missions conventions. In the next few years there were several announcements of missionary conventions that Short attended and led before he returned to missions work.[56] But by the 1951 General Council the mood for large missionary conventions had swung back to the importance of local church annual conventions. The report of the foreign missions committee said, "It is through the concentrated missionary emphasis of local conventions that many of our strongest missionary churches have raised their annual missionary budget pledge."[57]

These six goals, while not realized fully, encouraged the AG to think strategically and collectively. They led to some longer-range results.

51. "Missionary Service at General Council," 10.
52. Perkin, "Progress in Crisis," 11–12.
53. Perkin, "Missions Department Report," 46.
54. "The Missionary Conference," 8.
55. "Introducing New Members," 10.
56. No author, "Forth Coming Meetings," 7; and "Future Meetings: Missionary Convention," 14.
57. "Report of the Foreign Missions Committee," 14.

LASTING CONTRIBUTIONS OF THE MARCH 1943 MISSIONARY CONFERENCE

The last reference in the *Pentecostal Evangel* to the specific goal of five hundred new missionaries was in September 1945.[58] It appeared in a small sidebar along with goals of having five thousand native evangelists, fifty thousand prayer warriors, and five hundred million pieces of gospel literature. There was no mention of the five million dollar goal. Though the 1943 conference's goals were not reached there were two important results.

One result was the simple value of gathering missionaries together to share experiences, successes, and challenges. The face-to-face interaction with people facing similar missiological challenges was a great encouragement. Later conferences such as the one in 1948 had the same purpose and result.[59] By 1955 Perkin had established an annual "school of missions" at Central Bible Institute.[60] It continues to this day under the name "Missionary Training and Renewal" as a "boot camp" for new candidates as well as seminar training for those on furlough.[61]

A second result of the 1943 conference was embracing the principle of strategizing at an organizational level while maintaining initiative at the individual missionary level. Gary B. McGee's study referred to the remaining years of Perkin's mission administration as "The Era of Strategic Planning (1943–1959)."[62] Concerning finances, this strategic question was asked: How could the missionary vision of the AG be supported by the constituency? By 1945 the five million dollar fund for a special post-war effort had not come in, so the missions department decided to break their financial goals into more individual amounts by suggesting that each AG member set aside three cents a day for missions.[63] Later, the suggestion was for each congregation to adopt a formula for its missions giving: 70 percent to foreign missions, 5 percent to national home missions, 20 percent to district home missions, and 5 percent to administrative costs.[64]

In the area of missions planning, Perkin continued to strategize. His 1953 report at General Council focused on reaching urban centers, using

---

58. No author, "Lest We Forget," 4.

59. The one in June 1948 was also at Central Bible Institute with 100 in attendance, "The Missionary Conference," 8.

60. Carpenter, *Mandate and Mission*, 182–83.

61. Perkin used that military term to describe this annual conference in an undated letter from the 1950s, AGWM Archives.

62. McGee, *This Gospel Shall be Preached*, 163–203.

63. Perkin, "Report of the Foreign Missions Department," 67.

64. Carpenter, *Mandate and Missions*, 182–83.

radio, establishing more Bible schools, aiding the sick, establishing national organizations, and joining other Pentecostal organizations for coordinated efforts.[65] In 1957 Perkin prepared a new AG missions campaign, "Global Conquests," that again would focus on strategic cities for concentrated efforts.[66] When J. Philip Hogan replaced Perkin in 1959, the program was aggressively promoted.

The era of mission planning had begun, and the 1943 missionary conference launched the AG on a trajectory that continued well past those three March days in the middle of World War Two. Kenneth Short's message at the September 1943 General Council heralded a call to the AG to prepare and begin implementation of the plans that had emerged from this conference. It is a fitting summary of the spirit of that conference called by this Spirit-focused missionary agency:

> What will be the place of the Assemblies of God in the post-war world? Just the place that we earnestly, consistently, intelligently, and prayerfully prepare for TODAY! "Occupy till I come," is the command of the Lord. In other words, "Go forward till I return." Work as if His coming will be delayed a thousand years, but live as if He may come in the next ten minutes.[67]

Abbreviations
AG   Assemblies of God
AGWM   Assemblies of God World Missions
FPHC   Flower Pentecostal Heritage Center
NIDC   North India District Council of the Assemblies of God
PE   *Pentecostal Evangel*

BIBLIOGRAPHY

Bechtel, John. "Postwar Missionary Plans for South China." *The Alliance Weekly*, October 21, 1944. http://www.cmalliance.org/resources/ archives/alliance-magazine.
Beck, Ida. "Problems and Opportunities in Palestine." *PE* (July 3, 1943) 10–11.
Bergunder, Michael. *The South Indian Pentecostal Movement in the Twentieth Century*. Studies in History of Christian Missions. Grand Rapids: Eerdmans, 2008.
Blakeney, A. A. "The Full Gospel in North India." Unpublished paper of the AG Missionary Conference, March 16–18, 1943. FPHC Archives.
Brubaker, Malcolm R. "Evolving Models of Missions: A Case Study of the Assemblies of God in North India: 1918–1949." PhD diss., Regent University, 2012.

65. Perkin, "Foreign Missions Secretary's Report," 11.
66. Carpenter, *Mandate and Missions*, 182–83.
67. "Missionary Service at General Council," 11.

Bryant, Sydney. Letter to Mary Schoonmaker, NIDC secretary. May 29, 1941. AGWM Archives.
Carpenter, Harold R. *Mandate and Mission: The Theory and Practice of AG Missions*. Springfield, MO: CBC, 1999.
Cummings, Robert W. "Christ's Living Ministry." *PE* (October 30, 1943) 6–7, 12.
"The Diary of a Delegate to the General Council at Springfield, Missouri." *PE* (September 18, 1943) 2–3, 9.
Editorial announcement. *PE* (June 5, 1943) 10.
"Forthcoming Meetings: World Missionary Convention." *PE* (March 25, 1944) 7.
Franklin, John. "Latin America Calling." *PE* (June 5, 1943) 1, 8–9.
"Future Meetings: Missionary Convention." *PE* (December 22, 1945) 14.
Gannon, Raymond L. "The Shifting Romance with Israel: American Pentecostal Ideology of Zionism and the Jewish State." PhD diss., Jerusalem: Hebrew University, 2003.
"Introducing New Members of Our Missionary Department Staff." *PE* (November 27, 1943) 10.
Ketcham, Maynard. "Chairman's Report 1941–42." Unpublished paper of the AG Missionary Conference, March 16–18, 1943. FPHC Archives.
———. Letter to NIDC Executive Committee. August 17, 1942. AGWM Archives.
———. Letter to NIDC Members. February 4, 1942. AGWM Archives.
———. Recorded Audio Interview with Gary B. McGee, July 13, 1983. *Missionary Recollections*. Springfield, MO: FPHC, 2001.
"Keeping Up to Date." *PE* (December 6, 1947) 9.
"Lest We Forget." *PE* (September 8, 1945) 4.
Luce, Alice E. "Paul's Missionary Methods." Three-part series: *PE*, January 8, 1921, 6–7; January 22, 1921, 6, 11; February 5, 1921, 6–7.
Maloney, C. T. "Missionary Conference: Report on South India and Ceylon." Unpublished paper of the AG Missionary Conference, March 16–18, 1943. FPHC Archives.
McGee, Gary B. *This Gospel Shall Be Preached*. Vol. 1, *A History and Theology of Assemblies of God Foreign Missions to 1959*. Springfield, MO: Gospel, 1986.
———. *Miracles, Missions, and American Pentecostalism*. Maryknoll, NY: Orbis, 2010.
———. "Pentecostals and Their Strategies for Global Missions." In *Called and Empowered: Global Mission in Pentecostal Perspective*, edited by Murray A. Dempster et al., 203–24. Peabody, MA: Hendrickson, 1991.
"Ministers Directory of the General Council of the Assemblies of God." Springfield, MO: Gospel, 1914–2013. http://ifphc.org/index.cfm?fuseaction=publicationsGuide.generalcouncilministersdirectory.
"The Mission Field Needs You!" *PE* (May 29, 1943) 7.
"Missionaries by Country: North India." AGWM Archives, 2008.
"The Missionary Conference." *PE* (July 10, 1948) 8.
"Missionary Service at General Council." *PE* (September 25, 1943) 10–11.
Mueller, J. J. Letter to John Lewis. February 26, 1943. AGWM Archives.
———. "Minutes of the NIDC Executive Committee Meeting at Rupaidiha, April 3–5, 1933." AGWM Archives.
Newberg, Eric N. *The Pentecostal Mission in Palestine: The Legacy of Pentecostal Zionism*. Eugene, OR: Pickwick, 2012.

Nikoloff, N. "Missionary Conference: Report on Europe—Confidential." Unpublished paper of the AG Missionary Conference, March 16-18, 1943. FPHC Archives.

Osgood, Howard C. "Thoughts on the Evangelization of China." Unpublished paper of the AG Missionary Conference, March 16-18, 1943. FPHC Archives.

Perkin, Noel. "Foreign Missions Secretary's Report to the 1953 General Council." *PE* (September 27, 1953) 11.

———. Letter to "Beloved Co-workers." September 30, 1942. AGWM Archives.

———. Letter to "Beloved Co-worker." February 27, 1943. AGWM Archives.

———. Letter to "Our Missionaries Abroad." December 31, 1942. AGWM Archives.

———. "Missions Department Report." In *Minutes of the Twentieth General Council of the Assemblies of God*, 43–53. Springfield, MO: Gospel, 1943. http://ifphc.org/index.cfm?fuseaction=publicationsGuide.generalcouncilminutes.

———. "Onward to Victory." *PE* (April 10, 1943) 1, 6.

———. "Progress in Crisis (1940-1944)." *PE* (September 19, 1965) 11–12.

———. "Report of the Foreign Missions Department." In *Minutes of the Twenty-First General Council of the Assemblies of God*, 59–68. Springfield, MO: Gospel, 1945. http://ifphc.org/index.cfm?fuseaction=publicationsGuide.generalcouncilminutes.

———. Undated letter ca. 1950s. AGWM Archives.

"Recommendations of the North India Committee." Unsigned report from North India missionaries attending 1943 AG missionary conference at CBI. AGWM Archives.

"Report of the Foreign Missions Committee." In *Minutes of the Twenty-Fourth General Council with Constitution and Bylaws*, 11–15. Springfield, MO: Gospel, 1951. http://ifphc.org/index.cfm?fuseaction=publicationsGuide.generalcouncilminutes.

Shirer, Lloyd. "The Power of Gospel Literature in Africa." *PE* (January 30, 1943) 1–2, 5–7.

Short, Kenneth G. "Proving God in Borneo." *PE* (August 7, 1943) 2–3, 8–9.

Warner, Wayne, et al. "Fifty Years Ago: The Assemblies of God & World War Two." *Assemblies of God Heritage* 11, no. 4 (1991–1992) 4–15, 31. http://ifphc.org/index.cfm?fuseaction=publicationsGuide.assembliesOfGodHeritage.

Wilson, A. E. "Report on West Africa." Unpublished paper of the AG Missionary Conference, March 16-18, 1943. FPHC Archives.

Wilson, Everett A. *Strategy of the Spirit: J. Philip Hogan and the Growth of the Assemblies of God, 1960–1990*. Carlisle, UK: Paternoster, 1997.

Wilson, Lewis F. "Bible Institutes, Colleges, Universities." In *The New International Dictionary of Pentecostal and Charismatic Movements*. Rev. ed. Edited by Stanley M. Burgess and Eduard M. van der Maas. Rev. ed. Grand Rapids: Zondervan, 2002.

"Wishing You a Happy, *Missionary* New Year!" *PE* (January 1, 1944) 8–9.

15

Baptism in the Holy Spirit:
A Spiritual and Theological Journey

—Peter Hocken

In 1988 a book was published by Henry Lederle, *Treasures Old and New*, of which the subtitle well indicates its contents: "Interpretations of 'Spirit-Baptism' in the Charismatic Renewal Movement."[1] I was one of the authors surveyed, in my view very perceptively, though at the time I did not welcome my understanding of baptism in the Holy Spirit being classified as "neo-Pentecostal." Toward the end of his survey, Lederle wrote: "It is to be hoped that Hocken will in time develop his unique perspectives more fully in a monograph so that his ideas (which have here been gleaned from various articles) can be elaborated on, systematized and presented to a broader audience."[2]

In this Festschrift to honor Dr. Stanley Burgess, with whom I was pleased to work on the *The New International Dictionary of the Pentecostal and Charismatic Movements* (NIDPCM),[3] for which he was the chief editor, I want to clarify how my understanding of baptism in the Spirit has developed since my charismatic initiation in 1971. I hope to show how this theo-

---

1. Lederle, *Treasures*, 85–90.
2. Ibid., 89.
3. Burgess and van der Maas, *NIDPCM*.

logical development arose directly from my life situations, my participation in charismatic renewal, and my engagement with Pentecostal and charismatic studies.[4] In this development, I see four main phases: (1) First Years in England (1971–76); (2) Mother of God Community (1976–88); (3) The Influence of Louis Dallière (from 1989); and (4) Redaction of the document on baptism in the Holy Spirit for International Catholic Charismatic Renewal Services [ICCRS] (from 2008).[5]

FIRST YEARS IN ENGLAND (1971–76)

My first exposure to things charismatic was at a weekend on prophecy in October 1971 led by Fr Simon Tugwell, OP, whose book *Did You Receive the Spirit?*[6] appeared in 1972. Together with some other young Dominicans from Oxford, Tugwell had come into contact with Pentecostals at a weekly prayer meeting at the home of Joan Steele in Denton, a village just outside Oxford.[7] The weekend I attended at Spode House north of Birmingham brought together some thirty people impacted through Tugwell's ministry. A few days later I was baptized in the Spirit in Birmingham without any imposition of hands, while praying with a few others I had met at Spode House. Through the influence of Denton, my new Birmingham friends had been attending the Saturday evening revival nights at Hockley Pentecostal Church in the inner city of Birmingham, where some had been Spirit-baptized.

At that time what later came to be known as Catholic charismatic renewal (CCR) was just beginning in England. Tugwell had been fascinated by his encounter with flesh-and-blood Pentecostal faith, and was uninterested in the new movement arriving from the United States, which he saw as prepackaged and highly organized. I first went to Hockley Pentecostal Church soon after my baptism in the Spirit. I immediately recognized that here was something powerful that was distinctively different from other Christian patterns of worship and ministry that I had encountered.[8] This sense was fed at first by Tugwell's teaching and writings, but less as he began to pull away from anything overtly charismatic—partly by his refusing the role of

---

4. Particularly in the Society for Pentecostal Studies (from 1980) and in the European Pentecostal Charismatic Research Association (from 1983).

5. This booklet was published in 2012 and is available in the United States from Catholic Charismatic Renewal National Service Committee, Chariscenter USA, P. O. Box 628, Locust Grove, VA 22508.

6. Tugwell, *Did You Receive?*

7. See Hocken, "Joan Steele," 39–40.

8. I was much involved in ecumenical activities at the time and so I had some familiarity with Anglican, United Reformed, Methodist, and Baptist patterns.

foremost charismatic priest in which many wanted to cast him. Tugwell did not approve the terminology of "baptism in the Spirit," but he appreciated Spirit-led Pentecostals, and he saw the importance of speaking in tongues.[9]

From 1971 to 1973, I was learning much from Tugwell, who soon invited me to share in the leadership of his thrice-yearly weekends at Spode House. I shared his view that the Pentecostal understanding of Spirit-baptism was unacceptable for a Catholic, but fully endorsed his recognition of the importance of Pentecostalism. During this phase the Roman Catholic Archbishop of Birmingham, George Patrick Dwyer, asked me to write a report on Catholic Pentecostalism, as it was still called. My report was published in two parts in *The Heythrop Journal*.[10] I find it interesting today that in this report I expressed my unease concerning what was emerging as the dominant Catholic account of baptism in the Spirit: "I am suggesting then that any Catholic attempt to formulate a doctrine of 'Spirit-baptism' that can be harmonized with Catholic teaching on the sacraments of baptism and confirmation is a misguided enterprise."[11]

However by 1974 I was rethinking my attitude to CCR. Despite my lack of enthusiasm for "organized renewal," I was being invited to teach at renewal gatherings. I saw that the reticence to speak of baptism in the Spirit led to very few people receiving. So in 1975 at a national CCR conference at Hopwood Hall, Manchester, I inwardly committed myself to identify with and to serve this renewal whatever its defects and limitations.

MOTHER OF GOD COMMUNITY (1976–88)

In the summer of 1976, I paid a visit to the Mother of God Community in Maryland, USA that led to a prolonged stay.[12] The Mother of God community was strongly convinced of the importance of baptism in the Spirit, both the reality and this terminology. There I became convinced that the search for alternative terms was a mistake. One element in this conviction, also shared by the community, was that the same grace of baptism in the

---

9. Lederle struggles to fit Tugwell into his classifications (see Lederle, *Treasures*, 119–24). He could not have known the background I am mentioning, but nonetheless his account is very fair.

10. Hocken, "Catholic Pentecostalism."

11. Hocken, "Catholic Pentecostalism," 140. At that time, this expressed my reservations about the terminology. Later when I accepted the rightness of the terminology, I objected to the attempt to subsume baptism in the Spirit within the framework of Christian initiation.

12. At that time, the community had its meetings in Potomac, Maryland, but it soon began to cluster in households and later hold its meetings in Gaithersburg, Maryland.

Spirit had been poured out across all the churches, and was given in God's purpose as a major impulse for Christian unity. For charismatics to seek an alternative terminology was equivalent to denying the same work of God across the Christian spectrum.[13]

During this visit I had a profound experience of the cross and was deeply convicted of some patterns of sin. The leaders saw that many Catholics being prayed over for baptism in the Spirit had never been properly evangelized and never truly converted. The result, they were convinced, was producing many excited charismatics with undealt-with sin in their lives. My experience confirmed this diagnosis. Soon after my arrival the community began to develop a seminar known as Growing in Faith, whose purpose was to bring people to repentance and conversion, before they were introduced to baptism in the Spirit and the spiritual gifts through the Life in the Spirit seminar. In retrospect several of those involved see the Growing in Faith seminar as one of the best things to come out of the Mother of God Community.[14]

Another constant emphasis in the Mother of God Community was that baptism in the Spirit opened up the Christian to receive revelation. This was not understood primarily as receiving prophetic words or words of knowledge but as the Holy Spirit writing on our hearts the revelation of Jesus once given to the apostles at the beginning.[15] This understanding is prominent in my paper, "A Survey of the Worldwide Charismatic Movement," presented to the World Council of Churches (WCC) consultation on "Charismatic Movements" at Bossey, Switzerland in March, 1980.[16] It was most developed in two papers presented to the Society for Pentecostal Studies in 1982 and 1984, especially the second.[17] This view is expressed in the 1984 paper: "the meaning of baptism in the Spirit is the total immersion of the believer by the agency of the Spirit into the being and mystery of Christ to the glory of the Father."[18] A similar account is found in my doctoral dissertation (1984), published two years later as *Streams of Renewal*.[19]

---

13. This dimension was brought out in Hocken, "Charismatic Renewal," 310–21, the last writing cited by Lederle.

14. For example, Fr. Thomas Weinandy, OFM Cap.

15. A text that best explains this emphasis is John 16:15, "All that the Father has is mine; therefore I said that he will take what is mine and declare it to you."

16. See Bittlinger, ed., *Church*, 117–47, esp. 124.

17. Hocken, "Jesus Christ," 1–16; and "Meaning," 125–33.

18. Hocken, "Meaning," 131.

19. Hocken, *Streams*, contains an additional chapter to the dissertation comparing the origins in the United States to the origins in Britain.

The section entitled "The Centrality of Baptism in the Spirit"[20] has the same emphasis, and criticizes the widespread Pentecostal view that baptism in the Spirit is empowerment for ministry, ending with the statement that "a more comprehensive understanding and definition of baptism in the Spirit is needed that attributes primary place to the inward revelation of the person of Jesus as the incarnate Son of God. This would then see the visible effects of praise and empowerment for ministry as consequences of the changed relationship to Jesus."[21]

The emphasis on revelation through the Holy Spirit fits totally with the fact that Jesus is the baptizer in/with the Holy Spirit, a point constantly made by David du Plessis. It also stresses that baptism in the Spirit is a sovereign work of God through the risen and exalted Christ. While its sovereign aspect was certainly taught at the Mother of God Community, this word does not appear in these written accounts. In the WCC paper I had listed "the salient features of Charismatic Renewal,"[22] of which a shortened version is presented in *Streams of Renewal*.[23] In *One Lord One Spirit One Body* (1987), baptism in the Spirit is again treated within an account of the whole phenomenon of the charismatic movement, within which baptism in the Spirit and the spiritual gifts are the most distinctive features.[24] Here a similar though not identical list of characteristic features are presented as "the central elements in this spiritual transformation called the baptism in the Spirit."[25] A central point in all these presentations was the ecumenical character of the whole movement, as the salient features listed could be found across the entire Christian spectrum from the historic churches to the free churches and independent movements not affiliated to any existing Christian tradition.[26]

THE INFLUENCE OF LOUIS DALLIÈRE (FROM 1989)

Although I remained in the Mother of God Community until 1996, the developments in my understanding of baptism in the Spirit after 1988 came primarily from influences outside the community. In January 1989, I made

20. Ibid, 166–71 (in the revised edition of 1997, 163–69).
21. Ibid., 171.
22. Bittlinger, *Church*, 123–32.
23. Hocken, *Streams*, 154–56 (1997) 148–51.
24. Hocken, *One Lord*, especially 49–56.
25. Ibid., 25.
26. The subtitle of *One Lord One Spirit One Body* was the "Ecumenical Grace of the Charismatic Movement."

my first visit to Charmes-sur-Rhône in the south of France, the home of the Union de Prière (Prayer Union),[27] founded by Pastor Louis Dallière in 1946.[28] Although I had heard of Dallière during my doctoral studies with Professor Walter Hollenweger in Birmingham, England and had read two articles on his early years by David Bundy, I was unfamiliar with his teaching before my visit. In Charmes I was given copies of most of Dallière's teachings given to the Union de Prière, mostly during their annual August retreats.[29]

The Union de Prière has four prayer subjects that shape the life of their dispersed community: (1) revival and the conversion of souls; (2) the illumination of Israel; (3) the organic unity of the body of Christ; (4) the coming of the Lord Jesus in glory and the resurrection of the dead. In the teaching of Dallière the first three are all oriented to the fourth, the coming of the Lord. I came to see that "These four topics were not simply recommended subjects for intercession, but they represented Dallière's understanding of God's purposes in pouring out the Holy Spirit in what he called 'le Réveil de Pentecôte' (the Pentecostal revival)."[30] As I studied Dallière's teaching on the second coming of the Lord, I began to see the essentially eschatological significance of baptism in the Spirit. This made sense of the deep longing for the Lord's coming unleashed at the start of the Pentecostal revival, of which D. William Faupel has written: "The second coming of Jesus was the central concern of the initial Pentecostal message."[31] I sensed without being able to articulate it clearly at this stage that here was the missing link that explained why I found so unsatisfactory the dominant Catholic account of baptism in the Spirit—that it is a coming to conscious experience or the release of graces objectively conferred in the sacraments of initiation. Dallière understood that the Pentecostal outpouring of the Spirit and the specific grace of baptism in the Spirit deeply challenge the received theology and practice of the sacrament of baptism that Pentecostals call "water baptism." A major reason for my dissatisfaction with the received Catholic accounts of baptism in the Spirit was the assumption that Catholics were in possession of a totally adequate theology of sacramental baptism, and that baptism in the Spirit simply brought the doctrine to life. But I also sensed that the

---

27. See Hocken, "Union," 1156.

28. Dallière died in 1976. See Hocken, "Dallière," 569–70.

29. Dallière's teachings—all in French—are not currently available in book or digital form, as in 1938 he made a resolution only to teach those who came to him, since the authorities of the French Reformed Church, to whom he always remained loyal, had said his teachings disturbed the faithful.

30. Hocken, "Prophetic Contribution," 253–70.

31. Faupel, *Everlasting Gospel*, 20.

Catholic explanations did not do justice to the sovereign character of the Lord's action in baptizing with Holy Spirit.

In *The Glory and the Shame* (GS), published in 1994,[32] I reflected on the twentieth-century outpouring of the Holy Spirit in the Pentecostal and charismatic movements. In the second chapter I outlined the successive surprises of the Holy Spirit in this outpouring or outpourings, at the end of which I drew the following conclusions:

1. all the churches have a significance in God's plan;

2. the reappearance of Jewish Christianity is an essential component in this work of God;[33]

3. the non-denominational groupings also belong to the over-all pattern;

4. the Pentecostal movement was the mother of these surprises;

5. baptism in the Spirit is the common grace.[34]

In GS I was moving beyond description and a criticism of prevalent Pentecostal and Catholic presentations to sketch a distinctive theological account of baptism in the Spirit. The description is still there, as I remained convinced that the theology had to reflect on the data of Christian experience, as well as on the biblical texts. But in GS the reflection on the data of Christian experience has become a reflection on the movements as a whole, more than an analysis of a particular experience. In my view, it is a weakness of many Pentecostal accounts that in their attempt to develop a biblical teaching they do not pay enough attention to contemporary experience. Perhaps a Catholic author has a greater freedom to reflect theologically on the present reality, not being under the same pressure as Pentecostals to prove that everything written is really biblical.

GS has two chapters devoted to baptism in the Spirit.[35] In the first I examine the New Testament usage of the phrase "baptized in Holy Spirit," always in the verbal form, noting, "we are dealing with an act of God not with a thing or object."[36] The prophetic context of the statements of John the Baptist is noted, pointing to the eschatological character of this work

---

32. Hocken, *Glory and Shame*.

33. In this book, I present the Messianic Jewish movement as part of this outpouring, but I was only beginning to understand this component, as the phrase "Jewish Christianity" indicates. This dimension is more fully developed in Hocken, *Challenges*.

34. Ibid., 22.

35. Chapters titled "Baptism in the Spirit" (chap. 5) and "Understanding Baptism in the Spirit" (chap. 6).

36. Ibid., 41.

of the Spirit.[37] The role of Jesus as baptizer with the Holy Spirit is a heavenly ministry, which may explain why "the only fulfillments suggested are the dramatic events of the day of Pentecost in Jerusalem and the 'Gentile Pentecost' at Caesarea."[38] Maybe the most original suggestion in this presentation is what I would call a prophetic understanding of baptism in the Spirit. "It is an interpretation of contemporary experience in the light of the Scriptures rather than exegesis of the Scriptures illuminated by present circumstances. The designation of this work as baptism in the Spirit was not simply the result of study of the New Testament, but was a spiritual interpretation and prophetic proclamation that 'This is That' which was spoken of by the prophet Joel and initially experienced on the day of Pentecost."[39] This prophetic account of baptism in the Spirit enables us to say that the Pentecostal terminology concerning Spirit-baptism was profoundly right, but the rightness lay in prophetic insight grounded in the biblical witness rather than in biblical exegesis.

This prophetic understanding means that baptism in the Spirit "refers to a sovereign intervention of God in the life of the church, and points to a particular work of God at a specific point in Christian history."[40] Here I pick up the church dimension, convinced that a major defect in all the debates on baptism in the Spirit is limiting the focus on the experience of individual Christians. Baptism in the Spirit is not just the individual experience of millions of believers, it points to an ecclesial event. So I wrote that "a Christian baptized in the Spirit has been plunged by the risen Lord Jesus into the unlimited torrent of the Spirit's life, and thereby participates in a sovereign grace being poured out upon the church."[41] The ecclesial and the historical dimensions help to explain why I have never had much interest in the ongoing Pentecostal debate on subsequence and initial evidence seeking to prove everything from the book of Acts.

In the following chapter, I looked at the Pentecostal and charismatic accounts of baptism in the Spirit. Putting together the key data of the New Testament "can help us to avoid the problems created on the one hand by collapsing baptism in the Spirit into ritual initiation, whether Evangelical conversion or Catholic baptism-confirmation, and on the other hand by positing two baptisms, one in water and one in Spirit, in the manner of

---

37. Ibid., 41–43.
38. Ibid., 44.
39. Ibid., 46.
40. Ibid., 47.
41. Ibid.

the Pentecostals."[42] The New Testament references to being "baptized in/with Holy Spirit" are prophetic in character, whereas the references to being baptized in water are narrative-descriptive.

This eschatological and prophetic understanding was presented in more ordered form in an article published in 2005.[43] Norbert Baumert, a German Jesuit biblical scholar active for many years in CCR, had firmly criticized the dominant Catholic accounts of baptism in the Spirit. His position was only made available in English in 2004.[44] In my response to Baumert, I summarized the normal Pentecostal account, the dominant Catholic explanation offered by Kilian McDonnell, OSB, and George Montague, SM, and the position presented by Baumert. I limit myself here to my comments on Baumert, as my earlier writings had taken issue with the first two positions. I found myself in agreement with Baumert on the strongly experiential and irruptive character of Pentecostal-charismatic Spirit-baptism and the historical specificity of the modern outpouring of the Spirit. But I had problems with his conclusion that Spirit-baptism is for some, but not for all. So I wrote, "I see this as a privatizing of the outpouring of the Holy Spirit that ultimately makes impossible a 'charismatic renewal' of the whole church."[45] It runs the same risk as the tendency found among some early Catholic writers on the Renewal to designate it as a distinctive "spirituality," which inherently makes it one option among many.[46] So in this 2005 article, I examine in turn the advantages and the disadvantages of three theologies of Spirit-baptism: the Pentecostal, the sacramental and that of Baumert. I then offer an alternative proposal, which may be called the eschatological model, that I suggested "allows for the integration of what is right and insightful in the other positions."[47] The eschatological understanding of the Pentecostal outpouring of the Spirit was further developed in *The Challenges of the Pentecostal Charismatic and Messianic Jewish Movements* (2009), especially in the final chapter.

At this point I should note that Frank Macchia's ground-breaking study *Baptized in the Spirit*[48] (2006) for the first time presents a fully-round-

42. Ibid., 59.
43. Hocken, "Baptized in Spirit," 257–68.
44. Baumert, "'Charism' and 'Spirit–Baptism,'" 147–79.
45. Hocken, "Baptized in Spirit," 262.
46. It is instructive that as significant a theological commentator on Catholic charismatic renewal as Kilian McDonnell OSB initially classified it as a "distinctive spirituality," as for example in *Catholic Pentecostalism: Problems in Evaluation*, 17; and in "The Distinguishing Features of the Pentecostal–Charismatic Spirituality," 117–28.
47. Ibid., 267.
48. Macchia, *Baptized*.

ed Christian theology flowing from the role of Jesus as Spirit-baptizer[49] and recognizes its fundamentally eschatological character.

REDACTION OF THE ICCRS DOCUMENT ON BAPTISM IN THE HOLY SPIRIT (FROM 2008)

In 2003, I was invited to join the newly established ICCRS doctrinal commission. Aware that my ecumenical-eschatological approach was not shared by all in ICCRS, I was hesitant, but in the end I felt the reasons for joining outweighed the reasons against. It was a decision that I did not regret, as my participation opened the door to a significant advance in my understanding of baptism in the Spirit.

ICCRS had helped to organize an international colloquium on Prayer for Healing in 2001.[50] Bishop Joseph Grech from Sandhurst, Australia, the chairperson of the committee, said its first task was to prepare Guidelines on Prayers for Healing. Then in 2008, a consultation on Charisms in the Life of the Church was organized by ICCRS in collaboration with the Pontifical Council for the Laity, and it was anticipated that the doctrinal commission would then prepare a document on charisms. Instead, a clear majority at the consultation wanted a document on baptism in the Spirit. In effect, there was not really a functioning commission by this time, and Bishop Grech asked Dr. Mary Healy, of Sacred Heart seminary in Detroit, Michigan, and myself, who had done the basic work on the Guidelines on Prayers for Healing, to work together on the new document.[51]

The ICCRS document on baptism in the Holy Spirit was completed in September, 2011, following a consultation near Rome in March, 2011, and it was published in 2012.[52] As a document of ICCRS this booklet is likely to become a standard point of reference for charismatic Catholics. It integrates the truth embodied in the previous explanations, without accepting either (the actualization of the graces of sacramental baptism or a new sending of the Spirit) as adequate on its own. So the document states,

> although baptism in the Spirit is inherently related to the sacraments, it cannot be described solely as a release of dormant sacramental graces through the removal of obstacles. The idea

---

49. Macchia comments positively on Hocken, "Baptism in the Spirit" (see Macchia, *Baptized*, 46–47).

50. The papers from this consultation were published in *Prayer for Healing*.

51. It is an interesting detail that Mary Healy and I had both been members of the Mother of God community in Gaithersburg, Maryland.

52. *Baptism in the Holy Spirit*.

of release expresses one dimension of baptism in the Spirit: the coming forth into consciousness and effective power of that which was already within. But it does not address another aspect: the Spirit of God coming in a new way into a person's life and bestowing new gifts ... It involves not only the 'already given' but the 'new from above'.[53]

The ICCRS document illustrates a new phase in Catholic reflection on the charismatic renewal, a passing from the predominantly apologetic focus of the earlier literature, seeking to obtain official approval for the movement, to a freedom to explore its full significance.

However, for me personally the prolonged reflection required by the work on the document aided in my overall understanding. Particularly important was the inclusion of the key distinction between the institutional and the charismatic dimensions of the Church made by Pope John Paul II in Rome at Pentecost, 1998.[54] One section in Part III (the theological reflection) was devoted to this distinction, from which I cite a key passage:

> The institutional (or hierarchical) dimension refers to all that was instituted by Jesus during his earthly life, including his choice of the Twelve apostles; his conferral of authority upon them; his command to preach the gospel, to baptize, and to celebrate the Eucharist "in memory of me"; the power to forgive sins; and other structural elements that belong to the deposit of faith. The charismatic dimension refers to the gifts poured out spontaneously at Pentecost and afterward by the Holy Spirit, who freely distributes his graces when and where he wills. The institutional is passed down from generation to generation and belongs to the permanent visible structure of the Church. The charismatic is given by the Lord in an unpredictable way and cannot be codified. *Baptism in the Spirit, as a manifestation of the spontaneous working of the Spirit, belongs to the charismatic dimension*, but at the same time it brings new life and dynamism to the institutional dimension grounded in the sacraments.[55]

The more I considered baptism in the Spirit as belonging to the charismatic dimension of the church, the more I saw how this distinction provides a conceptual framework to support my longstanding resistance to baptism

---

53. Ibid., 72–73.

54. The occasion was a gathering of the new ecclesial movements and new communities in the Catholic Church that have predominantly arisen since the time of the Second Vatican Council.

55. *Baptism in the Holy Spirit*, 69; author's italics.

in the Spirit being subsumed within the sacramental framework of the church. I developed my thoughts further in a recent paper:

> It would seem that doctrine subsequent to the apostolic age that is binding on all cannot be based on charismatic elements, for the charismatic elements come and go. Theological reflection is needed on the charismatic irruptions, but they cannot form the basis of new doctrine. In this light, I suggest that any attempt to formulate a doctrine of baptism in the Spirit is misguided, being based on a confusion of categories.[56]

The institutional-charismatic distinction enables full justice to be done both to the permanent foundation in the sacrament of baptism, and to the distinctive character of baptism in the Spirit as it has been experienced in the Pentecostal and charismatic movements. This distinction saves Catholics from every anachronistic attempt to read back this experience into the lives of the saints of past generations, while doing full justice to the ways in which the Lord is preparing the church for the coming fulfillment. "This understanding prompts us to ask what on the one hand is a distinctive grace for our age, for this moment in the history of the church, and what on the other hand is the restoration of normality, the realization of what ought always to have been happening during the celebration of baptism."[57] In this way, I suggest that proper recognition is being given to the distinctive insights of the first Pentecostals and to the constant Catholic witness to the foundational character of sacramental baptism.

In conclusion, the Pentecostal outpouring of the twentieth century is to be understood as a charismatic grace to move the whole body of Christ toward the eschatological completion, while at the same time necessarily building on the foundation expressed in sacramental baptism, whose own eschatological significance it helps to bring back into focus.

BIBLIOGRAPHY

Baumert, Norbert. "'Charism' and 'Spirit-Baptism': Presentation of an Analysis." *Journal of Pentecostal Theology* 12 (2004) 147–79.
Bittlinger, Arnold, ed. *The Church Is Charismatic*. Geneva: WCC, 1981.
Burgess, Stanley M., and Eduard van der Maas, eds. *New International Dictionary of Pentecostal and Charismatic Movements*. Grand Rapids: Zondervan, 2002.

---

56. This paper has appeared in French translation in a future issue of the review *Istina*.
57. Ibid.

Faupel, D. William. *The Everlasting Gospel: The Significance of Eschatology in the Development of Pentecostal Thought*. Sheffield: Sheffield Academic, 1996.

Guidelines on Prayers for Healing. Vatican City: International Catholic Charismatic Renewal Services, 2007.

Hocken, Peter. "Baptism in the Spirit as Prophetic Statement." Paper presented at the annual meeting of the Society for Pentecostal Studies, Springfield, Missouri, November 12–14, 1992.

———. "Baptized in Spirit—An Eschatological Concept: A Response to Norbert Baumert and His Interlocutors." *Journal of Pentecostal Theology* 13 (2005) 147–79.

———. "Catholic Charismatic Renewal: Sources, Histoire, Défies." Symposium on Baptism in the Holy Spirit, St Niklausen, Switzerland, March 2013. Published in French translation in *Istina* 59, nos. 2–3 (2014) 179–92.

———. "Catholic Pentecostalism: Some Key Questions." *Heythrop Journal* 15, no. 2 (1974) 131–43; 15, no. 3 (1974) 271–84.

———. *The Challenges of the Pentecostal Charismatic and Messianic Jewish Movements*. Farnham, UK: Ashgate, 2009.

———. "Charismatic Renewal, the Churches and Unity." *One in Christ* 15 (1979) 310–21.

———. "The Distinguishing Features of the Pentecostal-Charismatic Spirituality." *One in Christ* 10 (1974) 117–28.

———. *The Glory and the Shame*. Guildford, UK: Eagle, 1994.

———. "Jesus Christ and the Gifts of the Spirit." *Pneuma* 5 (1983) 1–16.

———. "Joan Steele and the Denton Prayer Meeting." *Renewal* 199 (1992) 39–40.

———. "Louis Dallière." In *New International Dictionary of Pentecostal and Charismatic Movements*, edited by Stanley M. Burgess and Eduard M. van der Maas, 569–70. Grand Rapids: Zondervan, 2002.

———. "The Meaning and Purpose of 'Baptism in the Spirit.'" *Pneuma* 7 (1985) 125–33.

———. *One Lord One Spirit One Body*. Gaithersburg, MD: Word Among Us, 1987.

———. "The Prophetic Contribution of Pastor Louis Dallière." In *The Spirit and Spirituality: Essays in Honour of Russell P. Spittler*, edited by Wonsuk Ma and Robert P. Menzies, 253–70. London: T. & T. Clark, 2004.

———. *Streams of Renewal*. Exeter: Paternoster, 1986.

———. "Union de Prière." In *New International Dictionary of Pentecostal and Charismatic Movements*. Rev. ed. Edited by Stanley M. Burgess and Eduard M. van der Maas, 1156. Grand Rapids: Zondervan, 2002.

ICCRS Doctrinal Commission. "Baptism in the Holy Spirit." Locust Grove, Virginia, 2012.

Lederle, Henry. *Treasures Old and New*. Peabody, MA: Hendrickson, 1988.

Macchia, Frank. *Baptized in the Spirit: A Global Pentecostal Theology*. Grand Rapids: Zondervan, 2006.

McDonnell, Kilian. *Catholic Pentecostalism: Problems in Evaluation*. Watchung, NJ: Charisma, 1971.

Prayer for Healing. Vatican City: International Catholic Charismatic Renewal Services, 2003.

Tugwell, Simon. *Did You Receive the Spirit?* London: Darton, Longman & Todd, 1972.

16

The Ecumenical Imperative and the Catholic Charismatic Renewal

—Kevin M. Ranaghan and Dorothy Garrity Ranaghan

Ecumenism... is not an optional choice, but a sacred obligation.[1]

ONE IN THE SPIRIT

At a conference at the University of Notre Dame in June of 1983, Pentecostal historian Vinson Synan said he first heard the full, rich, heavenly harmony of singing in tongues at a previous Catholic charismatic conference at Notre Dame. It was a staggering experience for him. It was equally surprising for us to hear this statement coming from a renowned and lifelong Pentecostal. Singing in tongues! We thought we "learned" it from the Pentecostals, but here is at least one Pentecostal who insists he "learned" it, experientially, from us.[2] Such reciprocity has characterized the ecumenical relationships of the Catholic charismatic renewal from the beginning.[3]

---

1. Kasper, "Our Current Ecumenical Situation."
2. Synan, *Eyewitness Remembers*, 65.
3. This chapter details some Catholic charismatic renewal history seen from the perspective of our personal experience since 1967. It is more of a memoir than an academic paper. It is meant to stir up the pursuit of Christian unity among Pentecostals and charismatics of all types.

Protestant neo-Pentecostals had a major role in bringing the Pentecostal dimension to Catholic awareness. Mutual understanding and respect, a spirit of cooperation, and genuine relationships of brotherly love quickly grew up among us. We had our differences, and we knew they were not trivial. Our common experience, as powerful as it was, did not solve the issues of serious division in the church. We did, however, accept one another and the renewal that God was bringing about in all our churches.

Our experience of this Pentecostal/charismatic movement reveals that we are all descendants of the 1906 Azusa Street Revival. Until the 1960s, Christians in the mainline churches who encountered this Pentecostal experience tended to leave their churches and join in one of the new Pentecostal churches. But when Episcopalians, Presbyterians, and others began to be baptized in the Holy Spirit in great numbers and chose to stay within their own denominations, the Pentecostal movement as a whole took a giant leap forward. It is among such Protestant charismatics that the first Catholics we know were baptized in the Spirit in Pittsburgh, Pennsylvania in 1967.

The early history of the Catholic renewal is recounted in our book, *Catholic Pentecostals*.[4] In the fall of 1966, several Catholic laymen on the faculty of Duquesne University in Pittsburgh found themselves powerless to confront many problems of renewal in the Church. Knowing that the Holy Spirit is the power source of Christian life, they began to pray that the Holy Spirit would renew in them the grace of their baptism and confirmation. Each day they prayed for one another the sequence from the liturgy of Pentecost Sunday. During this time, they were casually introduced to *The Cross and the Switchblade*,[5] which recounts the work of David Wilkerson among drug addicts in New York City. They were intrigued by what he called a "baptism in the Spirit," which was at the root of his amazing results. One of the men then read John Sherril's *They Speak with Other Tongues*,[6] which persuaded them to seek out some people who had experienced these things. They were leery of actually contacting Pentecostals since they were thought to be "wild and wooly." But they remembered an Episcopalian priest, William Lewis, who had once lectured at Duquesne. They called him to see if he knew of any reliable people who had had this Pentecostal experience. He had also read the books by John Sherrill and said that in his parish there was a group that met every Friday night. On January 6, 1967 (interestingly enough the Catholic liturgical feast of the Epiphany), he introduced these

---

4. Ranaghan and Ranaghan, *Catholic Pentecostals*. See also O'Connor, *The Pentecostal Movement in the Catholic Church*.

5. Wilkerson with Sherrill, *Cross and Switchblade*.

6. Sherrill, *They Speak with Other Tongues*.

men to Mrs. Betty Schomaker, his parishioner. She then invited them on January 13 (the Catholic liturgical feast of the baptism of Jesus in the Jordan when the Holy Spirit came upon Him) to a prayer meeting in the home of Miss Florence Dodge, a Presbyterian who had organized the prayer group some time previously. It was in the context of this ecumenical group that these Catholic men from Pittsburgh were baptized in the Holy Spirit.

The new zeal and enthusiasm of these men, whom we both knew, was remarkable and visible. Over several visits with two of these men from Duquesne University to us at the University of Notre Dame, we and some friends also came—after an extensive period of prayer, questioning and study—to ask for this baptism in the Holy Spirit. After one of the men prayed with us on March 5, 1967, our own zeal, love for the Lord, faith, and boldness dramatically increased, but we had not yet manifested the charisms listed in 1 Corinthians 12. And so the second set of ecumenical relationships occurred. We contacted the president of the South Bend chapter of the Full Gospel Businessmen's Fellowship International, an interfaith group of laymen who promote the experience of the baptism in the Holy Spirit. On Monday, March 13, a group of us met at the home of Ray and Mabel Bullard in nearby Mishawaka, Indiana. We were a group of Roman Catholics, all university trained "intellectual types." The people with whom we were meeting included many Pentecostal pastors invited by Ray; since as a layman he was a bit intimidated to take on all these Catholics. They spoke in scriptural and theological categories that were foreign to us. Everything about that evening was so different that at first it was very disturbing. But those were primarily cultural differences. In spite of those differences, we were able to come together in common faith in Jesus and in one experience of his Holy Spirit to worship our Father together. Most of the Catholics present that night received the gift of tongues. Even more importantly for ecumenical relationships, we received encouragement, especially from Roy Wead, then the pastor of Calvary Temple Assembly of God in South Bend. The specific encouragement was to remain in the Catholic Church. Now, as Catholics we had never thought about doing anything except remaining Catholics, but he knew that many of the Pentecostals with whom we were and would be associating considered it necessary for us to "come out" of our church and join a Pentecostal fellowship. He and others who took his lead were ecumenically sensitive and quite convinced that we would do more for the Lord by remaining in the Church and working from within to bring others to the baptism in the Holy Spirit.

RELATIONSHIPS

From its inception, therefore, the Catholic charismatic renewal had an ecumenical character. This continued in the early prayer meetings at Notre Dame. Soon we began to receive requests locally, nationally, and internationally from both Catholic and Pentecostal groups to speak about our experience. In particular, the many invitations from the chapters of the Full Gospel Businessmen's Association advertised a Catholic speaker (often Kevin), and fueled the rapid growth of the renewal among Catholics.

One of the more powerful moments of ecumenical exchange occurred when Mennonite Bishop Nelson Litwiller came to a Catholic prayer meeting. He was over seventy years old, had retired in 1967, and felt burnt out. In August of 1970 at our prayer meeting in South Bend, he asked to be prayed with for the baptism in the Holy Spirit. He was so profoundly changed that rather than retire he went on (with his wife Ada) from 1970 until 1985 to serve as an itinerant minister primarily throughout North and South America, but also in Africa, Europe and the Far and Near East. His knowledge of English, Spanish, German, and Portuguese increased his ability to minister the baptism in the Holy Spirit throughout the world. In 1975 he helped established Mennonite Renewal Services.[7] According to Peter Hocken,

> The Mennonite Renewal Services came into being as a result of letters sent by Kevin Ranaghan to Litwiller and Harold Bauman, inviting the Mennonites to participate in a great ecumenical conference in Kansas City in 1977. Litwiller then invited a group of Mennonite charismatic leaders to meet in Youngstown, Ohio to consider the invitation. At this meeting the Mennonite Renewal Services was born.[8]

The baptism in the Holy Spirit has been called an "ecumenical grace"[9] for the Church. Walls of separation, division, and suspicion began to crumble in the wake of this Pentecostal outpouring, and it happened because of relationships. The urgent desire for Christian unity did not arise in the context of theological studies or ecclesiastical relationships. Rather, it has been our experience to know and to know richly the growing unity of the body of Christ on the grass roots level. It has been in person-to-person relationships, as brothers and sisters together, that we have come to know that we from the many streams of Christianity are already significantly one and are called to deepen that reality.

7. Hewett, "Litwiller, Nelson," 843.
8. Synan, *Century of the Holy Spirit*, 197.
9. Hocken, "Ecumenical Grace," 6–8.

Today there are large segments of the Catholic renewal, particularly in Europe and Latin America, but also in the United States, that have never had any practical, firsthand experience of ecumenical charismatic relationships. But especially in the early years of the renewal, the leadership, major activities, prayer groups, and communities in the United States were highly ecumenical. These ecumenical efforts were not without difficulties. Some have used ecumenical openness to launch attempts at proselytization, for example, to get Catholics to "come out" and join Pentecostal or nondenominational churches. Some attempts at ecumenism have degenerated into unthinking indifferentism, cheaply substituting a feeling of unity for genuine commitment to faith, and pretending that doctrinal differences do not matter. Nevertheless, many Catholic charismatic prayer groups maintained a healthy ecumenical dimension that welcomed Christians of other traditions, celebrated what we have in common, and acknowledged the serious differences that still exist. Furthermore, there are ecumenical charismatic associations and communities[10] living out their specific calls to foster unity in real commitment to the faith of their members.

There are at least two different levels of ecumenism. One is the level of official discussion between churches or of formal dialogue among representatives and theologians of different groups. The Catholic charismatic renewal has rarely dealt with "official" ecumenism.[11] Rather, we have had years of experience with grass roots ecumenism or what Cardinal Walter Kasper has called an "ecumenism of exchange," a "spiritual ecumenism" based on prayer and the sharing of one's spiritual gifts and resources with one another. It is an ecumenism that, Kasper notes, is based on relationships of truth and love.[12] Particularly in the early years of the renewal when there was one national movement, it had a highly ecumenical character that reflected the experience of its leadership at that time. It was almost a universal practice, for example, that a Protestant charismatic leader would be a speaker at regional and national conferences and that Catholic speakers were invited to Protestant charismatic conferences.

---

10. For example, see the websites of our community, The People of Praise, accessed May 29, 2013, http://www.peopleofpraise.org/, other ecumenical communities such as the Sword of the Spirit, accessed May 29, 2013, http://www.swordofthespirit.net/communities.html, and the Alleluia Community, accessed May 29, 2013, http://www.yeslord.com/.

11. The exception is the official Catholic/Pentecostal Vatican dialogue, which began in 1972 and has continued in five phases through 2003. "Pentecostal-Roman Catholic Dialogue," Centro Pro Unione, accessed June 17, 2013, http://www.prounione.urbe.it/dia-int/pe-rc/e_pe-rc-info.html.

12. Putney, "Churches and Ecumenism, 2008."

DISTRUST AND DIALOGUE

The booming of the renewal in both Catholic and mainline Protestant denominations in the eighties caused leaders to become very concerned with the state of the renewal in their own groups. The former emphasis on mutual ecumenical sensitivity without compromise of faith began to give way to concentration on denominational charismatic renewals that appear to have become increasingly separate. There are some in the Catholic renewal who see this decrease in interest in the pursuit of ecumenical charismatic relationships as a sign that the renewal is becoming "more Catholic," and they think that is a good thing. But backing away from ecumenism is not a sign of becoming more Catholic. To be fully Catholic is to be properly committed to ecumenism. Because of the ecumenical history of baptism in the Spirit and spiritual gifts being experienced in all the churches simultaneously, there is, we believe, an ecumenical imperative, an ecumenical responsibility in the Catholic charismatic renewal movement that is strong and immediate.

Pope John Paul II wrote concerning unity in 1995, "ecumenism, the movement promoting Christian unity, is not just some sort of 'appendix' which is added to the Church's traditional activity. Rather, ecumenism is an organic part of her life and work, and consequently must pervade all that she is and does."[13] To ensure that the deep dynamism of the Spirit is not lost, and to ensure that the renewal remains both Catholic and ecumenical, Fr. Peter Hocken suggests that Catholics need to acquire a new post-Vatican II sense of Catholic identity defined in terms of Catholic fullness, not by what we are against.[14] Furthermore, Catholics need to ask what gifts the others bring to the fullness that unity requires. As Pope John Paul II said, "Dialogue is not simply an exchange of ideas. In some way it is always an 'exchange of gifts.'"[15] That we have gifts to offer one another has not always been recognized. There is a painful history, centuries of mutual injury and distrust that blocked our awareness. But, Pope John Paul II avers,

> besides the doctrinal differences needing to be resolved, Christians cannot underestimate the burden of long standing misgivings inherited from the past, and of mutual misunderstandings and prejudices . . .With the grace of the Holy Spirit, the Lord's disciples, inspired by love, by the power of the truth and by a sincere desire for mutual forgiveness and reconciliation, are

---

13. Pope John Paul II, *Ut Unum Sint*, #20.
14. Hocken, "Ecumenical Grace," 6–9.
15. Pope John Paul II, *Ut Unim Sint*, #28.

called to re-examine together their painful past and the hurt which that past regrettably continues to provoke even today.[16]

PREPARED BY THE SPIRIT

The ecumenical openness within the Catholic Church to the Pentecostal experience did not happen in a vacuum. There were precedents that paved the way for its acceptance. Several major factors here were the biblical and liturgical revivals within the Catholic Church and the Second Vatican Council. In the 1950s and sixties, advances in biblical scholarship began to open a renewed appreciation for, and an accessibility to, Scripture among Catholics. In a book published in 1959, *Some Schools of Catholic Spirituality*, Fr. Eugene Masure, Director of the *Grand Seminaire* of Lille, France, commented on the renewed appreciation then surging throughout the Church for Scripture and liturgy. "What," he asked, "will a renewed interest in Scripture and a fresh understanding of the Paschal mystery now among us, come to mean for the church of tomorrow? . . . *Tomorrow, they will open to us the full meaning of the coming of the Holy Spirit, and the significance of this coming in the life of the church.*"[17] What was a prophetic statement that held promise in 1959 has since then been realized.

Furthermore, the biblical and liturgical revivals that paved the way for the Second Vatican Council enabled the Catholic charismatic renewal to develop because of the non-cessationist gateway given to us at the Second Vatican Council. Cessationism was never much of a problem for us in the Catholic Church. It is not just because there have been many miracles and healings associated with saints throughout our history, but because at the Second Vatican Council, the possibility of the gifts of the Spirit being active in the church today was explicitly acknowledged. Of course there are some Catholic cessationists in theory and practice. The question of charisms, however, was introduced at the Second Vatican Council through an intervention made by Cardinal Ruffini. He relegated charisms to the past and warned against overemphasizing them in the conciliar documents for fear that the institutional church would be endangered. In reply, Cardinal Suenens, who later became a great friend and mentor to the Catholic renewal, pointed out that the charismatic dimension was necessary to the church. He said, "What would become of our Church without the charisms of the doctors,

---

16. Pope John Paul II, *Ut Unim Sint*, #3.
17. Masure, *Some Schools of Catholic Spirituality*, 56.

the theologians, the prophets?"[18] The Council then adopted an open and receptive attitude to the charisms, ordinary and extraordinary, in both the *Dogmatic Constitution on the Church* in paragraphs 7 and 12, and in the decree on *The Apostolate of the Laity*. In the same vein, the 1994 *Catechism of the Catholic Church* reads: "Whether extraordinary or simple and humble, charisms are graces of the Holy Spirit which directly or indirectly benefit the Church, ordered as they are to her building up, to the good of men and to the needs of the world."[19] Because of these theological statements, there has been no serious impediment to the growth of the charismatic/ Pentecostal movement among Catholics. In fact, they have highlighted its ecumenical imperative.

Any exploration of the history of the ecumenical nature of the relationships in the Catholic charismatic renewal has its originating point and theological rationale in these statements from the Second Vatican Council. When Roman Catholics first heard of the baptism in the Holy Spirit and what was happening in the Pentecostal movement, their openness to learn from classical and neo-Pentecostals found its roots in these documents. Subsequently, the Catholic mentality has been shaped by the encouragement of Pope Paul VI, Pope John Paul II, Pope Benedict and the current Holy Father, Pope Francis, who was quoted in this exchange by Archbishop Rino Fisichella, president of the Pontifical Council for Promoting the New Evangelization:

> Before I left this morning, I was with Pope Francis, and I told him: 'Holy Father, I have to leave soon. I'm going to Rimini where there are thousands of faithful of the Charismatic Renewal: men, women and young people.' With a great smile, the Pope said: 'Tell them that I love them very much!' Upon leaving the Holy Father, Archbishop Fisichella recounted, the Holy Father added: 'Look, tell them that I love them very much because I was responsible for Charismatic Renewal in Argentina and that's why I love them very much.'[20]

From the very first year of the Catholic renewal, there was a desire to gather to share, pray, and learn together with others who were becoming baptized in the Spirit. Conferences, though small at first, became massive gatherings of more than 30,000 people. A network of relationships began

---

18. Suenens, *A New Pentecost?*, 30.

19. United States Catholic Conference of Bishops, *Catechism of the Catholic Church*, #799.

20. Garcia, "Pope to Catholic Charismatic Renewal."

to grow. Three of these many conferences are pivotal in the Catholic charismatic experience.

THE ROME CONFERENCE

In 1975, thirteen thousand Catholic charismatics gathered in Rome for a conference that found them singing in tongues, prophesying, and dancing at the Catacombs of Saint Callixtus and inside St. Peter's Basilica. Pope Paul VI joined the throng in the basilica and declared that the renewal was a "chance" for the church. Immediately following the Rome Conference, a theology panel discussion was held. Seventy theologians and members of the Roman Curia attended. At that meeting no one raised any serious objection to the renewal, an encouraging fact that soon became widely known throughout Rome. One of the realizations springing from this conference in Rome was that the Catholic charismatic renewal was now thoroughly international and not just a North American phenomenon.

THE KANSAS CITY CONFERENCE

The origin of this conference begins with the formation of a Charismatic Concerns Committee convened by Rev. Dennis Bennett in Seattle, Washington. Pentecostal, mainline Protestant, and Catholic renewal leaders, later joined by nondenominational leaders, began to meet annually in fellowship to discuss issues in the renewal, to air disagreements and to seek harmony. Though dealing with controversies, there was a sense of urgency for unity. This CCC moved its meeting to the Marianist Apostolic Center in Glencoe, Missouri, and from that time the gathering was referred to as the Glencoe meeting.[21] Over the years both its purpose and membership have evolved. There is now less discussion of issues within the streams of the renewal and more discussion of issues in the wider church and society. It is now called the Charismatic Leaders Fellowship (CLF) and meets annually at places like Regent University.

In June of 1974, at the National Catholic Charismatic Conference at Notre Dame, Indiana, Ralph Martin spoke of what God was doing in the world in terms of the three streams of renewal: classical Pentecostalism, neo-Pentecostalism and the Catholic renewal. These streams, he said, have been flowing separately, but God is moving the riverbeds enabling these

---

21. MacNutt, "Reflections," private paper.

streams to flow together.[22] In a meeting of the CCC in 1974, Vinson Synan suggested that it was time for all the various charismatic groups to gather for a "conference of conferences."[23] In 1975, a small group of CCC members who had been organizing successful ecumenical men's leaders' events proposed that a large general conference be called and recommended Kansas City as the site. The People of Praise community in South Bend offered to organize such a conference with its conference arm, Charismatic Renewal Services providing the seed money and administration. An ecumenical planning committee representing four streams of the renewal, Pentecostals, mainline Protestants, non-denominational charismatics, and Catholics was formed. Its executive committee consisted of a representative of each of three streams: Kevin Ranaghan, a Roman Catholic, who served as chairman of the conference; Larry Christenson, a mainline Protestant; and Vinson Synan, a Pentecostal. The relationships on the planning committee and the agreement they forged was the reason for the success of this historic conference. The structure of the conference reflected its ecumenical nature. Ten different denominational and non-denominational groups held sessions and workshops during the day on Thursday, Friday, and Saturday. General Sessions for all participants were held in the evenings at Arrowhead stadium. One of these sessions found Cardinal Leon Joseph Suenens sharing the platform with J. O. Patterson, presiding bishop of the Church of God in Christ. Suenens noted, "You are here together and at the same time you are keeping your identity. That's exactly what ecumenism means."[24]

A statement of unity was drafted by Kevin Ranaghan and adopted by the planning committee. This "statement of policy" required all committee members, speakers, performers, exhibitors, and advertisers to sign.[25] While acknowledging serious division and disagreement in the body of Christ, it proclaims that the conference is a wonderful work of the Holy Spirit. It promises mutual love and respect, speaking well of one another and solving our difficulties not contentiously, but in love. Paul DeCelles, of the People of Praise community, noted that, "The unity in the stands took place because of the unity on the planning committee."[26] This statement has since been adopted by other national and international conferences and ecumenical groups in their statements of purpose.

---

22. Martin, "God Is Restoring," 3–6.
23. Synan, *Century of the Holy Spirit*, 364.
24. Suenens,"Cardinal Suenens Applauds Ecumenism," 3.
25. Statement of Unity.
26. Rath, 3.

Attended by fifty thousand people, the Kansas City conference was the largest ecumenical conference in the nation's history. Among the registrants 46 percent identified themselves as Catholics, 31 percent as non-denominational, and the rest as mainline Protestant, Classical Pentecostal, or "other." The leadership of the Kansas City Conference and of Glencoe continued to foster the ecumenical impulse of Kansas City at subsequent conferences in New Orleans (1985 and 1987), Indianapolis (1990), Orlando (1995), and in St. Louis (2000).[27]

The evening sessions of the Kansas City Conference held in Arrowhead Stadium were hot. Crickets were jumping everywhere, but they were mere distractions, as both weeping and rejoicing occurred at different points in these sessions. One of the prophecies given by Catholic Ralph Martin broke our hearts: "Mourn and weep for the body of my Son is broken." It caused repentance for the sins of disunity and stirred desire to pursue unity afresh. But at one point as everyone was listening to Rev. Bob Mumford, a nondenominational evangelist who listed all the troubles in the world, he stopped, held up his Bible, and said, "We don't need to worry. If you sneak a look in the back of this book . . . you find out that Jesus wins!" He then began to shout, "Glory to God! Jesus is Lord!" The entire crowd of fifty thousand broke into an exuberant, deafening, fifteen-minute period of uninterrupted praise and worship that has since been called a "Holy Ghost breakdown."

A number of significant events occurred as a result of the Kansas City Conference, two of which are worthy of mention. The first is the so-called Memphis Miracle. One of the extraordinary fruits of the relationships in the Glencoe meetings and on the planning committee came seventeen years later. It was the historic "Miracle in Memphis." It grew from the deep fellowship formed at the Glencoe meeting between Bishop Ithiel Clemmons of the Church of God in Christ and Bishop B. E. Underwood of the Pentecostal Holiness Church. An audio recording of the story behind this event by one of the participants, Donald Evans, is available on the website of the Flower Pentecostal Heritage Center. Darrin Rogers, director of the Flower Center, writes,

> Recognizing the need to heal the racial divisions within Pentecostalism, church leaders came together in Memphis on October 18, 1994 and dissolved the Pentecostal Fellowship of North America. The next day the Pentecostal and Charismatic Churches of North America (PCCNA) was formed by both

---

27. The planning committee for the Kansas City Conference morphed into NARSC, the North American Renewal Service Committee and it is this group that planned the conferences in New Orleans, Indianapolis, Orlando, and St. Louis.

white and black denominations. The meetings surrounding this monumental act of racial reconciliation came to a climax when, on October 18, a white Assemblies of God pastor, Donald Evans, approached the platform. He tearfully explained that he felt God's leading to wash the feet of Church of God in Christ Bishop Ithiel Clemmons, while begging forgiveness for the sins of the whites against their black brothers and sisters. A wave of weeping swept over the auditorium. Participants sensed that this was the final seal of the Holy Spirit's approval from the heart of God over the proceedings. This event, which became known as the "Memphis Miracle," is a significant milestone in the annals of Pentecostal history.[28]

The second event brings to light an indirect connection with Pope Francis. One of the participants at the Kansas City Conference was Fr. Raniero Cantalamessa. He was an Italian Franciscan Capuchin theologian teaching scripture at the Catholic University of the Sacred Heart in Milan. He was visiting the conference with an intellectual curiosity. Leaving the conference inspired, he stopped in Fr. Jim Ferry's Catholic House of Prayer in New Jersey and asked to receive the baptism in the Holy Spirit. Shortly afterwards he asked permission of his religious superiors to leave the university and take up a full time ministry of preaching. He was later appointed the official preacher to the papal household by Pope John Paul the II, a position he retains to this day with Pope Francis. He has also preached to groups all over the world and has written several books on the Spirit-filled life. A brief visit to Amazon.com will reveal his prolific writings.

The Brighton Conference

1991 marked perhaps the most significant ecumenical event in the history of the charismatic renewal. While Kansas City was larger and remains pivotal in the history of the movement particularly in the United States, a conference held in Brighton, England was the most significant ecumenical, international, interracial conference to that point in the renewal. It sprang from a vision of three charismatic leaders: the then Anglican Fr. Michael Harper, Lutheran Larry Christenson, and Catholic Fr. Tom Forrest. Michael Harper, realizing that the charismatic renewal had achieved an international presence and that there were relationships linking the people and ecclesial communions involved, arranged for what is now called the "gang of three"

---

28. Rodgers, "Story Behind Foot Washing."

to have a cup of tea together at the 1983 "All African Conference"[29] in the hills of Limuru, Kenya, to discuss ways in which their three networks might share in the future. The next step was the first meeting of what became known as the "gang of nine," which met in May of 1984 in Rome. Some of the "gang" included Rev. Terry Fullam, Kevin Ranaghan, Bishop Arne Rudvin, Archbishop Bill Burnett, and the original three. In England in 1985, the representation was widened to include leaders from the Pentecostal and non-denominational streams. Invitations to a subsequent meeting in Singapore in February of 1987 were sent to about eighty leaders. This Singapore Consultation endorsed a call for a world conference to launch a decade of evangelization. When the continuing committee met in Jerusalem in 1989, they decided to change the name from the Singapore Consultation to the International Charismatic Consultation on World Evangelism (ICCOWE).

It was ICCOWE that sponsored the Brighton world conference, which drew over 3,000 people from all over the world. There were about 1500 Anglican/Protestant, 800 Roman Catholic, 730 Pentecostal/Non-denominational, and ten Orthodox participants. There was good representation from Africa (370), Asia (320) Latin America (50), North America (480), and Oceania (180) with the remainder from Europe and the UK.[30] Because of the recent fall of the Berlin wall, participants from Eastern Europe were able to attend an international charismatic conference for the first time. In all, 110 countries were represented.

Anglican Archbishop of Canterbury, George Carey, and Catholic Cardinal Basil Hume, Archbishop of Westminster, both addressed the conference. But beyond the depth of internationally recognized speakers, unity was palpable behind the scenes. Protestant and Catholic charismatics from Northern Ireland met in small groups where reconciliation took place. Iranian and Iraqi charismatics whose countries were then at war met together in secret as did Messianic Jews and Palestinian Christians. Profound interdenominational, international, and interracial unity was not just being talked about, but realized.

The importance of the theological track within the Brighton conference cannot be overstated. A new initiative was to bring together Catholic,

---

29. The AACC is a fellowship of churches and institutions working together in their common witness to the gospel.

30. Rev. Michael Harper was the chair of the Brighton Conference and the president of ICCOWE. ICCOWE changed its name to the International Charismatic Council (ICC), and its president since 2000 has been Charles Whitehead. Charles Whitehead was the president of the Vatican based International Catholic Charismatic Renewal Services (ICCRS) at the time of the Brighton Conference. International Charismatic Consultation, *A Brief History*, 3.

Protestant, and Orthodox theologians. Never before had such a gathering of theologians been part of such a conference. Charismatics and Pentecostals had been accused of being without serious theology. At Brighton it was demonstrated that they take theology seriously. Of the 150 scholars attending, several were theologians, exegetes, or historians of world renown. Many were participants in these movements. "Most striking was the range of nationalities and of Church traditions represented: these ranged from Latin American Pentecostals to a Coptic Orthodox bishop, from Scandinavian Lutheran to New Zealand Open Brother, from Afro American Pentecostal to Syrian rite Catholic."[31] At this theological symposium, the contributions from South Africa with the presentation of "The Relevant Pentecostal Witness," as well as the papers on liberation theology, spoke to the myth that Pentecostal and charismatic Christians and theologians are indifferent to social injustice. There was virtual unanimity among participants that this scholarly collaboration across continents and ecclesial communions should continue. Dr. Harold Hunter, Dr. Cecil M. Robeck, Jr., and Fr. Peter Hocken are among those who continue to foster continual scholarly collaboration.

CONTINUING EFFORTS

Beyond Brighton, under ICCOWE's new name, the International Charismatic Consultation (ICC), there have been many ecumenical events.[32]

- September 1997 (With the European Charismatic Consultation) in Prague, Czech Republic "Building Bridges, Breaking Barriers."
- March 2000: Penang, Malaysia "Celebrate Jesus 2000."
- January 2004: The Malta Consultation on the Suffering Church throughout the world.
- August 2005: Meeting with Latin American representatives in Buenos Aires to discuss ways to make ecumenical relationships work in the context of their acrimonious history. A highlight of that event was a one-hour meeting with Cardinal Jorge Bergoglio, now Pope Francis.

Currently, another of the more promising international ecumenical groups we know is called the "Gathering in the Holy Spirit." It originated from a meeting in Rome in 1998 between Catholic Kim Catherine Marie

31. Hunter and Hocken, "All Together in One Place."
32. At these and at all of the ecumenical events mentioned so far, it is important to note that in every case; close to 50 percent of the participants were Catholic.

Kollins and non-denominational Pastor Peter Dippl with Fr. Jim Puglisi, director of Centro Pro Unione.[33] The "Centro" (founded in 1968 by the Franciscan Friars of the Atonement), which sponsors this initiative, is an ecumenical research and documentation center in Rome. The "Gathering," which began in 2001 and has met every two years in Rome, is an informal encounter between global non-denominational and Roman Catholic leaders and theologians—all who share a charismatic/Pentecostal experience. Its goal is to enable better mutual understanding in Christ between some non-denominationals (now termed the new charismatic churches) and Catholics. One of the highlights of the each of the meetings thus far has been a session of the Gathering participants with representatives of the Pontifical Council for Promoting Christian Unity. In addition, growing out of these contacts an informal conversation between the Pontifical Council for Promoting Christian Unity and representatives of the new charismatic churches was begun in 2010 and has recently been extended through 2017.

As mentioned earlier, an official Roman Catholic dialogue with Classical Pentecostals continues to this day. Formally, an official Roman Catholic Dialogue with the Classical Pentecostals has existed since 1972. The dialogue was initiated by Fr. Kilian McDonnell and David du Plessis, who had been the only Pentecostal to attend the Second Vatican Council as an official Protestant observer. According to the Berkley Center of Georgetown University,

> Roman Catholic and Pentecostal dialogue has spanned five phases . . . and covered issues such as evangelization, baptism, discipleship, and community; the most recent phase addressed the process of conversion and Christian formation. One source of unity has been a common reliance on the theological insights of the patristic fathers, though the two sides hold divergent views on the relative authority of more recent Spirit-inspired interventions. As dialogue continues the Roman Catholic Church also intends to expand its contacts to include Pentecostal partners beyond North America. More recently the issue of healing through grace and faith has emerged as a locus of both agreement and tension in this ongoing dialogue.[34]

---

33. "Centro Pro Unione."
34. Berkley Center, "Roman Catholic Dialogue with Pentecostal Churches."

CONCLUSION

In our experience, ecumenism, especially an ecumenism of relationships, has been a significant characteristic of the Catholic charismatic renewal since its beginning. While most visible in the early years and in large conferences, it has continued undiminished in smaller, less well known projects and events, as well as in ecumenical associations and communities. Many Protestant charismatics and Pentecostals, especially leaders, maintain their interest in promoting Christian unity with Catholics. We realize that our experience, recounted here, is only part of the story. We encourage others to write of their experiences so we can understand this work for unity more fully. As the Catholic renewal approaches its fiftieth anniversary in 2017, it is our earnest prayer that a fresh longing for ecumenical relationships will develop in all the streams of the Pentecostal/charismatic movement.

BIBLIOGRAPHY

The Alleluia Community. http://yeslord.com.

Berkley Center. "Roman Catholic Dialogue with Pentecostal Churches." *Resources on Faith, Ethics, and Public Life*, Berkley Center for Religion, Peace, and World Affairs, Georgetown University. http://berkleycenter.georgetown.edu/resources/programs/roman-catholic-dialogue-with-pentecostal-churches.

"Centro Pro Unione." Franciscan Friars of the Atonement. http://www.atonementfriars.org/our_missions_and_ministries/centro_pro_unione.html.

Garcia, Roccio Lancho. "Pope to Catholic Charismatic Renewal: Tell Them I Love Them Very Much." Zenit.org. http://www.zenit.org/en/articles/pope-to-catholic-charismatic-renewal-tell-them-i-love-them-very-much.

Hewett, J. A. "Littwiller, Nelsen." In *New International Dictionary of Pentecostal and Charismatic Movement*, edited by Stanley M. Burgess and Eduard M. van der Maas, 842–43. Grand Rapids: Zondervan, 2002.

Hocken, Peter. "The Ecumenical Grace of Charismatic Renewal." *Pentecost Today* (2009) 6–8.

Hunter, Harold, and Peter Hocken. "All Together in One Place." Pentecostal-Charismatic Theological Inquiry International. http://www.pctii.org/edit.html.

International Charismatic Consultation. *A Brief History, 1984–2004*. Coventry, UK: ICC, 2004.

Kasper, Cardinal Walter. "Our Current Ecumenical Situation." *Catholic Online*, 2005. http://www.freerepublic.com/focus/f-religion/1935017/posts.

MacNutt, Francis. "Reflections on the History and Purpose of the Charismatic Leaders' Fellowship." Private paper.

Martin, Ralph. "God Is Restoring His People." *New Covenant Magazine*. South Bend: Charismatic Renewal Services, September, 1974.

Masure, Eugene. *Some Schools of Catholic Spirituality*. Edited by Jean Gautier. Paris: Desclée de Brouwer, 1959.

O'Connor, Edward. *The Pentecostal Movement in the Catholic Church*. Notre Dame: Ave Maria, 1971.

Pentecostal-Charismatic Theological Inquiry International. "All Together in One Place." http://www.pctii.org/edit.html.

"Pentecostal-Roman Catholic Dialogue." Centro Pro Unione. http://www.prounione.urbe.it/dia-int/pe-rc/e_pe-rc-info.html.

The People of Praise. http://www.peopleofpraise.org/.

Pope John Paul II. *Ut Unum Sint*. May 25, 1995. http://www.vatican.va/holy_father/john_paul_ii/encyclicals/documents/hf_jp-ii_enc_25051995_ut-unum-sint_en.html.

Putney, Michael. "The Churches and Ecumenism, 2008." *Compass: A Review of Topical Theology* 42 (2008). http://compassreview.org/spring08/6.html.

Ranaghan, Kevin, and Dorothy Ranaghan. *Catholic Pentecostals*. New York: Paulist, 1969.

Rath, Ralph. "Ecumenism at Conference," Editorial. *National Communications Office Newsletter*. South Bend: National Service Committee, September/October, 1977.

Rodgers, Darrin. "The Story Behind the Foot Washing at the 1994 'Memphis Miracle.'" Flower Pentecostal Heritage Center. http://ifphc.wordpress.com/2011/07/13/donaldevans/.

Sherrill, John. *They Speak with other Tongues*. Grand Rapids: Chosen, 1964.

Statement of Unity. *Chariscenter USA*. South Bend: National Service Committee, January/February, 1995.

Suenens, Cardinal Leon Joseph. "Cardinal Suenens Applauds Ecumenism at Conference." *National Communications Office Newsletter*. South Bend: National Service Committee, Summer, 1977.

———. *A New Pentecost?* New York: Seabury, 1974.

The Sword of the Spirit. http://www.swordofthespirit.net/communities.html.

Synan, Vinson. *The Century of the Holy Spirit: 100 Years of Pentecostal and Charismatic Renewal*. Nashville: Nelson, 2001.

———. *An Eyewitness Remembers the Century of the Holy Spirit*. Grand Rapids: Chosen, 2010.

United States Catholic Conference. *Catechism of the Catholic Church*. Washington, DC: USCC, 1994.

Wilkerson, David, with John and Elizabeth Sherrill. *The Cross and the Switchblade*. New York: Penguin Putnam, 1962.

17

Looking Back on the Forward Way
—Karl Luckert

MEMORY MORSELS FROM THE TWENTIETH CENTURY

Of course I will accept the honor, and the challenge, to write some words for this Festschrift as a tribute to Stanley and Ruth Burgess. Twenty years I occupied working space somewhere within earshot of Stanley. Twenty happy academic years these were, and they were blessed by friendships among a dozen and more colleagues in the general Religious Studies field. Other friendly relationships also flourished with people in other departments. For a few of these years Stanley was our chairman. It was he who would know precisely how many full-time or part-time professors we were at any one moment. At my level, as an ordinary professor in the history of religions, I never needed to count those numbers. After all, God only asked Adam to *name* the creatures, not to count them.

    We often chanced to meet each other in the hallways, one or two at a time, at random, for sporadic conversations to catch up on what seemed necessary—yes, we managed to keep official bureaucracy at a harmless level. And sometimes we sat down together for mental romps and somersaults. Thanks to Gerrit J. tenZythoff's canny and flexible strategies, a group of survivalists had been assembled at Missouri State to teach Religious Studies, right there at the buckle of the Bible Belt. All of Gerrit's people loved to build sandcastles anywhere between Springfield and the other side of the planet.

We all believed, and we knew, that our personal work was important for the healthy survival of humankind. Unabashedly we shared our goals and our discoveries with each other, and we inspired each other to render our own work a trifle more relevant than what we knew it to be before we started talking. After all, there is room for a little hope and faith at any dip in an academic life. Our friend Gerrit mastered the art of how to twist ordinary political obligations, including faculty meetings, into hobby ventures and into delightful shapes of pretzels.

This was the environment in which we lived and moved and had our being together, next to colleagues whom over the decades we learned to appreciate as family. It was a situation as close to paradise as could be found anywhere in academia; close enough to ignore purgatory. And now that I have been asked to share some of these memories for a *Festschrift*, the overall tone of our accustomed proceedings need not be noticeably altered. We simply continue in the mood in which we left off back in those days, at bits of subject matter that seemed interesting to share. The methodology is simple: *that with which the heart is filled the mouth overfloweth*—it also touches keyboards.

When I first inquired of Stanley what type of subject matter might be welcome here, he gave me two sample hints: 1) Order of the Golden Sloth and 2) Departmental Pants. Hmm! These hints made me scrape the curb for a moment. I am not good at narrating warmed-over hilarities, out of context. But under the circumstances I cannot refuse, really, because the "Order of the Golden Sloth" was actually Stanley's idea, and I was drawn into the affair only as his playwright and supporting actor. The redeeming element of telling this story may be, perhaps, that later generations of teachers will see how in the olden days, in our Religious Studies environment, serious bureaucratic issues were handled. And then also, my narration may demonstrate a practical dimension of Religious Studies itself. As professors we all understood, and therefore occasionally utilized, the power of ritual and of ritualistic communication. We also knew that an academic department that plays together stays together.

"ORDER OF THE GOLDEN SLOTH," AN ISSUE OF TENURE

In many academic organizations there is being cultivated an official status category of employment, which for some faculty looms higher than their professorial rank. This status level is called "tenure." It happens to be something about which I personally was not concerned at Missouri State, because in an earlier life, somewhere, I noticed how having tenure can be worse than having no tenure. For example, if an administration opined that their university would be happier without having a certain professor around, such a teacher without tenure would be able to leave more peacefully than one who had it. When I came to Missouri State I never asked for tenure and promptly forgot when it was given to me. In any case we did not celebrate. But along came Professor Ramsey Michaels. His notion of "tenure" was loftier than mine, because he had learned about it in a more sublime environment. He seemed "exceedingly happy" (Gerrit's words) when he saw his assurance of tenure on paper. Stanley was our department head at the time, and he suggested to me that inasmuch as Ramsey was so happy about his tenure, we should help him celebrate and induct him into our special Order of tenured faculty. This was the first time I heard about the existence of such an order. So, when Stanley noticed my astonishment, he elaborated that the time had come to establish the name of that organization as "Supreme Order of the Golden Sloth." Only a workaholic could have come up with a designation of that magnitude.

Alright then! Because Professor Ramsey Michael's induction into our ancient order was to happen in connection with a scheduled potluck dinner at our home, the tasks of writing a liturgy and providing ceremonial paraphernalia fell on me. At a potluck in any other home someone else would have done these chores better. It seems that we required full academic regalia for all tenured participants as well as for the novice who matriculated. I took some expired campaign buttons from the Eisenhower era and covered them with a Golden Sloth insignia—and we pinned one of those things on the professor. The tulip tree in our back yard furnished the branch that all of us held above our heads. Then, the only requirement that any of us has gotten obligated to during this solemn ceremony—for being privileged members of the Supreme Order of the Golden Sloth—was expressed in the refrain, "I will hang in there." Ramsey commented afterward that our ritual turned out to be "more meaningful than some of the others by which he matriculated here and there during his long career."

This ceremonial occasion placed "tenure" into an enduring sublime perspective for the entire department. Nobody expressed the wish of having a tenure ceremony performed on his or her behalf thereafter. I am confident that tenure documents were issued over the years on time. But inasmuch as everyone was afraid of my tulip-tree branch, they would not mention the word "tenure" anymore, at least not in my presence. So you see, in Religious Studies we actually took the subject matter we taught—rites and ceremonies—very seriously. We utilized rituals and believed in their efficacy.

THE ISSUE OF GENDER EQUALITY

It happened one more time that the need for a "tenure celebration" rose to the surface and became an issue. I cannot remember all the details. But it happened when Dr. Kathy J. Pulley, our longtime colleague, joined our faculty full-time. The occasion was multi-dimensional and entailed issues linked to American gender equality in general. Before this story can be told I must describe the tentacles of our quandary in a somewhat wider context. No historian can fully escape his or her own past.

Sometime after the ice of the Cold War had thawed between East and West, a new wind of crisis blew across Anglo-Saxon and American civilization. It was a flu-like epidemic that spread right from an infected cavity in the English language. It struck at the highest Ivy League university levels first. As a native speaker of German I noticed this peculiar English storm cloud accumulating for some time. So, to render this situation somewhat plausible, I must testify here from my personal uniquely constricted German perspective. If English is your only language, you may not yet have noticed that your native tongue lacks the essential noun for inter-human references and conversation. If approached from the German perspective, specifically, English lacks an equivalent for the word *Mensch*. And so it came to pass that in English you only could be politically correct if you referred to men in general with double-minted words. You needed to refer to them either as "human beings," or as "homines sapientes," or plug the word-cavity with some vague generality like "humankind." While I do like the sound of Pacific double homonymous syllables, I never felt comfortable with modern English doubling contrivances. If humans are indeed "beings," then sticks and stones are "beings" too. And if humans are of a "kind," then there must also be acknowledged many kinds of many things. In addition, I never could see the point of letting Linnaean Greek corrupt American street language with the basically false claim of "Homo sapiens." That name is surely a lie!

I also remember from university and divinity school days, how some female students recoiled from all theologies and theologians that used the English "God" to refer to someone fatherly or male. I failed to fully understand these fellow students, and for a while I was not even able to take them seriously. Why? With my upbringing, which admittedly happened at the rear end of the globe, I felt that every thought that was indecent to think in regard to human beings—such as to wonder excessively about mysteries hidden beneath Near Eastern robes and wrappings—was also indecent while thinking about God or angels. If questions of such a magnitude are permitted, where will they end? Is that famous archangel a Gabriel or a Gabrielle, or a Gabi? Or was Michael really a Michelle? Now we know why

English is unfit to be the official language of the Vatican. The effects would indeed have been unimaginable. Popes would have started retiring decades earlier over such questions.

Inasmuch as God is Creator of our procreators, his/her gender never really registered in my still young naive German mind. Besides, in accordance with German pious poetry, the German *Gott* has a *Schoß* (the grave) to which all mortals return after they die. *Der Schoß des Vaters* means both "lap" and "womb of the Father." It is by this linguistic route, by the grace of God and the courtesy of German poets, that Germany was not severely poked by the Anglo-Saxon gender revolution—and not even by the problem that American creationists still are having with "evolution" and the concepts of "nature" or "Mother Nature."

Obviously, the English concepts of "man" and "woman" got shaped over a background that featured more distinct pairings of opposites—perhaps a background of English trousers and dresses, contrasted with Scottish kilts, has been what predestined English gender oppositions so succinctly. On that account, convincing the entire world to return to using unisex loincloths again could have been one of the remedies we should have considered. It was foolish thinking on my part, of course. The core of gender misunderstandings lies deeper—far deeper in the nature of the universe than the human subconscious can fathom. But then, proverbially speaking, the chickens came home to roost on me in Springfield, one nice day, when friendly colleagues critiqued my written sentences for being sexist and not sufficiently gender-neutral. I had not sufficiently been doubling my pronouns. Instead of "he" I was supposed to have written "he and she," "him and her," or in successive sentences I should have alternated "he" with "she" and should have pretended that I did not really know or care about gender differences. I was asked to pretend these things after years of having had three children sit around our kitchen table. In addition to maintaining the rational poise of a university professor I was asked to do the impossible—pretend to be confused about gender duality and abandon time-proven ambiguities that had intentionally been built into theological systems millennia ago. Gender mysteries were hopelessly conflicting with our mandated fairness toward English language fashions. As a resolute guest to the English language, I was searching for a better way to communicate non-offensively.

When increasingly more fair and proud English-speaking ladies refused to be counted among "men in general" (as *Menschen*)—and when in protest they shoved that status exclusively unto bipeds who traditionally wore trousers—I proceeded to modify my English vocabulary to help distinguish all ladies as being nevertheless very "special men"—whether they liked it or not. And by special men I meant "women"—or more precisely, men who own a womb and who therefore should be acknowledged explicitly as "wombmen." They should so be recognized as full "men" who are given additional honors and recognition for owning the womb. Of course, I realized that in regard to all status questions there sooner or later lingers the problem of envy. Therefore, if some day in the future it should happen that the womb-less portion of humankind begins to feel slighted too, and should demand proper recognition, we could simply find a way of adding the appropriate "pe" prefix to their basic designation as "-men"—that is, to balance the "womb" feature that is there for the other half of the humanoid population. In this manner all together could again be "men in general," i.e. *Menschen*, who live happily ever after—or at least try to do so.

The problem resolved itself in our Missouri State Religious Studies Department at a practical symbolic level, on this one nice day when our dear friend Dr. Kathy J. Pulley was given tenure and professorial status in the Department. Having already done a tenure celebration in the department for Professor Ramsey Michaels—who is a male man—it dawned on some of us that current equal rights concerns and contemporary gender politics required some kind of a match-up adjustment. The celebration was scheduled to be in Professor Hodgson's home. Robert Hodgson was being asked to provide the liturgy, and he chose *Lieder ohne Worte* (music without words). Stanley then, as my superior, asked me to come up with the proper paraphernalia.

The six preceding paragraphs all needed to be written to explain to our readers the peculiar circumstances in which our second tenure celebration needed to be planned and staged. The ancient Order of the Golden Sloth could never be resurrected again. It did not seem proper to welcome lady professors to join a pack of male professors, who are thinking of themselves as climbing about slowly in the branches of a tree. Our new ceremonial paraphernalia needed to help keep feet planted solidly on the ground. Everyone needed to keep at least one foot on the floor. In actual performance, later, this plan was compromised slightly by allowing a little more elevation of one or the other leg here and there, in proper alternation.

I asked Dora to buy a length of cloth—of the Missouri State maroon color—and to sew a gigantic pair of integrated departmental slip-on pants or kilts, that would be large enough to hold the full row of full-time professors in the department, including Kathy. It was the largest pair of drawers I have ever seen—and it was made of an uncut piece of fabric just like the robe of Jesus for which Roman soldiers played dice. The doubled length of it reached almost across the width of Robert's living room. Divisions were stitched to keep all wearers distinct from one another. At one end we tried to fit our fearless leader, Gerrit. His back ailment permitted him to insert only his right leg—his left leg and his cane were tapping in their accustomed state of freedom. The entire row was arranged in the order of seniority. So at the new end position, Kathy was suited just like the rest of us. Then Robert had Mary push a button to play a snappy tune on his sound machine, and the entire full-time Religious Studies Faculty improvised a tap dance in a somewhat unified ecumenical rhythm. Gerrit confided to me afterward that it made him "exceedingly happy."

And so it came to pass that even though to this day none of us could ever agree on how to write gender-neutral English, or how to explain chauvinistic theologies in a gender-neutral mode without distorting ancient core denotations, the Department was sufficiently integrated and unified after that to coast along together, until the next stoppage would demand another type of ancient ritual.

The problem of gender specificity happens to be endemic not only to the English language, but also to most of the religions we are teaching "about" in English-speaking lands. It is a fact that most organized religions on this planet were founded by males, as atonement gestures for the original sins that our apish ancestral huntsmen have committed and have established as a long enduring heritage of curses for our species. Yes indeed, by men came death, and some of these men therefore also needed to contribute religious solutions by which some kind of life could again be re-affirmed.

I happen to be convinced that among all the white robes that await us in heaven, at least on the yearly anniversary of Kathy's tenure, up there, a few of us will be permitted to wear maroon or blue for a day. But I doubt very much whether any of those many mansions there will be painted in maroon. The symbolic value of our MSU academic color is just still a little too close to the hue of blood.

Well, my dear friend Stanley! I do not know whether I understood your suggestions well enough. If I took your words more literally than I should have, perhaps some good will come of it anyhow. In spite of misunderstandings, future students of Religious Studies will be given some practical examples of how—under Gerrit J. tenZythoff's lasting aura and patriarchal levity, many issues in the world could be resolved in an academic Religious Studies environment—along the path of efficacious ritual. So much of my reminiscences from the twentieth century for this essay! The past twelve years in the present century, since I left Missouri State, have not been spent on memories at all, but rather on fascinating field encounters, anticipations, and discoveries.

RETIREMENT, MY RESEARCH GRANT FOR THE REMAINDER

In linear time, the major portion of my learning life went as follows: During the first ten years of study—which followed house-painting and military service—I studied to be admitted someday to teach at universities. Because I was a late starter in academia, I only had thirty years of teaching left to give. Twenty of these, fortunately, I was able to spend in the company of friends at Missouri State. Looking back at my teaching years, I remember occasions when over-preparation of the lectures made them all the more difficult to communicate. In hindsight, however, I still wish I had prepared my thirty years of presentations more evenly. In hindsight I also wish I had known earlier all the things that I learned during the last dozen years of free-roaming research in retirement—especially what I learned during the last two years. Had I known what I know now I could have done a better job explaining the history of religions. Or per chance this improved knowledge could also have placed my subject matter farther out of reach for my students. The book I just finished writing, indeed, turned out a little better than any of my previous volumes—but precisely for this reason it now proves to be more difficult to find a publisher. The same population dynamic that bestows student responses also governs the book market. So, whereas for a while I was suggesting to Almighty God to let Religious Studies professors have some retirement years prior to granting them teaching tenure, I can now see that such an arrangement might only have pushed good teaching farther down the pike of dreams. Moreover, it is easier to write books on huge topics while knowledge is still limited. Less knowledge is easier to organize.

About the ins and the outs of how I changed my research interests from Navajo Indian religion and from the greater American Southwest to Middle America, and to ancient Egypt and China during the 1970s and 1980s, you are probably sufficiently informed—my learning curve is basically reflected in the sequence of my earlier publications. Between 1987 and 2000 I was travelling to the Middle Kingdom to learn more about Muslims in China. This Chinese dimension of my curiosity took on new form with events that followed 9/11 in 2001. From my contacts with Muslim friends in Ningxia and Xinjiang I noticed, in these western provinces, a rising fear of Al Qaida intrusions into their domains.

It was around 2003 when, at the deathbed of my research partner Li Shujiang I modified my Islam-oriented research in the direction of helping my Muslim friends, there, in their tasks of liberalizing theological education. In 2006, with the help of five board members, we incorporated a new type of educational program in the State of Oregon and called it "Road to Peace Inc." It was a non-profit institution. MSU's emeritus president, John H. Keizer was kind enough to accept the role of being our president, and a prominent local lawyer from Portland volunteered to serve as our corporate attorney. Our goal was to take young imams (*ahongs*) from China on bus tours across the United States, for historical, cultural, and theological conversations with the general aim of advancing inter-religious and inter-cultural understanding. Our planning trip was made during spring of 2007, by car, with two young Hui Muslim professors from Ningxia and Qinghai. We visited universities, historical sites and religious institutions between San Francisco and Georgetown University. After that fact-finding tour our decision was to get our program rolling. By the spring of 2008 sufficient funds were promised to take a group of six Muslim professors and mullahs on the road. All seemed well, and our path into the future lay open. The participants were chosen, and visa applications were started. But then something unforeseen happened—whether it happened by or against the will of Allah or God I do not know. In any case, it must have happened by some kind of divine levity. This was the year of the Beijing Olympics. Superficially religion-motivated rebellions started to flare up in the diverse Buddhist and Muslim western provinces. The apprehensive Chinese government did not wish to jeopardize its Olympic moment of national glory. All passports for western Chinese religious professionals were cancelled. Our plans needed to be put on hold, and our Road to Peace Inc. non-profit corporation lingered for a year and a half in waiting after that. The passports were not approved in time for us to restart our operation. We dissolved our organization and I decided to continue my efforts for China in other ways.

During our planning stages I have promised some Muslim educators of the University of Ningxia to write a textbook that might be useful in their program of educating young mullahs as well as secular cadres. This happens to be the same book that will be mentioned again below as a first release in English in the near future. Its general content will be Stone Age religion in evolution, at Göbekli Tepe.

All the while, between 2002 and 2009 I continued travelling to China every summer to gain a better understanding of the ancient shamanic beginnings and about the early centuries of this mega-civilization. What lured me to China during the 1980s, in the first place, was the happenstance that since my graduate school days at Chicago the English textbooks about religions of China failed to ring true. To derive ancient religions from more ancient philosophies just went against the flow of evolution everywhere else in the world, and against any historical common sense. Religions precede philosophies—they cannot very well have appeared as fallout effects from philosophies. So now, finally, after my sixteenth trip to China I felt confident enough to write a chapter concerning the early Chinese history of religion—at least a part if it now measures up to my own standards for historiography.

But even those insights about China would probably not have occurred had it not been possible to achieve a breakthrough for the prehistory of religions regarding Stone Age Religion in eastern Anatolia—along the Fertile Crescent. This breakthrough turned out to be the crowning moment of my academic career so far. It happened while writing a preliminary sketch about the general evolution of human culture and religion. Over the decades I have made several starts on this project, trying to fulfill promises I made to my students at Missouri State long ago. On January 11, 2011, I was writing on that project again when I followed some traces on the Internet and found a reference to the oldest Neolithic temples in eastern Anatolia—an assemblage of some twenty or more temples on a hill called Göbekli Tepe. Immediately I ordered the lead archaeologist's book in German—Klaus Schmidt, *Sie bauten die ersten Tempel*.[1] Most other published reports on that subject matter offered little help and added far too much confusion pulled from thin air. After reading Klaus Schmidt's data book the first time, two puzzles remained for me—the significance of "Göbekli Tepe" (*Bauch Berg*) and the meaning of the menhirs, which the archaeologists had designated as *T-Pfeiler* (T-shaped pillars). During my second reading the meaning of the Turkish name *Göbekli Tepe* (*Xerawrēk* in Kurdish) came into focus, and I translated "Abdomen Hill" as my best solution for English. And while no illumination came during the third reading, all the core pieces of the puzzle that had evoked my curiosity assembled nicely during a fourth reading. There was no question about it; I needed to visit Göbekli Tepe in person. I made this trip to eastern Anatolia—a place about thirty miles from the Harran of Terah and Abraham—during the fall excavation campaign in 2011.

When all the pieces were assembled, what emerged was the profile of a Neolithic culture and an atonement religion in transition. The Göbekli Tepe cult started a little after twelve thousand years ago, and it began preparing the last generations of the Neolithic huntsmen for what in archaeological circles has become known as the Neolithic Revolution. It turns out that this revolution in Neolithic culture was driven mostly by religious sentiments, by an atonement cult that hitherto had been unsuspected by pre-historians. The more I worked on decoding its sculpted limestone symbolism, the more I realized that this body of insights comprised precisely the knowledge that I had been seeking all my life.

1. Schmidt, *Sie bauten die ersten Tempel*.

Like most western historians of religions, I too began with asking my general evolutionary questions from a biblical perspective. The approach back then was valid out of necessity, because the Mesopotamian, Egyptian, Mediterranean, and Abrahamic traditions were all we had to start with. But then, in America I spent much of the spare time of my fifty-year career decoding the puzzles of Neolithic hunter religions in transition to domestication culture. And now, amazingly, at Göbekli Tepe, we are walking on temple floors, and we puzzle about sculpted paraphernalia that are seven to nine millennia older than anything we were able to learn from hints in the Bible—and five to seven millennia older than what we had in Mesopotamia and Egypt. And from that distant yonder point in time, looking forward in the direction of time's flow, the biblical initiatives come into focus as logical historical results within the context of the larger evolution of religions.

Göbekli Tepe religion needed to happen before our humanoid ancestors could systematically domesticate plants and animals—and before they could discover most of the deities that helped regulate the lives of domesticators. It needed to happen before there could be farmers and herdsmen in the Near East or anywhere else on the planet. It needed to happen before remnants of stalwart orthodox huntsmen could sink into obsolescence as drifters, bandits and warriors, and before some of them could rise millennia later as aristocrats to bestow on humankind progressive warfare and the spider-webs called "civilization." This broad realization forced me to re-conceptualize all the connotations of "civilization" within the larger evolutionary process and to re-label its complexity with "hyper-domestication." Hyper-domestication, essentially corresponds to what in an earlier book, *Egyptian Light and Hebrew Fire: Theological and Philosophical Roots of Christendom in Evolutionary Perspective*,[2] I named "grand-domestication" and "over-domestication."

In brief: the excavation of Göbekli Tepe led to the discovery of a hitherto unknown religion. Almost twelve thousand years ago the cult got established at a hill sanctuary in southeastern Anatolia. Its priests were shamans, hunters, miners of flint, knappers of weapon points, and sculptors of limestone. As heirs of a hunter culture, millions of years in the making, they entered upon their greatest transformation ever. Their improved weapon industry encouraged overhunting. It generated a temporary surplus of food and far too many hunters. Prey animal populations fell off, and the shortage elicited a cult that would mind the regeneration of life. Priestly wisdom and ritual thereby pre-justified the domestication of plants and animals. Over time, persistent hunters degenerated into hungry drifters, bandits, and

---

2. Luckert, *Egyptian Light and Hebrew Fire*.

warriors. Some rose as aristocrats, to bestow upon humanity warfare and hyper-domestication. The latter category entailed taking control not only of minerals, plants, and animals, but also of humankind. Hyper-domestication entailed large-scale warfare, slavery, and human sacrifice. Driven by fear for security, hyper-domesticated humankind sought safety in numbers and therefore overpopulated—mostly to win advantages in competition and in warfare. Thus, the world's problems of overpopulation were driven by violence and the fear thereof, and by hope for security, to overcome lethal dangers with the blessings of greater numbers. We all know by now what happened to that hope for more security by greater numbers and improved weapons.

My allotted space for this assignment is filled. Fortunately I can promise that, God willing, within the year there will appear a new kind of history of religions book, through the agency of some still unknown publisher. It will appear under my authorship and will be titled something like *Stone Age Religion at Göbekli Tepe and Beyond: Twelve Thousand Years Ago and around the Planet*.

BIBLIOGRAPHY

Luckert, Karl. *Egyptian Light and Hebrew Fire: Theological and Philosophical Roots of Christendom in Evolutionary Perspective.* SUNY Series in Religious Studies. Albany: State University of New York Press, 1991.

Schmidt, Klaus. *Sie bauten die ersten Tempel: das rätselhafte Heiligtum der Steinzeitjäger.* München: Beck, 2006; dtv edition 2008.

Epilogue
—Stanley M. Burgess and Ruth Vassar Burgess

Often words seem limited to express heartfelt thoughts and emotions. With this in mind, we extend our gratitude to friends, colleagues, and former students for sharing your friendship, thoughts, and scholarship in *Children of the Calling*. Beyond this, you have listened to our words that blew in the winds from the east to the west. Certainly our memories hold fast to the times we have spent with you. We shared beliefs that we could modify this world by preserving the past and providing just visions for more equitable futures.

The word "Calling" required reflection to the early times in Pentecostalism in North America. Those who were "called" by the Holy Spirit understood this to mean that God would bless and empower them to complete their divine missions both in the United States and abroad. Two young couples, John and Bernice Burgess as well as Ted and Estelle Vassar, were pioneers in the "new wave of this twentieth-century Pentecostal movement." These two couples felt the imprint of a divine calling. The question emerges, How do children of parents who were called adapt to life within changing multicultural settings? They were not missionary children, but they were children of missionaries. Their outlooks and understandings created a phenomenon called "children of the third culture." Where and to whom do these children belong and find a place of meaning and belonging?

First, using the skills that a Doctor of Philosophy provided, Stanley saw his primary mission as a historian of Pentecostal and Charismatic Movements, and not as a Pentecostal historian. Through encyclopaedias, dictionaries, and a plethora of books and journal articles, one hears the resonance of heritage voices. This documentation spreads across time, space, and cultural differences. Perhaps Stan had accepted part of his parents' calling because he carried within him the knowledge of being both an outsider and an insider.

Because Ruth's upbringing was somewhat mystical, she echoed her mother's voice, "You can do all things through Christ who strengtheneth you." Taking advantage of the academic and social discipline learned in boarding school, she earned a Doctor of Philosophy degree in Speech and Language Pathology. Ruth's professional life included research in psycholinguistics, cognitive psychology, and inclusion rights for those with disabilities and their families. Her concern about social justice issues led her to become involved in peacemaking in the land of her birth—Mother India.

Five children graced Stan and Ruth Burgess's home on Burgess Acres, a rural farm in Southwest Missouri. All were encouraged to travel abroad and to be savvy concerning different societal issues. Critical and creative thinking and discussion times were common around the kitchen table.

As parents and professionals, Ruth Vassar and Stanley Burgess have seized each moment to bless the significance of their intergenerational callings. They have managed the concepts of continuity and change. In the process, they have been challenged to remember how transcendence affects both the present and the future.

It is evident when one reads the chapters in *Children of the Calling* that our valued friends too come from a wide variety of scholarship and social justice areas. Thank you, Lois Olena and Eric Newberg, for sharing your time and professional editorial expertise. Then, as a fellow journeyman, we hail the kind words and friendship of Russell Spittler.

Index of Names and Subjects

-A-

Abraham, K. E., 265, 267–8, 279
Abrams, Minnie F., 264, 272, 287
Alopen, 114–17, 119, 212
Aristotle, 199–201, 203–04, 206, 212
Assemblies of God (AG), ix, xv, xxvi, 7, 33, 38, 41, 43, 61, 220
   Churches, xv, 30, 33, 45, 55
   Department of Foreign Missions (DFM), xxxiv, 32, 38, 283
   Ministerial Credentials, 6, 228
   Missionaries, ix, xvii, xxvi, 4, 264, 282
   Missionary Conference (1943), xxxiii, 281–95
   Missions, xv, xxxiv
   South India District Council, 286
   Theological Seminary (AGTS), xiv, xvii, xix
Augustine of Hippo, 12, 17, 170, 174–180
Azusa Street Revival, xxiv–xxv, xxxiv, 61, 312

-B-

Baptism in the Holy Spirit, xxv–xxvi, xxxiv, 6, 17, 264, 298–309, 313–14, 318, 322
Barnett, Elizabeth Byrd, 31
Basil of Caesarea, 12
Bethel Bible Institute, 4, 35
Braidotti, Rosi, 222–23, 225, 228, 233
Bresson, Bernard, 10–11, 15, 23

Brown, David, xv, xxxii–xxxiii, 235–36, 249, 251
Brubaker, Malcolm, xv, xxxiii, 281–95
Buddhism, 121, 126–27
Bundy, David D., 12–14, 23, 303
Burgess, Bernice, 4, 341
Burgess, John, xviii, xxiv, xxxiii, 4–5, 41, 265, 286
Burgess, Ruth Vassar, x, xiii–ix, 7, 29–64, 67–68, 71–78
   activism, x, 342
   childhood, 5
   education, x, 42–44, 46–48
   grants, x, 43–44, 59
   mentor, x–xi, xxxii, xxxv, 34, 81, 128, 223
   presentations, 46, 52, 57, 60–61, 76, 249, 252–54
   publications, 34, 63
   teaching, xiii, xviii, 9
   tributes, 81, 186, 199, 328
Burgess, Stanley Milton, ix–x, 3–28, 69–70, 72–78
   activism, x
   childhood, 4–6
   education, 6–7, 42
   ecumenical endeavors, 7, 19, 23, 43, 50, 61, 76
   mentor, x–xi, xxxv, 81, 128
   publications, xxix, 18, 24–25
   teaching, xi, xv, 7–9, 46
   tributes, ix, x, 3, 8–9, 23, 81, 186, 199, 328
Burgess Children and Grandchildren, 7, 42, 44–46, 74, 77

344 Index of Names and Subjects

-C-

Calling, xxiii–xxiv, xxxv, 26, 32, 43, 207–208, 211
  missionary calling, 36, 341
  Pentecostal missionary calling, xiv–xvi, xxiv–xxvi
  scholarship, xxvi–xxviii, 23
Cappadocian Fathers, 12
Catholic Charismatic Renewal, xvii, xx, 36–37, 299, 306, 311, 314–19, 323, 326
  Rome Conference, 31
Catholic Pentecostals, xx, 312, 327
Center for Research and Service, 55–56, 236
Charismatic, xxvi, xxxiv
  gifts, xiii, 11, 14, 18
  history, 10, 18, 22
  scholars, xi
  spirituality, 4, 17
  tradition, x–xi
Children of the Calling, ix, xxiii, xxiv, xxviii, xxix, 23, 341–42
Charismatic Movement, xi, 21, 262, 266, 274, 301–02, 304, 309, 312, 319, 326, 341
  Brighton Conference, 322–24
  Kansas City Conference, 319–22
  statistics, 21
Charismatic Renewal, 20
China, xxv, xxx, xxxv, 111–14, 118, 126–27, 282, 284–86, 291–92
China Inland Mission, 282
Christ, xxiv, xxv, xxxiv, 6, 14, 15, 17, 37, 38, 126, 129–31, 134, 150, 157, 170, 171, 175, 181, 182–83, 185, 187, 194–96, 204–05, 208, 210–11, 301–03, 309–10, 314, 320, 325, 342
Christian East (Eastern Christianity), xxiii, xxxi, 13–14, 23, 50, 173, 178–83
Christian Missionary Society (CMS), 263
Christian West (Western Christianity), 173

Christology, xxx, 12, 14, 17, 125, 179
Church of God (Cleveland), 265, 272
Church of God in Christ (COGIC), 220, 320–22
Church of the East (COTE), xxx, 112, 117, 125–27
Cicero, 200, 201, 203, 206, 208
Civil Rights, 220
Cleeton, Elaine, xv–xvi, xxxii, 219
Cognitve Map, xxxiii, 51, 60, 256–60
Community, xxviii, xxxi, 31, 36, 53, 59, 113, 126, 138, 148, 161, 170, 189, 193, 211, 221, 232, 240, 244, 246–47, 251–52, 254, 287, 300–303, 315, 320, 325
Cook, Robert F., 264–64
Crossan, John Dominic, 142, 165
Curriculum, xiv, xxxii–iii, xxxv, 51, 236–38, 241–44, 246, 248–50, 252–55, 272
"Cutting the Taproot," 19, 21, 24
Cyprian, 12

-D-

Dalliere, Louis, xxxiv, 299, 302–03
Daoism, 115, 121, 125, 127
Decalogue, 147
Diaspora, Keralite, xxxiii, 262
Dictionary of Pentecostal and Charismatic Movements, xviii, 21, 25, 63
Divine Representation, xxx
Divine Writing, 88, 94, 96, 102–03
Doak, Brian, xvi, xxx, 81
Dunhuang Documents, 121–22
Duquesne University, 312–13

-E-

Ecumenical, xiii, xvii, xxiii, xxxi, xxxiv, 7, 18–19, 23, 43, 61, 173, 174, 180–81
Emmert, Athanasios F. S., 13
Ephrem the Syrian, xxx, 111
Evangel College (University), xv, xix, 6–7, 10, 42–44, 46–47, 223

Index of Names and Subjects   345

- F -

Faith, xiv, xxvi, xxxi, 6-7, 30, 32-33, 43, 60, 123, 158-60, 170, 187, 192, 204, 221, 266, 274, 276, 287, 299, 301, 308, 313, 315-16, 325, 329
Faupel, D. William, 303
Feminism, 31, 55, 63, 219-20, 228-30
Feuerstein, Reuven, x, xiii, xxiii, xxix, xxxii-xxiii, 8-9, 31, 49-54, 58-61, 238, 255-61
Fichte, Gottlieb, xxvii, xxxv
Filioque Clause, xxxi, 12, 15, 18, 173-74, 178, 180-82
Finger of God, xxx, 81, 95, 99, 102
Flower Pentecostal Heritage Center (FPHC), xxxv, 281, 321, 327
Forgiveness, xxxi, 14, 154, 156, 158-61, 163, 168, 170, 188, 191-93, 196, 316, 322
Friedan, Betty, 222, 233

- G -

Gandhi, Mahatma, 33, 276
Gannon, Raymond L., 288, 296
Gender issues, x, xxiii-ix, 31-32, 55-56, 220, 223, 226, 229-31, 233, 331-34
Göbekli Tepe, xviii, xxxv, 336-39
Gospel of Thomas, 134, 144
Grace, xxix, xxx-xxxi, xxxiv, 8, 29, 46, 152-54, 157-59, 161-66, 168, 170-71, 300, 303-05, 309, 312, 314, 316, 318, 325, 332
Greenwood Laboratory School, 47, 49, 235-38, 242, 244, 247-48, 250, 252-54
Gregory of Nazianzus, 12
Gregory of Nyssa, 12
Gros, Brother Jeffrey, 3, 26
Guinness, Os, xxiv, xxxvi

- H -

Hadassah-WIZO-Canada Research Institute, Jerusalem, 8, 49
Hattie, John, 256-57, 260, 261

Healing, xxxi, 18, 20, 158-59, 161, 188, 190, 192-93, 196, 227, 232, 289, 307, 317, 325
Hebrew Bible, 81, 84, 89-90, 93, 96, 101, 106, 143
Hedrick, Charles, xvi, xxx, 8-9, 133
Heritage, xxiii, xxix, xxxiii, 29-31, 36, 48, 60, 62, 178, 201, 203, 233, 235, 238, 240-41, 246-48, 251-54, 262, 334, 341
Herzog, William R., 149
Hinch, Steven, xvi, xxxii-xxxiii, 235-36, 242-43, 246, 249-53
Hinduism, 4, 32, 34, 38, 60, 277, 287
Historiography, xiii, xxix, 10, 16, 20, 23, 337
Hocken, Peter, xvii, xxxiv, 298, 310, 314, 316, 324
Hodges, Melvin, 290
Holy Spirit, xiii, xxv-xxvi, xxix, xxxiv, 5-6, 10-21, 23, 120, 123, 156, 160, 181, 220, 263-66, 277-78, 291, 298-99, 301-09, 312-14, 316-318, 320, 322, 324, 341
The Holy Spirit: Ancient Christian Traditions, 10
The Holy Spirit: Eastern Christian Traditions, xiii, 13
The Holy Spirit in Medieval Roman Catholic and Reformation Traditions, 17
Horton, Stanley M., xi, xix, 46
Hunter, Harold, 324, 326

- I -

Incarnation, 176, 178-79
India, ix, xv, xviii, xxiii-xxvii, xxix, xxxii, xxxiv, 4-5, 10, 29-39, 42-43, 45, 48-49, 52, 60, 263-67, 276, 283, 286-87, 292
Kerala (Travancore), 4, 49, 262-63, 267
Kodaikanal, xxiv, 34
Mavelikara, 65, 265, 282
Nagercoil, 4
Pune, 31
India Christian Assembly, 268-69

Index of Names and Subjects

Indian culture, 223–24, 263
Indian Pentecostal Church (IPC), 265, 271
Indian Pentecostalism, xxxiii, 4–5, 262, 265, 267–79
Initial Evidence, xxv–vi, 6, 17, 305
Instrumental Enrichment (IE), xxiii, xxxii, 51–52, 57, 61, 236, 261
International Center for the Enhancement of Learning Potential (ICELP), xxxii, 52, 238
Israel, xxxii, 10, 29, 39, 49–53, 58–59, 75, 81, 83–84, 86, 89, 93, 95, 101, 105, 160, 169, 192, 238, 303
Israelites, 87, 89–90, 94, 143, 148–49, 202

-J-

Jeremias, Joachim, 154
Jerusalem, x, xxxii, 8, 13, 49, 50–51, 58, 125, 221, 238, 278, 305, 323
Jews, 58–59, 97, 156, 159, 193, 201, 273, 323
Jingjiao, 113–15, 118, 120–22, 126
John, K. C., xxxiii, 265
Jones, E. Stanley, 268
Junnar Boys Home (orphanage), 33, 37–38, 68, 74, 282

-K-

Kansas City Conference, 319–22
Kärkkäinen, Veli-Matti, xvii, xxxi, 173, 184
Kasper, Cardinal Walter, 315
Keralite Pentecostals, 265–74
Kingdom of God, xxi, 3, 145, 152, 154, 169, 188, 193, 195
Kistler, Judy, 236, 238, 242–43, 249

-L-

Larbi, E. Kingsley, 22
Learning Potential Assessment Device (LPAD), 51
Legacy, x, xviii, xxix, xxxv, 4, 19, 21, 37, 174, 176–78, 254

Lewis, Idell, 26, 31
Luce, Alice, 290
Luckert, Karl, xviii, xxxv, 328–341
Luoyang Monument, xxx, 112–13, 121

-M-

Ma, Wonsuk, xi, 310
Marriage, xxix, xxxii, 7, 42, 169, 190, 202, 204–07, 209–11
Marshall, I. Howard, 187
Martin, Ralph, 319, 321
Mathew, K. T., 265
Mathew, Thomson, xviii, xxxiii, 262
McGee, Gary B., 3, 13, 21–22, 25, 264, 294
Mediated Learning Experience (MLE), xxiii, 8–9, 51
Memphis Miracle, 321–22, 327
Messiah, 115–16, 119, 121–27, 187
Messianic, xvii, 163, 304–06, 323
Millet, Kate, 222
Missiology, xvii, xxxvi, 290
Missionary kids, xxiv, 5, 38, 46
MissouriFind Project, xxxii–xxxiii, 34, 55, 235–55
Missouri State University (MSU). See Southwest Missouri State University, x, xv–xvi, xviii, xix, xxxii, xxxv, 3, 7–9, 26, 47, 76, 81, 199, 236, 242, 252, 254, 328–30, 333–35, 337
Moltmann, Jürgen, 182
Moralism, xxxi, 39, 169–70
Moses, 82–83, 87–94, 97–104, 106, 124
Mother of God Community, xxxiv, 299–302, 307

-N-

Narrative, xvi, xxx, xxxv, 59–60, 82, 84, 88, 90, 94–95, 100, 103, 105–06, 119, 126, 133–36, 138, 141–45, 149, 158, 189, 193, 222, 227, 232, 243, 246, 249, 253, 306
National Association of Evangelicals, 20, 43

Index of Names and Subjects   347

Nazareth, 134–35, 155, 188, 191–92
Nestorian(s), xxx, 112–124, 126
The New International Dictionary of Pentecostal and Charismatic Movements, 4, 21–22, 25, 265–66, 279, 297–98, 309–10
New Testament, 11, 18, 20, 101, 186, 190–91, 199, 201, 287, 304–06
  Acts, xxvi, xxxi, 124, 170, 186, 190–96, 200–01, 278, 305
  Luke, xxx–xxxi, 134–39, 142, 144–47, 153, 155–56, 158–162, 166, 168–69, 171, 186–97
  1 Corinthians, xxxi–xxxii, 18, 199–212, 313
Newberg, Eric, x, xviii, xix, xxiii–xxxvi, 3–28, 51, 59, 64, 127, 288, 296, 342
Nixon, Carolyn, ix, xxxiii, 51, 256–61
Notre Dame University, 311, 313–14, 319

- O -

O'Collins, Gerald, 18–19
Old Testament, 191
  Genesis, 84, 103
  Exodus, xxx, 81–83, 86–91, 93, 95–99, 101, 103–06
  Daniel, 84, 88, 97
  Deuteronomy, 88, 124
  Isaiah, 18, 89, 103, 122, 124, 160, 188–90
  Joshua, 89–90, 143
  Leviticus, 96, 124
Olena, Lois E., xiii, xix, xx, xxix, 29–64, 78, 127, 342
Oral Roberts University, xi, xiv, 270, 272, 274
"Order of the Golden Sloth," xxxv, 329–30, 333

- P -

Parables of Jesus, xxx, 120, 126, 133–35, 145–46, 154–57, 159, 166, 168, 193
  Dishonest Manager, xxx, 133, 135
  Pharisee and Publican, 162
  Two Debtors, 138–39, 156, 166
  Unmerciful Servant, 161
  Workers in the Vineyard, 163
Parham, Charles, xxv
Pedagogy, xiii, xxviii, xxxii, 9, 50, 81, 228
Pentecost, Day of, xxvi, 305
Pentecostal(ism), ix–x, xiii, xxiii–xxvi, 3, 6, 10, 14–15, 17, 19–22, 31, 219–20, 262–64, 266, 274, 300, 303–04, 309, 312–15, 318–20, 341
Pentecostal Conference of North American Keralites (PCNAK), 270
Pentecostal Evangel, 5, 284, 288–90, 292, 294
Pentecostal Holiness Church, 321
Perichoresis, 176
Perkin, Noel, 32, 282–84, 291, 293–95
Pharisees, 155, 157, 169
Plato (Platonic), 83, 94, 174, 200, 206, 240
Pneumatology, xxviii, 8, 10–15, 17–19, 23
Pope Benedict XVI, 318
Pope Francis I, 318, 322, 324
Pope John Paul II, xxxiv, 308, 316–18, 322
Puglisi, Father Jim, 19, 76, 325
Pulley, Kathy J., 9, 331, 333
Puskas, Charles, xx, xxxi–xxxii, 199–215

- Q -

Quintillian, 201–04, 206, 209

- R -

Ramabai, Pandita, 58, 63, 264
Ranaghan, Dorothy Garrity, xx, xxxiv, 311–27
Ranaghan, Kevin, xx, xxxiv, 311–27
Rance, DeLonn, xxv
Receptive Syntax Semantics Test (RSST), 47

Index of Names and Subjects

Regent University, v, xiii–xiv, xxix, 8, 22, 58–59, 76, 186, 319
Repentance, xxxi, 152, 159–61, 166, 168, 171, 193, 301, 321
Revival(s), xxiv, xxv, xxxiv, 21, 170, 263–64, 299, 303, 312, 317
Rhetoric, xxxi–xxxii, 41, 137, 165, 199–207, 209–10, 212
Righteousness, xxx–xxxi, 56, 134–35, 146, 152–53, 155, 162, 166–69, 171
Robeck, Cecil ("Mel"), xxv, xxvi, xxxvi, 28, 324
Roberts, Oral, 274
Roman Catholic/Pentecostal Ecumenical Dialogue, 315, 325
Russell, Jeffrey B., 11, 18

-S-

Salvation, xxxi, 13–14, 40, 115–16, 124, 126, 159–161, 168, 179–82, 186–98
Samuel, K. J., 266
Savior, xxxi, 17, 45, 187–87, 189, 192–93, 195–96
Scholar(ship), x–xi, xiii–xiv, xxiii, xxvi–xxix, xxxv, 3, 7–12, 15–16, 19, 21–23, 40, 42, 44, 46, 50, 56, 60–61, 85, 112, 114–15, 119, 133–34, 146, 175, 199, 201–02, 306, 317, 324, 341–42
Second Vatican Council, 184, 308, 316–18, 325
Seraphim of Sarov, 14
Seymour, William, xxv,
ShantiStan, xxix, 58–60
Sinai, 82, 87–88, 92–94, 98–99, 100–03, 106
Social justice, x, xiii, xxi, xxiii, 19, 25, 36, 55, 63, 342
Society for Pentecostal Studies (SPS), xiv, xvii, xx, 3, 13, 23, 299, 301, 310

Southwest Missouri State University (SMSU). *See* Missouri State University (MSU), v, x, xix, xxxii, xxxv, 3, 7–9, 25, 26, 47, 199, 236, 242, 252
Southwestern Assemblies of God University (SAGU), 30, 38
Speech Pathology, x, xxxii, 223–24
Spirituality, xi, xii, xxiii, xxvi, xxviii–xi, 4–5, 10, 15–16, 23, 50, 179, 306, 317
Spittler, Russell P., ix–xi, 25, 27, 310, 342
Story, Lyle, xx, xxx, 152–172
Structural Cognitive Modifiability, 8, 50–52, 60
Swete, Henry B., 11, 13, 23, 28
Symeon the New Theologian, 14
Synan, Vinson, 311, 320
Syriac, 111–12, 114, 120, 122–25, 127

-T-

Tang Dynasty, 111–15, 121, 126–27
Tantur Ecumenical Institute, xiii, 8, 13, 50
Tenure, ix, 7, 19, 47, 58, 223, 228, 329–331, 333–35
tenZythoff, Gerrit, 7, 328, 334
Tertullian, 12, 194, 199, 209, 215
Texas Tech University, 41
Third Culture Kids, 36, 38, 46, 64, 341
Thomas, P. J., 266
Torah, 59, 82–83, 88, 93, 97, 99, 104, 106
Tournier, Paul, 152, 169
Trinity, xvii, xxxi, 6, 12, 17–19, 115, 120, 173–182
Tugwell, Simon, xxxiv, 299, 300, 310
Twelftree, Graham, xiv, xxi, xxxi, 186–198

-U-

Unity, xvii, 61, 76, 123, 174–75, 177–79, 183, 228, 273, 301, 303, 310–11, 314–16, 320–21, 323, 325–26

Index of Names and Subjects   349

University of Michigan, 6, 42
University of Missouri, ix, 7, 25, 44, 46, 48, 63

-V-

Vassar, Estelle Barnett, xxiv, 30, 32–35, 37, 70
Vassar, Lenora, 37
Vassar, Ted, xxiv, 30, 32–35, 37–38, 45
Vatican, 61, 63, 76, 310, 315, 323, 327, 332

-W-

Watkin-Jones, Howard, 16
Wood, George O., 3

-X-

Xi'ang Stele, xxx, 112–19, 122, 124, 127, 129

-Y-

YHWH, 84, 89–93, 96, 98, 100–05, 225

-Z-

Zacchaeus, 155, 160
Zarins, Juris, 9, 25
Zimmerman, Thomas, 7, 22